MEDITERRANEAN FASCISM, 1919-1945

Edited by CHARLES F. DELZELL

HARPER & ROW / HR 1507

Mediterranean Fascism,
1919–1945

A volume
in
DOCUMENTARY HISTORY
of
WESTERN CIVILIZATION

DOCUMENTARY HISTORY OF WESTERN CIVILIZATION
Edited by Eugene C. Black and Leonard W. Levy

Mediterranean Fascism
1919–1945

Edited by

CHARLES F. DELZELL

HARPER & ROW, PUBLISHERS

New York, Evanston, and London

MEDITERRANEAN FASCISM, 1919–1945

Introduction, editorial notes, translations by the editor, and compilation copyright © 1970 by Charles F. Delzell.

A clothbound edition of this book is published in the United States and Canada by Walker and Company.

First HARPER TORCHBOOK edition published 1970

STANDARD BOOK NUMBER: 06–138475–5

D
7265
.D44
1971

ABD-5890

Contents

II. FASCISM IN SPAIN

III. SALAZAR'S PORTUGAL

Introduction

IN THE aftermath of World War I much of Europe found itself engaged in a three-cornered ideological struggle, while the United States withdrew into smug isolationism. Parliamentary and democratic liberalism, undergirded by commercial capitalism and agrarianism, was in serious crisis in a continent that was rapidly becoming disrupted by the impact of industrialization and the problems and frustrations brought about by modern "mass" society and aggravated by the war. On the left it was challenged by Marxism, which burst upon the political scene in totalitarian Communist garb in Russia in November, 1917, and in milder democratic-socialist forms elsewhere in Europe. On the right it was attacked by a militantly ultranationalist and radical ideology that emerged as a reaction to the threat (real or imagined) of Communism, the frustrations of the war and peace settlement, the economic dislocation, and the political breakdown of liberal parliamentary government. Coming to be known as fascism, this radicalism of the right manifested itself chiefly in three areas: the Mediterranean region in its original and most authentic dress; in east-central Europe in a somewhat mixed and often racist guise; and in Germany in a strongly racist form and with dreams of unlimited conquest.

The fascistic movements pushed forward in three distinct waves —from 1919 to 1923; from 1929 to the mid-1930's; and again from 1939 to 1943. Italy was the major beachhead of the first wave, Benito Mussolini's Fascist party gaining political power by the end of October, 1922. In Germany, Adolf Hitler's Nazis were frustrated in the Munich Beer Hall *Putsch* of November, 1923. The coming of the Great Depression, however, served to resuscitate Hitler's National Socialist movement and to stimulate a variety of other fascistic movements throughout Europe. Finally, the years of the Axis military offensive in World War II saw the temporary imposition of other more or less fascistic regimes in many parts of the Continent.

It is the Mediterranean region, and more precisely the Italian and Iberian peninsulas, with which this documentary history is concerned. Mussolini's Italy was, of course, the country par excellence of authentic fascism. In contrast to the very brutal National Socialism of Hitler's Germany, Mussolini's regime seemed to many foreigners relatively moderate and respectable, at least until the last half of the 1930's, when it, too, became bellicose and racist. Mussolini's much-touted Charter of Labor and various socio-economic innovations, along with several aspects of his political mystique and Party-Militia-State structure, attracted a number of willing imitators, especially in the Latin world (though Hitler's movement also found converts in Spain and elsewhere).

Drawing much of his initial support from returning World War I veterans who were outraged by "leftist" subversion, Mussolini and his handful of backers soon organized blackshirted *squadristi* (militiamen) to fight the "Reds" (and also the democratic liberals and Catholics) and to impose their own peculiar brand of "law and order." Hoodlums and semicriminal elements of the cities and countryside were drawn to fascism by the opportunities for violent action. Starting out with a program that was a curious blend of republicanism, anticlericalism, and socio-economic reformism, the Italian Fascists soon discovered that they could gain political power much faster by working out opportunistic and cynical bargains with such "established" power groups as the large landholders, industrialists, Army, Monarchy, and Church. Many leaders of these latter groups were inclined to pursue a misguided strategy: they were willing to let the Fascist *squadristi* demolish the left-wing labor and farm organizations, expecting that afterward the Fascists could be "tamed" and brought into the existing political "system." In due course the Fascist movement fused with the prewar Nationalist party, thereby gaining new strength and a more respectable philosophical foundation.

Meanwhile, the Fascists came to espouse a tightly regimented, patriotic program of "national syndicalism" that would preserve private property while at the same time eliminating free labor unions and the threat of strikes and lockouts. In this way they made a peculiar appeal not only to well-to-do conservatives but also to a good many white-collar and lower-middle-class people who stood in fear of Bolshevism and who were often the greatest victims of inflation and other economic crises. Eventually Fascist national syndicalism evolved into the so-called Corporative State, which sought to regiment the dominant economic and political institutions of Italy under the supreme control of the Fascist party.

From the outset the Fascists made a concerted effort to recruit and mobilize the youth into their movement. They achieved much success, though this attraction subsided in later years as the movement crystallized into a hierarchic and bureaucratic party. The Fascists managed also to gain a substantial following from some of the working class (though by no means all), to whom they offered various social and psychological surrogates for their former economic and political freedoms. There was, to be sure, considerable resistance to the emerging Fascist dictatorship, and this was most conspicuous among the ranks of the outlawed leftist political parties and labor organizations, stifled journalists, and harassed academicians and professional people. But eventually millions of Italians were swept off their feet by the way in which Mussolini, a most effective and charismatic orator, played on their emotions. There was always a strong element of irrationalism in the Fascist appeal. Mussolini, in his role as the infallible leader (*Duce*) of the party, proved to be a consummate propagandizer of the "myths" of nationalism and imperialism, evoking past glories like the Roman Empire and utilizing such ancient symbols of authority as the *fasci* of the Roman Republic. At first Fascism was presented to the Italians for domestic consumption; but by the early 1930's Mussolini was openly extolling the desirability of Fascism "for export." Soon Italian Fascism became synonymous with war, and Mussolini's fate came to be inextricably tied to that of Hitler.

Mussolini's "March on Rome" occurred in October, 1922. It was not until three years later that he was in a position to nail down the so-called totalitarian state. This came about in the wake of his successful surmounting of the great Aventine crisis of the last half of 1924—the brutal assassination of the reformist Socialist leader, Giacomo Matteotti. The *Duce's* triumph was in no small measure due to the ready availability of the Fascists' Blackshirt private army. In establishing their own totalitarian Party-State, the Fascists were to borrow many of the techniques of the Communist party of Soviet Russia. And in their common hostility to democratic parliamentary government, the Fascists and Communists often found themselves appealing to the same kinds of alienated people. A good many Fascists (beginning with Mussolini himself) came from the ranks of left-wing Marxism and syndicalism; and when the Fascist regime was overthrown in 1943–45 it was not hard for a certain number of ex-Blackshirts to swing to left-wing political extremism.

The Fascists owed a good deal of their mystique and emphasis on the creative role of violence to Georges Sorel's revolutionary syndicalism and to the integral nationalism of Charles Maurras's Action Française, both of which had emerged at the turn of the century and proved quite influential, particularly in the Latin world.[1] In a general sort of way and in diverse measure, they also were indebted to the doctrines of Niccolò Machiavelli, Georg F. W. Hegel, Friedrich Nietzsche, Vilfredo Pareto, Gaetano Mosca, Maurice Barrès, and even William James, to name but the most obvious. But theory was never the long suit of the Fascists; they preferred activism. Theories could be rationalized later; in any case, they must always remain subject to pragmatic change. Thus Mussolini's ideology should be studied genetically; its platforms changed considerably over the years. There were relatively few "constants" except for nationalism and anti-Bolshevism. It was always easier to pinpoint what fascism was opposed to than what it stood for.

Spain saw the emergence of fascistic National Syndicalist and Falangist groups in the early 1930's—in the midst of the Depression and the political extremism that erupted with the overthrow of the Bourbon Monarchy in 1931. There were a good many similarities between the blue-shirted Falangist movement of José Antonio Primo de Rivera and Mussolini's Blackshirts. One can only speculate how the Falangist movement might have fared had its attractive leader not been killed in 1936. As it was, the Falangists and their various ideological allies were rather speedily and cynically "subjugated" by General Francisco Franco and the old-line army elements during the Civil War. Despite their setback, however, the Falangists continued to be a not inconsiderable political force in Nationalist Spain—certainly until the defeat of the Axis powers in 1945. But Franco was always determined to utilize the Falange only to the degree that it suited his own political purposes, and for a quarter of a century he has demonstrated how skillful he can be at playing them off against the Monarchists.

1. Action Française was in many respects a kind of halfway station on the ideological road to fascism. This protofascist movement emerged at the turn of the century in hostility to the Dreyfusards and looked back nostalgically to the pre-Revolutionary era when "forty kings in a thousand years" had made France. Regarding it, see especially Eugen Weber, *Action Française: Royalism and Reaction in Twentieth-Century France* (Stanford: Stanford University, 1962); and Ernst Nolte, *Three Faces of Fascism: Action Française, Italian Fascism, National Socialism* (New York: Holt, Rinehart & Winston, 1966).

Portugal is a somewhat different case. In the wake of a series of incompetent military dictatorships after the advent of the Republic in 1910, that country's generals in 1928 invited a mild-mannered professor of economics, Dr. António de Oliveira Salazar, to take unrestricted political power. He thereupon established a one-party, clerico-corporativist regime labeled the Estado Novo (New State). Though the title seemed to suggest a kind of Portuguese replica of Mussolini's one-party Corporative State, Salazar's system drew most of its inspiration not so much from the examples of twentieth-century totalitarian dictatorship as from an earlier age. Like Maurras's Action Française, Salazar found inspiration in his own country's imperial and Catholic traditions. He also paid close attention to the modern Church's social encyclicals—e.g., *Rerum novarum*, issued in 1891 by Pope Leo XIII and updated forty years later by Pius XI. Salazar's regime was authoritarian and semifascist; it stopped short of being totalitarian.

After the fall of the French Third Republic in June, 1940, there was, to a limited degree, a kind of reverse flow of political ideas from Portugal to France. At least some of the organizers of Marshal Philippe Pétain's Vichy regime—or, to be more precise, his series of Vichy regimes—were impressed by certain features of Salazar's clerico-corporative state as well as by Action Française and other models. Limitations of space in this volume, however, preclude any insertion of documents that are illustrative of the authoritarian and ramshackle Vichy regime of 1940–44 that extolled the traditional virtues of "Work, Family, Country."[2] Nor is it possible here to include documentary examples of the numerous right-wing radical movements and leagues that mushroomed in France during the Depression years in conscious imitation of Mussolini's and Hitler's ideologies, and that gained renewed vigor in Paris under the German occupation.[3]

2. For an introduction to the complex history of the Vichy regime, see especially Robert Aron, *The Vichy Regime, 1940–44* (London: Putnam, 1958); and René Rémond, *The Right Wing in France from 1815 to De Gaulle* (Philadelphia: Univ. of Pennsylvania, 1966).

3. Such leagues included Marcel Bucard's Francistes; Pierre Taittinger's Jeunesses Patriotes; Major Jean Renaud's Solidarité Française; Jacques Doriot's quite large Parti Populaire Français; the Comité Secret d'Action Révolutionnaire ("Cagoulards"); and numerous others. In the war years the gulf between Vichy and Paris grew wider—at least until 1944, when the Paris totalitarians managed to cross it and establish a measure of influence within the Vichy government.

Likewise, no attempt can be made in this book to discuss the rather old-fashioned military dictatorship that General John Metaxas established in Greece between 1936 and 1941. His regime was not fascist in the strict sense of the term.

Indeed, the label "fascism" should not be confused with old-style royalist or military regimes. One of the noteworthy characteristics of fascist regimes was that they had their own party militia, and this often acted as a rival to the regular armed forces of the state. Fascist dictatorships aspired to endure, in Hitler's grandiose vision, for at least "a thousand years," whereas military dictatorships were usually intended to be temporary affairs. Moreover, military dictatorships did not usually have their origins in the problems of the new "mass" societies in the way that fascist regimes did; after all, military dictatorships have come and gone with frequency over the centuries.

It is important also to emphasize that fascism is a "post-liberal" ideology. It presupposes the existence of a liberal political system that has fallen into a state of crisis with the concomitant threat of a left-wing revolution. Thus, it would be incorrect to label as "fascist" the authoritarian, secular, and Westernizing regime of Mustafa Kemal Atatürk in Turkey after the overthrow of the Ottoman Empire. The Young Turks had had insufficient time to get a truly "liberal" system into operation prior to Mustafa Kemal's takeover; nor was there any serious threat of a Communist victory.

In differentiating fascistic regimes from backward-looking authoritarian systems it is important to keep in mind that demagogic leaders like Hitler and Mussolini did not emerge from the traditional ruling classes. Instead they usually rose from a different and humbler social stratum (though there were some exceptions, such as the aristocratic José Antonio Primo de Rivera in Spain and Sir Oswald Mosley in Britain). Moreover, they intended to create a new ruling class. Yet in spite of the fact that fascist parties were strongly "elitist" in theory, they did not always maintain high selectivity; in Italy, for example, there was to be a considerable influx of the masses as time went on. The fascists intended to eliminate the existing "liberal" and "socialist" political parties and replace them by a single-party system that often made use of some form of the "corporative state." Ideally, there was to be an identity of Party and State; in practice, however, friction sometimes occurred.

In none of the Mediterranean countries did fascism become truly "totalitarian," despite the fact that Mussolini coined the term. Certainly the *Duce*'s Italy was nowhere nearly so "totalitarian" or "monolithic" as Stalin's Russia—or even Hitler's Germany (which we now know had a surprising number of competing agencies and contradictory sources of authority beneath the *Führer*). This was partly because of Mussolini's frequent deference to the machinery of the state: "Everything in the State, nothing outside the State, nothing against the State!"[4] And that, in turn, was probably the result of the philosophical influence of the older, conservative Nationalist party of Alfredo Rocco and Luigi Federzoni that merged with the Fascists in 1923. The chronic chaos of the bureaucracy and the humanitarian, almost anarchistic tendencies of the Italian people were also factors. Lastly and most obviously, the failure to achieve complete totalitarianism in Italy was due to Mussolini's inability to get rid of the House of Savoy and the Church. King Victor Emmanuel III, to be sure, never made a public show of hostility to the *Duce* for more than two decades, but in July, 1943, he became the instrument for overthrowing Mussolini, just as he had been the instrument for bringing him to power in October, 1922. The Church, on the other hand, did find itself occasionally at odds with the regime after the euphoria of the Lateran pacts of 1929; this was true in the clash over Catholic Action in 1931 and again when Mussolini announced the anti-Semitic decrees in 1938. In the case of the Iberian countries, the failure to achieve complete totalitarianism was even more apparent, given the powerful position of the Church, the army, and other conservative forces.

For many years three more or less "standard" interpretations of fascism have dominated the scene: (1) the rather dogmatic assertion of Communist spokesmen in the 1920's and early 1930's that fascism was the inevitable and final stage of dying capitalism; (2) the contention of liberal-conservatives (*e.g.*, Benedetto Croce and Friedrich Meinecke) that fascism was a moral sickness that suddenly afflicted an essentially healthy body politic and, once cured, would not likely recur; and (3) the democratic-radical thesis (set forth by Luigi Salvatorelli, Angelo Tasca, and others) that fascism should be considered as one of several possible forms of political and social organization that may emerge in modern mass society at

4. Speech of October 28, 1925, quoted in *Opera Omnia di Benito Mussolini*, ed. by Edoardo and Duilio Susmel (Florence: La Fenice, 1951–63), Vol. XXI, p. 425.

a certain stage in its development and under certain crisis conditions. To these three may be added various Catholic historiographi-
cal currents (*e.g.*, Jacques Maritain and Augusto Del Noce); the
contention that fascism can be subsumed under the category of
"totalitarianism" (*e.g.*, Hannah Arendt and Carl Friedrich); and a
variety of other interpretations stemming from the disciplines of
the social sciences (*e.g.*, Erich Fromm and Seymour Lipset). The
author of this volume finds elements to commend themselves in
several of the categories mentioned above, and especially in the
democratic-radical one, but he is unwilling to restrict himself to
any single-track approach to the complex problem. This documentary collection, however, is not directly concerned with the
interpretations of fascism set forth by its critics; that is a topic for
another book.[5] Here the editor has generally chosen to let various
fascists speak for themselves.

As the title indicates, this study covers the years 1919 to 1945—
the classic "age of fascism" in the Mediterranean region. What
about fascism since that time? In Spain and Portugal a factitious
and attenuated form of the ideology managed to survive the shock
of World War II—perhaps more because of the isolation of these
countries (and physical exhaustion in the case of Spain) than
through the positive achievements of their regimes. At this writing
in 1969 there seem to be signs of a decision to whittle away more
of the façade of fascism in both Iberian nations; but if past experience is a guide, the foreign observer will be well advised to wait
and see.

In Italy Mussolini came to a violent death in April, 1945, but his
movement had already largely fallen apart several years before.
There continues to be a small neo-fascist party (the Italian Social
Movement, MSI), but at least at this time it does not pose a major
threat. The factors that favored the growth of fascism after World
War I have not been operative in the same measure after the
second world conflict. In the latter case the transition to economic
reconstruction was facilitated by massive American assistance.
After World War II, moreover, it became increasingly clear that
capitalism had far more possibilities for renovation than anyone

---

5. Pioneering efforts in this field include Renzo De Felice, *Le interpretazioni del fascismo* (Bari: Laterza, 1969); Ernst Nolte (ed.), *Theorien über
den Faschismus* (Cologne: Verlag Kiepenheuer & Witsch, 1967); and
Costanzo Casucci (ed.), *Il Fascismo: Antologia di scritti critici* (Bologna:
Il Mulino, 1961).

had thought possible back in 1919. Though Communism has remained a powerful and subversive force since 1945, the currents that prefer to use the label "Socialist" have generally become quite democratic and no longer frighten the middle and upper classes in the way they did half a century ago. Anti-Communism has become "internationalized" by the Cold War and is no longer the monopoly of a particular rightist movement. Although parliamentary government is still far from being robust in Italy, there is at least greater popular participation in and control over government than was possible fifty years ago. There has also been a shoring up of free institutions thanks to the safeguards written into the new Constitution of the Italian Republic, the development of European "communities," and the security provided by NATO. Italy has grown accustomed to the peace settlement of 1947; irredentism no longer occupies center stage in her politics, and certainly no one seriously proposes to revive imperialism. So far neither the Church nor the army has shown much inclination to play ball with neo-fascism in Italy, though the latter movement does enjoy some cooperation from the dwindling remnants of monarchists.

Yet even if old-style Fascism with its Blackshirt militia and identification of Party and State is not likely to return to power in Italy in the foreseeable future, it would be foolhardy to say that never again could some related form of nativist right-wing political extremism find favor. This might occur under some combination of circumstances such as the appearance of a magnetic new demagogue, or mounting popular disgust with the inability of parliamentary government to cope with housing shortages and to bring about the renovation of political and educational institutions, or soaring frustration with the inconveniences brought about by spiraling strikes on the part of Communist-dominated organized labor, or anger over the disruptive behavior of thousands of alienated university students. The course of events in Greece since the *coup d'état* of the colonels in April, 1967, underscores the latent danger of new manifestations of right-wing extremism in the Mediterranean region.

It is the editor's hope that the documents in this volume will help to guide the reader through the shifting and often far from crystalline currents of Mediterranean fascism. Many of them have been translated by the editor and are published here for the first time in English. Headnotes and connecting narrative are designed to place the selections in their historic context.

For Mussolini's Italy the documents are arranged in seven chapters. These include the period of the advent of fascism; the path to totalitarianism; the emergence of the corporative state; the socio-economic and youth programs; the relationship with the Roman Catholic Church and later with the Jews; the increasingly aggressive foreign policy; and finally the *coup d'état* of July 25, 1943, and the brutal epilogue of neo-fascism in the German-occupied northern Italian Social Republic.

Spain presents a different problem. Here the materials are of three types: documents that explain the nature of the Falange party during the brief life of its founder, José Antonio Primo de Rivera; speeches and decrees of Generalissimo Franco, who imposed his own will on the Falange during the Civil War; and finally diplomatic agreements and reports that point up the often difficult relationship between Nationalist Spain and the Axis powers.

In the case of Portugal, where the clerico-corporativist regime of Salazar was not brought into being by an already existent fascist party, the documents are fewer in number. They consist of excerpts from the dictator's speeches setting forth his political and economic philosophy, and key portions of the Constitution of 1933 that laid the basis for his new corporative state (Estado Novo).

The editor wishes to express his gratitude to Pilar Primo de Rivera, sister of the founder of the Falange Española; Jesús Unciti, director of Editora Nacional of the Spanish Ministry of Information and Tourism; the United States Catholic Conference; the Carnegie Endowment for International Peace; the Bruce Publishing Company; the Cambridge University Press; Giulio Einaudi Editore; Harcourt, Brace & World, Inc.; Giangiacomo Feltrinelli Editore; Arnaldo Mondadori Editore; and others for kindly permitting him to include in English translation certain documents and excerpts that originally appeared elsewhere.

I

Fascism in Italy

1. The Birth of Fascism

AT THE end of the Great War Italy's liberal political system was sickly; as a matter of fact, it had never been robust. After all, the country had been unified for only half a century, and the newly established state had been confronted by gargantuan problems—parliamentary inexperience, intense regional jealousies, hostility from the papacy, widespread illiteracy (especially in the south), economic underdevelopment, a high birth rate, and a tightly stratified social structure. Until 1912 the right to vote was restricted to a small proportion of the population; thereafter a democratic franchise was put into effect for all male literates over the age of twenty-one and for illiterates over the age of thirty if they had seen military service. In the years just before the war Catholics began to participate at last in national politics, now that the Church was worried by the growth of Marxism.

By the turn of the century an industrial revolution had begun to take place, particularly in the triangle bounded by Turin, Milan, and Genoa. This led to the emergence of two Italian societies living side by side in a state of uneasy tension. In the northern cities an industrialized form of capitalism was becoming superimposed on a commercial and agrarian society, while in the more feudalistic south the latter kind of society continued to predominate. Concomitantly, anarcho-syndicalist and socialist currents grew in strength, while landless peasants and urban masses seethed with discontent and erupted in violence from time to time.

After the death of Cavour in 1861 Italy's liberal politicians were mostly third-rate, with the exception of Giovanni Giolitti, who dominated the decade before World War I and instituted some significant reforms, though remaining cynical about electoral procedures. King Victor Emmanuel III, on the throne since the assassination of his father in 1900, was indecisive, uncommunicative, and physically unimpressive.

In retrospect it is easy to see that liberal Italy sealed its fate when it permitted itself to be dragged into the war in 1915 by a willful minority that included the King and some of his ministers, the superheated patriot-poet Gabriele D'Annunzio, and the renegade socialist Benito Mussolini. If Italy had stayed neutral, it is conceivable that in due course she could have stabilized her democratic institutions. As it turned out, however, Parliament receded into the background, while the Council of Ministers ruled largely by decree. As the war dragged on, neutralist-minded Socialists became ever more alienated, while the restive Catholics displayed a growing lack of enthusiasm for the struggle. The news of the Russian revolutions of 1917 caught the imagination of millions of Italian workers, who naïvely thought that Lenin's Bolshevist regime was simply Western-style Marxism "with a dash of Tartar sauce." The great military debacle at Caporetto in the fall of 1917 fanned the internal discontent of the country, though in the end, upon the advent to power of Premier Vittorio Emanuele Orlando, it reinforced the conservative nationalist groups.

In 1917 and 1918 Allied grain shipments and economic assistance helped Italy pull through the struggle. Unfortunately, this aid quickly terminated with the armistice. After World War I there was nothing comparable to the Marshall Plan that was to save Europe from economic and political chaos after the Second World War; instead, discontent soared. In the face of monopoly-minded industrialists who paid low wages while reaping huge wartime profits, labor began to organize in rapidly expanding labor unions. These engaged in a wave of strikes that aggravated an already bad inflationary situation and thoroughly alarmed the employers. On the large agricultural estates of the lower Po Valley and elsewhere, landowners were disturbed by the increasingly strident demands of migratory farm hands who were being organized by both Catholics and Socialists. Everywhere newly enfranchised industrial and farm workers were flocking into the two "mass" parties—either the Socialists or the brand-new Catholic Popular party (Partito Popolare Italiano), organized at war's end by the Sicilian priest Don Luigi Sturzo. If these two parties could have agreed to form a center-left coalition government, Italian democracy might still have succeeded; but at this stage of history only a handful of leaders in either party were that imaginative. The parliamentary elections of 1919, conducted for the first time under a system of proportional representation, resulted in the new *partiti di massa* torpedoing the elitist liberal parties that had been manipulated by the old ruling class.

Compounding the economic and political disaffection of the working people was a widespread psychological malaise. Returning servicemen were infuriated by the failure of "stay-at-homes" to appreciate their wartime sacrifices. Their sense of frustration was augmented by their resentment of Italy's inability to gather all of the Adriatic, Mediterranean, and African plums she desired at the peace harvest. The unwillingness of President Woodrow Wilson to concede her the Adriatic port of Fiume was particularly galling to ultrapatriotic veterans. To such people it seemed indeed that Italy had suffered a "mutilated victory." Their fury was exploited by Gabriele D'Annunzio, who in a melodramatic, filibustering expedition seized Fiume from September, 1919, to December, 1920—an episode that further fanned the flames of frustration and facilitated the growth of Fascism.

Italy had moved from the Great War into a kind of civil war that was to last from 1919 to 1922. During the first two years of strife the leftist political forces seemed to predominate, but after the failure of the workers' sit-down strike in the northern metallurgical plants in September, 1920, the forces of the Right gained the upper hand. The Socialist party fell asunder. A separate Communist party was formed in January, 1921, while right-wing Socialists split away to form still a third Marxist current. Whatever the danger of Communism's coming to power may have been prior to 1920–21, it was virtually nonexistent thereafter, though this was clearer in retrospect than at the time. As many of the workers began to learn the bitter truth about conditions in Soviet Russia, they became discouraged at the failure to achieve a postwar utopia either there or at home. In the face of this disillusionment, the initiative passed from the Marxists to frightened and determined reactionary forces on the radical right. And now that D'Annunzio was no longer in the limelight, Benito Mussolini, who had been steadily sidling toward the right, was able to emerge as the principal spokesman of this radical nationalist movement.

Born in 1883 in the village of Predappio in the notoriously "Red" region of Romagna in the lower Po Valley, Mussolini was the son of an anarchist blacksmith and religious-minded mother. He was named in honor of Benito Juárez, leader of Mexico's social revolution. Five feet, six inches tall, with jutting jaw and flashing eyes, Mussolini's pugnacious appearance suggested his revolutionary outlook. Largely self-educated, intensely anticlerical, antimonarchist, and antimilitarist, the young man got a job in 1902 as a substitute teacher in an elementary school. Partly to avoid military service he spent the next two years as a vagabond in Switzerland, working as a stonemason and absorbing some of the elitist ideas expressed in the writings of Nietzsche, the sociologist Pareto, and the syndicalist Sorel. The latter's emphasis on the need for overthrowing decadent liberal democracy and capitalism by the use of violence, direct action, and the general strike made a deep impression on Mussolini, as did also his neo-Machiavellian ideas for manipulating the masses by appealing to their emotions.

Returning to Italy in 1904 with a speaking knowledge of French and a smattering of German, Mussolini decided to serve his two-year term in the army, after which he returned to teaching. Soon he joined the Marxian Socialist movement and for a time in 1909 lived in the Austrian city of Trent, where he was secretary of the local chamber of labor. While there he wrote *The Cardinal's Mistress*, a bitterly anticlerical pamphlet that had to be withdrawn from circulation when he made his truce with the Vatican. By 1910 Mussolini returned to Forlì, where he edited the weekly *Lotta di classe*. He was now one of Italy's most prominent Socialists. In 1911 he bitterly denounced the "imperialist war" to gain Tripoli, an action which earned him a five-month jail term. After his release he helped expel from the ranks of the Socialist party two "revisionists" who had supported the war, Ivanoe Bonomi and Leonida Bissolati. For that he was rewarded in December, 1912, with the editorship of the Socialist party newspaper *Avanti!* Its circulation soon rose from 20,000 to 100,000.

The following document summarizes Mussolini's activities from then until the formation of his Fasci di Combattimento. It is an excerpt from a police report prepared for Premier Orlando in June, 1919, by the Inspector-General of Public Security in Milan.

Report of Inspector-General of Public Security, G. Gasti, Regarding Mussolini (June 4, 1919)

BIOGRAPHICAL OBSERVATIONS (Mussolini)

PROFESSOR BENITO MUSSOLINI, son of the late Alessandro, born in Predappio (Forlì) on July 29, 1883; now residing in Milan at Foro Bonaparte 38; revolutionary socialist; has a police record; elementary schoolteacher qualified to teach in secondary schools; former first secretary of the Chambers of Labor in Cesena, Forlì, and Ravenna; after 1912 editor of the newspaper *Avanti!* to which he gave a violent, suggestive, and intransigent orientation. In October, 1914, finding himself in opposition to the directorate of the Italian Socialist party because he advocated a kind of active neutrality on the part of Italy in the War by the Nations against the party's tendency of absolute neutrality, he withdrew on the twentieth of that month from the directorate of *Avanti!*

Then on the fifteenth of November thereafter he initiated publication of the newspaper *Il Popolo d'Italia,* in which he supported—in sharp contrast to *Avanti!* and amid bitter polemics against that newspaper and its chief backers—the thesis of Italian intervention in the war against the militarism of the Central Empires.

For this reason he was accused of moral and political unworthiness, and the party thereupon decided to expel him.

Thereafter he . . . undertook a very active campaign in behalf of Italian intervention, participating in demonstrations in the

SOURCE: Translated by permission of Harcourt, Brace & World, Inc., from Renzo De Felice, *Mussolini il rivoluzionario, 1883–1920* (© 1965 by Giulio Einaudi editore, Turin), pp. 730–735 *passim.*

piazzas and writing quite violent articles in *Popolo d'Italia*. Called into military service, he was sent to the zone of operations and was seriously wounded by the explosion of a grenade.

He was promoted to the rank of corporal "for merit of war." The promotion was recommended because of his exemplary conduct and fighting quality, his mental calmness and lack of concern for discomfort, his zeal and regularity in carrying out his assignments, where he was always first in every task involving labor and fortitude. On December 25, 1915, in Treviglio he contracted a marriage with his fellow countrywoman Rachele Guidi, who had already borne him a daughter, Edda, at Forlì in 1910.

He also had a mistress, the thirty-year-old Ida Irene Dalser, . . . by whom he had a son born in November, 1915, and legally recognized by Mussolini on January 11, 1916. . . . After being abandoned by Mussolini, [Miss Dalser] spoke badly of him to everybody. . . .

PHYSICAL AND PSYCHOLOGICAL CHARACTERISTICS

Benito Mussolini is of strong physical build even though he has been afflicted by syphilis. His robustness enables him to work continuously. He rests until a late hour in the morning, leaves his home at noon, but does not return again until 3 A.M., and those fifteen hours, except for a brief pause for meals, are devoted to newspaper and political work.

He is a sensual type, and this is revealed by the various relationships he has contracted with women. . . . He is an emotional, impulsive type, and these characteristics cause him to be suggestive and persuasive in his speeches, although it cannot be said that he is an orator, even though he speaks well.

Basically he is a sentimental type—a fact which results in much sympathy and friendship for him. He is disinterested, generous with the money that he has available, and this has given him a reputation for altruism and philanthropy.

He is very intelligent, shrewd, cautious, reflective, a good judge of men and of their strengths and weaknesses.

Quick friendships and dislikes come easily for him, and he is capable of making sacrifices for friends, and is stubborn in his dislikes and hatreds.

He is courageous and bold; he has organizing ability, and is capable of making quick decisions; but he is not equally tenacious in standing by his convictions and proposals.

He is very ambitious. He is motivated by the conviction that he represents a significant force in the destiny of Italy, and he is determined to make this prevail. He is a man who does not resign himself to positions of secondary rank. He intends to rate first and to dominate.

Within the ranks of official socialism he rose rapidly from obscure origins to an eminent position. He was the ideal editor of *Avanti!* for the socialists. In that line of work he was greatly esteemed and beloved. Some of his former comrades and admirers still confess that there was no one who understood better than he how to interpret the spirit of the proletariat, and there was no one who did not observe his apostasy with sorrow.

This came about not for reasons of self-interest or money. He was a sincere and passionate advocate, first of vigilant and armed neutrality, and later of war; and he did not believe that he was compromising with his personal and political honesty by making use of every means—no matter where they came from or wherever he might obtain them—to pay for his newspaper, his program and line of action.

This was his initial line. It is difficult to say to what extent, later on, his socialist convictions (which never did he either openly or privately abjure) may have been sacrificed in the course of the indispensable financial deals that were necessary for the continuation of the struggle in which he was engaged. . . . But assuming these modifications did take place . . . , he always wanted to give the appearance of still being a socialist, and he fooled himself into thinking that this was the case. . . .

According to my investigations, this is the moral figure of the man—in contrast to the opinion of his former political comrades and of those who belong to parties of "order" and regard him as somebody who has sold out, is corrupt, and can be corrupted; and in contrast to others who think he has remained firmly attached to his socialist principles of an earlier period.

Soon after the armistice Mussolini sensed the political potentialities of launching at home such a struggle as hitherto had been waged against the foreign enemy. A civil war against neutralists and "Bolsheviks" might well enable him to gain political power. With encouragement from the syndicalist Michele Bianchi (later to become one of the quadrumvirs of the Fascist March on Rome) and a few Arditi[1] veterans like Captain Ferruccio Vecchi, Mussolini summoned a meeting to take place in Milan on Sunday, March 23, 1919. The Industrial and Commercial Alliance, located at Piazza San Sepolcro 9, made available its second-floor salon.

The audience of about 120 people consisted chiefly of Arditi and Futurists[2] from Milan, with a sprinkling of republicans, national-syndicalists, and revisionist socialists. The meeting, which was presided over by Captain Vecchi and included speeches by Mussolini, Filippo Marinetti, and a few others, proclaimed the birth of the Fasci di Combattimento (Combat Fascio). The term *fascio* derived from the insignia that the lictors of ancient Rome carried (a bundle of rods with ax blade protruding, symbolizing authority and discipline) as they cleared the way for the chief magistrates in public. The so-called "Fascism of the first hour" that was proclaimed on March 23 anticipated in large measure the official program that was to be published on June 6. Mussolini spoke both in the morning and in the afternoon. In his first appearance he made a threefold programmatic declaration. In the afternoon he explained the position of the Fascist movement on a variety of political and socio-economic points.[3] According to the account in his own newspaper, *Popolo d'Italia*, Mussolini spoke nervously in short bursts, the audience paying rapt attention and interrupting often with applause.

The Birth of the Fascist Movement
(Piazza San Sepolcro 9, Milan, March 23, 1919)

MUSSOLINI'S MORNING SPEECH

First of all, a few words regarding the agenda.

Without undue formality or pedantry, I shall read to you three declarations that seem to me to be worthy of discussion and a vote.

SOURCE: Milan *Il Popolo d'Italia*, Vol. VI, No. 83 (March 24, 1919); reprinted in *Opera Omnia di Benito Mussolini*, ed. by Edoardo and Duilio Susmel (Florence: La Fenice, 1953), Vol. XII, pp. 321–4 *passim*. My translation.

1. The Arditi were a daredevil military corps assigned to especially hazardous tasks.
2. The Italian Futurist movement, made up of a small number of artistic, literary, and political nonconformists, was launched in February, 1909, by Filippo Marinetti (a friend of Captain Vecchi's). It extolled anticlericalism, nationalism, militarism, and imperialist expansion.
3. Some of his ideas about national syndicalism derived from talks with Alceste DeAmbris, head of the national-syndicalist labor union (Unione Italiano del Lavoro). DeAmbris was to be one of D'Annunzio's closest economic advisers in Fiume.

Later, in the afternoon, we can resume discussion of our platform declaration. I must tell you right off that we dare not bog down in details; if we wish to act, we must grasp reality in its broad essentials, without going into minute details.

FIRST DECLARATION

"The meeting of March 23 extends its greetings and its reverent and unforgetful thoughts first of all to those sons of Italy who have given their lives for the grandeur of the fatherland and the freedom of the world, to the wounded and sick, to all the fighters and ex-prisoners who carried out their duty; and it declares that it is ready to give energetic support to claims of both a material and moral nature that may be set forth by the servicemen's associations." . . .

SECOND DECLARATION

"The meeting of March 23 declares that it is opposed to the imperialism of other peoples at the expense of Italy, and declares that it is opposed to any eventual Italian imperialism that works to the detriment of other people. It accepts the supreme postulate of a League of Nations, which presupposes the integrity of each nation —integrity which, so far as Italy is concerned, must be realized in the Alps and along the Adriatic through her claim to Fiume and Dalmatia." . . .

THIRD DECLARATION

"The meeting of March 23 pledges the Fascists to sabotage in every way the candidates of neutralists in all the various parties." . . .

MUSSOLINI'S AFTERNOON SPEECH

I shall dispense with the idea of delivering a long speech. We don't need to place ourselves programmatically on a revolutionary footing because, in a historic sense, we already did so in 1915. It isn't necessary to set forth too analytical a program.

If Bolshevism could prove to us that it guarantees a people's greatness and that its regime is better than others, we wouldn't be frightened by it. But it has now been demonstrated beyond a doubt that Bolshevism has ruined the economic life of Russia. Over there, every kind of economic activity, from agriculture to industry, is completely paralyzed. Famine and hunger prevail. Not only that, but Bolshevism is a peculiarly Russian phenomenon, to which our

Western civilizations, starting with that of the Germans, have been resistant. We declare war against socialism, not because it is socialist but because it has opposed nationalism. Although we can discuss the question of what is socialism, what is its program, and what are its tactics, one thing is obvious: the official Italian Socialist party has been reactionary and absolutely conservative. If its views had prevailed, our survival in the world of today would be impossible. It is clear that the Socialist party will not be able to assume leadership of a program of renewal and reconstruction. We who have led the attack against political life in these past few years are going to expose the responsibilities of the official Socialist party.

It is inevitable that majorities become static, whereas minorities are dynamic. We intend to be an active minority, to attract the proletariat away from the official Socialist party. But if the middle class thinks that we are going to be their lightning rods, they are mistaken. We must go halfway toward meeting the workers. Right at the time of the armistice I wrote that we must approach the workers who were returning from the trenches, because it would be odious and Bolshevik not to recognize the rights of those who had fought in the war. We must, therefore, accept the demands of the working classes. Do they want an eight-hour day? Tomorrow will the miners and laborers who work at night demand six hours? Sickness and old-age insurance? Worker control over industry? We shall support these demands, partly because we want the workers to get accustomed to responsibilities of management and to learn as a result that it isn't easy to operate a business successfully.

These are our postulates, ours for the reasons that I said before and because in history there are inevitable cycles whereby everything is renewed and changed. If syndicalist doctrines maintain that one can find among the masses the necessary leadership capable of taking over the management of labor, we shall not object, especially if this movement takes into account two basic facts: the true nature of the productive process and the reality of the nation.

As for economic democracy, we favor national syndicalism and reject state intervention whenever it aims at throttling the creation of wealth.

We shall fight against technological and moral backwardness. There are industrialists who shun both technological and moral innovations. If they don't find the strength to transform themselves, they will be swept aside. We must impress upon the workers, however, that it is one thing to destroy, and quite another to build. Destruction can be the work of an hour, but construction may require years or centuries.

Economic democracy—this must be our motto. And now let us turn to the subject of political democracy.

I have the impression that the present regime in Italy has failed. It is clear to everyone that a crisis now exists. During the war all of us sensed the inadequacy of the government; today we know that our victory was due solely to the virtues of the Italian people, not to the intelligence and ability of its leaders.

We must not be fainthearted, now that the future nature of the political system is to be determined. We must act fast. If the present regime is going to be superseded, we must be ready to take its place. For this reason, we are establishing the Fasci as organs of creativity and agitation that will be ready to rush into the piazzas and cry out, "The right to the political succession belongs to us, because we were the ones who pushed the country into the war and led it to victory!"

Our program includes political reforms. The Senate must be abolished. But while we draw up this death certificate, let us add that in recent months the Senate has proved itself to be much superior to the Chamber. [A voice: "That doesn't take much!"] True enough, but even that little bit is a fact. In any case, we want to abolish that feudal organism.

We demand universal suffrage for both men and women; a system of voting by list on a regional basis; and proportional representation. New elections will produce a national assembly, and we insist that it must decide the question of what form of government the Italian state is to have. It will choose between a republic and a monarchy; and we who have always been inclined toward republicanism declare right here and now that we favor a republic! We are not going to . . . make a retrospective, historical indictment of the monarchy, however. The existing system of political representation cannot satisfy us; we want every distinct interest group to be represented directly. Since I, as a citizen, can vote according to my beliefs, then in the same manner I, as a professional man, should be permitted to vote according to my occupational outlook.

It may be objected that such a program implies a return to the corporations [guilds]. That is not important. The problem is to organize occupational councils that will complement an authentically political system of representation.

But let us not dwell on details. Of all the questions to be resolved, the one that interests us most is that of creating a governing class and endowing it with the necessary powers. For it is quite useless to raise more or less urgent issues if leaders who are capable of coping with them have not been produced.

Our program, upon examination, may be found to resemble others. In particular, one may discover some premises that are analogous to those of the official Socialists. But our position is different in spirit, because it is based on the war and the victory. This enables us to face everything boldly. I should even like to see the Socialists assume power for a while, because it is so very easy to promise paradise and so difficult to produce it. No government tomorrow can demobilize all the soldiers in a few days, nor increase the food supply when it doesn't exist. But in actuality we cannot allow such an experiment; for, once in power, the official Socialists would want to give Italy an imitation of the Russian phenomenon. And to this all socialist thinkers are opposed, from Branting and Thomas to Bernstein, because the Bolshevik experience, far from abolishing classes, entails a ferocious dictatorship. We are strongly opposed to all forms of dictatorship, whether they be of the saber or the cocked hat, of wealth or numbers. The only dictatorship we acknowledge is that of the will and intelligence.

Therefore, I hope that this assembly will agree to the resolution that accepts the economic demands advanced by the national syndicalists.

With this compass as our guide, we shall quickly succeed in creating a number of Fasci di Combattimento. Tomorrow we shall co-ordinate their activity simultaneously in all the centers of Italy. We are not static people; we are dynamic, and we intend to take our rightful place, which must always be in the vanguard.

In mid-April, 1919, the Fascists engaged in their first clash with Socialists, sacking the Milan offices of their newspaper, *Avanti!* By June 6 the Fascists decided the time had come to publish their own program in *Popolo d'Italia*. The new statement was generally in line with the March 23 announcement, though it now omitted all mention of the League of Nations or of cosmopolitanism. It was also more outspoken about the need for a National Constituent Assembly and national councils of experts in labor, industry, transportation, and other fields. Nowhere was there comment about the problem of education. Although still quite radical (perhaps more so than Mussolini himself would have liked), the June 6 program showed a tendency to shift to the right. The 17-point version printed below is the slightly revised one that was circulated in the form of a manifesto in the summer of 1919.

Program of the Italian Fascist Movement

ITALIAN FASCI DI COMBATTIMENTO
CENTRAL COMMITTEE
MILAN—VIA PAOLO DA CANNOBBIO, 37—TELEPHONE 7156

Italians!

This is the national program of a movement that is soundly Italian.

Revolution, because it is antidogmatic and antidemagogic; strongly innovating because it ignores a priori objections.

We regard the success of the revolutionary war as standing above everything and everybody.

The other problems—bureaucracy, administration, judiciary, school system, colonies, etc.—we shall consider after we have created a new ruling class.

Consequently, WE INSIST UPON:

For the political problem:

(a) Universal suffrage with a system of regional voting by list, with proportional representation, and woman suffrage and eligibility for office.

(b) Reduction of the age of voters to eighteen years; and that of eligibility for membership in the Chamber of Deputies to twenty-five years.

(c) Abolition of the Senate.

(d) Convocation of a National Assembly to sit for three years, *its primary task to be the establishment of a new constitutional structure for the state.*

(e) *Formation of National Technical Councils* for labor, industry, transportation, public health, communications, etc., to be elected by either professional or trades collectivities, and provided with legislative powers and the right to elect a Commissioner General who shall have the powers of a Minister.

SOURCE: Translated by permission of Harcourt, Brace & World, Inc., from Renzo De Felice, *Mussolini il rivoluzionario, 1883–1920* (© 1965 by Giulio Einaudi editore, Turin), pp. 744–745.

For the social problem:

WE INSIST UPON:

(a) Prompt promulgation of a state law that makes compulsory for *all workers* an eight-hour working day.

(b) Minimum wage scales.

(c) *Participation of workers' representatives in the technical management of industry.*

(d) Transfer to such proletarian organizations as are morally and technically qualified for it the responsibility for operating industries and public services.

(e) Prompt and complete satisfaction of the claims of the railroad workers and all employees in the transportation industry.

(f) Appropriate revision of the draft law regarding insurance for sickness and old age, and reduction of the presently proposed age eligibility from sixty-five to fifty-five.

For the military problem:

WE INSIST UPON:

(a) *Creation of a National Militia,* with short periods of training, and designed purely for a defensive role.

(b) Nationalization of all arms and munitions factories.

(c) A foreign policy calculated to improve Italy's position in the peaceful competition of the civilized nations.

For the financial problem:

WE INSIST UPON:

(a) A heavy and progressive tax on capital which would take the form of a meaningful PARTIAL EXPROPRIATION of all kinds of wealth.

(b) *Confiscation of all the properties belonging to religious congregations* and abolition of all the revenues of episcopal sees, which at present constitute an enormous burden on the nation while serving as a prerogative for a few privileged persons.

(c) Revision of all contracts for supplying war matériel, and confiscation of 85 per cent of war profits.

During most of 1919 Mussolini remained the journalist, orator, and theoretician of Fascism, leaving to others the task of organizing the movement. In the elections in Milan on November 16 of that year Mussolini was able to gain only 5,000 votes out of 270,000 cast. The workers apparently despised him as a renegade.

When the second congress of the Fasci di Combattimento met in

Milan on May 24–25, 1920, Mussolini and Cesare Rossi emerged as the leaders. Mussolini's inaugural speech, expressed in generic and flexible terms, urged the Fascists to avoid becoming too conservative and detached from the workers. For reasons of expediency he swallowed his earlier republicanism, asserting that this problem must not be viewed dogmatically; and in a brief interview he also backtracked on the subject of the papacy. Such watering-down of antimonarchism and anticlericalism proved too much for Marinetti, Captain Vecchi, and several of the Futurists, who quickly pulled out of the Fascist movement. Rossi also assumed a flexible stance that in effect pushed Fascism further to the right. The congress approved his call for revision of the platform in anticipation of local elections, but postponed discussion of the agricultural problem. The new program softened some of the earlier planks. For example, talk of proportional representation was dropped (the government of F. S. Nitti had already granted it); nor was there any longer a demand to eliminate the Senate and convene a National Constituent Assembly. Instead of calling for confiscation of 85 per cent of war profits, the new program recommended sequestration only of profits that were "left unproductive." It also virtually repudiated the General Confederation of Labor, calling instead for support of "those minority groups of the proletariat who can harmonize defense of class with the national interest"—the first clear step along the path that would lead to creation of strictly Fascist labor unions.

Postulates of the Fascist Program
(May, 1920)

The Fasci di Combattimento do not intend—in the present historical situation—to become a new party. Thus, they do not feel tied to any particular doctrinal form, nor to any traditional dogma. The intangible, shifting, complex currents of thought as well as the almost daily modifications of tactics that are necessitated by the reality of the situation cannot be reduced to narrow, artificial formulas.

The broad lines of the immediate tasks that confront the Fasci di Combattimento can be sketched under the following major headings: —*Support for our recent national war.* —*Winning the peace.* —*Resistance and opposition to the theoretical and practical degenerations of politically oriented socialism.*

SOURCE: Translated by permission of Harcourt, Brace & World, Inc., from Renzo De Felice, *Mussolini il rivoluzionario, 1883–1920* (© 1965 by Giulio Einaudi editore, Turin), pp. 746–748.

Against Political Parasitism

With the hope of mobilizing all our national energies to win the peace, the Fasci di Combattimento express their disgust for those men and agencies of the political bourgeoisie who have shown that they are incapable of handling domestic and foreign problems, that they are hostile to every profound renovation and to every spontaneous recognition of popular rights, and that they are inclined to make only those concessions that are dictated by calculations of parliamentary advantage.

For a Bourgeoisie of Labor

The Fasci recognize the very great value of the "bourgeoisie of labor," which in all fields of human endeavor (from that of industry and agriculture to that of science and the professions) constitutes a precious and indispensable element for bringing about progressive development and the triumph of national aspirations.

Against the Degenerations of the Labor Struggle

The Fasci di Combattimento, which are anxious to support the moral improvement of the proletariat and to help in the establishment of syndical organizations that will increase the self-consciousness of labor, feel that it is their duty to maintain an attitude of staunch opposition to those labor struggles in which strictly economic goals are submerged and confused by considerations of pure demagoguery.

The Problem of the Kind of Regime

For the Fasci di Combattimento the question of what kind of regime the country should have is subordinate to the present and future moral and material interests of the nation, as understood both in its present situation and in its historic destiny. Thus they express no prejudice either for or against existing institutions.

Our Postulates of a Financial Character

(a) A heavy, extraordinary tax of a progressive character on capital, which will assume the form of real but partial expropriation of all the wealth, and which will be paid within a very short period of time;

(b) The confiscation of all properties belonging to religious congregations and the abolition of all the revenues of episcopal sees, which at present constitute an enormous burden on the nation while serving as a prerogative for a few privileged persons;

(c) Revision of all contracts for supplying war matériel, and the confiscation of those excess war profits that are left unproductive.

THE FASCI AND LABOR ORGANIZATIONS

The Fasci express their sympathy and intention of supporting every initiative of those minority groups of the proletariat who seek to harmonize the safeguarding of their class interests with the interests of the nation. With respect to syndical tactics, they advise the proletariat to make use of whatever forms of struggle assure the development of the whole and the well-being of the various producers, without any special prejudices and without any dogmatic exclusiveness.

FOR AN ECONOMY OF MAXIMUM PRODUCTION

In contrast to theological proposals for reconstructing the economy on a rigidly collectivist basis, the Fasci di Combattimento assume a realistic position and do not express approval of any particular form of self-management. Instead, they declare their support for whatever system guarantees maximum production and maximum prosperity, whether it be individualist, collectivist, or something else.

OUR DEMANDS FOR SAFEGUARDING THE PROLETARIAT

(a) The prompt promulgation of a national law that will impose an eight-hour day for all kinds of labor;

(b) Representation of workers in industrial management, but restricted to matters regarding personnel;

(c) Transfer to such proletarian organizations as are morally and technically qualified for it the responsibility for managing industries and public utilities;

(d) Formation of National Technical Councils of Labor, composed of representatives from industry, agriculture and transportation, intellectual labor, public health, communications, etc., to be elected by the professional and trades bodies and endowed with legislative powers.

For the Military Problem

The Fasci di Combattimento call for the institution of a National Militia, with short periods of training and designed purely for a defensive role; and for the immediate acceptance of all the demands set forth by the associations of ex-soldiers and wounded veterans, to whom we express in a clear-cut and tangible manner the fatherland's gratitude.

The Means of Struggle of the Fasci di Combattimento

Regarding tactics to be adopted in support of the above program, the Fasci Italiani di Combattimento reserve the right to make contacts and agreements, as the situation requires, with all those groups and parties who occupy the same ground in their fight against demagoguery, bureaucracy, and plutocracy, and in favor of creating all kinds of forces for national reconstruction.

A token of things to come in Fascist foreign policy was Mussolini's success in getting the 1920 congress to approve his resolution calling for effective implementation of the 1915 Secret Treaty of London, annexation of Fiume, gradual withdrawal from the group of "Western plutocratic nations," establishment of closer ties with erstwhile enemy nations and with peoples of southeastern Europe, and support of the nation's need for and right to colonies.

At first the Fascists were concentrated in Milan and a few other cities. They gained ground quite slowly between 1919 and 1920; not until after the scare brought about by the workers' "occupation of the factories" in the late summer of 1920 did Fascism become really widespread. The industrialists then began to throw their financial support to it. Moreover, toward the end of 1920 Fascism started to spread into the countryside, bidding for the support of large landowners, particularly in the area between Bologna and Ferrara, a traditional stronghold of the Left and scene of frequent violence. Socialist and Catholic organizers of farm hands in that region, Venezia Giulia, Tuscany, and even distant Apulia were soon attacked by squads of Fascists, armed with castor oil, blackjacks, and more lethal weapons. The era of *squadrismo* and nightly expeditions to burn Socialist and Catholic political and labor headquarters had begun.

To enable the Fascists to take a clear-cut stand on agricultural problems, Mussolini ordered Gaetano Polverelli to prepare a report. By way of guidelines he advised him that they must categorically reject the socialist slogan of "land for the peasants" and proclaim instead that land belongs not simply to him who works it but to him whose mone-

tary investment makes it flourish. The document was completed in
January, 1921.

Fascist Agrarian Program
(January, 1921)

BROAD LINES FOR A SOLUTION

In tackling the agrarian problem, let us say first of all that in view
of the political nature and brevity of this present report, we cannot
and shall not make a theoretical, detailed exposition of our views.
. . . In any case, conditions in Italy vary greatly from region to
region. . . . We shall discuss the question in its broad political
aspects in order to chart our course of action during 1921. . . .

1. *Land for him who works it* can be a superficial, demagogic,
and harmful formula if promises are made to apply it with the
accompaniment of beating drums. In reality, the question is complex, and the application of this principle requires very careful
preparation. Let us begin with the *latifondo*. It is impossible today
to divide up the *latifondo*, because we cannot divide up malaria or
divide up a desert that is characterized by lack of roads, drinking
water, irrigation ditches, farm equipment, livestock, capital, and
houses. . . . A few socialists . . . are in favor of the *latifondo!*
But we are against it, resolutely against it, for an infinite number of
reasons, and chiefly because we must provide greater opportunities
to a steadily increasing population.

But we declare that before land division takes place [the state]
must provide roads, drinking water, irrigation systems, public
safety, housing, and capital for the development of agriculture.
. . . Moreover, we must have a well-organized and well-
developed mutual credit system, with both small agencies and large
banks. Increased productivity, of which there has been too much
talk, will take place only after this transformation of the system of
agricultural loans. . . .

The proper utilization of lands in the *latifondi* must be a slow,
gradual, and expensive process. If it were done tumultuously, it
would be disastrous. . . .

SOURCE: Translated by permission of Harcourt, Brace & World,
Inc., from Renzo De Felice, *Mussolini il fascista*, Vol. I: *La
conquista del potere, 1921–1925* (© 1966 by Giulio Einaudi
editore, Turin), pp. 736–740.

2. *Large-scale farming.* Generally speaking, large-scale industrial enterprises are *healthy.* Only ignorance could confuse them with the *latifondo.* Large-scale enterprises involve minimum expense and maximum income. . . . They cannot be divided without increasing expenses and reducing income, and this would result in serious social harm. Moreover, the large-scale type of undertaking permits cultivation of marginal lands, with the utilization of labor by old people, women, and children. Here, too, just as in the case of the factories, it is a question of maturity. One cannot improvise *technical advantages.* A co-operative can replace a large-scale industrialized agricultural enterprise with no national harm . . . only in those cases where such a new entity actually possesses technical and administrative advantages. . . .

3. *Breaking up of estates.* Not only is a system of *latifondi* harmful to the nation, so too is the breaking up of estates into scattered bits. Anyone who has to travel to distant plots of land scattered about the four points of the compass loses a great deal of time. It is imperative for us to establish a legal limit to land division, and to reform inheritance rights so as to facilitate compact plots of land around a farmhouse by exchanging those that are scattered about elsewhere.

4. *Parliamentary and ministerial bankruptcy.* The entire parliamentary and ministerial program in this field is bankrupt because of the incompetence of the deputies and ministers, the constant inspection and myopia of the bureaucrats, and the artificiality and rigidity of measures taken.

We must decentralize, and above all *we must not wait for Rome to act;* instead *we must present to and impose upon Rome* measures which have their own logic and local usefulness. . . .

5. *Opera Nazionale Combattenti* [National Land Program for Veterans]. Instead of creating colossal new central and regional authorities to regulate agricultural policy, it would be better to support the development and improvement of those that already exist and especially the Opera Nazionale Combattenti, which is also carrying out an agricultural policy. It has received many funds from the Crown as well as from private sources for the promotion of land cultivation, and it makes such funds available to war veterans. It has more than 300 million lire of capital.

The work of the Opera is meritorious. We do not share the views of those who assert that it has not accomplished very much.

Suffice to say that it must create everything *ex novo* and organize not only the farmers but also itself in every region. Obstacles have arisen not only because of the cultural and political backwardness of the masses but also because of technological backwardness in Italy. . . .

As for rural co-operation in the south, everything has yet to be done. . . .

But anyone who has a creative mind will set out with greater determination to overcome these difficulties. . . . We oppose the breakup and scattering of estates. There should be over-all quotas for co-operatives and families, but not for individuals; otherwise a new problem will arise for veterans who have large families.

In Italy it is important to build homesteads, because our people do not have a historical background of individualism such as the Anglo-Saxons; instead, they have the tradition of the clan. It is impossible, therefore, to force a family to live in an isolated home.

The only solution is that of colonies. The Germans migrated to South America and colonized it by means of organized platoons, with an expert in charge and a Protestant pastor as well. Without trying to copy the Germans, we have our own Roman tradition. Caius Gracchus sent 6,000 proletarian soldiers into Africa to build the colony of Giunonia, according to the historian Mommsen. We must translate (unfortunately from German!) specialized studies regarding the Roman colonies.

We must also decentralize the Opera and expropriate the estates of public agencies. . . .

6. *Against socialism and communism.* The first characteristic that we must give to our agrarian program is that of implacable hostility to social-communist propaganda. Socialism and communism applied to the agricultural problem would end up in nationalization of the lands—that is, in the collectivist transformation of all Italy into a single administrative *latifondo.* There is no question but that the social-communist party members have a vested interest in nationalization, because they would not do the work and they would furnish the cadres for the bureaucracy, making of themselves a parasitic caste of exploiters. But the notion that we must create an enormous, incompetent, parasitical bureaucracy to administer Italian agriculture is terrifying. The disasters resulting from state administration of the railroads and the postal system should be sufficient warning! . . .

We must explain that the Soviet commissars in Russia have carried out pitiless raids in the countryside, and have shot the muzhiks who sought to defend themselves. Social-communism, in short, tends to bring about privileged urban political organizations, which the farmers have to pay for. A similar theory leads to this choice: either the farmers rebel and starve out the cities, or else they limit their work to their own subsistence needs. In either case, communism is the father of famine.

In the south it would also lead to political separatism. That is why when we give land to the farmers, they become our most dependable and determined auxiliary forces in the struggle against socialism and communism, regimes which we shall leave to the ants and bees and to other lower forms of life.

Agricultural Fasci

Let us address ourselves to *Homo rusticus*, who is the best, healthiest, and most dependable type of *Homo sapiens*. But let us do it with determination and through organized action. The problem cannot be resolved by tourist expeditions.

We propose that an *Agricultural Section* be created within the Fasci for the purpose of propagandizing, organizing, and looking after the welfare of the farmers. . . .

We propose the organization of Agrarian Fasci (Fasci Colonici), which will act on the basis of clearly established principles. . . .

The Fasci, which are opposed to social-communist misery, seek the general prosperity of a people who in their two thousand years of history and in their present-day life are too great to be compared to primitive tribes on the steppes.

In May, 1921, Mussolini and 34 other Fascists were elected to the Chamber of Deputies. Ostensibly they belonged to a pro-government bloc of candidates that extended from the extreme right to various gradations of democratic liberalism. Premier Giolitti had called the election and given his blessing to this national bloc in the hope primarily of cutting the strength of his opponents among the Socialist and Popular parties who were making it impossible for him to govern according to the prewar methods. But the results were not very encouraging. Although the Socialists fell from 156 to 122 seats, the new Communist party elected 16. The Populars gained 7 seats, increasing their total from 100 to 107.

Giolitti has been roundly criticized for helping make possible Fascism's first success at the polls. By bringing the Fascists into Parliament, he had hoped to domesticate and absorb them. But Fascism was not a political force of the old stamp that could be blandished and brought into the liberal constitutional system. The Fascists had no intention of becoming beholden to Giolitti, as the maiden speech of Mussolini in the Chamber of Deputies on June 21, 1921, made clear. The address revealed how greatly his views had shifted since March, 1919.

*Mussolini's First Speech
in the Chamber of Deputies
(June 21, 1921)*

[*Signs of attention.*] Honorable colleagues, I am not unhappy to begin my speech from the benches of the extreme right. . . . Let me tell you at once, with that supreme contempt I hold for all labels, that in my speech I shall advocate reactionary theses. I am not sure, therefore, just how parliamentary my speech will be in its form; but in its substance it will be clearly antidemocratic and antisocialist. [*Approval from the extreme right.*] And when I say antisocialist, I also mean anti-Giolitti [*laughter*], because never so much as in these recent days has there been so assiduous an exchange of loving feelings between the Honorable Giolitti and the Socialist Parliamentary Group. . . .

And now to the argument. In the speech from the Throne, Honorable Giolitti, you had the King say that all of the Alpine frontier is now in our power. I challenge the geographical and political accuracy of that assertion. Only a few kilometers from Milan we still lack an Alpine frontier that could defend Lombardy and the entire Po Valley. . . . And the policy of this Government with respect to the Alto Adige is one of the saddest you can imagine. . . . And I deplore the fact that in the speech from the Throne no mention was made of the action carried out by Gabriele D'Annunzio and his legionnaires. [*Applause from the extreme right.*] . . .

In short, what is our foreign policy with respect to the vast, smoldering mixture of disagreements which the peace treaty, or rather the various treaties of nonpeace, have left in every part of the world? . . . So long as Count Sforza is in charge of foreign policy in the Giolitti cabinet, we cannot but be in the opposition. [*Comments.*]

SOURCE: *Atti del Parlamento Italiano. Camera dei Deputati. Legislatura XXVI, Sessione del 1921, Discussioni,* June 21, 1921 (Rome: Tipografia della Camera dei Deputati, 1921), pp. 89–98 *passim.* My translation.

And now I turn to domestic policies. Let me clarify the attitude of Fascism toward the various parties. [*Signs of attention.*] I shall begin with the Communist party. . . . I know the Communists. I know them because some of them are children of mine . . . spiritually speaking, of course. [*Laughter; comments.*] . . . And I recognize with a candor that may appear cynical that I was the first to infect these people, when I introduced into Italian socialism something of Bergson mixed with much of Blanqui. . . . These friends or enemies of mine. [*Voices from the extreme left:* "Enemies! Enemies!"] All right, the matter is settled! Enemies of mine. . . . So long as the Communists speak of dictatorship of the proletariat, . . . of soviets and other absurdities, there can only be combat between us. [*Interruptions from the extreme left.*] . . .

Our attitude toward the Socialist party is different. First of all, we insist on distinguishing between the labor movement and the political party. . . . We recognize that the General Confederation of Labor did not share the attitude of hostility to the war that was adopted by a large part of the Official Socialist party. . . . We also recognize the fact that because of their daily contact with the complex realities of economic life, the organizers of the General Confederation of Labor are quite reasonable. [*Interruptions from the extreme left; comments.*]

. . . If you present a bill for the eight-hour day, we shall vote for it. [*Comments from the extreme left; interruptions.*] We shall not oppose; indeed, we shall vote in favor of all measures intended to improve our body of social legislation. Nor shall we oppose experiments in co-operativism. But let me warn you at once that we shall resist with all our strength any attempt at socialization, collectivization, and state socialism! [*Applause from the extreme right.* . . .]

We deny that there are two classes; there are many more [*comments*]; we deny that all of human history can be explained by economic determinism. [*Applause from the extreme right.*] We deny your internationalism, because it is a luxury item [*comments from the extreme left*], that can be enjoyed only by upper classes, whereas the people are desperately attached to their native land. [*Applause from the extreme right.*]

Furthermore, we assert—and on the basis of the most recent socialist literature that you cannot deny [*comments*]—that the real history of capitalism is only now beginning, because capitalism is not just a system of oppression; it also represents a choice of values, a co-ordination of hierarchies, a more amply developed sense of individual responsibility. [*Approval.*] This is so true that Lenin, after establishing factory councils, has abolished them and replaced them with dictators. It is so true that after nationalizing commerce, he has restored a system of free exchange. And you who have been to Russia know that after having suppressed the bourgeoisie physically, he is today begging them to come back, because without capitalism and its technical systems of production, Russia can never get back on her feet again. [*Applause from the extreme right; comments.*] . . .

And now I come to the Popular party. [*Comments.*] Let me remind the Popolari that in the history of Fascism there are no invasions of churches. . . . I confess that there have been some beatings [*comments*], and there has been a burning, as a sacred act, of one newspaper that defined Fascism as an association of criminals. [*Comments; interruptions from the center; rumblings.*] Fascism does not preach and does not practice anticlericalism. And this too we can say: Fascism is not linked to Freemasonry, which really does not deserve the fear it seems to arouse among some members of the Popular party. . . .

But let us come to specific problems. References have been made here to the problem of divorce. Fundamentally, I am not in favor of divorce because I believe that problems of a sentimental nature cannot be resolved by juridical formulas. But I ask the Popolari to consider whether it is fair for the rich to obtain divorces by going to Hungary, while some poor devil has to drag a ball and chain all his life.

We agree with the Popolari on the issue of freedom of the schools. We are very close to them on the agrarian question, because we think that it is useless to sabotage small property holdings where these exist. Indeed, where it is possible to create them, it is proper to do so; but in cases where that system is unproductive, other forms of landholding should be adopted, even more or less collectivist co-operatives. We are in agreement regarding administrative decentralization, provided there is no talk of federalism or autonomies, because under a system of provincial federalism and everything that goes along with it, Italy would revert to where she was a century ago.

But there is one problem that transcends all these . . . , the problem of relations that may exist . . . between Italy and the Vatican. [*Signs of attention.*] . . . I affirm here and now that today the Latin and imperial tradition of Rome is represented by

Catholicism. [*Approval.*] . . . I believe and affirm that the universal idea that exists in Rome today is that which radiates from the Vatican. [*Approval.*] . . . I believe that if the Vatican were to renounce once for all its dreams of temporal power—and I think it is going to—profane or lay Italy would furnish the Vatican with material aid for its schools, churches, and hospitals. . . .

I have now reached the last part of my speech, and I wish to touch upon a very difficult question that, given the present situation, should arouse the attention of the Chamber. I refer to the struggle, the civil war that is taking place in Italy. First of all, and with regard to foreign opinion, it is necessary not to exaggerate the extent of this struggle. . . . All the nations of Europe have had some civil war. . . .

The function of the state is to provide us with a police force to protect honest men from rogues, a well-organized judicial system, an army ready for all eventualities, and a foreign policy in tune with the nation's needs. All the rest—and I do not even exclude secondary education—must be returned to the individual's private initiative. . . .

The civil war is worsening because all the parties are tending to organize militarily. A confrontation then ensues—something which was not very dangerous when political parties were in a nebulous state, but which has become much more dangerous now that parties are clearly organized, led, and controlled. On the one hand, it is now obvious that the working masses will be beaten. . . . On the other hand, risk, danger, and a taste for adventure have always been the duty and privilege of small aristocracies. [*Approval from the extreme right.*] . . . For us, violence is not a system, it is not a form of aesthetics, and even less is it a sport. It is a hard necessity to which we have had to submit. [*Comments.*] Let me say further that we are ready to disarm if you disarm as well. . . . I have spoken clearly. I await an equally elevated and clear reply from you. I have finished. [*Very lively and repeated applause from the extreme right; prolonged comments; many congratulations.*]

A major stronghold of Fascism came to be the region between Bologna and Ferrara, where Italo Balbo and Dino Grandi were the movement's most resolute leaders. Balbo was one of the main organizers of Fascism on the military level; Grandi correctly appraised the significance of recruiting and organizing labor. Until this time most of Italy's labor organizations had been either Socialist or Catholic; henceforth Fascist labor unions or syndicates also appeared.

Deplorable acts of violence increased markedly during the first six months of 1921 in Emilia and Romagna, with Tuscany running a close second. Things reached such a pitch in the summer that the new premier, Ivanoe Bonomi, helped persuade Mussolini that a truce must be achieved. A "peace pact" with the Socialists and General Confederation of Labor was signed by the Fascists on August 3. But Grandi and Balbo refused to recognize it, thereby precipitating a serious split with Mussolini. The latter retaliated by resigning as a member of the executive group of the Central Committee, though not from the movement. Mussolini's resignation was rejected by the Fascist National Council, which recognized that his rivals were all inexperienced, but the price that was paid was Fascist denunciation of the "peace pact" in November.

The true explanation for this repudiation was that the large landowners had intervened. Behind the efforts of the Fascists to organize labor unions were the landowners, anxious to avenge the farm workers' occupation of their lands and determined to put an end once for all to the cry "Land for the peasants!" The new Fascist syndicates drew up contracts that in effect favored the landowners and obliged the workers to take a cut in pay. Thus agrarian reaction set in, perhaps even more intense and shortsighted than that of the industrialists who had already reacted in favor of Fascism. The punitive raids of the *squadristi* increased in tempo. The movement was now making its greatest strides—at the very time when the danger of socialist revolution was over and there was a possibility that the government might even balance the budget.

The Fascist "movement" officially became the National Fascist Party (Partito Nazionale Fascista, PNF) at the Rome congress of November 7–10, 1921. Despite the compound title, the conservative Nationalist party (founded in 1910 by Enrico Corradini and others) was as yet only informally associated with the Fascists; the complete merger of these two parties did not take place until 1923 after Mussolini came to power. In the weeks before the Rome conclave Mussolini had expressed preference for the label "Fascist Labor Party" and had hoped to win support from the General Confederation of Labor; but by the time the congress convened he was forced by the Grandis and Balbos to drop the word "labor." Moreover, the party was not to be based on a coalition of labor syndicates, as Mussolini had once envisaged, but rather on an association of the *fasci* and their storm squads. Mussolini was also overruled as to the location of the congress, the opposition elements preferring not to let it be held in his stronghold of Milan.

The Rome congress was informed that there were now 2,200 *fasci* and 320,000 members in the PNF, recruited chiefly from the landowners and middle classes. This figure compared with only 100 *fasci* and 30,000 supporters in 1920. An analysis that was made of about half of the members in November, 1921, revealed the following occupational breakdown: 18,084 landowners; 13,878 tradesmen; 4,269 manufacturers; 9,981 members of learned professions; 7,209 state employees; 14,988 private employees; 1,680 teachers; 36,847 agricultural laborers; and 23,418 industrial workers. Probably most of the farm workers had previously been identified with Socialist or Catholic "leagues" and were forced into the *fasci* by the *squadristi*, while a good many of the industrial workers were taken from the civil service, unemployed dock workers, and districts under Fascist military occupation. The mass of workers in the towns and even in the rural areas, though paralyzed by fear, generally remained loyal to their Socialist or Catholic organizations.

From the point of view of structure and style, the PNF represented something new in comparison to traditional parties. It possessed a military organization whose guiding figures in the early stages were Balbo, Count Cesare Maria De Vecchi (an elderly monarchist landowner), and Emilio DeBono (an Italian army general who had gone over to Fascism). The talent for military and revolutionary strategy was to be seen in the importance the Fascists assigned to securing control of such major railway junctions as Bologna, Verona, and Alessandria.

It is clear from the text of the new Fascist program adopted in November, 1921, at the Rome congress that the tenuous "socialism" of 1919 had given way to "integral" nationalism.[4] The abolition of "demagogic" fiscal measures such as taxes on inheritances and bondholders was called for, as were strikes in the public services. The program advocated National Technical Councils with legislative powers alongside Parliament. It demanded complete freedom for the Catholic Church in the exercise of its spiritual office. It repudiated the League of Nations and called for a large standing army instead of the short-term militia that had been favored in 1919.

New Program of the National Fascist Party (PNF)
(Adopted at the Third Congress in Rome, November 7–10, 1921)

BASES

Fascism has now become a political party in order to tighten its discipline and clarify its "creed."

The Nation is not simply a sum of individual beings, nor is it an

SOURCE: Translated by permission of Harcourt, Brace & World, Inc., from Renzo De Felice, *Mussolini il fascista*, Vol. I: *La conquista del potere, 1921–1925* (© 1966 by Giulio Einaudi editore, Turin), pp. 756–763.

4. "Integral nationalism" may be defined, in the words of Charles Maurras, as "the exclusive pursuit of national policies, the absolute maintenance of national integrity, and the steady increase of national power—for a nation declines when it loses military might." Quoted in Carlton J. H. Hayes, *The Historical Evolution of Modern Nationalism* (New York, 1931), pp. 165–166.

instrumentality of parties for attaining their own goals. It is rather an organism made up of an endless series of generations whose individual members are but transient elements. It is the supreme synthesis of the material and immaterial values of the race.

The State is the juridical incarnation of the Nation. Political institutions are effective instrumentalities to the extent that national values find expression and security therein.

The autonomous values of the individual and those that are common to most individuals—expressed through such organized collective personalities as families, towns, corporations, etc.—are to be promoted, developed, and defended, but always within the context of the Nation, to which they occupy a subordinate place.

The National Fascist Party declares that at this moment in history the dominant form of social organization in the world is *national society*; and the essential law of life in the world is not the consolidation of different societies into one single, immense society called "Humanity," as internationalist-minded theoreticians believe, but is rather a fruitful and, let us hope, peaceful competition among different national societies.

The State

The State should be reduced to its essential function of preserving the political and juridical order.

The State must grant legal powers and responsibility to a variety of Associations, and must also confer upon such professional and economic corporations the right to elect representatives to the National Technical Councils.

Consequently, the powers and functions that now appertain to Parliament must be restricted. Problems that concern the individual as a citizen of the State, and concern the State as the organism for achieving and defending the supreme national interests, fall within the competence of Parliament; but problems that affect various kinds of activity by individuals in their role as producers lie within the competence of the National Technical Councils.

The State is sovereign. Such sovereignty cannot and must not be infringed or diminished by the Church, and the latter, for its part, must be guaranteed the broadest freedom in the exercise of its spiritual mission.

With respect to the specific form of political institutions,[5] the

5. *I.e.*, a republic or a monarchy.—*Ed.*

National Fascist Party subordinates its own attitude to the moral and material interests of the Nation as understood in all aspects of its historic destiny.

THE CORPORATIONS

Fascism does not deny the historic fact of the development of corporations, and it intends to co-ordinate this development in the best national interest.

Corporations must be promoted for two basic purposes—as the expression of national solidarity, and as the means for increasing production.

Corporations should not submerge the individual within the collectivity. They should not arbitrarily level his opportunities and strength, but should instead develop and maximize these qualities.

The National Fascist Party intends to fight for the following principles in behalf of the working and white-collar class:

1. The promulgation of a national law that specifies the eight-hour day as the average legal working day for all wage earners (*salariati*), with such possible exceptions as may be deemed advisable as a result of either agricultural or industrial requirements.

2. Social legislation that is brought up to date to conform to present-day needs, and especially in order to give agricultural, industrial, and white-collar workers protection against accidents, sickness, and old age, so long as this does not hamper productivity.

3. Labor representation in the management of all industries, but restricted to personnel matters.

4. Assignment of managerial responsibilities in industries and public services to those syndical organizations that are morally worthy and technically qualified.

5. Encouragement of the system of ownership of small farms wherever this is economically beneficial.

CARDINAL PRINCIPLES OF DOMESTIC POLICY

The National Fascist Party intends to improve and dignify the level of political behavior so that public and private morality will cease to be at odds in our national life.

The Party aspires to the supreme honor of becoming the Government of the Nation; and of restoring the ethical concept that Government should administer public affairs not in the selfish interests of parties and clienteles but in the supreme interests of the Nation.

The prestige of the Nation-State must be restored. Therefore, the State must not watch with indifference the unleashing of arrogant forces that attack and otherwise threaten to weaken the material and spiritual qualities of our national life. Instead, it must act scrupulously as the custodian, defender, and promoter of our national traditions, national feeling, and national will.

The citizen's freedom is limited in two ways. It must take into account the freedom of other juridical persons, and it must recognize the sovereign right of the Nation to live and develop itself.

The State must encourage the development of the Nation, not by monopolizing but by promoting every activity that seeks to bring about the ethical, intellectual, religious, artistic, juridical, social, economic, and physical progress of the national collectivity.

Cardinal Principles of Foreign Policy

Let Italy reaffirm its right to complete historic and geographic unification, even where this has not yet been achieved. Let it carry out its rôle as a bulwark of Latin civilization in the Mediterranean. Let it impose firmly and resolutely the authority of its law over the peoples of various nationalities who have been annexed to Italy. Let it give effective support to those Italians abroad to whom right of political representation should be granted.

Fascism does not believe in the validity of the principles that inspire the so-called League of Nations, because not every nation is represented in it, and those that are in it do not enjoy equal status.

Fascism does not believe in either the validity or the usefulness of a Red International, or a White one, or any other kind, since these are artificial creations that attract small minorities of more or less committed individuals in contrast to the great mass of people who, in the course of the progress and setbacks in their lives, finally bring about the kind of realignment of interest groups against which all internationalist-type contrivances are doomed to failure, as recent historical experiences have proved.

Our international treaties should seek through commercial expansion and political influence to bring about a greater diffusion of *italianità* in the world. International treaties should be revised and modified whenever they have become clearly inapplicable, and they should be regulated according to the needs of the economy of the nation and the world.

The State must develop Italy's colonies in the Mediterranean and overseas by means of economic and cultural institutions and a system of rapid communications.

The National Fascist Party proclaims its support of a policy of friendly relations with all the peoples of the Near East and the Far East.

The defense and development of Italy overseas should be assigned to an Army and a Navy that are adequate to the needs of this policy and sufficiently strong in comparison to other nations. Our diplomatic service should also be made aware of its responsibilities and endowed with the requisite training, attitudes, and facilities for expressing in both a symbolic and a material way Italy's grandeur in the world.

Cardinal Principles of Financial Policy and of National Economic Reconstruction

The National Fascist Party will take steps to bring about the following things:

1. The true responsibility of either individuals or corporations will be clearly publicized in cases of violations of labor agreements that have been freely negotiated.

2. Officials in public administration will bear civil responsibility for any acts of negligence on their part that cause injury to others.

3. Publicity will be given to incomes that are subject to taxation as well as to the appraised value of inherited property, so that a control will exist over the financial obligations of all citizens to the State.

4. State intervention, which may be absolutely necessary to protect certain branches of agriculture and manufacturing from excessively dangerous foreign competition, will be of such a nature as to stimulate the productive forces of the country rather than to ensure parasitical exploitation of the national economy by plutocratic groups.

The immediate objectives of the National Fascist Party include the following:

1. Balancing the budgets of State and local public agencies, to be achieved through rigorous economies in all parasitical and superfluous bodies, and through paring of expenditures that are not absolutely necessary for the well-being of the recipients or for the needs of society as a whole.

2. Administrative decentralization in order to simplify services and facilitate reduction of the size of the bureaucracy—but we resolutely oppose any form of political regionalism.

3. Rigid safeguarding of taxpayers' money, eliminating every subsidy or special favor on the part of the State or any other public agency to consortiums, co-operatives, industries, clienteles, and other entities which even though they may be incapable of managing their own affairs are not indispensable to the nation.

4. Simplification of machinery for collecting taxes and distributing revenues. Instead of progressive and confiscatory taxation, the principle of proportionality must apply, with no preference being shown either for or against particular categories of citizens.

5. Opposition to the kind of financial and tax demagoguery that discourages initiative and sterilizes the very sources of saving and of national productivity.

6. Halting of the political practice of ill-conceived, "pork-barrel" public works projects that are undertaken either for vote-getting purposes or for alleged reasons of public need, and are often unproductive because of their hit-or-miss location.

7. Preparation of an organic plan for public works to conform to the nation's new economic, technical, and military needs, a plan that will be undertaken primarily for the purpose of:

(a) Completion and reorganization of the Italian railroad network in such a way as better to link the newly redeemed regions to the trunk lines of the peninsula, as well as to improve communications within the peninsula itself, and particularly those lines that run north and south over the Apennines.

(b) Acceleration insofar as possible of the electrification of the railways, and the general development of the country's water resources by means of mountain reservoirs, which will also be of help to industry and agriculture.

(c) Systematization and extension of the network of highways, especially in the south, where this is the prerequisite to solving innumerable economic and social problems.

(d) Establishment and enlargement of the system of maritime communications between the peninsula, the islands, the eastern shore of the Adriatic, and our Mediterranean colonies, as well as between the northern and southern halves of the peninsula itself— for the dual purpose of providing a supplement to our railroad network and of encouraging Italians in the art of navigation.

(e) Concentration of expenditures and efforts in just a few ports on the three seas, installing the most modern equipment in them.

(f) Opposition and resistance to local particularisms, which lead to dispersion of efforts especially in the field of public works and are an obstacle to really great undertakings of national interest.

8. The return to private enterprise of those industrial plants whose management by the State has proved unsatisfactory—especially the telephone and railway systems. In the case of the railroads, competition should be encouraged among the major lines, in contrast to local lines which can be operated in a variety of ways.

9. The termination of the monopoly for the post and telegraph system so that private initiative can move into this field and eventually replace state control.

Cardinal Principles of Social Policy

Fascism recognizes the social utility of private property, which involves both a right and a duty. This is the form of administration that society historically has assigned to the individual for the increment of his patrimony.

In contrast to socialist proposals for reconstructing the economy along purely collectivist lines, the National Fascist Party takes the position, based on historic and national realism, that there is no single ideal form of agricultural and industrial economy. Instead it declares its support of whatever economic pattern—individualistic or otherwise—guarantees maximum production and prosperity.

The National Fascist Party is in favor of a regime that encourages the growth of national wealth by spurring individual initiative and energy (which constitute the most powerful and fruitful element in economic production), and it absolutely repudiates the motley, costly, and uneconomic machinery of state control, socialization, and municipalization. The National Fascist Party will therefore support any undertaking that seeks to improve productivity and aims at eliminating all forms of individual and group parasitism.

The National Fascist Party will take steps:

(a) To discipline the disorderly struggles between classes and occupational interests. It favors therefore the juridical recognition of and the assignment of responsibility to the various organizations of workers and employers.

(b) To enact and enforce in every way a law prohibiting strikes in the public services. At the same time, arbitrational courts must be organized, to consist of one representative for management, one representative from the category of workers and white-collar employees, and one representative of the general public, since it is they who pay the bill.

EDUCATIONAL POLICY

The general goal of schools must be the education of those persons who will be capable of guaranteeing the Nation's economic and historic progress; of raising the moral and cultural level of the masses, and of training the best elements in all the various classes so as to ensure a continuous renewal of the governing groups.

To this end we urge the following measures:

1. Intensify the struggle against illiteracy through the construction of schools and access roads. Let the State take responsibility for whatever measures are necessary.

2. Extend compulsory education through and including the sixth elementary grade in those communes that are in a position to provide the necessary schools, and for all those who, after taking the "maturity examination," do not enter the middle school (*scuola media*); compulsory education through and including the fourth elementary grade in all the other communes.

3. Introduce a rigorously national character into the elementary schools so that they will also provide Italy's future soldiers with physical and moral training. Thus there must be rigid State control over the curricula, the hiring of teachers, and the supervision of their work, especially in those communes that are dominated by antinationalist parties.

4. Freely operated middle schools (*scuole medie*) and universities, except for State control over the programs and the spirit of instruction, and the State's duty to provide premilitary instruction for the purpose of training officers.

5. Normal schools should be guided by the same criteria that have been extablished for the schools to which the future teachers are going to be sent. This implies a rigorously national program, even in the institutes which train elementary teachers.

6. Professional schools and industrial and agricultural institutes should be placed under an organic plan that will make use of the financial contribution and experience of industrialists and agriculturalists, and that will exist for the purpose of increasing national productivity and of creating a class of technicians standing midway between the executors and the directors of production. To this end, the State will have to integrate and co-ordinate various private initiatives, and wherever these are lacking, substitute itself for them.

7. A predominantly classical type of curriculum should be offered in the lower and upper middle schools (*scuole medie inferiori e superiori*). In the case of the lower ones, there should be consolidations and reforms so that all students must study Latin. French is no longer to be the only possible secondary language to Italian. Instead, the possibility shall exist of choosing and adapting the secondary language requirement in accordance with the needs of specific regions, especially those along the frontiers.

8. Consolidate all forms of financial assistance for education, scholarships, and the like, into one institute which will be controlled and organized by the State and have the power to select the most intelligent and ambitious pupils from the elementary grades upward and assure them a superior education, and which may overrule parental selfishness, if need be, and make available an appropriate subsidy wherever this is necessary.

9. Financial and moral rewards should be given to teachers and professors and also to Army officers (who are the military educators of the Nation) so as to ensure them self-respect and opportunities for improving their own skills, and to inspire them and the public with a consciousness of the national importance of their mission.

JUSTICE

There must be intensive support for both preventive and reformatory measures in handling delinquency (reformatories, training schools, mental hospitals for the criminally insane, etc.). Penalties —which are the means whereby National Society defends itself against lawbreakers—should have both a punitive and a corrective function. With respect to the second of these, the penitentiary system must be improved hygienically and renovated in a socially useful manner—for example, by developing prison workshops.

Special magistracies must be abolished. The National Fascist Party favors revision of the military penal code.

Court procedures must be expedited.

NATIONAL DEFENSE

Every citizen has the obligation of military service. Steps must be taken to convert the Army into a kind of Nation in Arms, wherein all individual, collective, economic, industrial, and agricultural forces will be fully integrated for the supreme purpose of defending our national interests.

To this end, the National Fascist Party proposes the immediate recruitment of an Army which, as the result of a fully perfected system of training, will vigilantly exercise surveillance over our newly won frontiers. And simultaneously, in hours of danger and of glory, it will make sure that the men, means, and will power which our Nation can draw from its unlimited resources will be kept ready, properly trained, and organized.

To these same ends, the Army, together with the school system and various sports organizations, must seek to develop in the bodies and minds of citizens, from childhood on, an aptitude and habit for combat and sacrifice in behalf of the fatherland (*i.e.*, premilitary training).

ORGANIZATION

Present-day Fascism is:

    (a) a political organism;
    (b) an economic organism;
    (c) a combat organism.

In the political field, it welcomes without sectarianism all those who sincerely subscribe to its principles and obey its discipline. It stimulates and develops individual talents and brings them together in appropriate groups according to their aptitudes. It participates intensely and constantly in every manifestation of political life, thereby putting into effect whatever can properly be extracted from its theories, while simultaneously reaffirming the integral nature of all of them.

In the economic sector, it promotes the formation of professional corporations—some purely Fascist, some autonomous—in accordance with the requirements of time and place, so long as these are in essential agreement with the Party's national policy that the Nation must always stand above classes.

As regards organization for combat, the National Fascist Party forms a single entity with its own squads, and these constitute a voluntary militia in the service of the Nation-State, a living force embodying and defending the Fascist Idea.

In February, 1922, Premier Bonomi decided to resign when he lost key support among the moderate left over a minor issue. Giolitti would have been the logical successor, but opposition from Sturzo of the Popular party prevented this. Instead, Luigi Facta, a second-rate lieutenant of Giolitti's, was chosen. He scarcely tried to maintain the peace. The Fascists, for their part, accelerated their violence during the spring and summer. For example, after a Fascist had been killed in a brawl in Ravenna, Balbo took revenge, setting fire to one of the "Red" buildings:

Italo Balbo's Squadrismo

I [then] announced to [the chief of police] that I would burn down and destroy the houses of all Socialists in Ravenna if he did not give me within half an hour the means required for transporting the Fascists elsewhere. It was a dramatic moment. I demanded a whole fleet of trucks. The police officers completely lost their heads; but after half an hour they told me where I could find trucks already filled with gasoline. Some of them actually belonged to the office of the chief of police. My ostensible reason was that I wanted to get the exasperated Fascists out of the town; in reality, I was organizing a "column of fire" . . . to extend our reprisals throughout the province. . . . We went through . . . all the towns and centers in the provinces of Forlì and Ravenna and destroyed and burned all the Red buildings. . . . It was a terrible night. Our passage was marked by huge columns of fire and smoke.

Meanwhile in a speech delivered in Udine on September 20, 1922, Mussolini, ever the opportunist, made a highly significant policy statement. Posing as a defender of order, he indicated that the Fascists were ready to renounce their republicanism and preserve the House of Savoy if the King and the Army made no hostile move against what he called the "Fascist revolution."

SOURCE: Italo Balbo, *Diario 1922* (Milan: A. Mondadori, 1932), pp. 103, 109 (July 28–30, 1922). My translation.

Mussolini's Speech Regarding
the House of Savoy
(September 20, 1922)

In the speech that I am about to deliver I shall make an exception to
the rule that I have always followed—of limiting so far as possible
the demonstrations of my eloquence. Oh, if it were only possible,
as a poet has recommended, to strangle this verbose, prolix, endless,
democratic eloquence that has gotten us off the track so long! I am
sure, therefore, . . . that you would not expect from me a speech
that was not exquisitely Fascist—harsh, frank, tough, and cut to
the bare bones. . . .

Let us turn to another theme—discipline. I am in favor of rigid
discipline. We must impose on ourselves the most ironclad discipline, because otherwise we shall not have the right to impose it on
the nation. And it is only through discipline of the nation that Italy
can make itself felt in the arena of other nations. Discipline must be
accepted, and when it is not accepted, it must be imposed. . . .

And now I come to the subject of violence. Violence is not
immoral. Violence is sometimes moral. We deny the right of all
our enemies to complain about our violence, because compared to
what was committed during the unhappy years of 1919 and 1920,
and compared to what the Bolsheviks did in Russia, where two
million people were executed and another two million are languish-
ing in prison, our violence is child's play. On the other hand, our
violence is effective. . . . When our violence is effective in a
cancerous situation, it is most moral, sacrosanct, and necessary.
But, O my Fascist friends, . . . it is necessary that our violence
have specifically Fascist characteristics. The violence of ten against
one is to be repudiated and condemned. [*Applause.*] . . . Violence must be adapted to the needs of the moment, not made into a
cult, a doctrine, or a sport. . . .

Another theme which may lend hope to our enemies is that of

SOURCE: Delivered at the Teatro Sociale in Udine the morning of
September 20, 1922, at the convention of the Fasci Friulani di
Combattimento. Published in *Il Popolo d'Italia* (Milan), Vol. IX,
No. 226 (Sept. 21, 1922); reprinted in *Opera Omnia di Benito
Mussolini*, ed. by Edoardo and Duilio Susmel (Florence: La
Fenice, 1956), Vol. XVIII, pp. 411–421 *passim*. My translation.

the masses. You know that I do not worship the new divinity—the masses. It is a creation of democracy and of socialism. . . . History teaches that it is always minorities, small at the beginning, who have produced profound upheavals in human society. We do not worship the masses, even if they come endowed with every kind of sacrosanct callus on their hands and brains. . . .

We have had to practice syndicalism, and we continue to do so. Some say, "Your syndicalism will end up by becoming just like socialist syndicalism; you will be forced by the logic of events to embark upon class struggle." . . . In actuality, our syndicalism differs from that of others because we absolutely deny the right to strike in the public services. We are in favor of class collaboration, especially in a period like the present one of very acute economic crisis. Therefore we are trying to imbue our own syndicates with this truth, this theory. However, it is necessary to say with equal frankness that the industrialists and employers must not blackmail us, because there is a limit beyond which they can't go. . . .

And now I have come to the theme that is of the utmost importance at this moment. . . . It is a great fortune [for] our foreign policy, it a great fortune that alongside an army that has very glorious traditions, our National Army, there is also the Fascist Army. Our ministers of foreign affairs must learn how to play this card and throw it down on the green table and say: "Take note of the fact that no matter what it costs, Italy no longer will pursue a policy of renunciation and weakness!" [*Prolonged applause.* . . .]

. . . They ask us what is our program. . . . Our program is simple. We want to govern Italy. . . . It isn't programs of salvation that Italy needs. It is men and determination! [*Applause.*] . . .

Let us take up the delicate and burning question of the regime. . . . Is it possible—and here is the big question—for a profound transformation of our political regime to take place without tampering with the institution of monarchy? In other words, is it possible for Italy to be renovated without jeopardizing the monarchy? And what is the over-all attitude of Fascism toward political institutions?

Our attitude in the face of political institutions is not binding in any sense. After all, perfect regimes exist only in the books of philosophers. . . . Political forms cannot be approved or disapproved on permanent grounds, but must be examined in the light of the relationship they have to the state of the economy and to the

spiritual outlook of a given people. . . . Now, I really believe that
the regime can be profoundly altered without touching the monarchy. . . . Therefore, we shall not make the monarchy a part of
our campaign, for we have other more visible and formidable
targets. Moreover, we believe that a large part of the country
would view with suspicion any transformation of the regime that
went as far as that. We would probably stir up some regional
separatism, for it always works out that way. Today many are
indifferent toward the monarchy, but tomorrow they may well be
sympathetic and favorable, and find very respectable reasons to
attack Fascism if it has attacked that target.

I am basically of the opinion that the monarchy has no reason
whatever to oppose what one must already call the Fascist revolution. It can gain nothing, for by doing so, it would become a target,
and if it became the target, it is certain that we would surely not be
able to save it. . . .

One month later the Fascists held a huge party congress in the San
Carlo opera house in Naples. Mussolini and others advocated a "march
on Rome" to intimidate Facta's weak government and open the way
for Mussolini to become premier. Thereafter Mussolini hurried back to
his Milan newspaper office (where he would also be close to Switzerland in case things went wrong), leaving four quadrumvirs (Italo
Balbo, General Emilio DeBono, Count Cesare Maria DeVecchi, and
Michele Bianchi, the young PNF secretary) to organize the "march."
Following are excerpts from Mussolini's speech at the San Carlo opera
house on October 24, 1922.

Prelude to the
March on Rome: Mussolini's Speech
(San Carlo Opera House, Naples, October 24, 1922)

Fascists! Citizens! . . . We have come to Naples from every part
of Italy in order to carry out a rite of fraternalism and love. . . .
All of Italy is looking at our convention because—let me say it
without that false modesty which is sometimes the umbrella of
imbeciles—there does not exist in postwar Europe or the world a

SOURCE: From Il Popolo d'Italia (Milan), Vol. IX, No. 255 (Oct.
    25, 1922); reprinted in Opera Omnia di Benito Mussolini, ed. by
    Edoardo and Duilio Susmel (Florence: La Fenice, 1956), Vol.
    XVIII, pp. 453–459 passim. My translation.

phenomenon that is more interesting, more original, more powerful than Italian Fascism. . . .

Because of the extraordinarily grave situation confronting us, I think it is desirable to spell out with maximum precision the terms of the problem. . . . In short, we are at the point when either the arrow shoots forth from the bow or the tightly drawn bowstring breaks! [*Applause.*] You will recall that in the Chamber of Deputies . . . I propounded a question which concerns Italy as well as Fascism: legality or illegality? Victory by means of Parliament, or through insurrection? Through what paths will Fascism become the State? For we mean to become the State! . . . To the question, "Fascists, what do you want?" we have already replied very simply: We want the dissolution of the Chamber, electoral reform, elections in the very near future. We have asked that the State abandon its grotesque attitude of neutrality toward the national and antinational forces within it. We have asked for drastic financial measures, the postponement of the evacuation of Dalmatia, five portfolios, and also the Commissariat of Aviation. We have asked specifically for the Ministries of Foreign Affairs, War, Navy, Labor, and Public Works. I am sure that none of you will think these demands excessive; and I may add that by the terms of this "legalitarian" solution, I was to have no personal share in the government. And the reasons are quite clear if you but consider that to keep Fascism in my grip I must have great freedom of movement in journalism and in discussions.

What was the reply? Nothing! Worse still, they answered in a ridiculous way. . . . They made a quick calculation of our forces and talked of ministries without portfolio . . . and of assistant ministries—all of which is contemptible. We Fascists have no intention of getting into the government through the back door, of selling our wonderful birthright for a miserable mess of ministerial pottage! [*Vigorous, prolonged applause.*] For we take what can be termed a historical view of the problem, in contrast to what can be called a purely political and parliamentary one. . . .

Gentlemen, this problem . . . has to be faced as a problem of force. Every time in history that strong clashes of interests and ideas occur, it is force that ultimately decides the matter. That is why we have gathered and powerfully equipped and resolutely disciplined our legions—so that if a clash must decide the matter on the level of force, victory will be ours. . . .

The rulers in Rome are trying to create misunderstandings . . .

and confront us with other problems—problems that go under the heading of Monarchy, Army, and pacification. . . . [Let me] now clarify once more the historic and political position of Fascism with respect to the Monarchy. . . .

There can be no doubt that the unitary regime of Italian life rests solidly on the House of Savoy. [*Prolonged applause.*] . . .

Let me add that we don't want to deprive the people of their toy (the Parliament). We say "toy" because a large part of the Italian nation so regards it. Could you tell me, for example, why only six out of eleven million voters bother to go to the polls? . . .

In the final analysis, what separates us from democracy is our mentality, our method. Democracy holds that principles are fixed, that they are applicable at all times, in all places, in all eventualities. We don't believe that history repeats itself; we don't believe that history follows a hard and fast itinerary; we don't believe that after democracy there must ensue super-democracy! If democracy was useful and profitable for the nation in the nineteenth century, it may well be that in the twentieth century some other political system will give greater strength to the national community. ["Fine!"] . . .

As for the other institutions that personify the regime, that exalt the nation—I am speaking now of the Army—the Army should know that we—our bands of small numbers of brave men—defended it when the ministers were advising its officers to go about in civilian dress in order to avoid clashes! [*Prolonged applause.*]

We have created our own myth. That myth is a faith, it is a passion. It isn't necessary that it be a reality. It is a reality by virtue of the fact that it is a fist, that it is a hope, that it is a faith, that it is courage. Our myth is the nation, our myth is the greatness of the nation! ["Very good!"] And it is this myth, this grandeur, that we want to translate into a comprehensive reality and subordinate everything to it.

For us the nation is not just a territorial thing; above everything else, it is a spiritual thing. There have been states that possessed immense territories that did not leave behind the slightest trace in human history. It isn't a mere question of numbers, because there have been in history some very small, microscopic states that have left behind memorable and imperishable documents in art and philosophy.

The greatness of the nation is the complex of all these manly virtues, of all these conditions. A nation is great when it translates the strength of its spirit into reality. Rome became great when the small, rural democracy slowly extended the rhythm of its spirit throughout Italy, and then confronted the warriors of Carthage and gave battle to them. It was the first war of history, one of the first. Then, little by little, it carried the eagles to the far corners of the earth. Nevertheless, the Roman Empire was and is a spiritual creation, since it was the spirit of the Roman legionnaires that ordered their physical arms to thrust out the spears. Now, therefore, we want the greatness of the nation to exist in both the material and the spiritual senses.

And that is why we practice syndicalism. We do not practice it because we believe that the masses, just because of their numbers, their quantity, can create something lasting in history. We reject this fable of low-class socialist literature. But the working masses do exist within the nation; they are a great portion of the nation; they are necessary for the life of the nation in both peace and war. They cannot and should not be rejected. They can and should be educated; their legitimate interests can and should be protected! [*Applause.*]

There are some who say, "So you wish to perpetuate this state of civil strife that torments the nation?" No. . . . We are in favor of pacification. . . . On the other hand, we cannot sacrifice our rights, or the interests and future of the nation, to the idea of pacification (which we loyally propose) unless the other side accepts this with corresponding loyalty. Peace with those who really want peace. But with those who are a threat to us and especially to the nation, peace can come only after victory!

And now, Fascists and citizens of Naples, I thank you for the attention you have paid to my speech. Naples is providing a strong and fine spectacle of strength, discipline, and austerity. It is good that we have been able to come from every corner of the land to get acquainted with you and see you as you are, a courageous people who face up to life's struggle Roman-style. . . . And so, O standard-bearers of all the Fasci of Italy, raise your banners and salute Naples, metropolis of the south, queen of the Mediterranean! [. . . *Loud, interminable applause. Everyone is on his feet, applauding the* Duce *of Fascism, who moves off stage amid a forest of banners and shouts of* "Long live Italy! Long live Fascism!"]

2. The Path to the Totalitarian State

On October 27, 1922, some 50,000 Blackshirts began to converge on Rome, while others hurriedly seized prefectural buildings in surrounding provinces. In the capital many political leaders still misjudged the nature of Fascism and assumed they could channel it into the liberal constitutional system. Failure to perceive the true danger in time was the main cause of what happened at the end of October. The Fascist conquest of power did not require an authentic "revolution." Indeed, when the news of the March on Rome reached the capital, the King refused to sign the proclamation of martial law that his Council of Ministers had prepared; instead he sought to entrust the task of forming a new government to a team headed by the conservative ex-premier, Antonio Salandra, and Mussolini. When the latter rejected that formula, the King had an aide telephone the Fascist *Duce*, inviting him to come down from Milan on the overnight train. Thus by the time the Blackshirts actually sloshed their way down Rome's rain-swept streets, their entry was a parade, not a battle.

Why did Victor Emmanuel III refuse to have a showdown? The answer seems to be that, first of all, he doubted the determination of Premier Facta to resist. Moreover, he was uncertain the Army would back him in such a move. In addition, he feared the possibility of losing his throne to an ambitious cousin, the Duke of Aosta, who enjoyed great popularity because of his war record and could be sure of Fascist backing if the King caused trouble. Finally, there was the influence of Queen Mother Margherita, who beneath her attractive outward appearance was a woman of iron, completely reactionary, and by this time ardently pro-Fascist.

The King was by no means the only person responsible for bringing the Fascists to power. According to the memoirs of Marcello Soleri, Minister of War in 1922, it seems that Premier Facta himself advised the King not to sign the decree proposed by the cabinet, lest it provoke the intervention of the Army against the Fascists. Facta had started negotiations with one of the quadrumvirs, Michele Bianchi, in the hope of bringing the Fascists into his government and avoiding bloodshed. Giolitti too had embarked on negotiations with Mussolini, through the prefect of Milan, and with the same purpose in mind. For his part, Mussolini was quite ready to talk, as he did not wish to preclude a parliamentary solution in the old style if that seemed the most practical course of action. He was a man who never slammed any door against himself.

On the morning of October 29 the thirty-nine-year-old Mussolini arrived by *wagon-lit* in Rome. When he saw the King for the first time that day, he deliberately wore his black shirt. "Excuse my dress," he explained. "I have come from the battlefield." But a few hours later he returned in more traditional attire, and on the thirtieth announced the formation of a coalition cabinet. Retaining personal control of such key portfolios as Interior and Foreign Affairs, the new president of the Council of Ministers allowed a few misguided Liberals, Nationalists, Populars, and Social Democrats to hold other ministries. (Mussolini had only 35 Fascist party members in Parliament on whom to draw.)

Technically he had come to power by legal means, and his government was a "compromise" arrangement. Despite the propagandistic claims of the Blackshirts, the Fascist March on Rome was not yet a real "revolution." That was to come after January 3, 1925. As of October 30, 1922, the future was by no means clear. Yet some intimation of what Premier Mussolini had in mind was revealed in the truculent maiden speeches he delivered in the Chamber and Senate on November 16.

Mussolini's First Speech as Premier to the Chamber of Deputies (November 16, 1922)

GENTLEMEN! What I am doing now in this hall is an act of formal deference to you, for which I ask no special sign of gratitude. . . .

To the melancholy zealots of super-constitutionalism I shall leave the task of making their more or less pitiful lamentations about recent events. For my part, I insist that revolution has its rights. And so that everyone may know, I should like to add that I am here to defend and enforce in the highest degree the Blackshirts' revolution, and to inject it into the history of the nation as a force for development, progress, and equilibrium. [*Lively applause from the right.*]

I could have abused my victory, but I refused to do so. I imposed limits on myself. I told myself that the better wisdom is that which does not lose control of itself after victory. With 300,000 youths armed to the teeth, fully determined and almost mystically ready to act on any command of mine, I could have punished all those who defamed and tried to sully Fascism. [*Approval from the right.*] I could have transformed this drab, silent hall into a bivouac for my squads. . . . [*Loud applause from the right; noise; comments;*

SOURCE: *Atti del Parlamento italiano. Camera dei deputati. Sessione 1921–23. Legislatura XXVI. Discussioni* (Rome: Tipografia della Camera dei Deputati, 1923), Vol. IX, pp. 8389–8394. My translation.

Modigliani: "Long live Parliament! Long live Parliament!" *Noise and shouts from the right; applause from the extreme left.*] . . . I could have barred the doors of Parliament and formed a government exclusively of Fascists. I could have done so; but I chose not to, at least not for the present.

Our enemies have held on to their hiding places; and they have emerged from them without trouble and have enjoyed freedom of movement. And already they are profiting from this by spitting out poison again. . . .

I have formed a coalition government, not indeed with the object of obtaining a parliamentary majority—which I can now get along very well without [*applause from the extreme right and extreme left; comments*]—but in order to rally to the support of this suffocating nation all those who, regardless of nuances of party, wish to save this nation.

From the bottom of my heart I thank my collaborators, ministers, and undersecretaries. . . . And I cannot help recalling with pleasure the attitude of the laboring masses of Italians who have strengthened the Fascist motto by both their active and passive solidarity.

I believe that I also express the thought of a large part of this assembly, and certainly the majority of the Italian people, when I pay warm homage to the Sovereign who refused to take part in futile, last-minute reactionary maneuvers, who averted civil war and allowed the new and impetuous Fascist current, springing from the war and inspired by victory, to flow into the weakened arteries of the parliamentary state. [*Shouts of* "Long live the King!" *Ministers and many deputies rise to their feet for warm, prolonged applause.*]

Before attaining this position I was asked on all sides for a program. Alas! It is not programs that are lacking in Italy; it is the men and the willingness to apply the programs. All the problems of Italian life, all of them I say, have been solved on paper. What is lacking is the will to translate them into fact. Today the Government represents this firm and decisive will.

What preoccupies us most, especially at this moment, is foreign policy. I shall not deal here with all the problems, for in this field too I prefer action to words.

The fundamental guidelines of our foreign policy are the following things. Treaties of peace, whether good or bad, must be carried out once they have been signed and ratified. A self-respecting state can have no other doctrine. [*Lively approval.*] But treaties are not eternal; they are not irreparable. They are chapters of history, not its epilogue. Execution of them is the acid test. If in executing them their absurdity becomes evident, this may be the new fact that leads to a re-examination of the signatories' respective positions. Thus, I shall place before the Parliament the Treaty of Rapallo, as well as the agreements of Santa Margherita that derive from it.

. . . Let me now move on to establish another guideline of our foreign policy—viz., the repudiation of all "revisionist" ideological smoke screens.

We agree that there is a kind of unity, or better yet, an interdependence in Europe's economic life. We agree that this economy must be reconstructed, but we deny that the methods hitherto adopted are working toward this end.

For the purpose of European economic reconstruction, bilateral commercial accords, based on the broadest kind of economic relations among peoples, are worth more than the bureaucratic and confused plenary conferences whose sad history everybody knows. As far as Italy is concerned, we intend to follow a policy of dignity and national self-interest. [*Lively approval from the right.*] . . .

We do not indulge in the bad taste of exaggerating our power. But neither do we intend by excessive and false modesty to minimize it. My formula is simple: nothing for nothing. Whoever wants to have concrete evidence from us of friendship must also give us concrete evidence of friendship. [*Approval from the right.*]

Just as Fascist Italy has no intention of tearing up the peace treaties, so, for political, economic, and moral reasons, she also has no intention of abandoning her wartime allies. Rome is on the side of Paris and London, but Italy must show the Allies that it is embarking upon a courageous and severe examination of conscience such as has not been faced from the armistice to the present. [*Lively approval.*]

Does an Entente, in the real meaning of the word, still exist? What is the Entente's position toward Germany, toward Russia, toward a Russo-German alliance? What is Italy's position in the Entente? . . .

In the talks that I shall undertake with the prime ministers of France and England, I intend to face clearly the whole complex problem of the Entente and the resulting problem of Italy's position within the Entente. [*Lively applause.*]

. . . Either the Entente heals up its internal ills and contradictions and becomes a truly homogeneous bloc that is balanced and equal in strength, and with equal rights and equal duties; or else its end will have come, and Italy, resuming her freedom of action, will loyally adopt another policy that will safeguard her interests. [*Lively approval.*]

I hope that the first alternative takes place—for many reasons, including the outbreak of new turbulence throughout the Eastern world and the growing intimacy among the Russians, Turks, and Germans. But in order for that to be, it is necessary once for all to get away from hackneyed phrases. . . .

A foreign policy such as ours—a policy of national self-interest, of respect for treaties, of equitable clarification of Italy's position within the Entente—cannot be passed off as adventurous or imperialistic in the vulgar sense of the word. We wish to pursue a policy of peace; but not one of suicide. . . .

As regards Austria, Italy will remain faithful to her pledges, and will not overlook promoting agreements of an economic nature also with Hungary and Bulgaria.

We feel that as regards Turkey, the Lausanne Conference must recognize what is already an accomplished fact, and provide the necessary guarantees for traffic through the Straits, for European interests, and for the Christian minorities. The situation that has resulted in the Balkans and in Islam must be watched carefully. When Turkey obtains what is due her, she must not demand more. . . .

As regards Russia, Italy feels that the time has now come to consider in their present reality our relations with that state, leaving aside its internal conditions in which, as a government, we do not intend to interfere, just as we do not permit foreign intervention in our affairs. We are therefore ready to examine the possibility of a definitive solution. And with respect to the participation of Russia in the Lausanne Conference, Italy has argued in favor of the most liberal position and does not despair of seeing it triumph, though up to now Russia has been invited only to discuss the question of the Straits.

Our relations with the United States are excellent, and it will be my responsibility to improve them, especially in the field of a desirable and close collaboration in economic matters.

. . . Our relations are cordial with the republics of Central and South America, and especially with Brazil and Argentina, where millions of Italians live, to whom must not be denied the possibilities of sharing in local life, which by enhancing their importance will not estrange them but link them more closely to the motherland.

As for the economic and financial problem, Italy will argue at the forthcoming Brussels meeting that war debts and reparations are indivisible. For this policy of dignity and national well-being we must have in the [Ministry of Foreign Affairs] both central and subsidiary agencies that are adequate for the new needs of national life and the growing prestige of Italy in the world.

The guidelines of our domestic policy may be summarized in these words: economy, labor, discipline. The financial problem is basic. It is imperative to balance the budget with the greatest possible speed. We shall pursue a regime of austerity; we shall spend wisely; we shall assist all the productive forces of the nation; we shall put an end to all restrictions remaining from the war. [*Lively approval.*] . . .

Whoever uses the word "labor" means the productive bourgeoisie and the urban and rural working classes. We believe in no special privileges for the former, and none for the latter; but rather the safeguarding of the interests of all, so that they may be harmonized with those of production and of the entire nation. [*Loud applause.*]

The working proletariat, with whose status we are concerned, though not with demagogic or blameworthy indulgence, has nothing to fear and nothing to lose, but everything to gain from a financial policy that preserves the solvency of the state and prevents that bankruptcy that could make itself felt in a disastrous way, especially among the poorest strata of the population. . . . The Italian citizen who emigrates must know that he will be carefully looked after by this nation's representatives abroad.

The increase of a nation's prestige in the world is proportionate to the discipline that the country displays at home. There is no doubt but that the domestic situation has improved, but not as much as I should like. . . . The large cities and, in general, all our cities are calm; acts of violence are sporadic and peripheral, but they must come to an end. All citizens, regardless of party, must be able to move about freely.

All religious beliefs must be respected, with particular consideration for the dominant one, Catholicism. Fundamental freedoms must not be impaired; respect for the law must be exacted at whatever cost. The state is strong, and it intends to show its strength against everyone, even against any eventual Fascist illegality, for this would be an irresponsible and impure illegality wholly lacking in justification. [*Lively applause.*] I must add, however, that nearly all Fascists have given complete support to the new order of things.

The state does not intend to abdicate its authority before anyone. Whoever defies the state will be punished. This explicit warning is addressed to all citizens. . . . You must not forget that apart from the militant minority elements, there are forty million first-rate Italians who are working to perpetuate the deep foundations of our race, and who demand and have a right to demand that they not be thrown into chronic disorder, the sure prelude to general ruin. [*Vigorous, prolonged applause.*]

Since it is clear that sermons are not enough, the state will undertake to prune and perfect the armed forces that guard it. The Fascist State will organize perhaps one single police force, fully equipped and with great mobility and high morale. When the Army and Navy—which are most glorious and dear to every Italian—are freed from the changeableness of parliamentary politics and reorganized and strengthened, they will provide the nation with the supreme reserve force for service both at home and abroad. [*Very loud applause. Shouts of* "Long live the Army!" *Ministers and deputies on the right, center, and left rise and applaud vigorously at length.*]

Gentlemen! Later communications will inform you of the Fascist program in its details and as regards every ministry. So long as it is possible for me, I do not want to govern against the Chamber; but the Chamber must understand its special situation, something which makes it liable to dissolution within maybe two days or maybe two years. [*Laughter. Applause on the right and extreme left. Comments.*]

We ask for full powers because we wish to assume full responsibility. Without full powers, you know very well that it would be impossible to achieve a single lira—I repeat, a single lira—of economy. This does not mean we intend to exclude voluntary co-operation, which we shall accept cordially whether it comes from deputies, senators, or competent private citizens.

All of us have a religious conception of our difficult task. The country encourages us and is waiting for us. Let us not give it mere words but deeds. We formally and solemnly pledge to rebalance the budget; and we shall rebalance it. We intend to have a foreign policy of peace but at the same time one of dignity and firmness; and we shall have it. We propose to give discipline to the nation; and we shall do so. Let none of our adversaries of yesterday, today, or tomorrow deceive themselves as to our stay in power. [*Laughter; comments; applause from the right.*] That would be a childish and foolish delusion, just as were those of the past. Our government has a formidable base in the nation's conscience and is upheld by the better and fresh Italian generations.

There is no doubt that in these recent days an enormous step has been taken toward the unification of their minds. Once again the Italian fatherland has found itself, from the north to the south, from the continent to our numerous islands which will never again be forgotten [*applause*], from the metropolis to the busy colonies of the Mediterranean and Atlantic. Gentlemen! Don't shower the country with any more useless chatter! Fifty-two members scheduled to speak on my remarks are too many! [*Hilarity; comments.*] Instead, let us get to work with pure hearts and alert minds in order to assure prosperity and grandeur to the fatherland. May God help me bring my arduous task to a victorious end! [*Very vigorous applause from the right and other benches. . . .*]

Mussolini's First Speech as Premier to the Senate (November 16, 1922)

Honorable Senators! All of the first portion of the statements that I read a short time ago to the Chamber of Deputies does not in the least affect the Senate. ["Good!"] I must not use in front of the Senate the necessarily harsh language that I had to employ before the honorable deputies. [*Vigorous, prolonged applause, joined in also by the galleries.*] Not only today but for several years, I can safely say, I have regarded the Senate not as a superfluous institution. . . . Instead, I consider the Senate a bulwark of the state, a reserve force of the state ["Fine!"], a necessary organ for the just and sagacious administration of the state. [*Vigorous, prolonged applause.*] . . .

SOURCE: *Atti parlamentari della Camera dei Senatori. Prima Sessione 1921–23. Legislatura XXVI. Discussioni* (Rome: Tipografia del Senato, 1923), Vol. IX, p. 3999. My translation.

After his first speech as premier, Mussolini won a vote of confidence (306 to 116) from the Chamber of Deputies. Only the Socialists and Communists voted compactly against him. Simultaneously he was granted emergency powers to reform the tax structure, achieve economies, and reorganize public services. Yet even with these powers the Fascists did not feel sufficiently safe to give up their privileged position of being the only political party allowed to maintain a private army. On January 13, 1923, at the first meeting of the Fascist Grand Council after the March on Rome, the problem arose of how to utilize the Blackshirt action squads. Mussolini had no intention of abandoning this instrument, which formed the real basis of his power. So he created a permanent Fascist militia—the Volunteer Militia for National Security, MVSN—by means of the following royal decree.

Decree Establishing the Fascist Militia (MVSN)
(January 14, 1923)

Art. 1: The Voluntary Militia for National Security is hereby established.

Art. 2: The Militia for National Security will serve God and the Italian fatherland, and will be under the orders of the Head of the Government. With the help of the Armed Corps of Public Security and the Royal Army, it will be responsible for maintaining public order within the nation; and it will train and organize citizens for the defense of Italy's interests in the world.

Art. 3: Recruitment will be voluntary, and all men between the ages of seventeen and fifty who apply may be admitted . . . , provided that in the judgment of the president of the Council of Ministers or of the hierarchical authorities designated by him they possess the physical and moral prerequisites.

Art. 4: Organic and disciplinary norms for the formation and operation of the Militia will be established by special regulations, to be prepared in harmony with existing laws by the president of the council. . . .

Art. 5: Nomination of officers and their promotion will be effected by royal decree upon recommendation of the Ministers of Interior and War.

Art. 6: The Militia for National Security offers its services free of charge. The state will pay for service performed outside the corps' commune of residence.

SOURCE: Royal Decree No. 31, January 14, 1923, in the *Gazzetta Ufficiale del Regno*, No. 16 (Jan. 20, 1923). My translation.

Art. 7: In case of partial or full mobilization of either the Army or the Navy, the Fascist Militia is to be absorbed by the Army and Navy, and in accordance with the obligations and military grades of its various members.

Art. 8: Expenses for establishment and operation of the Militia for National Security are to be charged to the budget of the Ministry of Interior.

Art. 9: All parties whatsoever shall be forbidden to have formations of a military character after the present decree goes into effect. Violators will be subject to punishment by law.

Art. 10: The present decree will be presented to Parliament for enactment into law and will go into force on February 1, 1923.

No mention was made in the decree of swearing allegiance to the King; the militiamen would remain under the orders of Mussolini. Thus there was introduced in Italy one of the politically armed forces that were to be so typical of fascistic regimes. Indeed, such a party army was one of the most significant differences between twentieth-century fascistic dictatorships and previous authoritarian regimes. Other dictators in the past had restricted freedom of the press or condemned political foes into exile, and they had made use of the regular army in carrying out their *coups d'état;* but the Fascists and Nazis secured power thanks in large measure to a military organization of their own, especially prepared for the purpose and destined to remain in existence side by side with the regular army. The presence of the MVSN was one of the key factors that enabled Mussolini to remain at his post during the great crisis of 1924. Membership in the MVSN was 251,000 by 1927; by 1934 it was 461,000; and with the impact of the Ethiopian War it grew rapidly to 763,000 in 1938.

Another portent of totalitarianism was a decree of July 15, 1923, setting up fairly rigid control of the Italian press. After 1925 these regulations were tightened to such an extent that great newspapers like *La Stampa* of Turin and *Corriere della Sera* of Milan passed into Fascist hands. The text of the decree follows.

Decree Regulating the Press

Art. 1: In addition to the conditions prescribed by Articles 36 and 37 of the edict on the press dated March 26, 1848, the managing editor of a newspaper or other periodical publication must be either the director or one of the principal regular editors of this

SOURCE: Royal Decree No. 3288 of July 15, 1923, in *Gazzetta Ufficiale,* No. 159 (July 18, 1923). My translation.

newspaper or publication, and he must obtain the recognition of the prefect of the province wherein the newspaper or publication is printed.

Senators and Deputies may not serve as managing editors. Anyone who has been sentenced on two occasions for crimes involving the press is ineligible to be managing editor, and he will lose this position if he has assumed it.

The decision of the prefect who refuses to recognize a managing editor must be based upon evidence. An appeal from this decision may be made to the Ministry of Interior. The decision of this minister may be appealed on legal grounds to the Fourth Section of the Council of State.

Art. 2: The prefect of a province is empowered, except where penal action prevents it, to address a warning to the managing editor of a newspaper or a periodical:

(a) If by means of false or tendentious news the newspaper or periodical impedes the diplomatic action of the Government in its foreign relations, or injures the national honor at home or abroad, or creates unjustifiable alarm in the population, or disturbs public order;

(b) If by means of articles, comments, notes, headlines, or illustrations it incites to crime or excites class hatred or disobedience to the laws and orders of public authorities, or compromises the discipline of public servants, or favors the interests of foreign states, societies, or individuals to the detriment of Italian interests, or holds up to opprobrium the King, the Royal Family, the Sovereign Pontiff, the religion of the state, or the institutions and organs of the state or of friendly powers.

This warning is to be issued by a decree resting upon evidence and in accordance with the recommendation of a committee that consists of the following people: a judge, who presides over it; a substitute for the King's procurator in the court of the locality or prefectural seat, appointed respectively by the first president and by the procurator general of the Court of Appeal; and a representative of the category of journalists, to be designated either by the local press association or, in its absence, by the president of the local tribunal. The committee will hold office for one year.

Art. 3: On the advice of the committee referred to above, the prefect may cancel the recognition of a managing editor who has received two warnings in one year.

The prefect may refuse to recognize a new managing editor

whenever the previous one has been dismissed or condemned for any kind of press abuse twice in the space of two years to a penalty depriving him of his liberty for a period of six months or more; or whenever the newspapers or periodicals affected by the prefect's decisions have assumed new titles in order to continue their publication.

The decisions of the prefect are subject to the recourse set forth in Article 1.

Art. 4: Newspapers or other periodical publications printed in contravention of the previous regulations may be sequestered.

The sequestration is to be carried out by police authorities with no further need for special authorization.

Those who are guilty of abusive publication are to be punished in accordance with the laws in force. . . .

Despite such measures as a Fascist militia and control of the press, many citizens were still under the illusion that Fascism had not radically changed the political pattern of Italy. The monarchical institution, for example, remained intact. Some of the leading Fascists—including the quadrumvir, DeVecchi—were royalists, as were all of the adherents of the older National party which formally merged with the Fascists in 1923 and thereby imparted a veneer of intellectual respectability to the Partito Nazionale Fascista. Furthermore, during the first year or two of his rule Mussolini still grudgingly accepted the collaboration of Liberals and Populars in the cabinet. The representatives of the latter party, to be sure, were excluded in April, 1923, after left-wing Populars expressed reservations about the way Mussolini was ruling, but the Liberals stayed in the government until the end of 1924. Thus in the initial months it was still possible to speak of formal cooperation between Fascism and some representatives of other parties—"some representatives," because Mussolini quickly decided not to enter into agreements with the parties as such. But this type of collaboration was the reverse of what Giolitti and some of the older political leaders had envisaged. It was not the traditional parties which were domesticating and canalizing Fascism into the "system," but rather the Fascists who were accepting for a little longer, and with ill grace, the cooperation of the others. Meanwhile, they continued to employ violence against the Socialists, Communists, and Populars—in short, against anyone who was not Fascist. Local party bosses, the *ras*, acquired in most places a pre-eminent position vis-à-vis the government-appointed prefects. In this way the substance of things began to change rapidly even though the form of things thus far was modified only in part.

Parliament was co-operative in these initial months; nevertheless Mussolini was displeased to have but 35 Fascist party deputies at his call. Determined to prepare the way for electing a Chamber that would be unmistakably controlled by his own party, he had one of his lieutenants, Giacomo Acerbo, draft a new electoral law. Enacted on November 18, 1923, this bill provided that whichever list received the largest number of votes would obtain two-thirds of the seats in the Chamber. "Unproportional representation" would thus replace the system of proportional representation that had come into operation in 1919 with such damaging effects upon the traditional forces. Fascism now needed to obtain only a plurality in order to gain clear-cut parliamentary control. Effective means existed to secure that result by hamstringing the oppositionists and making it very difficult for voters to carry out their electoral duty. In this manner, in the ensuing elections of April 6, 1924, the Fascist (or "National") list got 64.9 per cent of the votes and 374 seats. In spite of their general success, however, the Fascists failed to gain a majority of the popular vote in the regions of Piedmont, Liguria, Lombardy, and Venetia.

On May 30, 1924, Giacomo Matteotti, the young secretary of the "revisionist" Unitary Socialist party, delivered a vigorous and well-documented speech in the Chamber in which he denounced the abuses perpetrated by Fascists during the election campaign and challenged the official results. Suddenly on June 10 he was kidnapped by Fascist gangsters in the center of Rome and brutally stabbed to death. Matteotti's body was not found for several weeks. A tremendous storm of indignation arose immediately; for the next six months Mussolini faced a political crisis of the first magnitude. Temporarily he was visibly shaken, for it was clear to everyone that, if not he himself, certainly several officials close to him were implicated.

In protest against the political murder, a substantial minority of deputies (mostly Socialists, Republicans, and Populars; the Communists only temporarily) withdrew from Parliament on June 27 to a symbolic "Aventine of their own conscience." The leader of the Aventinian secession was the liberal democrat, Giovanni Amendola. He and his group viewed the problem as one of morality and sought to bring about the moral isolation of the regime. They did not advocate violent revolution; rather they hoped to persuade Victor Emmanuel III to recognize his own blunder in bringing Mussolini to the premiership and to exercise his constitutional prerogative of dismissing the prime minister. But key Liberals like Giolitti and Salandra refused to join the Aventine, which engaged in endless talk and newspaper editorials. The King refused to take any action; he rationalized his behavior in later years on the ground that there was no effective opposition majority in Parliament. He was "blind" and "deaf," he declared, and the Chamber and Senate had to be his "eyes and ears." The failure of the Sovereign to be moved was the great reason why most of the political opposition was to become increasingly antimonarchist as well as anti-Fascist. As the weeks slipped by the Aventinians muffed their chances. By seceding they had weakened Parliament and actually made it easier for Mussolini to win his battle, for he did not have to expel the opposition with force as Hitler was to do.

Prodded by such firebrands as Roberto Farinacci, the *ras* of Cremona, Mussolini began to regain his composure and promised to clean up the regime. At last on January 3, 1925, he was ready to launch the counterattack. In an unusually bombastic speech before the Chamber of Deputies he took personal "political, moral, and historical responsibility for everything" that had happened. "Force is the only solution!" he cried, and promised to "clarify" everything within twenty-four hours.

Mussolini's Coup d'État of January 3, 1925

Gentlemen, the speech that I am about to deliver should not perhaps be classified, strictly speaking, as a parliamentary address. . . . A speech of this sort may or may not lead to a vote on policy. Let it be known that in any case I do not seek such a vote on policy. . . . I have had too many of them. ["Good!"]

Article 47 of the *Statuto* says: "The Chamber of Deputies has the right to impeach the King's Ministers and to bring them before the High Court of Justice [the Senate]." I ask formally whether there is anyone, either in or out of this Chamber, who wants to avail himself of Article 47? [*Vigorous, prolonged applause.* . . .]

My speech therefore will be very clear and such as to bring about absolute clarification. . . .

Gentlemen, it is I who raise in the hall the charges against myself. It is said that I have created a *Cheka*. Where? When? How? No one can answer! In Russia there has really been a *Cheka*, which has executed, without any trial, between 150 and 160,000 people. . . . In Russia there has been a *Cheka* which has systematically imposed terror on all the bourgeois class and on individual members of the bourgeoisie—a *Cheka* which is said to be the Red sword of the revolution. But an Italian *Cheka* has never existed.

Thus far nobody has ever denied me three qualities: a certain intelligence, much courage, and a sovereign disdain for filthy lucre. [*Vigorous, prolonged applause.*] If I had created a *Cheka*, I would have done so according to the criteria that I have always imposed on that degree of violence which cannot be eliminated from history. I have always said—and let those who have followed me through these five years of difficult battle remember this—that violence, to

SOURCE: *Atti del Parlamento Italiano. Camera dei Deputati. Legislatura XXVII. Sessione del 1924–25. Discussioni*, January 3, 1925 (Rome: Tipografia della Camera dei Deputati), Vol. III, pp. 2028–2032 *passim*. My translation.

be effective, must be surgical, intelligent, and chivalrous. [*Approval.*] Now the acts of this so-called *Cheka* have always been unintelligent, disorganized, and stupid. ["Very good!"] . . .

You certainly remember my speech of June 7 [1924]. You may find it easy to recall that week of heated political passions when in this Chamber the minority and majority were clashing every day, to the point that some despaired of establishing the necessary conditions for political and civil co-existence between the two hostile parts of the Chamber. . . . I then delivered a speech that completely clarified the atmosphere. I said to the opposition: I recognize your right in principle and even in fact. You may disregard Fascism as a historical experience; you may subject all the measures of the Fascist government to immediate criticism.

I recall and I still have before my eyes the sight of this part of the Chamber, where everyone understood and felt that at that moment I had uttered profound and living words and had established the terms of that necessary co-existence without which no political assembly of any kind is possible. [*Approval.*]

Now, after such a success . . . , how could I, unless I were struck by madness, think of committing a crime, or even giving the slightest, silliest affront to a foe whom I had respected because he possessed a certain *crânerie*, a certain courage that at times resembled my own courage and my own stubbornness in upholding my points of view? [*Lively applause.*]

What should I have done? Some cricket-brains demanded of me at that time cynical gestures that I did not feel like making because they were deeply repugnant to my conscience. [*Approval.*] Or should I have committed some act of force? What force? Against whom? For what purpose? . . .

It was at the end of that month—that month which is marked indelibly in my life—that I said: "I want peace for the Italian people." I wanted to bring political life back to normalcy.

But what was the reply to this principle of mine? First of all, there was the Aventine secession, an unconstitutional secession that was clearly revolutionary. [*Lively approval.*] Then there followed a press campaign that lasted through June, July, and August; a filthy and wretched campaign that dishonored us for three months. [*Vigorous, prolonged applause.*]

The most fantastic, most horrendous, most macabre lies were widely published in all the papers! A veritable outbreak of necro-

THE PATH TO THE TOTALITARIAN STATE

philia took place. [*Approval.*] There were inquiries even into what takes place underground in the grave. They invented lies; they knew they were lying, but they went right on lying.

And I remained calm, tranquil in the midst of this storm, which will be remembered with a deep sense of shame by those who come after us. [*Signs of approval.*]

In the meanwhile, this campaign bore fruit. On September 11 someone sought to avenge the dead man and shot one of our best people, a man who died in poverty. . . .

Nevertheless, I continued my effort at normalization. I repressed illegal acts. It is no lie that today hundreds of Fascists are still in jail! [*Comments.*] It is no lie that Parliament was reconvened regularly at the prescribed date and that all the budgets were discussed no less regularly. It is no lie that the Militia swore an oath of loyalty, and that generals were appointed to all the zonal commands.

Finally, a question was raised that has been of great concern to us—a request that the parliamentary immunity of the Honorable Giunta[1] be lifted and that he resign and stand trial. The Chamber was shocked. I understood the meaning of this feeling of revolt. And yet, after forty-eight hours, I once more gave in, and relying on my prestige and growing strength, I bent this riotous and reluctant assembly to my will and said: "Let the resignation be accepted." It was accepted. But even that was not enough. I performed one last gesture of normalization. I proposed a reform of the electoral law.[2]

And how did they respond to all of this? They responded with an intensified campaign. They said that Fascism is a horde of barbarians encamped in the country, a movement of bandits and marauders! They raised a moral question, and we are familiar with the sad story of moral questions in Italy. [*Lively signs of approval.*] . . .

Very well, I now declare before this assembly and before the entire Italian people that I assume, I alone, full political, moral, and historical responsibility for all that has happened. [*Very vigorous and repeated applause. Shouts of* "We are with you! All with you!"]

1. Francesco Giunta was vice-president of the Chamber of Deputies and an ardent Fascist.—*Ed.*
2. The reform called for repeal of proportional representation and a return to single-member constituencies.—*Ed.*

If more or less distorted phrases are enough to hang a man, then bring out the gallows, bring out the rope! If Fascism has been nothing more than castor oil and the rubber truncheon, instead of being a proud passion of the best part of Italian youth, then I am to blame! [*Applause.*] If Fascism has been a criminal association, then I am the chief of this criminal association! [*Vigorous applause. . . .*]

If all the violence has been the result of a particular historical, political, and moral climate, then let me take the responsibility for this, because I have created this historical, political, and moral climate with a propaganda that has gone forth from the intervention until today.

In recent days not just the Fascists but many citizens have asked themselves: Do we have a government? [*Signs of approval.*] Are these men, or are they puppets? Do these men possess manly dignity? And do they also have a government that possesses it? [*Approval.*]

I deliberately wanted things to come to this extreme point. Enriched by my lifetime of experience, I tested out the party. And just as one must beat certain metals with a hammer to determine their temper, so I have tested the temper of certain men. . . . I have tested myself. And note well that I would not have resorted to such measures if the interests of the nation had not been at stake. But a people does not respect a government that lets itself be despised! [*Signs of approval.*] People want to see their own dignity reflected in that of the government, and people, even before I said it, were declaring: "Enough! We have gone far enough!"

And why have we gone far enough? Because the Aventine sedition has a republican background! [*Lively applause; shouts of* "Long live the King!" . . .] This sedition on the part of the Aventine has resulted in a situation in which any Fascist in Italy is in danger of his life! In the two months of November and December alone, eleven Fascists were killed. . . . And then three fires have taken place in one month, mysterious fires, fires in the railway system and yards in Rome, Parma, and Florence. . . . You see from this situation that the sedition of the Aventine has had profound repercussions throughout the country. For this reason, the moment has come when we must say, "Enough!"

When two irreducible elements are locked in a struggle, the solution is force. In history there never has been any other solution, and there never will be.

Right now, I make bold to declare that the problem will be re-solved. Fascism, the Government, and the Party are completely ready. Gentlemen, you have suffered from illusions! You thought that Fascism was finished because I was restraining it, that it was dead because I was punishing it and because I had the audacity to say so. But if I were to employ the hundredth part of the energy in unleashing it that I have used in restraining it, you would under-stand then. [*Vigorous applause.*] But there will be no need for this, because the Government is strong enough to break the Aventine's sedition completely and definitely. [*Vigorous, prolonged applause.*]

Gentlemen, Italy wants peace, tranquillity, calm in which to work. We shall give her this tranquillity and calm, by means of love if possible but by force if necessary. [*Lively applause.*]

You may be sure that within the next forty-eight hours after this speech, the situation will be clarified in every field. [*Vigorous, prolonged applause; comments.*] Everyone must realize that what I am planning to do is not the result of personal caprice, of a lust for power, or of an ignoble passion, but solely the expression of my unlimited and mighty love for the fatherland. [*Vigorous, pro-longed and reiterated applause. Repeated shouts of* "Long live Mussolini!" *The ministers and many deputies congratulate the Honorable President of the Council. The meeting is ended.*]

Mussolini's speech of January 3, 1925, was in effect a *coup d'état* and marked the beginning of a dictatorship that was to be riveted down by skillfully spaced decrees until Italy found herself under what the Fas-cists claimed to be a totalitarian state. Farinacci, who became PNF secretary in February, 1925, played a significant role in these events. All pretense at collaboration with non-Fascists was abandoned. In July, Amendola, the leader of the Aventine, was brutally beaten; his injuries resulted in death a few months later. Meanwhile, a series of attempts on the life of Mussolini provided pretexts for the government to suppress one political party after another, as well as the Masonic Lodge and all opposition newspapers.

One of the most fundamental decrees was that of December 24, 1925: henceforth the president of the Council of Ministers was to be "Head of the Government" (*Capo del Governo*) and no longer accountable to Parliament. The *Statuto* of 1848 had not envisaged the existence of a Head of the Government as distinct from the rest of the Council of Ministers. Thus the decree marked the end of "responsible parliamentary government" in Italy; only the King now had the power to dismiss the Prime Minister. It also declared that henceforth no question could be placed on the agenda for Parliament without the prior approval of the Head of the Government. Thus Mussolini could prevent all political debate in Parliament.

Decree on Powers
of the Head of the Government
(December 24, 1925)

Art. I: The executive power is exercised by His Majesty the King through his Government. The Government consists of the Prime Minister Secretary of State and the Ministers Secretaries of State.

The Prime Minister is the Head of the Government.

Art. II: The Head of the Government, who is Prime Minister and Secretary of State, is appointed and dismissed by the King, and is responsible to the King for the general policy of the Government.

The decree appointing the Head of the Government Prime Minister is countersigned by himself, and that of his dismissal by his successor.

The Ministers Secretaries of State are appointed and dismissed by the King upon proposal of the Head of the Government Prime Minister. They are responsible to the King and to the Head of the Government for all the acts and measures enforced by their Ministries.

The Undersecretaries of State are appointed and dismissed by the King upon the proposal of the Head of the Government in agreement with the Minister concerned.

Art. III: The Head of the Government Prime Minister directs and co-ordinates the work of the Ministers, decides whatever differences may arise among them, calls meetings of the Council of Ministers, and presides over them.

Art. IV: The number, constitution, and responsibilities of the Ministers are established by royal decree, upon proposal of the Head of the Government.

The Head of the Government may be entrusted by royal decree with the direction of one or more Ministries. In such cases, the Head of the Government by his own decree may delegate to

SOURCE: Law No. 2263 of December 24, 1925, "Attributions and prerogatives of the Head of the Government Prime Minister Secretary of State," in *Gazzetta Ufficiale*, No. 301 (Dec. 29, 1925). My translation.

the Undersecretaries of State a share of the responsibilities of the Minister.

Art. V: The Head of the Government is a member of the council for the guardianship of members of the Royal Family, and exercises the function of Notary of the Crown.

He is, furthermore, by right, Secretary of the Supreme Order of the Holy Annunciation.

Art. VI: No bill or motion may be placed on the agenda of either of the two Chambers without the consent of the Head of the Government.

The Head of the Government is empowered to request that a bill, rejected by one of the two Chambers, shall again be voted upon when at least three months have elapsed since the first vote. In such cases the bill is voted upon by secret ballot, without previous debate.

When, in submitting the bill for a second vote, the Government also submits amendments to the bill, there may be debate only upon the amendments, after which the bill will be voted upon by secret ballot.

The Head of the Government is also empowered to request that a bill, if rejected by one of the Chambers, be equally submitted to the other Chamber and voted upon, after due examination.

When a bill already passed by one Chamber is passed by the other with amendments, the debate in the Chamber to which it is submitted a second time is limited to the amendments, after which the vote on the measure will be by secret ballot.

Art. VII: The Head of the Government, during his tenure of office, takes precedence over the Knights of the Supreme Order of the Holy Annunciation at public functions and ceremonies.

He will receive from the State Treasury an annual appropriation to cover the expenses of his office, the sum being fixed by royal decree.

Art. VIII: The Head of the Government may designate from time to time the Minister who will substitute for him in case of absence or impediment; this designation is made separately for each given case.

Art. IX: Whosoever makes an attempt against the life, safety, or personal freedom of the Head of the Government is to be punished by a term of imprisonment of not less than fifteen years, and by life imprisonment if he succeeds in his attempt.

Whosoever offends the Head of the Government in words or deeds is to be punished by imprisonment or detention from six to thirty months, and by a fine of from 500 to 3,000 lire.[3]

Art. X: All regulations contrary to the present law are abrogated.

Soon the government was depriving Italians of their citizenship if they committed an act abroad that was calculated to damage Italy's prestige. The first victims of this decree were Professor Gaetano Salvemini of the University of Florence and an émigré editor of the Popular party, Giuseppe Donati. Another attempt on Mussolini's life in the spring of 1926 led to the abolition of local elective government organs. Finally, after the firing on Mussolini's car in Bologna, the *Duce* proclaimed in November, 1926, the "exceptional decrees" which nailed down totalitarianism. The decree of public safety of November 6, excerpts of which are printed below, was of great importance. The deputies who had withdrawn from the Chamber were now deprived of their parliamentary status and driven from the Aventine into the catacombs.

Decree on Public Safety
(November 6, 1926)

TITLE VI: REGULATIONS PERTAINING TO PERSONS WHO ENDANGER SOCIETY

CHAPTER II: REGARDING SUSPECTS, PERSONS RELEASED FROM PRISON . . . , ILLEGAL REPATRIATION, AND EXPATRIATION

Art. 158—Whoever outside his own commune arouses suspicion by his conduct, and cannot or will not identify himself to officers or agents of the Public Security by producing an identity card or some other trustworthy evidence, is to be taken before the local Public Security authority. The latter, in case the suspicions prove to be well founded, may require him to return to his home. . . .

Without need for further authorization, the Public Security can

SOURCE: Royal Decree-Law No. 1848 of November 6, 1926, published in *Gazzetta Ufficiale*, No. 257 (Nov. 8, 1926). My translation.

3. Modified by Law No. 2008 of November 25, 1926, regarding "Measures for the Defense of the State." Article I of this latter law declared: "Whosoever makes attempts against the life, safety, or personal freedom of the King or the Regent is to be punished by death. The same applies if the attempt be made against the life, safety, or personal freedom of the Queen, the Crown Prince, or the Head of the Government."

forbid anyone who has thus been sent home . . . from returning to the commune whence he was expelled.

Violators are to be arrested and punished by imprisonment ranging from one to six months, and upon completion of their sentence shall be conducted to their home.

Art. 159—The mayor must deliver to all persons who are fifteen years of age or older and habitually reside in the commune . . . an identity card conforming to the model that will be provided by the Ministry of the Interior. The identity card must include a photograph of the bearer and is valid for three years.

Art. 160—Whoever, for political reasons, leaves or tries to leave the country without a passport or equivalent document is punishable by imprisonment of not less than three years and a fine of not less than 20,000 lire.

Whoever in any way assists the preparation or execution of this crime is liable to the same penalty.

. . . The use of firearms is permitted to prevent illegal crossings of the frontier. . . .

CHAPTER III: REGARDING ADMONITIONS

Art. 166—The chief police officer of the district may, by written and documented report, request the prefect to present an admonition to idlers, habitual vagabonds . . . , pimps, vendors of harmful drugs, . . . and whoever are singled out by public rumor as being dangerous to the national order of the State. . . .

Art. 168—Such admonition is to be pronounced by a Provincial Commission made up of the prefect, the royal procurator, the superintendent of police (*Questore*), the provincial commander of the Royal Carabinieri, and a high-ranking officer of the Voluntary Militia for National Security who is designated by the commandant of the zone involved. The commission is presided over by the prefect. . . .

Art. 173—The Commission may require a person who is so admonished to find employment and observe the laws, avoid doing anything that might arouse suspicions in his regard, and not to leave his domicile without first informing the local Public Security authority.

Art. 174—The Commission may further prescribe that such persons, no matter what their category, may not associate with convicted or otherwise suspicious people, return home late at night, leave home in the morning before a specified hour, carry arms, habitually visit cafés, gambling places, or brothels, or attend public meetings. . . .

CHAPTER V: REGARDING COMPULSORY DOMICILE (DOMICILIO COATTO)

Art. 184—If they present a danger to public safety, the following persons may be assigned to compulsory domicile under police supervision, with an obligation to work:

1. Those who have received an admonition;

2. Those who have committed or have shown a deliberate intention of committing any act calculated to bring about violent disturbance to the national, social, or economic regulations of the State . . . , or to impede the carrying out of the functions of the State in such a manner as to injure in any way the national interests either at home or abroad.

Art. 185—A sentence of compulsory domicile will last no less than one nor more than five years, and will be carried out in either a colony or a commune of the Kingdom other than the normal residence of the sentenced person.

Art. 186—The sentence of compulsory domicile and the length of same will be handed down by the Provincial Commission described in Art. 168. The Commission may order the immediate arrest of whosoever is proposed for such confinement. . . .

Art. 190—Whosoever is assigned to compulsory domicile may be required to do the following things:

1. Not to leave the specified domicile without prior approval of the authority charged with looking after his surveillance;

2. Not to retire at night or go out in the morning either later than or earlier than the specified hour;

3. Not to possess or carry arms that belong to him, nor any other instruments that may be considered offensive;

4. Not to frequent bad places, cafés, or other public locales;

5. Not to frequent public meetings, shows, or entertainments;

6. To conduct himself well and give no cause for suspicion;

7. To present himself on specified days, as well as at any other summons, to the police authorities who are charged with his surveillance;

8. To carry with him at all times his residence card and to show it to police officers or agents whenever requested. . . .

Another decree, printed below, established the Special Tribunal for the Defense of the State to adjudicate so-called political crimes.

Appointed by Mussolini, the Special Tribunal began hearings on February 1, 1927. Cases were referred to it by specific recommendation of the Fascist head of the police. (Many more or less "political" cases also continued to come before the regular courts, where the accused could at least hope to get a fairer hearing.) Decisions of the Special Tribunal could not be appealed. Some 720 audiences were held between 1927 and 1943; approximately 5,319 individuals were brought to trial, and of these 5,155 were sentenced. All told, their prison terms added to 28,115 years. There were 29 death sentences and 7 for life imprisonment.

The Exceptional Decrees: Law for the Defense of the State (November 25, 1926)

Art. 1—Whoever commits any act aimed against the life, person, or personal freedom of either the King or the Regent is punishable by death.

The same penalty applies if the act is aimed against the life, person, or personal freedom of the Queen, the heir to the throne, or the Head of the Government.

Art. 2—Crimes specified in Articles 104, 107, 108, 120, and 252 of the Penal Code are equally punishable by death.

Art. 3—If two or more persons conspire to commit one of the acts referred to in the preceding articles, they are liable, by the mere fact of conspiracy, to imprisonment ranging from five to fifteen years.

The leaders, promoters, and organizers are liable to imprisonment ranging from fifteen to thirty years.

Whoever publicly or in the press incites to one of the crimes referred to in the preceding articles or defends it is liable to imprisonment ranging from five to fifteen years.

Art. 4—Whoever reconstitutes, even under a different name, any association, organization, or party that has been dissolved by order of the public authority, is liable to imprisonment ranging from three to ten years and, moreover, is subject to permanent exclusion from public office.

Whoever is a member of such associations, organizations, or parties is liable, for the mere fact of this participation, to imprison-

SOURCE: Decree-Law No. 2008, November 25, 1926, published in *Gazzetta Ufficiale*, No. 281 (Dec. 6, 1926). My translation.

ment ranging from two to five years, and permanent exclusion from public office.

Whoever propagates by any means the doctrines, opinions, or methods of such associations is liable to the same penalty.

Art. 5—Any citizen who, outside the national territory, spreads or in any way communicates false, exaggerated, or tendentious rumors or information regarding the internal condition of the state in such manner as to lessen the credit or prestige of the state abroad, or who practices actions of any kind that tend to prejudice the national interests, is liable to imprisonment ranging from five to fifteen years, and permanent exclusion from public office.

In such case, a sentence pronounced in contumacy carries with it the loss of citizenship and the confiscation of property. The judge may substitute sequestration for confiscation. In this case, he will specify the duration of this action and the destination of the revenue from said property.

The loss of citizenship does not apply to the wife or the children of the sentenced person.

All alienations of property effected by the sentenced person after the execution of the crime, as well as one year prior thereto, are presumed to have been done to the detriment of the State; therefore, these properties are to be included in the confiscation or sequestration.

The effects of the sentence in contumacy as set forth in the above clauses will terminate with the surrender or arrest of the condemned person; and in such case, the properties are to be restituted in the condition in which they were found, except as regards the rights legitimately acquired by third parties.

Art. 6—Wherever, in the case of crimes set forth in the present law, the action is of attenuated gravity, or there are extenuating circumstances that make it appropriate to modify the terms of punishment set forth in the Penal Code, the judge is empowered to substitute imprisonment ranging from fifteen to thirty years for the death penalty; to substitute temporary for permanent exclusion from public office; and to reduce the other penalties by not more than one-half.

Whosoever helped, in whatever way, the commission of these same crimes is subject to the penalties established by the present law.

Art. 7—The crimes referred to in this law shall be brought before a Special Tribunal, to consist of a president chosen from among the general officers of the Royal Army, the Royal Navy, the Royal Air Force, and the Voluntary Militia for National Security, and five judges chosen from among the officers of the Voluntary Militia for National Security who hold the rank of consul. . . . The Special Tribunal may operate, if necessary, in more than one section, and the arguments may take place either at the seat of the tribunal or in any other commune of the Kingdom.

The formation of this tribunal is to be ordered by the Minister of War, who will determine its composition, seat, and the command under which it will function.

Whenever conditions envisaged by Article 559 of the Penal Code for the Army apply, extraordinary tribunals may also be established.

The provisions of the Military Penal Code regarding penal procedure in time of war shall apply in the procedure for crimes covered under the present law. All powers that by the terms of that code belong to the commander-in-chief are hereby conferred on the minister of war.

Sentences of the Special Tribunal are not subject to appeal, nor to any kind of impugnment except review.

The legal procedures for crimes covered under the present law, and that are in effect on the day it is promulgated, are hereby transferred to the competency of the Special Tribunal that is described in the first part of the present article.

Art. 8—Nothing is altered with respect to the powers conferred on the Government by Law No. 2260 of December 24, 1925.

The present law goes into effect the day it is published in the *Gazzetta Ufficiale* of the Kingdom, and it ceases to be in effect after the expiration of five years from that date, except as regards the carrying out of sentences already handed down.

Within that same period of time the Government of the King has the right to promulgate norms for the carrying out of the present law, and for co-ordinating it with the Penal Code, the Code of Penal Procedure, the Military Penal Code, and other laws.

The Acerbo electoral law of 1923 was replaced by a very different law on May 17, 1928, excerpts from which are printed below. The new measure provided for only a single list, for which candidates were to be nominated by the labor syndicates and other organizations. These entities were to put forward 800 names—twice as many as the number to be elected. From these the Fascist Grand Council would choose 400 and present this slate to the electorate for their approval *en bloc*. With the advent of this law Italy formally moved away not only from the parliamentary but from the constitutional system itself. Rubber-stamp plebiscites superseded the liberal system of choosing between candidates. Not even universal manhood suffrage was retained: to qualify to vote in the plebiscites one had to present evidence of having paid dues to a Fascist syndicate, a fact which automatically disqualified about three million men.

The first elections under this new system were not held until March 24, 1929, one month after the announcement of the Lateran Pacts. They produced 8,519,559 yes and 137,761 no votes. In Milan, however, the negative response amounted to 6 per cent of the total, whereas the national average was less than 2 per cent.

The Fascist Electoral Law of 1928

Art. 1—Electors must enjoy, through birth or origin, the civil and political rights of the Kingdom. Persons who do not belong to the Kingdom either through birth or origin may be electors if they have obtained naturalization by Royal Decree and have sworn allegiance to the King. . . .

Art. 2—All citizens may be electors who are twenty-one years of age, or eighteen years provided they are married or widowers with children, and attained these respective ages not later than May 31 of the year in which the revision of the electoral lists takes place. They must furthermore meet one of the following requirements:

(a) Payment of dues to a syndicate under Law No. 563 of April 3, 1926, except when the voter is an administrator or member of an organization or concern paying syndical dues in conformity with the aforesaid law. In the case of holders of stock in limited and unlimited companies, only registered shares which have been in his possession for at least one year confer the right to vote;

(b) Payment of at least 100 lire per annum of direct taxes to the State, province or commune, unless the voter has been for at least a year the owner or beneficiary of registered bonds of the public debt or of registered bonds of provincial or communal loans yielding an income of 500 lire annually;

SOURCE: Royal Decree of September 2, 1928, No. 1993, approving Electoral Law No. 1019 of May 17, 1928, published in *Gazzetta Ufficiale*, No. 118 (May 21, 1928). Printed in Benito Mussolini, *Fascism: Doctrine and Institutions* (Rome: "Ardita," 1935), pp. 182–194 *passim*.

(c) Receipt of a stipend, salary or pension, or other emolument of continuous character, provided in the budget of the State, province or commune, or any other body which is subject, by law, to the supervision of the State, province or commune;

(d) Membership of the Catholic clergy, secular or regular, or minister of another religion the exercise of which is admitted in the State. . . .

Art. 44—The number of deputies for the Kingdom shall be 400. The Kingdom shall form a single national constituency. . . .

Art. 46—The election of the deputies shall take place through:

1. the designation of candidates by the organizations mentioned in Articles 47 and 51;

2. the nomination of candidates by the Fascist Grand Council;

3. approval by the electoral body.

Art. 47—The right to designate candidates belongs first to the National Confederations of legally recognized syndicates, under Article 41 of the Royal Decree of July 1, 1926, No. 1130. . . .

The organizations mentioned above shall designate a total number of candidates which is double the number of deputies to be elected.

The distribution of this number among the various confederations is made in the table annexed to the present law.

The candidates shall be designated, for each confederation, by its general or national council regularly elected and convoked in accordance with the statutes.

The meetings called for the selection of candidates shall be held in Rome. The persons who receive the largest number of votes at these meetings shall be designated as candidates.

A notary shall draw up a record of the meeting and the result of the voting. . . .

Art. 51—Candidates may also be designated by legally recognized *enti morali*[4] and by *de facto* associations having national importance and pursuing ends of culture, education, assistance and propaganda, [provided that they are] recognized by royal decree . . . subject to revision every three years.

The above-mentioned organizations may propose a total number of candidates equal to one-half of the deputies to be elected. . . .

Art. 52—The period within which the organizations indicated in Arts. 47 and 51 are to submit the names of their candidates to the

---

4. Incorporated charitable and educational bodies.—*Ed.*

Fascist Grand Council is set forth in the decree announcing the elections. This period shall not be less than 20 nor more than 40 days from the date of publication of the decree just mentioned.

For each candidate put forward the organizations designating him must furnish certificates of birth, citizenship and criminal record, except in the case of ex-deputies.

The secretariat of the Fascist Grand Council, on receiving the names of the proposed candidates, shall form a single list of candidates in alphabetical order, indicating beside each name the organization proposing him. No attention shall be paid to the names of candidates received after the expiration of the time limit fixed in the decree calling the elections.

The Fascist Grand Council shall nominate a list of candidates, choosing freely from the list of those designated and even elsewhere if necessary, in order to include persons who have achieved fame in the sciences, letters, arts and politics, and in the defense services, who do not figure in the list of candidates.

A report on the deliberations of the Grand Council shall be drawn up under the direction of the Secretary of the Grand Council itself.

The list of nominated deputies bearing the emblem of the "Lictors' Fasces," on the model prescribed for the emblem of the State, shall be published free of cost in the *Gazzetta Ufficiale* and posted in all the communes of the Kingdom under the direction of the Minister of the Interior.

Art. 53—The elections for the approval of the list of deputies nominated shall take place on the third Sunday following the publication of the list in the *Gazzetta Ufficiale* of the Kingdom.

The vote shall be cast on ballots bearing the sign of the "Lictors' Fasces" and the formula: "Do you approve the list of deputies nominated by the Fascist Grand Council?" The vote shall be expressed beneath this formula by the word "Yes" or "No." . . .

Art. 88—Should the list of deputies nominated not be approved, the Court of Appeal of Rome, by a decree shall order new elections with competing lists of candidates, and shall set the date of the elections not sooner than 30 and not later than 45 days from the date of the decree. . . .

At the second election all associations and organizations having 5,000 voting members who are regularly registered in the electoral lists may present lists of candidates.

In deciding with regard to the lists of candidates proposed there shall be observed the rules and regulations established in the statutes of each association or organization. The persons receiving the largest number of votes at the meeting shall be proposed as candidates. A public notary shall draw up a report of the meeting and of the balloting. The report must also confirm that the meeting has been regularly convened. . . .

Art. 100—The Court of Appeal in Rome, acting as a national electoral office indicated in Article 83, upon receiving the acts . . . , shall count the votes obtained by each list and proclaim the result of the ballot.

All the candidates of the list which has received the majority of votes are declared elected.

Places reserved for minority representation shall be distributed among the other lists in proportion to the number of votes cast for each.

For this purpose, the total number of votes obtained by all the lists competing for the places reserved to the minority shall be divided by the total number of such places. The resulting figure is the minority quotient. The total number of votes received by each list is then divided by the said quotient and the result represents the number of places to be assigned to each list. The places eventually remaining unassigned shall be distributed respectively to the lists to which these last divisions have given the largest remainders and, in case of equality of remainders, to the minority list which has received the largest number of votes.

In each list the first on the list are declared elected within the limits of the number of places assigned to the list. . . .

Art. 106—All provisions regarding parliamentary incompatibilities are abrogated.

TABLE OF CANDIDATES

Number of candidates that each National Confederation of legally recognized syndical associations may propose for each hundred candidates presented by the Confederations:

1. National Confederation of Agriculturalists—12;
2. National Confederation of employees and workers in agriculture—12;
3. National Confederation of Industrialists—10;

4. National Confederation of employees and workers in industry—10;

5. National Confederation of Merchants—6;

6. National Confederation of employees and workers in commerce—6;

7. National Confederation of Persons Conducting Air and Sea Transport Services—5;

8. National Confederation of employees and workers in Air and Sea Transport Services—5;

9. National Confederation of Persons Conducting Transport Services by Land, Lakes and Rivers—4;

10. National Confederation of employees and workers in Transport Services by Land, Lakes and Rivers—4;

11. National Confederation of Credit and Insurance—3;

12. National Confederation of employees of Credit and Insurance—3;

13. National Confederation of Professionals and Artists—20.

The law on the Fascist Grand Council of December 9, 1928 (supplemented by a decree of December 14, 1929), put the finishing touches on the dictatorship. The Grand Council was instructed to keep always on hand a list of names to be presented to the Crown for the posts of Head of the Government and cabinet ministers; in this way the nomination passed from the hands of Parliament to the Fascist party. The Head of the Government was simultaneously the *Duce* of the PNF; his responsibility toward the King was only nominal, and was really effective only as regards the party. By this legislation, therefore, Italy became a party-state, the PNF structure being superimposed on that of the state. Under the new arrangement the party would have to be dissolved and the Grand Council come out in open opposition to Mussolini before the King could intervene. Among the constitutional questions lying within the purview of the Grand Council were the succession to the throne and the attributes and prerogatives of the Crown. Though privately he was irritated, Victor Emmanuel accepted this diminution of his power.

As things actually worked out, the task of the Grand Council consisted merely of approving what had already been decided by the *Duce*. Except for some debate over the racist decrees in 1938, the only time the Grand Council played a significant role was the night of July 24/25, 1943, when it appealed to the Crown against Mussolini.

The Fascist Grand Council
(December 9, 1928)

Art. 1—The Fascist Grand Council is the supreme organ which coordinates and integrates all the activities of the regime that emerged from the Revolution of October, 1922. It possesses deliberative powers in cases established by law, and is likewise empowered to give advice upon all other political, economic, and social questions of national interest whenever called upon to do so by the Head of the Government.

Art. 2—The Head of the Government, Prime Minister Secretary of State, is by right president of the Fascist Grand Council. He may summon it whenever he deems it necessary and fix its agenda.

Art. 3—The secretary of the National Fascist Party is also secretary of the Grand Council. The Head of the Government may delegate the secretary to preside over the meetings of the Grand Council in his absence, or whenever he is prevented from attending, or in case of vacancy.

Art. 4—The quadrumvirs of the March on Rome are members of the Fascist Grand Council for an indefinite period.

Art. 5—The following are ex officio members of the Grand Council for the duration of their office:

1. The President of the Senate and the President of the Chamber of Deputies;

2. The Ministers Secretaries of State for Foreign Affairs, Interior, Justice, Finance, National Education, Agriculture and Forestry, and Corporations;

3. The President of the Royal Academy of Italy;

4. The Secretary and the two Vice-Secretaries of the National Fascist Party;

5. The Commandant General of the Voluntary Militia for National Security;

6. The President of the Special Tribunal for the Defense of the State;

SOURCE: Law No. 2693 of December 9, 1928, published in *Gazzetta Ufficiale*, No. 287 (Dec. 11, 1928), as revised by Law No. 2099 of December 19, 1929. My translation.

7. The Presidents of the National Fascist Confederations and of the National Confederations of the Fascist Syndicates of Industry and Agriculture.

Art. 6—The appointment of the above-listed persons to the Grand Council is recognized by royal decree upon the recommendation of the Head of the Government. The appointment may be revoked by the same method at any time.

Art. 7—The Head of the Government may, by decree, appoint as members of the Fascist Grand Council, for a period of three years and with the possibility of reappointment, those persons who have, as members of the Government, or secretaries of the National Fascist Party since 1922, or for other merits, deserved well of the nation and of the cause of the Fascist Revolution. Such appointments may be revoked by the same method at any time.

Art. 8—Eligibility for membership in the Grand Council is compatible with that of Senator and Deputy.

Art. 9—No member of the Grand Council may be arrested, unless he be taken in the very act of a crime, nor submitted to legal or police proceedings, without the authorization of the Grand Council.

Art. 10—The members of the Grand Council receive no remuneration. The State incurs no expense for the Grand Council. The meetings of the Grand Council are secret. Its mode of procedure is fixed by by-laws which the Grand Council approves.

Art. 11—The Grand Council deliberates upon:

1. The list of Deputies designated for election under the terms of Art. 5 of Law No. 1019 of May 17, 1929 (*cf*. Art. 52 of the electoral law No. 1993 of Sept. 2, 1929);

2. The statutes, regulations, and political directives of the National Fascist Party;

3. The appointment and dismissal of the secretary, vice-secretaries, administrative secretary, and other members of the directory of the Fascist Party.

Art. 12—The advice of the Grand Council shall be requested upon all questions of a constitutional character. Proposed legislation on the following matters will be construed to have such constitutional character:

1. The succession to the Throne, and attributions and prerogatives of the Crown;

2. The composition and functions of the Grand Council, the Senate, and the Chamber of Deputies;

3. The attributions and prerogatives of the Head of the Government, Prime Minister Secretary of State;

4. The right of the Executive to issue rules having force of law;

5. The nature of syndical and corporative organization;

6. The relations between the State and the Holy See;

7. International treaties involving alteration in the territory of the State or of the colonies, or any surrender of territory.

Art. 13—The Grand Council, at the recommendation of the Head of the Government, draws up and keeps up to date a list of names to be submitted to the Crown, in the case of vacancy, for the position of Head of the Government. . . .

Although the elitist principle was followed ostensibly by the PNF (as was the case with the Communist party in Russia, whose example it copied), this was not always scrupulously observed. Until 1932 there were never more than one million party members (about 2.5 per cent of the population); beginning in 1932–33 Mussolini packed the party with a considerably larger number in order to bring about its "identification" with the nation. Civil servants and educators were coerced into it, while thousands of others joined for reasons of job security or avoidance of physical harm. Some cynics declared the initials really meant *Per Necessità Familiari* (For Family Necessity). After the early years of exaltation, "dry rot" and sycophancy set in by the late 1930's. In June, 1943, membership in the PNF was 4,770,770—of whom 1,600,140 were in the armed forces.

The PNF statute that went into effect on November 12, 1932, is printed below. It superseded that of December 20, 1929. Minor revisions were made in later years.

Statute of the National Fascist Party
(November 12, 1932)

NATURE OF THE PARTY

Art. 1—The National Fascist Party is a civil militia, under the orders of the DUCE, in the service of the Fascist State.

Art. 2—The National Fascist Party is composed of *Fasci di Combattimento*, which are grouped, in each province, into a Federation of *Fasci di Combattimento*.

The Secretary of a Federation of *Fasci ·di Combattimento*,

SOURCE: Benito Mussolini, *Fascism: Doctrine and Institutions* (Rome: "Ardita," 1935), pp. 198–217.

whenever he considers it necessary, is authorized to organize the *Fasci di Combattimento* into regional groups or sub-sections, each directed by a Leader (*Fiduciario*) and by a Board of five members, to one of whom will be entrusted administrative functions.

A *Fascio di Combattimento* cannot be formed or dissolved without the authority of the Secretary of the National Fascist Party.

In every provincial capital shall be established a University Fascist Group.

Attached to each *Fascio di Combattimento* shall be formed a *Fascio Giovanile di Combattimento* and a Women's *Fascio*. The latter shall in its turn establish a group of girl Fascists.

Attached to the Federation of *Fasci di Combattimento* shall be established the provincial associations of Schools, of Public Employment, of Railways, of Posts and Telegraphs, of Employees in State Industrial Concerns, and the Section of District Doctors belonging to the Association of Public Employment.

Art. 3—The Black Shirt is the Fascist uniform and must be worn only on prescribed occasions.

The Fascist must wear the badge of the National Fascist Party.

Art. 4—The standard is the emblem of the *Fascio di Combattimento* and is the symbol of Fascist faith.

The standard, which at official ceremonies is entrusted to a standard-bearer, is entitled to an escort of five Fascists chosen amongst those who took part in the March on Rome or have served the longest in the Party, commanded by the Vice-Secretary of the *Fascio di Combattimento*.

The standard of the National Directories of the National Fascist Party and the standard of the Federation of *Fasci di Combattimento*, to both of which military honors must be paid, are entitled to an escort of Fascist Militia (M.V.S.N.) under the command of an officer.

ORGANS AND HIERARCHY

Art. 5—The National Fascist Party through its collegiate organs and its officers carries out its activities under the guidance of the DUCE and in accordance with the directions traced by the Grand Council.

The hierarchy are:

1. The Secretary of the National Fascist Party;
2. The members of the National Directorate of the National

Fascist Party—the President of the Association of the Families of the Fascist Fallen and of Fascists Wounded or Disabled for the National Cause;

3. The Federal Secretary and the Federal Commander of the *Fasci Giovanili di Combattimento*—the Vice-Secretary of the University Fascist Groups;

4. The members of the Federal Directorates—the Secretaries of the University Fascist Groups—the Seconds-in-Command of the *Fasci Giovanili di Combattimento*—the Regional Inspectors—the Administrators of the Associations of the Families of the Fascist Fallen and of Fascists Wounded and Disabled for the National Cause—the provincial Administrators of the Women's *Fasci;*

5. The Secretaries of the *Fasci di Combattimento*—the members of the Directorate of the *Fasci di Combattimento*—the Administrators of the Regional Groups—the members of the Directorate of the University Fascist Groups—the Commanders of the *Fasci Giovanili di Combattimento*—the Administrators of the Sub-Sections—the Administrators of the Fascist University Nucleus—the Secretaries of the Women's *Fasci.*

The Collegiate organs are:

1. The National Directorate of the National Fascist Party;
2. The National Council of the National Fascist Party;
3. The Directorate of the Federations of *Fasci di Combattimento* (Federal Directorate);
4. The Directorate of the *Fasci di Combattimento;*
5. The Board of the Regional Groups;
6. The Directorate of the University Fascist Groups;
7. The Board of the Sub-Sections.

A Fascist who was present at the foundation of the *Fasci di Combattimento* (Piazza San Sepolcro, Milan, 23rd March 1919) shall have precedence over other Fascists of his category.

Art. 6—Positions of authority, commands or other offices must be entrusted to Black Shirts who have fought for or assisted the Revolution or to Fascists who have risen from the Youth Organizations.

THE CENTER

Art. 7—The National Directorate of the National Fascist Party, presided over by the Secretary of the National Fascist Party, consists of two Vice-Secretaries, an Administrative Secretary and six members.

The DUCE proposes to the King the nomination and dismissal of the Secretary of the National Fascist Party.[5] The Secretary of the National Fascist Party is a member of the Fascist Grand Council and is also its Secretary; he can be summoned to take part in the sessions of the Council of Ministers; he is a member of the Supreme Council of Defense, of the Superior Council of National Education, of the Administrative Council of the National Fascist Institute of Culture, of the National Council of Corporations and of the Central Corporative Committee; he is the President of the National Union of Italian Reserve Officers, of the Administrative Commission of National Employment Bureaus, Vice-President of the Central Board of University Activities, Secretary of the University Fascist Groups and Commander of the *Fasci Giovanili di Combattimento*.

The Secretary of the National Fascist Party, basing himself on the general instructions of the Grand Council of Fascism (set up by the law of December 9, 1928-VII, No. 2693) the supreme body issued from the Revolution, which co-ordinates and integrates all the activities of the regime, imparts instructions for the work to be carried out by the dependent organizations, reserving to himself the fullest control.

He presides over the activities of the National Directorate of the National Fascist Party and, subject always to his right eventually to make necessary changes, lays down the regulations for the setting up and working of the Departments, which are constituted as follows:

Political Secretariat;
Administrative Secretariat;
Association of the Families of Fascist Fallen;
Fascist University Groups;
Fasci Giovanili di Combattimento;
Women's *Fasci*;
Fascist Associations (Schools, Public Employees, State Railways, Posts and Telegraphs, Employees of the State Industrial organizations);
National Olympic Committee;

5. Mussolini dismissed Farinacci from the secretaryship in April, 1926. He was replaced by Augusto Turati until 1929; Giovanni Giuriati (1929–31); and Achille Starace (1931–39). Thereafter such mediocrities as Ettore Muti, A. Serena, Aldo Vidussoni, and Carlo Scorza held the post.—*Ed.*

National *Dopolavoro* Organization;
Press and Propaganda;
Historical Committee;
Archives.

On the proposal of the Federal Secretaries, he nominates the Federal Directors, the Secretaries of the University Fascist Groups, and the Administrators of the Women's *Fasci*.

Whenever, at his request, a Federal Secretary is removed, he has the right to dissolve the Federal Directorate and to proceed to the appointment of an Extraordinary Commissioner.

He controls the working of the non-central organizations, since all their actions are imbued with the spirit of Fascism; he maintains contact with the National Fascist Confederations of Employers and Workers, the National Fascist Confederation of Professional Workers and Artists, and the National Co-operative Organizations and, whenever necessary, collaborates in the field of labor and production; he maintains contact with the various organs of the State, with the Presidency of the Senate, with the Presidency of the Chamber of Deputies, with the General Command of the M.V.S.N. (Militia), and with the Secretary General of the Italian *Fasci* abroad.

He has under his direct orders the National Italian Olympic Committee and the National *Dopolavoro* Organization.

Subject to the decision of the DUCE he personally takes the Chair at their meetings or appoints others to do so.

Art. 8—The members of the National Directorate of the National Fascist Party are appointed and removed by the DUCE on the proposal of the Secretary of the National Party.

The Vice-Secretaries of the National Fascist Party are members of the Grand Council of Fascism and of the National Council of Corporations, and are Vice-Commanders of the *Fasci Giovanili di Combattimento*.

They assist the Secretary of the National Fascist Party and substitute him in case of need.

The Administrative Secretary of the National Fascist Party is a member of the Central Board of University Activities.

The National Directorate, summoned by the Secretary of the National Fascist Party, will normally meet once a month in the Littorio Palace, and whenever the Secretary of the National Fascist Party may deem it necessary.

When the meetings of the National Directorate of the National Fascist Party are ordered and presided over by the DUCE, the Minister of the Interior, the General Commandant of the M.V.S.N. (Militia), and the Minister of Corporations shall take part.

At meetings presided over by the Secretary of the National Fascist Party, the Under-Secretary of State for the Interior, the Under-Secretary of State for Corporations, and the Chief of Staff of the M.V.S.N. (Militia) have the right to be present.

As a general rule the decisions shall be published by means of the Order Sheet (*Foglio d'Ordine*).

Art. 9—The National Council is composed of the Federal Secretaries and is presided over by the Secretary of the National Fascist Party, who summons it with the previous authorization of the DUCE.

It examines the activity of the National Fascist Party, and receives general instructions for execution.

Art. 10—The DUCE summons to the General Meeting (*Gran Rapporto*) the members of the Grand Council of Fascism, the National Directorate of the National Fascist Party, the National Council of the National Fascist Party, and the Federal Directors.

IN THE PROVINCES

Art. 11—Federal Secretaries are appointed and removed by the DUCE, on the proposal of the Secretary of the National Fascist Party.

They carry out the orders of the Secretary of the National Fascist Party.

They promote and control the activities of the *Fasci di Combattimento* of the province and exercise a political control over all the institutions and organizations of the Regime.

They keep in touch with Senators and Deputies and with the Commandant of the Militia.

They preside over the Intersyndical Committee and the Joint Administrative Commission of the Provincial Employment Bureaus.

They are members of the Board of University Activities in cities where Universities or Higher Educational Institutes are established.

They preside over the Relief Organizations and the provincial *Dopolavoro*.

They promote and regulate sport in the subordinate organizations.

They convene the Federal Directorate at least once a month, and at least once a year summon the Secretaries of the *Fasci di Combattimento* and with them examine and illustrate the problems confronting the *Fasci di Combattimento* and the political, moral and economic problems of the province.

They control directly, or through their appointees, the keeping of the registers of membership (Federal and of the *Fasci di Combattimento*) and of the archives.

They propose to the Secretary of the National Fascist Party the names of the members of the Federal Directorate to the number of seven.

The Federal Directorate has consultative functions; to each member the Federal Secretary may entrust special duties in connection with the various branches of the National Fascist Party's activities and those of dependent organizations.

Two of the members of the Federal Directorate will respectively be delegated to conduct the Federal Secretariat (Federal Vice-Secretary) in the absence of the Federal Secretary, and the Federal Administrative Secretariat (Federal Administrative Secretary).

He (the Federal Secretary) may avail himself of the assistance of Regional Inspectors, whom he appoints himself.

He is Federal Commandant of the *Fasci Giovanili di Combattimento*.

He appoints the Political Secretary of each *Fascio di Combattimento*, and the latter, in turn, proposes to the Federal Secretary the names of members of the Directorate of the *Fascio di Combattimento*, to the number of five.

The number of members of the Directorate of the *Fascio di Combattimento* in the provincial capital is seven.

This number may, with the authorization of the Secretary of the National Fascist Party, be raised to nine if the membership (of the *Fascio di Combattimento*) exceeds 20,000.

Art. 12—At the headquarters of the Federation of the *Fasci di Combattimento* a register must be kept of those inscribed in each *Fascio di Combattimento*.

The making out of membership cards is entrusted to the Federation of the *Fasci di Combattimento* under the personal responsibility of the Federal Secretary.

Art. 13—It is incumbent on the Political Secretary of the *Fascio di Combattimento* and the leaders of district groups and sub-sections to know the political and moral antecedents as well as the means of subsistence of each member, and to insist that even in every day matters Fascist spirit and discipline be respected, reporting to the Federal Secretary whenever necessary those who fail in their duties.

He is personally responsible for the correctness of the register of membership.

The Political Secretary of the *Fascio di Combattimento* and the leaders, on receipt of orders from the Federal Secretary shall call together the Fascists on the opening of the Fascist year, to communicate and illustrate the program which they intend to follow, and upon which discussion is permitted. In the course of the year, they hold at least one other meeting, preferably on the anniversary of the constitution of the *Fascio di Combattimento* concerned.

THE FASCIST LEVY

Art. 14—The Fascist Levy takes place on April 21st, Labor Day.

The Fascist Levy consists in the promotion of *Balilla* to the ranks of the *Avanguardisti*, and of *Avanguardisti* to the ranks of the Young Fascists, as well as of the latter to the National Fascist Party and the Fascist Militia.

The arrangements for the Levy are agreed upon by the Secretary of the National Fascist Party, the Under-Secretary of State for the Education and Physical training of the young, the President of the National *Balilla* Organization, and the Chief of Staff of the Fascist Militia.

The Young Fascists who enter the National Fascist Party take the oath before the Political Secretary of the *Fascio di Combattimento* in the following form:

"In the name of God and of Italy I swear to carry out without discussion the orders of the Duce and to serve the Cause of the Fascist Revolution with all my might and if necessary with my life."

DISCIPLINE

Art. 15—In the National Directorate of the National Fascist Party is instituted the Court of Discipline, presided over by a Vice-Secretary and composed of two full members, two supplementary members chosen from the National Directorate and a Secretary, appointed from time to time by the Secretary of the National Fascist Party.

Only such cases will be deferred to the Court as the Secretary of the National Fascist Party considers call for special examination.

The findings of the Court of Discipline will be submitted to the Secretary of the National Fascist Party for his decisions.

Art. 16—In every Federation of *Fasci di Combattimento* is instituted a Federal Disciplinary Commission presided over by the Federal Vice-Secretary and composed of five full members and two supplementary members and a secretary, drawn from outside the Federal Directorate.

These appointments are made by the Federal Secretary.

The Federal Disciplinary Commission may inflict the penalties prescribed in paragraphs 1, 2, and 3 of Article 19.

When the findings of the Federal Disciplinary Commission involve the penalty of withdrawal of the membership card or expulsion, the proceedings will be referred to the Federal Secretary who, where he considers that expulsion from the National Fascist Party is advisable, submits a proposal to this effect to the Secretary of the National Fascist Party in accordance with Article 21.

Art. 17—When the Disciplinary Commission has to try officers or men of the Militia, Directors of the National *Balilla* Organization, and Directors of the Syndical or Co-operative organizations, the Federal Secretary will invite an officer or representative of the said organization to form part of the Commission.

(a) When a Fascist, officer or man of the Fascist Militia, incurs one of the disciplinary penalties prescribed by Article 19 of the present Statute, the qualified Command takes analogous action. Reprimands must be entered on the register sheets.

When a member of the Fascist Militia incurs one of the penalties prescribed by the disciplinary regulations laid down by the General Command, which imply removal from the Militia, he must be brought before the Federal Disciplinary Commission; whenever "removal from the roll" is in question owing to lack of those physical requirements or moral aptitudes called for in a member of the Militia, the decision is without effect insofar as membership of the National Fascist Party is concerned.

(b) When the Fascist Militia has to proceed against officers or men who hold office in the National Fascist Party, the Federal Secretary concerned will be consulted.

(c) When proceedings have to be taken against General Officers or Consuls of the Fascist Militia—in permanent service or on half pay—the General Command will be consulted.

(d) In disciplinary proceedings against higher (*Primi Seniori* and *Seniori*) and lower grade officers—in permanent service or on half pay—the Fascist Militia Command concerned (Group Command or Legion) will be consulted.

(e) When the Fascist Militia authorities have pronounced a decision which has subsequently been confirmed by the National Fascist Party, the delinquent's case may only be re-examined and eventually modified by the Command concerned, with the prior assent of the Federal Secretary.

Art. 18—The Fascist who fails in his duty through indiscipline or lack of those qualities which constitute the traditionally Fascist spirit will, except in cases of extreme urgency, be sent by the Federal Secretary before the Federal Disciplinary Commission.

In cases of extreme urgency the Federal Secretary himself imposes the penalty.

DISCIPLINARY PENALTIES

Art. 19—Disciplinary penalties are as follows:

1. Reprimand;
2. Suspension for a definite period of time (from a minimum of one month to a maximum of one year);
3. Suspension for an indefinite period of time;
4. Withdrawal of membership card;
5. Expulsion from the National Fascist Party.

Art. 20—The penalties referred to in Nos. 1, 2 and 3 of Article 19 are inflicted for disciplinary lapses which do not preclude reconsideration.

When penal proceedings are opened against a Fascist for offenses against personal honor, he is placed by the Federal Secretary in *suspension pending judgment*.

Loss of his membership card is incurred by a Fascist who is guilty of serious lapses of discipline or who shows that he does not possess those qualities which make up the traditionally Fascist spirit.

The punishment referred to in No. 5 of Article 19 is inflicted upon traitors to the Cause of the Fascist Revolution and upon those who have been sentenced for disgraceful crimes.

The Fascist who is expelled from the National Fascist Party must be outlawed from public life.

His position is not susceptible of revision except in cases where an error is shown to have been made by new facts or new evidence, and then only upon the order of the DUCE.

Art. 21—Disciplinary punishment must be accompanied by a brief but clear statement of reasons and must be noted upon the identification card of the person punished.

Upon this card must also be noted the expiration or revocation of the sentence.

The person punished has the right of appeal to the Federal Secretary in respect of punishments inflicted by the Federal Disciplinary Commission, and to the Secretary of the National Fascist Party for punishments inflicted by the Federal Secretary, within one month from the date of notification of the measure, which, despite such appeal, becomes immediately effective.

He does not possess the right of appeal when the punishment has been inflicted by the Secretary of the National Fascist Party, except in cases where an error is revealed by new facts or new evidence.

Expulsion from the National Fascist Party is inflicted directly by the Secretary of the National Fascist Party or upon the proposal of the Federal Secretary.

Art. 22—Fascists who hold public offices of particular importance cannot be subjected to proceedings or disciplinary penalties until they have left office.

Proceedings which it is proposed to take in regard to them will be brought, informally, to the notice of the National Fascist Party, and by the latter to the Government.

Disciplinary penalties may be inflicted upon Senators and Deputies only by the Secretary of the National Fascist Party.

Art. 23—A Fascist who has been suspended from the Party is obliged to abstain from all political activity and can take advantage of no right accruing to him by reason of his Fascist membership.

Within twenty-four hours from the time of notification of the sentence passed, he must deposit his membership card and badge in the Secretarial Office of the *Fascio di Combattimento* in which he is enrolled.

He is suspended from all offices or duties, unless instructions to the contrary have been given.

The Fascist whose membership card is withdrawn or who is expelled is obliged to resign from all offices, to relinquish all charges, and to return, within twenty-four hours from the time of notification of the sentence, his membership card and badge to the

Secretarial Office of the *Fascio di Combattimento* in which he was enrolled.

Art. 24—The Federal Secretary, upon his own initiative, upon the proposal of the political secretary of the *Fascio di Combattimento*, or upon the request of the person concerned, has authority to reconsider the position of the Fascist who has been punished.

A Fascist who, after having suffered the loss of his membership card, renders himself worthy of readmission has the right to claim his previous standing as regards length of service.

Readmission must be ratified by the Secretary of the National Fascist Party.

Art. 25—No punishment may be inflicted or proposed until the charges have been notified and the defense carefully examined.

ADMINISTRATION

Art. 26—The Administrative Secretary of the National Fascist Party administers the property of the National Fascist Party and is responsible therefor.

He is responsible for the compilation of a balance sheet, which he submits for examination by the National Fascist Party and for approval by the Secretary of the National Fascist Party.

Supervision of the accounts of the National Fascist Party devolves upon a board of accountants composed of three members elected each year by the National Directorate of the National Fascist Party from among persons outside the Directorate.

Each year the board will present to the National Directorate of the National Fascist Party its report.

The Administrative Secretary of the National Fascist Party is in charge of the employment and supervision of personnel.

The Administrative Secretary of the National Fascist Party approves the estimated and effective budgets of the Federations of the *Fasci di Combattimento* and of subordinate organizations and supervises the administration thereof through persons specially designated by him.

Art. 27—The Federal Administrative Secretary is in charge of the various property transactions of the Federation of the *Fasci di Combattimento* and is responsible therefor.

He draws up the estimates and accounts, which he must present annually for examination by the board of auditors and the Federal Directorate, and for approval by the Administrative Secretary of the National Fascist Party.

He provides, according to the instructions of the Federal Secretary, for the Administration of the Federation of the *Fasci di Combattimento*, and subordinate organizations (excluding the Relief organizations) upon the basis of their respective estimated budgets; for collections and payments within the various allotments made in the budget, and in the case of possible extraordinary expenditure he must consult the Federal Secretary, who will request the approval of the Administrative Secretary of the National Fascist Party.

He is responsible for the accuracy of the accounting.

Supervision of the administration and accounting of the Federation of the *Fasci di Combattimento* and of subordinate organizations (excluding the Relief organizations) devolves upon a board of three auditors appointed by the Federal Secretary from among persons outside the Federal Directorate. As regards the Relief organizations such functions are fulfilled by a board of auditors composed of one accountant in the employ of the Prefecture and two other members appointed by the Prefect.

The Federal Administrative Secretary makes provision directly and through representatives appointed for that specific purpose for surveillance and supervision of the administration of the *Fasci di Combattimento*.

He is responsible for the discipline of subordinate personnel.

Art. 28—The National Directorate of the National Fascist Party will at the opening of each Fascist year issue instructions regarding the financing of the Federations of the *Fasci di Combattimento* and subordinate organizations.

Art. 29—The Administrative Secretary of the *Fascio di Combattimento* has charge of and is responsible for the activities of the *Fascio di Combattimento*.

He compiles the estimated and effective budgets which he must present annually for examination by the Board of Auditors and the Directorate of the *Fascio di Combattimento* and for approval by the Federation of the *Fasci di Combattimento*.

He takes charge of obtaining membership cards from the Federal Administrative Secretarial Office.

He is responsible for the custody of liquid funds in the bank selected by him in agreement with the Federal Administrative Secretary.

He takes charge of collections and payments upon the basis of the estimated budget; he is responsible for the accuracy of the

accounting; he carries out the instructions of the Federal Administrative Secretary.

Supervision of the administration and accounting of the *Fascio di
Combattimento* devolves upon a board of three auditors appointed
by the Political Secretary of the *Fascio di Combattimento* from
among persons not members of the Directorate of the *Fascio di
Combattimento*.

MEMBERSHIP CARDS

Art. 30—The membership card of the National Fascist Party is
issued gratuitously by the Political Secretary of the *Fascio di
Combattimento* to:

(a) Disabled War Veterans;

(b) Disabled Fascists;

(c) Families of Fallen Fascists;

(d) Members who are fathers of families of seven or more
children.

Art. 31—The Fascist Year begins on October 29th.

After the fusion of the Fascist and Nationalist parties in 1923, members
of the latter contingent made a vigorous effort to give a more conservative, "statist" tone to the ideology of Fascism. The most noteworthy early such effort was the so-called *Manifesto of the Fascist
Intellectuals*, proclaimed on April 21, 1925, by Giovanni Gentile, a
distinguished neo-Hegelian philosopher who had served until 1924 as
Mussolini's first Minister of Education. His very rhetorical declaration
was signed by numerous figures of the cultural world, including Luigi
Pirandello and the poet Giuseppe Ungaretti.

Gentile's manifesto was too much for Benedetto Croce, a Liberal
Senator from Naples, to stomach. This eminent philosopher of history
(and former friend of Gentile's) penned a scathing *Countermanifesto*
on May 1, 1925. Years later he recalled with satisfaction that almost
everyone remembered his reply long after they had forgotten the
contents of Gentile's declaration. Signed by dozens of Italy's leading
anti-Fascist intellectuals (*e.g.*, Luigi Einaudi, Guido DeRuggiero, Luigi
Salvatorelli, and Guglielmo Ferrero), it was published in the national
press with the help of Amendola, leader of the Aventine. Croce ridi-
culed the "new religion" of Fascism as "an incoherent and bizarre
mishmash of appeals to both authority and demagogism, of professed
respect for the laws combined with violation of the laws, of reverence
for both ultramodern theories and moldy old notions, of fondness for
both absolutistic postures and Bolshevik tendencies, of unbelief alternating with flirtations with the Catholic Church, of a loathing for real
culture mixed with a sterile reaching after culture that has no founda-

tion, of mystical mawkishness on the one hand and cynicism on the other."[6]

Though intensely irritated, Mussolini never dared to arrest the renowned scholar, partly out of fear of foreign criticism; indeed, he sought to make the rest of the world think that the dictatorship could not be very brutal when a man like Croce was free to publish. The latter's review, *La Critica*, which dealt with philosophy, history, and literature, did manage to continue expressing publicly the editor's judgments, the outward cultural format serving to mask the frequently political substance. Thus if Croce jibed against the regimentation of culture by Russian Communists or Nazi Brownshirts, his Italian readers could discern that he also meant the pompous Blackshirt lictors at home. It has been reported that whenever Croce left Naples to visit other cities, his disciples welcomed him as the early Christians did St. Paul. He became the major and virtually the only voice of freedom and anti-Fascism within Italy during the next two decades.

Gentile was not the only intellectual to try to expound the philosophy of Fascism in 1925. Alfredo Rocco, a Nationalist party jurisprudent who espoused the organic state and became Mussolini's influential Minister of Justice, set down on paper the theory of a supreme, totalitarian state directed by the intuitive genius of an all-powerful *Duce*. Finally it was Mussolini's turn himself. After he had been in power a decade the editors of the new *Enciclopedia Italiana* asked for an authoritative article on Fascism. They invited Gentile to prepare it, but when PNF leaders heard of this they were incensed, for it was known that he had expressed hostility to Mussolini's Lateran Pacts with the Church. They insisted that the *Duce* himself write the article. Mussolini thereupon spent some three days reworking it, and the second portion was entirely his own. It is in this section that the "working ideology" of Fascism is stated most fully.

Mussolini's Doctrine of Fascism
(1932)

FUNDAMENTAL IDEAS

Like all sound political conceptions, Fascism is action and it is thought; action in which doctrine is immanent, and doctrine arising from a given system of historical forces in which it is inserted, and working on them from within. It has therefore a form correlated to

SOURCE: Benito Mussolini, *Fascism: Doctrine and Institutions* (Rome: "Ardita," 1935), pp. 7–14. Footnote references deleted.

6. Published in *Il Mondo* (Rome), May 1, 1925, and reprinted in Emilio R. Papa, *Storia di due manifesti: Il fascismo e la cultura italiana* (Milan: Feltrinelli, 1958), pp. 92–97. My translation. By permission of Feltrinelli Editore.

contingencies of time and space; but it has also an ideal content which makes it an expression of truth in the higher region of the history of thought. There is no way of exercising a spiritual influence in the world as a human will dominating the will of others, unless one has a conception both of the transient and the specific reality on which that action is to be exercised, and of the permanent and universal reality in which the transient dwells and has its being. To know men one must know man; and to know man one must be acquainted with reality and its laws. There can be no conception of the State which is not fundamentally a conception of life: philosophy or intuition, system of ideas evolving within the framework of logic or concentrated in a vision or a faith, but always, at least potentially, an organic conception of the world.

Thus many of the practical expressions of Fascism—such as party organization, system of education, discipline—can only be understood when considered in relation to its general attitude toward life. A spiritual attitude. Fascism sees in the world not only those superficial, material aspects in which man appears as an individual, standing by himself, self-centered, subject to natural law which instinctively urges him toward a life of selfish momentary pleasure; it sees not only the individual but the nation and the country; individuals and generations bound together by a moral law, with common traditions and a mission which, suppressing the instinct for life closed in a brief circle of pleasure, builds up a higher life, founded on duty, a life free from the limitations of time and space, in which the individual, by self-sacrifice, the renunciation of self-interest, by death itself, can achieve that purely spiritual existence in which his value as a man consists.

The conception is therefore a spiritual one, arising from the general reaction of the century against the flaccid materialistic positivism of the nineteenth century. Anti-positivistic but positive; neither skeptical nor agnostic; neither pessimistic nor supinely optimistic as are, generally speaking, the doctrines (all negative) which place the center of life outside man; whereas, by the exercise of his free will, man can and must create his own world.

Fascism wants man to be active and to engage in action with all his energies; it wants him to be manfully aware of the difficulties besetting him and ready to face them. It conceives of life as a struggle in which it behooves a man to win for himself a really worthy place, first of all by fitting himself (physically, morally, intellectually) to become the implement required for winning it. As for the individual, so for the nation, and so for mankind. Hence the high value of culture in all its forms (artistic, religious, scientific), and the outstanding importance of education. Hence also the essential value of work, by which man subjugates nature and creates the human world (economic, political, ethical, intellectual).

This positive conception of life is obviously an ethical one. It invests the whole field of reality as well as the human activities which master it. No action is exempt from moral judgment; no activity can be despoiled of the value which a moral purpose confers on all things. Therefore life, as conceived of by the Fascist, is serious, austere, religious; all its manifestations are poised in a world sustained by moral forces and subject to spiritual responsibilities. The Fascist disdains an "easy" life.

The Fascist conception of life is a religious one, in which man is viewed in his immanent relation to a higher law, endowed with an objective will transcending the individual and raising him to conscious membership in a spiritual society. Those who perceive nothing beyond opportunistic considerations in the religious policy of the Fascist regime fail to realize that Fascism is not only a system of government but also and above all a system of thought.

In the Fascist conception of history, man is man only by virtue of the spiritual process to which he contributes as a member of the family, the social group, the nation, and in function of history to which all nations bring their contribution. Hence the great value of tradition in records, in language, in customs, in the rules of social life. Outside history man is a nonentity. Fascism is therefore opposed to all individualistic abstractions based on eighteenth-century materialism; and it is opposed to all Jacobinistic utopias and innovations. It does not believe in the possibility of "happiness" on earth as conceived by the economistic literature of the eighteenth century, and it therefore rejects the teleological notion that at some future time the human family will secure a final settlement of all its difficulties. This notion runs counter to experience which teaches that life is in continual flux and in process of evolution. In politics Fascism aims at realism; in practice it desires to deal only with those problems which are the spontaneous product of historic conditions and which find or suggest their own solutions. Only by entering into the process of reality and taking possession of the forces at work within it, can man act on man and on nature.

Anti-individualistic, the Fascist conception of life stresses the importance of the State and accepts the individual only insofar as his interests coincide with those of the State, which stands for the conscience and the universal will of man as a historic entity. It is opposed to classical liberalism which arose as a reaction to absolutism and exhausted its historical function when the State became the expression of the conscience and will of the people. Liberalism denied the State in the name of the individual; Fascism reasserts the rights of the State as expressing the real essence of the individual. And if Liberty is to be the attribute of living men and not of abstract dummies invented by individualistic liberalism, then Fascism stands for liberty, and for the only liberty worth having, the liberty of the State and of the individual within the State. The Fascist conception of the State is all-embracing; outside of it no human or spiritual values can exist, much less have value. Thus understood, Fascism is totalitarian, and the Fascist State—a synthesis and a unit inclusive of all values—interprets, develops, and potentiates the whole life of a people.

No individuals or groups (political parties, cultural associations, economic unions, social classes) outside the State. Fascism is therefore opposed to Socialism to which unity within the State (which amalgamates classes into a single economic and ethical reality) is unknown, and which sees in history nothing but the class struggle. Fascism is likewise opposed to trade-unionism as a class weapon. But when brought within the orbit of the State, Fascism recognizes the real needs which gave rise to socialism and trade-unionism, giving them due weight in the guild or corporative system in which divergent interests are co-ordinated and harmonized in the unity of the State.

Grouped according to their several interests, individuals form classes; they form trade-unions when organized according to their several economic activities; but first and foremost they form the State, which is no mere matter of numbers, the sum of the individuals forming the majority. Fascism is therefore opposed to that form of democracy which equates a nation to the majority, lowering it to the level of the largest number; but it is the purest form of democracy if the nation be considered—as it should be—from the point of view of quality rather than quantity, as an idea, the mightiest because the most ethical, the most coherent, the truest, expressing itself in a people as the conscience and will of the few, if not, indeed, of one, and tending to express itself in the conscience and the will of the mass, of the whole group ethnically moulded by natural and historical conditions into a nation, advancing, as one conscience and one will, along the self-same line of development and spiritual formation. Not a race, nor a geographically defined region, but a people, historically perpetuating itself; a multitude unified by an idea and imbued with the will to live, the will to power, self-consciousness, personality.

Insofar as it is embodied in a State, this higher personality becomes a nation. It is not the nation which generates the State; that is an antiquated naturalistic concept which afforded a basis for nineteenth-century publicity in favor of national governments. Rather it is the State which creates the nation, conferring volition and therefore real life on a people made aware of their moral unity.

The right to national independence does not arise from any merely literary and idealistic form of self-consciousness; still less from a more or less passive and unconscious *de facto* situation, but from an active, self-conscious, political will expressing itself in action and ready to prove its rights. It arises, in short, from the existence, at least *in fieri*, of a State. Indeed, it is the State which, as the expression of a universal ethical will, creates the right to national independence.

A nation, as expressed in the State, is a living, ethical entity only insofar as it is progressive. Inactivity is death. Therefore the State is not only Authority which governs and confers legal form and spiritual value on individual wills, but it is also Power which makes its will felt and respected beyond its own frontiers, thus affording practical proof of the universal character of the decisions necessary to ensure its development. This implies organization and expansion, potential if not actual. Thus the State equates itself to the will of man, whose development cannot be checked by obstacles and which, by achieving self-expression, demonstrates its own infinity.

The Fascist State, as a higher and more powerful expression of personality, is a force, but a spiritual one. It sums up all the manifestations of the moral and intellectual life of man. Its functions cannot therefore be limited to those of enforcing order and keeping the peace, as the liberal doctrine had it. It is no mere mechanical device for defining the sphere within which the individual may duly exercise his supposed rights. The Fascist State is an inwardly accepted standard and rule of conduct, a discipline of the whole person; it permeates the will no less than the intellect. It stands for a principle which becomes the central motive of man as a member of civilized society, sinking deep down into his personality; it dwells in the heart of the man of action and of the thinker, of the artist and of the man of science: soul of the soul.

Fascism, in short, is not only a law-giver and a founder of institutions, but an educator and a promoter of spiritual life. It aims at refashioning not only the forms of life but their content—man, his character, and his faith. To achieve this purpose it enforces discipline and uses authority, entering into the soul and ruling with undisputed sway. Therefore it has chosen as its emblem the Lictor's rods, the symbol of unity, strength, and justice.

POLITICAL AND SOCIAL DOCTRINE

When, in the now distant March of 1919, I summoned a meeting at Milan through the columns of the *Popolo d'Italia* of the surviving members of the Interventionist Party who had themselves been in action, and who had followed me since the creation of the Fascist Revolutionary Party (which took place in the January of 1915), I had no specific doctrinal attitude in my mind. I had a living experience of one doctrine only—that of Socialism, from 1903–4 to the winter of 1914—that is to say, about a decade: and from Socialism itself, even though I had taken part in the movement first as a member of the rank and file and then later as a leader, yet I had no experience of its doctrine in practice. My own doctrine, even in this period, had always been a doctrine of action. A unanimous, universally accepted theory of Socialism did not exist after 1905, when the revisionist movement began in Germany under the leadership of Bernstein, while under pressure of the tendencies of the time, a Left Revolutionary movement also appeared, which though never getting further than talk in Italy, in Russian Socialistic circles laid the foundations of Bolshevism. Reformation, Revolution, Centralization—already the echoes of these terms are spent—while in the great stream of Fascism are to be found ideas which began with Sorel,[7] Péguy,[8] with Lagardelle[9] in the "Mouvement

SOURCE: Benito Mussolini, "The Political and Social Doctrine of Fascism," in *International Conciliation*, No. 306 (Jan. 1935), pp. 5–17, republished by courtesy of the Carnegie Endowment for International Peace.

7. Georges Sorel (1847–1922), French theorist of syndicalism. *Ed.*

8. Charles Péguy (1873–1914), French Marxian socialist who became a convert to Roman Catholicism. *Ed.*

9. Hubert Lagardelle (1874–1958), French theorist of revolutionary syndicalism and editor of *Le Mouvement Socialiste*. *Ed.*

Socialiste," and with the Italian trade union movement which throughout the period 1904–14 was sounding a new note in Italian Socialist circles (already weakened by the betrayal of Giolitti) through [Angelo] Olivetti's *Pagine Libere*, [Paolo] Orano's *La Lupa*, and Enrico Leone's *Divenire Sociale*.

After the War, in 1919, Socialism was already dead as a doctrine: it existed only as a hatred. There remained to it only one possibility of action, especially in Italy: reprisals against those who had desired the War and who must now be made to "expiate" its results. The *Popolo d'Italia* was then given the subtitle of "The newspaper of ex-servicemen and producers," and the word producers was already the expression of a mental attitude. Fascism was not the nursling of a doctrine worked out beforehand with detailed elaboration; it was born of the need for action and it was itself from the beginning practical rather than theoretical; it was not merely another political party but, even in the first two years, in opposition to all political parties as such, and itself a living movement. The name which I then gave to the organization fixed its character. And yet, if one were to re-read, in the now dusty columns of that date, the report of the meeting in which the *Fasci Italiani di Combattimento* were constituted, one would there find no ordered expression of doctrine, but a series of aphorisms, anticipations, and aspirations which, when refined by time from the original ore, were destined after some years to develop into an ordered series of doctrinal concepts, forming the Fascists' political doctrine —different from all others either of the past or the present day.

"If the bourgeoisie," I said then, "think that they will find lightning-conductors in us, they are the more deceived; we must start work at once. . . . We want to accustom the working-class to real and effectual leadership, and also to convince them that it is no easy thing to direct an industry or a commercial enterprise successfully. . . . We shall combat every retrograde idea, technical or spiritual. . . . When the succession to the seat of government is open, we must not be unwilling to fight for it. We must make haste; when the present régime breaks down, we must be ready at once to take its place. It is we who have the right to the succession, because it was we who forced the country into the War, and led her to victory. The present method of political representation cannot suffice, we must have a representation direct from the individuals concerned. It may be objected against this program that it is a return to the conception of the corporation, but that is no matter. . . . Therefore, I desire that this assembly shall accept the revindication of national trade-unionism from the economic point of view. . . ."

Now is it not a singular thing that even on the first day in the Piazza San Sepolcro that word "corporation" arose, which later, in the course of the Revolution, came to express one of the creations of social legislation at the very foundation of the régime?

The years which preceded the March to Rome were years of great difficulty, during which the necessity for action did not permit of research or any complete elaboration of doctrine. The battle had to be fought in the towns and villages. There was much discussion, but—what was more important and more sacred—men died. They knew how to die. Doctrine, beautifully defined and carefully elucidated, with headlines and paragraphs, might be lacking; but there was to take its place something more decisive—Faith. Even so, anyone who can recall the events of the time through the aid of books, articles, votes of congresses, and speeches of great and minor importance—anyone who knows how to research and weigh evidence—will find that the fundamentals of doctrine were cast during the years of conflict. It was precisely in those years that Fascist thought armed itself, was refined, and began the great task of organization. The problem of the relation between the individual citizen and the State; the allied problems of authority and liberty; political and social problems as well as those specifically national—a solution was being sought for all these while at the same time the struggle against Liberalism, Democracy, Socialism, and the Masonic bodies was being carried on, contemporaneously with the "punitive expedition." But, since there was inevitably some lack of system, the adversaries of Fascism have disingenuously denied that it had any capacity to produce a doctrine of its own, though that doctrine was growing and taking shape under their very eyes, even though tumultuously; first, as happens to all ideas in their beginnings, in the aspect of a violent and dogmatic negation, and then in the aspect of positive construction which has found its realization in the laws and institutions of the régime as enacted successively in the years 1926, 1927, and 1928.

Fascism is now a completely individual thing, not only as a régime but as a doctrine. And this means that today Fascism, exercising its critical sense upon itself and upon others, has formed its own distinct and peculiar point of view, to which it can refer and upon which, therefore, it can act in the face of all problems, practical or intellectual, which confront the world.

And above all, Fascism, the more it considers and observes the future and the development of humanity quite apart from political considerations of the moment, believes neither in the possibility nor the utility of perpetual peace. It thus repudiates the doctrine of Pacifism—born of a renunciation of the struggle and an act of cowardice in the face of sacrifice. War alone brings up to its highest tension all human energy and puts the stamp of nobility upon the peoples who have the courage to meet it. All other trials are substitutes, which never really put men into the position where they have to make the great decision—the alternative of life or death. Thus a doctrine which is founded upon this harmful postulate of peace is hostile to Fascism. And thus hostile to the spirit of Fascism, though accepted for what use they can be in dealing with particular political situations, are all the international leagues and societies which, as history will show, can be scattered to the winds when once strong national feeling is aroused by any motive—sentimental, ideal, or practical. This anti-pacifist spirit is carried by Fascism even into the life of the individual; the proud motto of the *Squadrista*, "Me ne frego,"[10] written on the bandage of the wound, is an act of philosophy not only stoic, the summary of a doctrine not only political—it is the education to combat, the acceptance of the risks which combat implies, and a new way of life for Italy. Thus the Fascist accepts life and loves it, knowing nothing of and despising suicide: he rather conceives of life as duty and struggle and conquest, life which should be high and full, lived for oneself, but above all for others—those who are at hand and those who are far distant, contemporaries, and those who will come after.

This "demographic" policy of the régime is the result of the above premise. Thus the Fascist loves in actual fact his neighbor, but this "neighbor" is not merely a vague and undefined concept, this love for one's neighbor puts no obstacle in the way of necessary educational severity, and still less to differentiation of status and to physical distance. Fascism repudiates any universal embrace, and in order to live worthily in the community of civilized peoples watches its contemporaries with vigilant eyes, takes good note of their state of mind and, in the changing trend of their interests,

10. "I don't give a damn!"—*Ed*.

does not allow itself to be deceived by temporary and fallacious appearances.

Such a conception of life makes Fascism the complete opposite of that doctrine, the base of so-called scientific and Marxian Socialism, the materialist conception of history; according to which the history of human civilization can be explained simply through the conflict of interests among the various social groups and by the change and development in the means and instruments of production. That the changes in the economic field—new discoveries of raw materials, new methods of working them, and the inventions of science—have their importance no one can deny; but that these factors are sufficient to explain the history of humanity excluding all others is an absurd delusion. Fascism, now and always, believes in holiness and in heroism; that is to say, in actions influenced by no economic motive, direct or indirect. And if the economic conception of history be denied, according to which theory men are no more than puppets, carried to and fro by the waves of chance, while the real directing forces are quite out of their control, it follows that the existence of an unchangeable and unchanging class-war is also denied—the natural progeny of the economic conception of history. And above all Fascism denies that class-war can be the preponderant force in the transformation of society. These two fundamental concepts of Socialism being thus refuted, nothing is left of it but the sentimental aspiration—as old as humanity itself—towards a social convention in which the sorrows and sufferings of the humblest shall be alleviated. But here again Fascism repudiates the conception of "economic" happiness, to be realized by Socialism and, as it were, at a given moment in economic evolution to assure to everyone the maximum of well-being. Fascism denies the materialist conception of happiness as a possibility, and abandons it to its inventors, the economists of the first half of the nineteenth century: that is to say, Fascism denies the validity of the equation, well-being = happiness, which would reduce men to the level of animals, caring for one thing only—to be fat and well-fed—and would thus degrade humanity to a purely physical existence.

After Socialism, Fascism combats the whole complex system of democratic ideology, and repudiates it, whether in its theoretical premises or in its practical application. Fascism denies that the majority, by the simple fact that it is a majority, can direct human society; it denies that numbers alone can govern by means of a periodical consultation, and it affirms the immutable, beneficial, and fruitful inequality of mankind, which can never be permanently leveled through the mere operation of a mechanical process such as universal suffrage. The democratic régime may be defined as from time to time giving the people the illusion of sovereignty, while the real effective sovereighty lies in the hands of other concealed and irresponsible forces. Democracy is a régime nominally without a king, but it is ruled by many kings—more absolute, tyrannical, and ruinous than one sole king, even though a tyrant. This explains why Fascism, having first in 1922 (for reasons of expediency) assumed an attitude tending towards republicanism, renounced this point of view before the March to Rome; being convinced that the question of political form is not today of prime importance, and after having studied the examples of monarchies and republics past and present reached the conclusion that monarchy or republicanism are not to be judged, as it were, by an absolute standard; but that they represent forms in which the evolution—political, historical, traditional, or psychological—of a particular country has expressed itself. . . .

Fascism has taken up an attitude of complete opposition to the doctrines of Liberalism, both in the political field and the field of economics. There should be no undue exaggeration (simply with the object of immediate success in controversy) of the importance of Liberalism in the last century, nor should what was but one among many theories which appeared in that period be put forward as a religion for humanity for all time, present and to come. Liberalism only flourished for half a century. It was born in 1830 in reaction against the Holy Alliance, which had been formed with the object of diverting the destinies of Europe back to the period before 1789, and the highest point of its success was the year 1848, when even Pius IX was a Liberal. Immediately after that date it began to decay, for if the year 1848 was a year of light and hope, the following year, 1849, was a year of darkness and tragedy. The Republic of Rome was dealt a mortal blow by a sister republic—that of France—and in the same year Marx launched the gospel of the Socialist religion, the famous *Communist Manifesto*. In 1851 Napoleon III carried out his far from liberal *coup d'état* and reigned in France until 1870, when he was deposed by a popular movement as the consequence of a military defeat which must be counted as one of the most decisive in history. The victor was Bismarck, who knew nothing of the religion of liberty, or the prophets by which that faith was revealed. And it is symptomatic that such a highly civilized people as the Germans were completely ignorant of the religion of liberty during the whole of the nineteenth century. It was nothing but a parenthesis, represented by that body which has been called "The ridiculous Parliament of Frankfort," which lasted only for a short period. Germany attained her national unity quite outside the doctrine of Liberalism—a doctrine which seems entirely foreign to the German mind, a mind essentially monarchic—while Liberalism is the logical and, indeed, historical forerunner of anarchy. The stages in the achievement of German unity are the three wars of '64, '66, and '70, which were guided by such "Liberals" as Von Moltke and Bismarck. As for Italian unity, its debt to Liberalism is completely inferior in contrast to that which it owes to the work of Mazzini and Garibaldi, who were not Liberals. Had it not been for the intervention of the anti-Liberal Bismarck at Sadowa and Sedan it is very probable that we should never have gained the province of Venice in '66, or been able to enter Rome in '70. From 1870 to 1914 a period began during which even the very high priests of the religion themselves had to recognize the gathering twilight of their faith—defeated as it was by the decadence of literature and atavism in practice—that is to say, Nationalism, Futurism, Fascism. The era of Liberalism, after having accumulated an infinity of Gordian knots, tried to untie them in the slaughter of the World War—and never has any religion demanded of its votaries such a monstrous sacrifice. Perhaps the Liberal Gods were athirst for Blood? But now, today, the Liberal faith must shut the doors of its deserted temples, deserted because the peoples of the world realize that its worship—agnostic in the field of economics and indifferent in the field of politics and morals—will lead, as it has already led, to certain ruin. In addition to this, let it be pointed out that all the political hopes of the present day are anti-Liberal, and it is therefore supremely ridiculous to try to classify this sole creed as outside the judgment of history, as though history were a hunting ground reserved for the professors of Liberalism alone—as though Liberalism were the final unalterable verdict of civilization.

But the Fascist negation of Socialism, Democracy, and Liberalism must not be taken to mean that Fascism desires to lead the world back to the state of affairs before 1789, the date which seems to be indicated as the opening year of the succeeding semi-Liberal century: we do not desire to turn back; Fascism has not chosen De Maistre for its high-priest. Absolute monarchy has been and can never return, any more than blind acceptance of ecclesiastical authority.

So, too, the privileges of the feudal system "have been," and the division of society into castes impenetrable from outside, and with no intercommunication among themselves: the Fascist conception of authority has nothing to do with such a polity. A party which entirely governs a nation is a fact entirely new to history, there are no possible references or parallels. Fascism uses in its construction whatever elements in the Liberal, Social, or Democratic doctrines still have a living value; it maintains what may be called the certainties which we owe to history, but it rejects all the rest—that is to say, the conception that there can be any doctrine of unquestioned efficacy for all times and all peoples. Given that the nineteenth century was the century of Socialism, of Liberalism, and of Democracy, it does not necessarily follow that the twentieth century must also be a century of Socialism, Liberalism, and Democracy: political doctrines pass, but humanity remains; and it may rather be expected that this will be a century of authority, a century of the Right, a century of Fascism. For if the nineteenth century was a century of individualism (Liberalism always signifying individualism) it may be expected that this will be the century of collectivism, and hence the century of the State. It is a perfectly logical deduction that a new doctrine can utilize all the still vital elements of previous doctrines.

No doctrine has ever been born completely new, completely defined and owing nothing to the past; no doctrine can boast a character of complete originality; it must always derive, if only historically, from the doctrines which have preceded it and develop into further doctrines which will follow. Thus the scientific Socialism of Marx is the heir of the Utopian Socialism of Fourier, of the Owens and of Saint-Simon; thus again the Liberalism of the eighteenth century is linked with all the advanced thought of the seventeenth century, and thus the doctrines of Democracy are the heirs of the Encyclopedists. Every doctrine tends to direct human activity towards a determined objective; but the action of men also reacts upon the doctrine, transforms it, adapts it to new needs, or supersedes it with something else. A doctrine then must be no mere exercise in words, but a living act; and thus the value of Fascism lies in the fact that it is veined with pragmatism, but at the same time has a will to exist and a will to power, a firm front in face of the reality of "violence."

The foundation of Fascism is the conception of the State, its character, its duty, and its aim. Fascism conceives of the State as an absolute, in comparison with which all individuals or groups are relative, only to be conceived of in their relation to the State. The conception of the Liberal State is not that of a directing force, guiding the play and development, both material and spiritual, of a collective body, but merely a force limited to the function of recording results: on the other hand, the Fascist State is itself conscious, and has itself a will and a personality—thus it may be called the "ethic" State. In 1929, at the first five-yearly assembly of the Fascist régime, I said:

"For us Fascists, the State is not merely a guardian, preoccupied solely with the duty of assuring the personal safety of the citizens; nor is it an organization with purely material aims, such as to guarantee a certain level of well-being and peaceful conditions of life; for a mere council of administration would be sufficient to realize such objects. Nor is it a purely political creation, divorced from all contact with the complex material reality which makes up the life of the individual and the life of the people as a whole. The State, as conceived of and as created by Fascism, is a spiritual and moral fact in itself, since its political, juridical, and economic organization of the nation is a concrete thing: and such an organization must be in its origins and development a manifestation of the spirit. The State is the guarantor of security both internal and external, but it is also the custodian and transmitter of the spirit of the people, as it has grown up through the centuries in language, in customs, and in faith. And the State is not only a living reality of the present, it is also linked with the past and above all with the future, and thus transcending the brief limits of individual life, it represents the immanent spirit of the nation. The forms in which States express themselves may change, but the necessity for such forms is eternal. It is the State which educates its citizens in civic virtue, gives them a consciousness of their mission and welds them into unity; harmonizing their various interests through justice, and transmitting to future generations the mental conquests of science, of art, of law and the solidarity of humanity. It leads men from primitive tribal life to the highest expression of human power which is Empire; it links up through the centuries the names of those of its members who have died for its existence and in obedience to its laws, it holds up the memory of the leaders who have increased its territory and the geniuses who have illuminated it with glory as an example to be followed by future generations. When the conception of the State declines, and disunifying and centrifugal tendencies prevail, whether of individuals or of particular groups, the nations where such phenomena appear are in their decline."

From 1929 until today, evolution, both political and economic, has everywhere gone to prove the validity of these doctrinal premises. Of such gigantic importance is the State. It is the force which alone can provide a solution to the dramatic contradictions of capitalism. . . . Fascism desires the State to be a strong and organic body, at the same time reposing upon broad and popular support. The Fascist State has drawn into itself even the economic activities of the nation, and, through the corporative social and educational institutions created by it, its influence reaches every aspect of the national life and includes, framed in their respective organizations, all the political, economic and spiritual forces of the nation. A State which reposes upon the support of millions of individuals who recognize its authority, are continually conscious of its power and are ready at once to serve it, is not the old tyrannical State of the medieval lord nor has it anything in common with the absolute governments either before or after 1789. The individual in the Fascist State is not annulled but rather multiplied, just in the same way that a soldier in a regiment is not diminished but rather increased by the number of his comrades. The Fascist State organizes the nation, but leaves a sufficient margin of liberty to the individual; the latter is deprived of all useless and possibly harmful freedom, but retains what is essential; the deciding power in this question cannot be the individual, but the State alone.

The Fascist State is not indifferent to the fact of religion in general, or to that particular and positive faith which is Italian Catholicism. The State professes no theology, but a morality, and in the Fascist State religion is considered as one of the deepest manifestations of the spirit of man; thus it is not only respected but defended and protected. The Fascist State has never tried to create its own God, as at one moment Robespierre and the wildest extremists of the Convention tried to do; nor does it vainly seek to obliterate religion from the hearts of men as does Bolshevism; Fascism respects the God of the ascetics, the saints and heroes, and equally, God, as He is perceived and worshipped by simple people.

The Fascist State is an embodied will to power and government; the Roman tradition is here an ideal of force in action. According to Fascism, government is not so much a thing to be expressed in territorial or military terms as in terms of morality and the spirit. It must be thought of as an empire—that is to say, a nation which directly or indirectly rules other nations, without the need for conquering a single square yard of territory. For Fascism, the growth of empire, that is to say the expansion of the nation, is an essential manifestation of vitality, and its opposite a sign of decadence. Peoples which are rising, or rising again after a period of decadence, are always imperialist: any renunciation is a sign of decay and of death.

Fascism is the doctrine best adapted to represent the tendencies and the aspirations of a people, like the people of Italy, who are rising again after many centuries of abasement and foreign servitude. But empire demands discipline, the co-ordination of all forces and a deeply felt sense of duty and sacrifice: this fact explains many aspects of the practical working of the régime, the character of many forces in the State, and the necessarily severe measures which must be taken against those who would oppose this spontaneous and inevitable movement of Italy in the twentieth century, and would oppose it by recalling the outworn ideology of the nineteenth century—repudiated wheresoever there has been the courage to undertake great experiments of social and political transformation: for never before has the nation stood more in need of authority, of direction, and of order. If every age has its own characteristic doctrine, there are a thousand signs which point to Fascism as the characteristic doctrine of our time. For if a doctrine must be a living thing, this is proved by the fact that Fascism has created a living faith; and that this faith is very powerful in the minds of men, is demonstrated by those who have suffered and died for it.

Fascism has henceforth in the world the universality of all those doctrines which, in realizing themselves, have represented a stage in the history of the human spirit.

3. *The Corporative State*

MUSSOLINI'S ESSAY of 1932 on the doctrine of Fascism had almost nothing to say about either the corporative state or economic autarky. Yet in the period since the war he had become intrigued with the possibility of harmonizing the interests of capital and labor with the overarching interests of the state, and instituting a system of representation that would rest on functional groupings organized in various kinds of national syndicates instead of the old parliamentary system based on geographical and numerical constituencies.

Such an idea was not new with Mussolini; it derived from two currents of thought. On the one hand, there was the Catholic tradition of corporativism, set forth in modern format by Leo XIII in his encyclical of 1891, *Rerum novarum*, as an answer to the Marxist challenge. The Catholic corporativists looked back with nostalgia toward a revival of medieval guilds or corporations, and argued in favor of class collaboration. They were willing to support the idea of joint consultation between employers and workers, profit-sharing schemes, and even part ownership. Thus the idea of a corporative state was in the air and enjoyed some measure of respectability.

The second current that contributed to Mussolini's eventual espousal of the corporative state was syndicalism, most cogently propagandized by Georges Sorel at the turn of the century. Originally the Sorelian syndicalists were not corporativists, but eventually some wound up in that camp. In the beginning the syndicalists espoused class warfare, stressed the importance of the myths of violence, sabotage, and the general strike, and called for government based on labor syndicates alone. In theory they rejected political parties and parliamentary institutions as well as the Marxist "dictatorship of the proletariat." Yet in practice they organized politically. In Italy they infiltrated the Socialist party until they were expelled in 1908. Thereafter they gravitated into curious new stances. Some became Communists; others became archnationalists. During the war some of these "national syndicalists" became friendly with Mussolini. One of them, Edmondo Rossoni, had spent some time in the United States. He conceived of a new kind of syndical organization that would include not just labor unions but parallel syndicates of the "producers" (*i.e.*, capitalists). Capitalism and private property would thus be preserved, though a laissez-faire economy and class struggle would be repudiated. National syndicalists came to advocate governmental co-ordination of both capital and labor. Labor must give up the right to strike; employers must renounce the lockout; the state must crack the whip over both capital and labor and adjudicate disputes by means of new labor courts. But in actual practice capital would be treated much more leniently than labor. This new

kind of national syndicalist corporative program was experimented
with by D'Annunzio and Alceste DeAmbris in Fiume in 1919–20.

A great deal of verbiage was to pour forth in Fascist Italy regarding
the corporative state, as efforts were made to amalgamate contradictory traditions. Many of the corporative institutions that were
eventually launched were rationalizations of accomplished facts; many
of them had few real powers and served chiefly as a façade to mask the
harsh features of continuing class rule in Italy. Certainly they became a
bureaucratic hodgepodge that enabled Rome to surpass Milan in
population for the first time since 1875. Most critics are convinced that
the corporative system rested upon one very important pragmatic
consideration: it was a process designed to win the employers over to
Fascism. Though the corporative state did not save Italy from the
ravages of the Depression, it aroused much interest on the part of
foreigners in those years in what seemed to be an imaginative new
pattern of economic and political organization.

There were several stages in the development of the Italian corporative state. The first occurred on December 21, 1923, when Mussolini
called to his office in Rome's Chigi Palace representatives of the
employers' organization (Confindustria) and representatives of the
new General Confederation of Fascist Corporations (the Fascist labor
syndicates) to name a permanent committee to study the relationship
of capital and labor. The text of this Palazzo Chigi Pact follows.

The Palazzo Chigi Pact
(December 21, 1923)

The General Confederation of Italian Industry [Confindustria]
and the General Confederation of Fascist Corporations,
acting for the purpose of
harmonizing their work by means of directives from the National
Government, which has repeatedly declared that it regards the
harmonious will to work by industrialists, technicians, and laborers
as offering the best means of increasing the prosperity of all classes
and the nation;

and recognizing
the complete accuracy of this political philosophy and the need for
the nation's productive forces to put it into effect;

SOURCE: Resolution approved under the chairmanship of Mussolini
at the meeting of December 21, 1923. Published in Alberto
Aquarone, *L'organizzazione dello stato totalitario* (Turin: Giulio
Einaudi Editore, 1965), Appendix No. 29, pp. 435–436. By permission of Giulio Einaudi Editore, Turin. My translation.

do hereby declare

that the nation's natural resources, which are the prerequisite for its political strength, can rapidly be increased; and that both laborers and industrialists can avoid the damages and losses caused by work interruptions if harmony between the various elements of production assures the continuity and tranquillity of industrial development;

and they do hereby affirm

the principle that syndical organization must not rest on the assumption of an insoluble conflict of interests between industry and labor, but must instead be based on the need to establish increasingly cordial relations among the various employers, workers, and their syndical organizations, and must assure to these productive elements the best possible conditions for developing their respective functions and obtaining a fairer compensation for their work —all of which will reflect the spirit of national syndicalism, even in the negotiation of labor contracts;

and they do hereby agree

(a) that the Confederation of Industry and the Confederation of Fascist Corporations should intensify their respective efforts toward organizing industrialists and workers for the purpose of mutual collaboration;

and (b) that a permanent Commission, consisting of five members for each side, be appointed to supervise the fulfillment of the above-mentioned principles both at the seat of government and in outlying regions, and to co-ordinate the major bodies of the two Confederations so that syndical activity will proceed in accordance with the directives set forth by the Head of the Government.

Two years later (October 2, 1925) came the Vidoni Palace Pact. In negotiating labor contracts henceforth, Gino Olivetti's Confindustria agreed to deal only with the Fascist labor syndicates (Confederation of Fascist Corporations) that were headed by Rossoni. The rival Socialist and Catholic labor unions would be outlawed. The Fascist regime would choose the officials of the Fascist labor syndicates rather than permit the workers to do so, whereas the Confindustria would continue to be self-managed in large measure. In this way Mussolini ingratiated himself with the big industrialists who thus far had not always been as pro-Fascist as the great landowners.

The Palazzo Vidoni Pact
(October 2, 1925)

The General Confederation of Industry recognizes in the Confederation of Fascist Corporations and its dependent organizations the exclusive right to represent the various labor forces.

The Confederation of Fascist Corporations recognizes in the Confederation of Industry and its dependent organizations the exclusive right to represent the industrialists.

All contractual relationships between industrialists and employees must be negotiated by the dependent organizations of the Confederation of Industry on the one hand and those of the Confederation of Corporations on the other.

Consequently, factory shop-steward committees (internal commissions) are hereby abolished, and their functions are handed over to the local syndicate which will exercise them only as regards the corresponding industrial organization.

Discussions will begin within ten days to lay down broad guidelines that will be embodied in regulations.

During 1925 political liberalism was largely scotched in Italy; in 1926 economic liberalism met a similar fate. On April 3 a very important decree-law prohibiting strikes and lockouts was proclaimed. It was drafted by Alfredo Rocco, the influential Nationalist party legal expert who had become Mussolini's Minister of Justice and close adviser. By this legislation the "syndical state" (though not yet the "corporative state") came into existence. The state, acting as umpire, officially recognized a pair of producers' and workers' syndicates in each of six fields (industry, agriculture, commerce, maritime and air transport, land and inland-waterway transport, and banking). In addition, there was a syndicate of intellectuals. Each syndicate would assess dues upon everyone in its category. They were placed under the control of a newly created Minister of Corporations, and Mussolini was given this portfolio to add to the many he already held. In due course some sixteen labor courts were established.

SOURCE: Alberto Aquarone, *L'organizzazione dello stato totalitario* (Turin: Giulio Einaudi Editore, 1965), Appendix No. 31, p. 439. By permission of Giulio Einaudi Editore. My translation.

The Rocco Labor and Antistrike Law
(April 3, 1926)

CHAPTER I: JURIDICAL RECOGNITION OF SYNDICATES
AND COLLECTIVE LABOR CONTRACTS

Art. 1—Syndical associations of employers and of workers, both intellectual and manual, may obtain legal recognition when they can prove that they comply with the following requirements:

1. In the case of associations of employers, that the employers who have voluntarily registered as members employ not less than one-tenth of the workers in the service of the concerns of the kind for which the association has been formed. This rule applies for each association within its district. In the case of employees' associations, that the employees who have voluntarily enrolled shall represent at least one-tenth of the total number of workers of the category for which the association is organized. This rule applies to each association within its district.

2. That the associations shall include among their aims not only the protection of the economic and moral interests of their members, but shall also aim to promote the welfare and education (especially the moral and national education) of their members.

3. That the directors of the associations shall give proof of their competence, good moral behavior, and sound national loyalty.

Art. 2—When the conditions prescribed in the previous article exist, legal recognition may be given to associations of persons independently exercising an art, trade, or profession.

Existing and legally recognized orders, institutes, and associations of artists, artisans, and professional men will continue to be regulated by existing laws and regulations. However, such laws and regulations may be revised by means of a royal decree issued after consulting the opinion of the Council of Ministers in order to harmonize them with the provisions of the present law.

The statutes of incorporated associations of artists and persons exercising the liberal professions and recognized as public institutions prior to the publication of the present law may also be revised in order to harmonize them with the provisions of this law.

SOURCE: Law No. 563 of April 3, 1926, published in *Gazzetta Ufficiale*, No. 87 (Apr. 14, 1926). My translation.

Art. 3—The membership of the associations mentioned in the preceding articles must include either employers or employees alone.

Associations of employers and of workers can be brought together by means of central liaison organs with a common higher organization. However, the representation of employers and employees shall always remain distinct; and in the case of associations representing several categories of workers, each category must be separately represented.

Art. 4—The recognition of the associations referred to in the preceding articles is conferred by a royal decree upon the proposal of the competent minister, acting jointly with the Minister of the Interior, and after consultation with the Council of State. The statute of the association is approved by the same decree, which is published, at the expense of the association, in the *Gazzetta Ufficiale* of the Kingdom.

The statute must set forth in detail the purposes of the association, the mode of procedure following in the appointment of its administrative officers, and the conditions laid down for the admission of members, one of which must be sound political conduct from the standpoint of national loyalty.

The statute may provide for the establishment of vocational schools, institutions for the economic assistance and moral and patriotic education of members, and of institutions aiming at promoting and improving national production, culture, or art.

Art. 5—Legally recognized associations possess juridical personality, and before the law they represent all the employers, employees, artists, and professional men of the category for which they are organized, regardless of whether or not there are any members enrolled within the jurisdiction of the territorial division in which they operate.

The legally recognized associations are entitled to levy annual dues on all employers, workers, employees, artists, and professional men whom they represent, whether they be registered members or not, for an amount not to exceed in the case of employers, one day's pay for each worker employed, and in the case of workers, employees, artists, and professional men, one day's pay. At least one-tenth of the sums thus collected must be set aside annually and paid into a capital fund to guarantee the liabilities incurred by the associations with reference to the collective contracts which they have negotiated. This fund is to be administered in accordance with the provisions of the regulation.

Employers are under obligation to report the number of employees to their associations not later than March 31 of each year. Those who fail to report, or who file a false or incomplete report, are punishable by a fine not to exceed 2,000 lire.

These dues are levied in accordance with the rules contained in the laws on the collection of municipal taxes. The contributions of employees are deducted from their wages or salaries and are turned over to the associations.

Only regularly registered members participate in the activities of the associations and in the election or nomination of administrative officers.

Only legally recognized associations can appoint representative of employers or workers to sit on all councils, guilds (corporations), or other bodies on which such representation is provided for by law.

Art. 6—The associations may be communal, district, provincial, regional, inter-regional, or national.

Recognition may also be granted, under the provisions of this law, to federations or unions of several associations, and to confederations of several federations. The recognition of these federations or confederations carries with it the right to recognize each association or affiliated federation. The federations or confederations exercise disciplinary powers over their member associations, as well as over the individual members of same, these rights being exercised in accordance with the rules laid down in their respective statutes.

Legal recognition can be granted to only one association for each class of employers, workers, artists, or professional men. Similarly, legal recognition can be given to only one federation or confederation of employers or workers or artists or professional men, referred to in the preceding paragraph, for the class or classes of employers or workers represented within the district assigned to each.

If recognition be granted to a national confederation of all classes of employers or workers in agriculture, industry, or trade, or for all categories of artists or professional men, recognition cannot be granted to federations or associations which are not affiliated with the said confederation.

In no case can associations be recognized which, without the prior authorization of the Government, have entered into disciplinary relations or have become affiliated with an international association.

Art. 7—Each association is required to have a president or secretary who directs and represents it, and is responsible for its activities. The president or secretary is elected or appointed in accordance with the provisions laid down in the statutes.

The appointment or the election of presidents or secretaries of national, inter-regional, and regional associations is not valid unless it is approved by royal decree on the proposal of the competent minister, in agreement with the Minister of the Interior. This approval may, at any time, be revoked.

The statutes must determine the organ empowered to exercise disciplinary powers over members and to expel them for unworthy moral or political conduct.

Art. 8—The presidents or secretaries are assisted by boards of directors elected by the members of the association in accordance with the provisions laid down in the statutes.

Communal, district, and provincial associations are subject to the supervision of the prefect and are under the trusteeship of the Administrative Provincial Council (*Giunta*). They exercise their respective powers in the manner and in accordance with the measures to be determined in the regulations. Regional, inter-regional, and national associations are subject to the supervision and control of the competent minister.

The competent minister, in agreement with the Minister of the Interior, may dissolve the boards of directors of associations and concentrate all authority in the hands of the president or secretary for a period not to exceed one year. He may also, in more serious cases, appoint a commissioner to look after the administration during the emergency.

In the case of associations affiliated with a federation or confederation, the decree recognizing the federation or confederation and approving its statute may prescribe that the powers of supervision and control be exercised in all or in part by the federation or confederation.

Art. 9—Similarly, in very serious cases, and in every case in which the conditions prescribed in the preceding articles for securing the recognition are not fulfilled, a royal decree to be issued on the proposal of the competent minister, in agreement with the

Minister of the Interior, after hearing the opinion of the Council of State, may revoke the recognition.

Art. 10—Collective labor contracts drawn up by the legally recognized associations of employers, workers, artists, and professional men are valid in respect to all employers, workers, artists, and professional men belonging to the category to which said contract refers and which the associations represent in accordance with the provisions of Art. 5 of this law.

Collective labor contracts must be made in writing under penalty of voidance. They are also held null and void if they fail to state the period for which they are valid.

The central liaison organs provided for under Art. 3 of this law can draw up, by agreement with the representatives of employers and workers, general rules applicable to conditions of labor in the concerns to which they refer. Such rules are valid for all the employers and all the workers belonging to the category to which said rules refer, and who are represented by the joint associations in accordance with the provisions of Art. 5 of this law.

A copy of the collective contracts drawn up in accordance with the provisions of the preceding paragraph must be deposited with the local prefecture and published in the official posters of the province, in the case of communal, district, or provincial associations; and filed at the Ministry of National Economy and published in the *Gazzetta Ufficiale* of the Kingdom, in the case of regional, inter-regional, or national associations.

Employers and employees who fail to abide by collective contracts and general rules to which they are parties are held civilly responsible for such failure both toward the associations of workers and toward the association of employers who negotiated the said contract.

Other regulations relative to the negotiation and application of collective labor contracts shall be issued by royal decree, on the proposal of the Minister of Justice.

Art. 11—The regulations of the present law on the juridical recognition of syndical associations are not applicable to associations composed of state, provincial, or municipal employees and employees of other public welfare institutions, for which provisions will be made by separate measures.

However, similar associations of officers, noncommissioned officers, and soldiers of the Royal Army, Royal Navy, Royal Air Force, and of the other armed bodies of the state, provinces, and communes, as well as associations of magistrates of the judiciary and administrative order, associations of professors of secondary and higher institutions, associations of officers and employees of the ministries of the Interior, Foreign Affairs, and Colonies are prohibited, under penalty of removal from rank and dismissal, and of other disciplinary punishments to be established by special regulations according to each individual case.

Art. 12—Associations of employers, employees, artists, and professional men which are not legally recognized continue to exist as *de facto* associations, regulated by existing laws, with the exception of those referred to in the second paragraph of the preceding article.

In these cases the regulations of the Royal Decree-Law of January 24, 1924, No. 64, are applicable.

CHAPTER II—THE LABOR COURTS

Art. 13—All disputes arising as to the regulation of collective contracts, or of other existing regulations, or the request for new conditions of labor, come within the jurisdiction of the Courts of Appeal acting as Labor Courts. The president of the court shall attempt to bring about conciliation before pronouncing his own decision.

Disputes referred to in the above provisions can be settled by arbitration, in accordance with the provisions of Art. 8 *et seq.* of the Code of Civil Procedure.

No modification is made in the jurisdiction of the boards of arbiters and of the provincial arbitration commissions for employers of private business concerns, as determined by the law of June 15, 1893, No. 295, and by the Royal Decree-Law of December 2, 1923, No. 2686, respectively.

Appeals against the decisions of such boards and commissions and of other jurisdictional bodies on individual labor contracts, insofar as they are subject to appeal under existing legislation, may be made to the Courts of Appeal functioning as Labor Courts.

Art. 14—To enable the Courts of Appeal to act as Labor Courts, a special section is established for each of the sixteen Courts of Appeal. Each section is composed of three magistrates, viz., a sectional president and two counselors of the Court of Appeal. Two citizens expert in problems of production and labor and selected by the first president in accordance with the regulations of the following article may be added to this body from time to time.

On the proposal of the Minister for Justice acting jointly with the Minister for Finance, a royal decree will enforce such modifications in the number of magistrates and in the staff of the chancelleries of the courts as are necessary to carry out the above provisions.

Art. 15—Each Court of Appeal will draw up a panel of experts on problems of production and labor, classified by groups and subgroups, according to the several kinds of business activities carried on within the jurisdiction of the court. This panel will be revised every two years.

On the proposal of the Minister for Justice acting jointly with the Minister for National Economy, a royal decree shall establish the regulations for the preparation and revision of these panels and shall fix the daily compensation and other indemnities for persons who are called upon to exercise judiciary functions.

Each year the first president designates for each group and subgroup the members of the panel who will be called on to act as expert advisers in cases concerning the enterprises included in the group or subgroup. Persons directly or indirectly concerned in the disputes can never act as members of the judicial board.

Art. 16—The Court of Appeal, acting as a Labor Court for the enforcement of existing contracts, shall deliver judgment according to the regulations of the law on the interpretation and enforcement of contracts, and in cases involving new conditions to be fixed for labor it shall judge in accordance with equity, harmonizing the interests of the employers with those of employees, and in every case protecting the higher interests of production.

The formulation of new conditions to be fixed for labor shall always specify the period of time during which they must be in force, which regularly shall be the same as that fixed in the case of agreements freely entered into.

The decisions of the court functioning as a Labor Court are issued after hearing the verbal opinion of the public prosecutor.

The decisions of the Court of Appeal acting as a Labor Court can be appealed against in the Court of Cassation on the grounds set forth in Art. 517 of the Code of Civil Procedure.

Rules of procedure to be promulgated by royal decree on the proposal of the Minister of Justice will determine the special procedure to be followed in taking cognizance of a case and in enforcing the decisions of the court, in derogation, if need be, of the ordinary procedure under the Code of Civil Procedure.

Art. 17—Only associations which are legally recognized may take action in disputes arising out of collective labor agreements, and such action must be taken against legally recognized associations, where they exist; otherwise such action shall be argued by a special administrator, appointed by the president of the Court of Appeal. In the latter case, the voluntary interpleading of the interested parties in the proceedings shall be permitted.

When associations of employers or employees are affiliated with federations or confederations, or when associations of employers and associations of workers have formed central liaison organs, action at law cannot be taken against them unless it can be shown that the federation or the confederation or the central liaison organ has attempted to bring about a friendly settlement of the dispute, and that the attempt has failed.

Only legally recognized associations can sue in the court in the name of all the employers or of all the employees of the category for which they are formed, within the territorial jurisdiction assigned to them.

Judgments given in their regard are valid for all concerned and are published, in the case of communal, district, and provincial associations, in the official legal posters of the province, and in the case of regional, inter-regional, or national associations in the *Gazzetta Ufficiale* of the Kingdom.

All the memoranda and documents relating to the proceedings of the Court of Appeal functioning as a Labor Court, and all the measures issued by it, are exempt from registration fees and stamp taxes.

Chapter III—Prohibition of Strikes and Lockouts

Art. 18—The lockout and the strike are prohibited.

Employers who suspend work in their factories, enterprises, and offices without justifiable reasons and for the sole object of compelling their employees to modify existing labor contracts are punishable by a fine of from 10,000 to 100,000 lire.

Employees and laborers who, in groups of three or more, cease work by agreement, or who work in such a manner as to disturb its continuity or regularity, in order to compel the employers to change the existing contracts, are punishable by a fine of from 100 to 1,000 lire. In the proceedings the regulations of Articles 298 *et seq.* of the Code of Penal Procedure are applicable.

When the persons guilty of the offenses covered in the above paragraphs are more numerous, the leaders, promoters, and organizers are liable to imprisonment for not less than one year, nor more than two years, in addition to the fines prescribed in the same paragraphs.

Art. 19—Persons in the employ of the State and of other public bodies or bodies performing essential public services who, in the number of three or more, by preconcerted agreement, leave their work or perform it in a manner likely to interfere with its continuity or regularity, render themselves liable to imprisonment for a period of not less than one month and not to exceed six months. The provisions of Art. 298 *et seq.* of the Code of Civil Procedure are applicable in the proceedings. The leaders, promoters, and organizers are liable to imprisonment for a period of from six months to two years and shall be barred from public offices for not less than three years.

The administrators of public services or of public utility enterprises who, without justifiable motives, suspend work in their establishments, enterprises, or offices, are punishable by imprisonment of from six months to a year and by a fine of from 5,000 to 10,000 lire, in addition to being barred temporarily from public offices.

When the action referred to in this article causes danger to personal safety the penalty incurred is that of imprisonment for a period of not less than one year. Should such action be the cause of death to one or more persons, the penalty incurred is that of imprisonment for a period of not less than three years.

Art. 20—Persons in the employ of the state and of other public bodies, persons carrying on public services and services essential to the public, and their dependents, who in the event of strikes or lockouts fail to do all in their power to secure the regular working or the resumption of a public service essential to the public, are liable to detention for a period of not less than one month and not more than six months.

Art. 21—When the stoppage of work by employers or the act of leaving work or performing it irregularly by worker aims at coercing the will or influencing the decisions of a department or organ of the State, provinces, or communes, or of a government official, the leaders, promoters, and organizers render themselves liable to imprisonment for a period of from three to seven years and to permanent debarment from public office, and the other persons concerned in such offense are liable to imprisonment for a period of from one to three years and to temporary debarment from public office.

Art. 22—Employers and employees who refuse to carry out the decisions of a Labor Court are punishable by imprisonment of from one month to one year and by a fine of from 100 to 500 lire. This does not affect the application of the regulations of common law on civil responsibility for carrying out and executing the sentences.

The directors of legally recognized associations who refuse to carry out the decisions of the Labor Court are punishable by imprisonment of from six months to two years and by a fine of from 2,000 to 10,000 lire, in addition to dismissal from office.

Should failure to carry out the decisions of the Labor Court be aggravated by strikes or lockouts on the part of the parties convicted, the provisions of the Penal Code on the relation between guilt and punishment are applicable.

Art. 23—All regulations contrary to the present law are repealed.

His Majesty's Government is authorized to promulgate by royal decree whatever measures are necessary for putting this law into effect, and for co-ordinating it with the provisions of the Royal Decree of October 19, 1923, No. 2311, of the Law of June 15, 1893, No. 2686, to be revised as needed, and with all other national laws.

As a kind of window dressing for the new system, Mussolini proclaimed a Labor Charter on April 21, 1927 (Fascist Labor Day). This vapid document contained thirty aphorisms, promising the workers such things as social insurance, vacations with pay, and extra compensation for night work. At least some of the workers appeared satisfied with these promises that were partly designed to take their minds off the loss of their right to strike. This Fascist Labor Charter was to be widely imitated in Salazar's Portugal, Franco's Spain, and elsewhere.

The Labor Charter
(April 21, 1927)

THE CORPORATE STATE AND ITS ORGANIZATION

Art. 1—The Italian nation is an organism possessing a purpose, a life, and instruments of action superior in power and duration to those possessed by the individuals or groups of individuals who

SOURCE: Promulgated by the Fascist Grand Council and published in *Gazzetta Ufficiale*, No. 100 (Apr. 30, 1927). My translation.

compose it. The nation is a moral, political, and economic unity integrally embodied in the Fascist State.

Art. 2—Labor in all its forms—intellectual, technical, manual, organizing, and executive—is a social duty. By virtue of this fact, and this fact alone, labor falls within the purview of the State. When considered from a national point of view, production in its manifold forms constitutes a unity, its many objectives coinciding and being generally definable as the well-being of those who produce, and the development of national power.

Art. 3—There is complete freedom of professional or syndical organization, but only the syndicate legally recognized by the State and subject to State control is empowered:

To legally represent the particular division of employers or employees for which it has been formed;

To protect the interests of these as against the State or as against other trade organizations;

To negotiate collective labor contracts binding upon all those engaged in the branch in question;

To levy assessments and to exercise, in connection with the branch, specified functions of public support.

Art. 4—Solidarity between the various factors of production is concretely expressed by the collective labor contract, which conciliates the opposing interests of employers and workers, subordinating them to the higher interests of production at large.

Art. 5—The Labor Court is the organ through which the State acts in settling labor controversies, whether these arise in connection with observances of rules or agreements already made or in connection with new conditions to be fixed for labor.

Art. 6—Legally recognized professional associations guarantee equality before the law to employers and employees alike. They maintain discipline in labor and production and promote measures of efficiency in both. The corporations constitute the unifying organization of all the elements of production (capital and labor) and represent the common interests of them all. By virtue of this joint representation, and since the interests of production are interests of the nation, the corporations are recognized by law as organs of the State.

As they represent the joint interests of production, the corporations may enforce binding regulations for the discipline of labor relations as well as for the co-ordination of production, whenever they are empowered to do so by the affiliated associations.

Art. 7—The Corporate State regards private initiative in the field of production as the most useful and efficient instrument for furthering the interests of the nation. Since private enterprise is a function of national concern, its management is responsible to the State for general policies of production. From the fact that the elements of production (labor and capital) are co-operators in a common enterprise, reciprocal rights and duties devolve upon them. The employee, whether laborer, clerk, or skilled workman, is an active partner in the economic enterprise, the management of which belongs to the employer who shoulders the responsibility for it.

Art. 8—Professional associations of employers are required to promote by all possible means the increase and improvement of production and a reduction of costs. The organizations representing practitioners of the liberal professions or of the arts, and the associations of State employees, should work together for furthering the interests of science, letters, and the arts, for improving the quality of production, and for realizing the moral ideals of the corporate organization of the State.

Art. 9—State intervention in economic production arises only when private initiative is lacking or insufficient, or when the political interests of the State are involved. Such intervention may take the form of supervision, of promotion, or of direct management.

Art. 10—In labor disputes involving groups, there can be no recourse to the Labor Court until the corporation has exhausted its efforts for conciliation. In disputes involving individuals in connection with applications or interpretations of collective contracts, professional associations may employ their good offices to attempt conciliation. Jurisdiction in such disputes belongs to the ordinary Labor Courts supplemented by the referees appointed by the professional associations concerned.

Collective Labor Contracts

Art. 11—Professional associations are required to regulate by means of collective contracts labor relations between the employers and the employees whom they represent. The collective contract is made between associations of primary grade, under the guidance and with the approval of the central organizations, with the provision that the association of higher grade may make amendments in cases specified in the constitutions of the associations or by law. All collective labor contracts must, under pain of nullity, contain precise rules on such matters as disciplinary relations, trial periods, amounts and manner of payment of wages, and schedules of working hours.

Art. 12—The operation of the syndicates, the mediation of the corporations, and the decisions of the Labor Court guarantee correspondence between wages and the normal.demands of living, the possibilities of production and the yield from labor. The fixing of wages is determined without reference to any general rule and is entrusted to agreements between parties in the collective contracts.

Art. 13—Losses occasioned by business crises and by variations of exchange must be equitably divided between the elements of production (capital and labor). Statistics relating to conditions of production and labor, to variations of exchange, to changes in standards of living, as issued by the various governmental departments, by the Central Bureau of Statistics, and by the legally recognized professional associations, and as co-ordinated and elaborated by the Ministry of Corporations, will constitute the criteria for adjusting the interests of the various branches of trade, and of harmonizing the interests of the various classes among themselves and with the higher interests of production in general.

Art. 14—Remuneration should be paid out in the form which best fills the needs of employers and workers. When remuneration is by piece rate and payments are, made at intervals of more than a fortnight, adequate weekly or fortnightly sums on account are due. Night work, with the exception of ordinary regular night shifts, shall be paid with a percentage over and above the wage settled for day work. In cases in which work is paid at piece rate, the rate must be such that a diligent workman, of a normal working capacity, will be able to earn a minimum amount over and above the basic wage.

Art. 15—The employee has the right to a weekly day of rest, falling on Sundays. Collective labor contracts will apply this principle so far as it is compatible with existing laws, and with the technical requirements of the enterprise concerned; and within the limits of these requirements, they will see that civil and religious holidays are observed according to local traditions. Working hours must be scrupulously and earnestly observed by employees.

Art. 16—After a year of uninterrupted service, the employee in enterprises that function the year around is entitled to an annual vacation with pay.

Art. 17—In concerns functioning throughout the year, the employee is entitled, in case of discharge through no fault of his own, to a compensation proportional to his years of service. Similar compensation is also due to his family or representatives in the event of the death of a worker.

Art. 18—Transfers of ownership of concerns offering continuous employment shall not put an end to the labor contract, and the employees of such concerns retain all their rights and claims against the new proprietors. Similarly, illness on the part of the employee, provided it does not exceed a specified period, shall not put an end to the labor contract. Call to service in the Army or Navy or Volunteer Militia for National Security does not constitute valid cause for dismissal.

Art. 19—Breaches of discipline on the part of employees and acts disturbing to the normal operation of a concern are punishable, according to the seriousness of the offense, by fine, by suspension, or in grave cases, by immediate discharge without compensation. The cases in which the employer may impose the respective penalties of fine, suspension, or discharge without compensation must be specified.

Art. 20—A newly hired worker is subject to a trial period, in the course of which both parties have a right to cancel the contract, the employee in such case being entitled to wages only for the time of actual service.

Art. 21—The benefits and discipline attaching to the collective labor contract extend also to home workers. Special rules shall be issued by the State to assure proper hygienic conditions for home labor.

EMPLOYMENT BUREAUS

Art. 22—The State has exclusive power to determine and control the factors of government employment and unemployment, since these are indices of the general conditions of production and labor.

Art. 23—Employment bureaus are to be managed by the corporations through commissions having equal representation of employers and employees. It is compulsory for employers to hire workers through these bureaus, freedom of choice being allowed them among the various registrants, with preference being given, however, to those who are members of the Fascist party and of the Fascist syndicates, according to their seniority of registration.

Art. 24—The professional associations of workers are required to exercise a process of selection among the workers with a view to improving their technical capacity and moral standards.

Art. 25—Corporative organs shall ensure the observance of the laws governing safety, accident prevention, and sanitation by the individuals belonging to the affiliated associations.

WELFARE, EDUCATION, AND INSTRUCTION

Art. 26—Insurance is another manifestation of the principle of collaboration. Employers and employees must bear proportionate shares of such burdens. The State, working through the corporations and the professional associations, will strive to co-ordinate and unify as far as is possible the agencies and the system of insurance.

Art. 27—The Fascist State is working for:

1. improvements in accident insurance;

2. improvements and extensions of maternity insurance;

3. insurance against occupational diseases and tuberculosis as a step toward insurance against all forms of disease;

4. improvements of insurance against involuntary unemployment;

5. adoption of special forms of endowment insurance for young workers.

Art. 28—The associations of workers are required to safeguard the interests of those they represent in administrative and judicial suits arising out of accident and social insurance. The collective labor contracts shall establish, whenever this is technically feasible, Mutual Sickness Funds, with contributions from employers and employees, to be administered by representatives of both classes under the general supervision of the corporations.

Art. 29—It is the right and duty of professional associations to give assistance to those they represent, whether members or nonmembers. These associations should exercise the functions of assistance directly through their own organs, and may not delegate them to other bodies or institutes except for purposes of a general nature which transcend the particular interests of the branch of production concerned.

Art. 30—Training and education, especially technical training of the workers they represent, whether these be members or nonmembers, is one of the principal duties of the professional associations. These associations must work side by side with the Dopola-voro[1] institution and other educational institutions.

By the early 1930's corporativism was the one political topic that could be discussed with some measure of freedom in Italy by university groups and young people. Many such youths who resented the idea of Mussolini's personal dictatorship felt that the evolution of the corporative system might lead to relaxation of the totalitarian regime. Some of the "left-wing" corporativists even insisted on the need for proclaiming a "war on capitalism." In the midst of such discussion, the embryonic corporative system underwent further change by the Law of February 5, 1934, which set up 22 corporations (or cycles of economic activity—e.g., wines and textiles). Mussolini explained their aim as twofold: "At home, to establish an organization which will gradually and inflexibly reduce the distance between the greatest and the least or nonexistent possibilities in life. This is what I call a higher 'social justice.' . . . In relation to the outer world, the object of the corporation is to increase constantly the global power of the nation to further the ends of its expansion in the world."[2] In the estimation of Marxist critics, Mussolini's corporative state was simply a smoke screen for his aggressive foreign policy.

Law on Formation
and Functions of the Corporations
(February 5, 1934)

Art. 1—Corporations, as provided for in Article VI of the Labor Charter, in the Law of April 3, 1926, No. 563, and in the Royal Decree of July 1, 1926, No. 1130, are instituted by decree of the Head of the Government, upon proposal of the Minister for Corporations and after consulting the Central Corporative Committee.

Art. 2—Corporations are presided over by a Minister or by an Undersecretary of State, or by the secretary of the Fascist party, to be appointed by decree of the Head of the Government, who is the president of the National Council of Corporations.

Art. 3—The decree instituting a corporation determines the number of members to be included in the board, and how many of

SOURCE: Law of February 5, 1934, No. 163, published in *Gazzetta Ufficiale*, No. 32 (Feb. 20, 1934). My translation.

1. See pp. 133–134.
2. Speech of November 10, 1933, *Opera Omnia di Benito Mussolini*, XXVI, 379.

them should be designated by each of the associations affiliated with the corporation.

The members designated shall be approved by decree of the Head of the Government, upon proposal of the Minister for Corporations.

Art. 4—In those corporations in which categories of different branches of economic activity are represented, special sections may be instituted, but the decisions taken by these sections shall be approved by the corporation.

Art. 5—In questions concerning different branches of economic activity, the Head of the Government may order the convocation of two or more corporations together.

With regard to these questions corporations sitting jointly have the same powers as, by the following articles, are attributed to single corporations.

Art. 6—The Head of the Government by his decree, upon proposal of the Minister for Corporations, after consulting the Central Corporative Committee, is authorized to constitute Corporative Committees for the regulation of economic activity concerning specified products. The Head of the Government may appoint representatives of economic categories, of state administrations concerned, and of the Fascist party, to be members of these committees. Decisions taken by these committees are subject to the approval of the corporations concerned, and of the General Assembly of the National Council of Corporations. . . .

Art. 8— . . . The corporation draws up rules . . . to regulate economic relations and the unitary discipline of production. . . .

Art. 10—The corporation is given, within its own field of competence, the power to fix salary scales for the work and economic services of its producers, as well as prices of consumers' goods offered to the public under privileged conditions.

Art. 11—Regulations, plans, and salary scales referred to in the foregoing articles are subject to the approval of the General Assembly of the National Council of Corporations, and become compulsory when published by decree of the Head of the Government, and are included as such in the official collection of laws and decrees of the Kingdom. The infringement of these regulations, plans, and salary scales is punishable according to rules applying to Collective Labor Contracts.

Art. 12—The corporation gives advice on all questions involving the branch of economic activity for which it is constituted, whenever advice is requested by the public agencies concerned. . . .

Art. 13—The attempt at conciliation in collective controversies of labor is made by the corporation through a Board of Conciliation composed of members of the corporation itself. In each separate case the members of this board are selected by the president of the corporation, with due regard to the nature and subject of the controversy.

Art. 14—All provisions conflicting or incompatible with the present law are abrogated. . . .

Art. 15—The composition of organs of the National Council of Corporations will be modified by royal decree, upon proposal of the Head of the Government, after approval by the Council of Ministers.

Between 1934 and 1939 the moribund Chamber of Deputies prepared to make way for a successor body, the Central Committee of Corporations, to consist of 824 members representing the 22 newly created corporations or cycles of economic activity. In each corporation the PNF, the employers, and the employees were represented. At last, on January 19, 1939, this Central Committee of Corporations rechristened itself the Chamber of Fasces and of Corporations (representing the PNF and the corporations), whereupon the old Chamber of Deputies committed suicide. Thus by the eve of World War II nothing was left of the old parliamentary structure described in the 1848 *Statuto Albertino* except the Senate. Nominally, Senators were still appointed for life by the King; in reality, however, the Senate had become subservient to Mussolini, who on one occasion had Victor Emmanuel appoint forty Fascist Senators in a single decree.

After all the verbiage of the corporative state has been cut away, one is left with two naked realities—the political dictatorship of the National Fascist Party, and the pre-eminent position of employers over employees (because capitalists remained largely self-organized, whereas labor was regimented by the state). Ironically, the industrialists began to desert Mussolini in these very years of the culmination of the corporative state. There was too much bureaucratic bungling and too much "proletarian" rhetoric by militants like Achille Starace, party secretary from 1931 to 1939, to suit their fancy.

Law Creating the Chamber
of Fasces and of Corporations
(January 19, 1939)

Art. 1—The Chamber of Deputies shall be abolished at the termination of the XXIX Legislative Session. In its stead shall be instituted the Chamber of Fasces and of Corporations.

Art. 2—The Senate of the Kingdom and the Chamber of Fasces and of Corporations shall collaborate with the Government in the formulation of laws.

Art. 3—The Chamber of Fasces and of Corporations shall be formed from the members of the National Council of the National Fascist Party and from the members of the National Council of Corporations, except in those cases of incompatibility specified in Art. 9.

Changes in the composition of the National Council of the National Fascist Party and of the National Council of Corporations shall be set forth by law.

Art. 4—The DUCE of Fascism, Head of the Government, is, by law, a member of the Chamber of Fasces and of Corporations.

Members of the Fascist Grand Council are also members thereof, except in cases of incompatibility specified in Art. 9.

Art. 5—The National Councilors who belong to the Chamber of Fasces and of Corporations must possess the prerequisites set forth in Art. 40 of the Constitution of the Kingdom, but the minimum age limit is set at twenty-five years as of the day they are sworn in, as specified in Art. 6.

The qualifications for National Councilor shall be set forth in a decree by the DUCE of Fascism, Head of the Government, to be published in the *Gazzetta Ufficiale* of the Kingdom.

Art. 6—The National Councilors, prior to being admitted to the exercise of their functions, shall take an oath in plenary assembly, according to the formula set forth in Art. 49 of the Constitution of the Kingdom.

Art. 7—The National Councilors shall enjoy the prerogatives

SOURCE: Law No. 129 of January 19, 1939, reprinted in Alberto Aquarone (ed.), *L'organizzazione dello stato totalitario* (Turin: Giulio Einaudi Editore, 1965), Appendix No. 62, pp. 567–70. By permission of Giulio Einaudi Editore. My translation.

previously established for Deputies by the Constitution of the Kingdom.

National Councilors shall be entitled to an annual indemnity, to be determined by law.

Art. 8—National Councilors shall cease to hold office upon the termination of the functions exercised in the Councils which are merging to form the Chamber of Fasces and of Corporations.

Art. 9—No one may simultaneously serve as National Councilor, Senator, or Academician of Italy.

Art. 10—The work of the Senate of the Kingdom and of the Chamber of Fasces and of Corporations shall be divided into legislative sessions (legislatures).

The termination of each legislature shall be set by royal decree, upon proposal of the DUCE of Fascism, Head of the Government. The decree shall also announce the date for convocation of the two legislative assemblies to meet in joint session for the purpose of hearing the speech from the Throne, which event shall mark the beginning of the ensuing legislature.

For the purpose of carrying out their normal legislative functions, the two assemblies shall periodically be convened by the DUCE of Fascism, Head of the Government.

Art. 11—The President of the Chamber of Fasces and of Corporations shall be appointed by royal decree. The Vice-Presidents shall likewise be appointed by royal decree.

The President of the Chamber of Fasces and of Corporations shall appoint the other officials who are listed in the by-laws of the Chamber.

Art. 12—The Chamber of Fasces and of Corporations shall exercise its functions by means of a plenary assembly, a General Budgetary Committee, and various other legislative committees.

Special committees may be formed for particular tasks.

Art. 13—The legislative committees shall be established by the President of the Chamber of Fasces and of Corporations in accordance with specific national needs. The President may convene them at any time.

The President shall also create and convene committees envisaged in the second part of Art. 12.

Art. 14—The President and, at his request, the Vice-Presidents of the Chamber of Fasces and of Corporations may participate in the work of the committees and preside over them.

The Ministers, and at their request, the Undersecretaries of State, may make interventions in them.

The provisions of the present article, as well as those in Articles 12 and 13, shall also apply to the Senate of the Kingdom.

Art. 15—Draft laws of a constitutional nature, as specified in Art. 12 of Law No. 2693 of December 9, 1928-VII; those matters specified in the last part of Art. 1 of Law No. 100 of January 31, 1926-IV; and those legislative powers of a general character, budgetary proposals, and balance sheets of the State as well as of the autonomous State enterprises and incorporated administrative entities of whatever type that are of national importance and are subsidized directly or indirectly by the State Treasury, shall be debated and voted upon by the Chamber of Fasces and of Corporations and by the Senate of the Kingdom in their respective plenary assemblies, upon the basis of reports submitted by their respective competent committees.

Similar discussion, as set forth in the paragraph above, shall take place for whatever draft legislation the Government asks to have considered by this method, or for whatever legislation may be proposed by the respective plenary assemblies or by the committees with the authorization of the DUCE of Fascism, Head of the Government.

Voting shall always take place in open fashion.

Art. 16—Draft laws that are not considered in accordance with the provisions of Art. 15 above shall be turned over to the legislative committees of the Chamber of Fasces and of Corporations and of the Senate of the Kingdom for their exclusive examination.

Draft laws that have been approved shall be placed before both assemblies by their respective presidents.

Within one month after the presentation of each draft law—a time limit that may be extended by the DUCE of Fascism, Head of the Government—the text that has been debated and approved by the legislative committees of the Chamber of Fasces and of Corporations and of the Senate shall be transmitted to the DUCE of Fascism, Head of the Government, who shall see to it that it is submitted for the approval of the Sovereign and promulgated in the usual manner established by law.

The introductory clauses in the law must indicate the fact that it has received the approval of the legislative committees and of the Chamber and the Senate.

The provisions thus promulgated have the force of law for all purposes.

Art. 17—The method of discussion and approval, as specified in Art. 16, may also be followed for the draft laws that are mentioned in Art. 15, whenever the DUCE of Fascism, Head of the Government, shall request same for urgent reasons.

Art. 18—In case of emergency caused by war or for urgent reasons of a financial or tax nature, it shall be permissible to proceed by means of royal decree without observing the procedure set forth under Art. 16.

The same procedure may be followed if the committees have not completed their task within the prescribed time.

In such instances the provisions contained in the second and succeeding clauses of Art. 3 of Law No. 100 of January 31, 1926-IV, shall be applied.

Art. 19—The corporative regulations elaborated by the corporations and the collective agreements negotiated by the interested associations, whenever they call for contributions of any sort or denomination at the expense of the members of the categories involved by these agreements and regulations, may be presented, at the discretion of the DUCE of Fascism, Head of the Government, after the examination of the Central Corporative Committee, to the Chamber of Fasces and of Corporations, in order that they be submitted to the examination and approval of the competent legislative committee or, if necessary, of joint committees.

In case the committee or joint committee should propose amendments to the text that was elaborated by the corporations, approval must be deferred to the plenary Assembly of the Chamber of Fasces and of Corporations.

The definitive text shall be transmitted by the President of the Chamber of Fasces and of Corporations to the DUCE of Fascism, Head of the Government, who shall promulgate it by his own decree, which is to be inserted in the *Raccolta Ufficiale delle Leggi e dei Decreti del Regno.*

Art. 20—Whenever the juridical provisions which are within the competence of the Government as set forth by Law No. 100 of January 31, 1926-IV, reflect matters of a technical or economic character falling within the specific purview of the corporations, they must be preceded, except in cases of urgency, by the opinion of the competent corporation or by the advisory committee set up within it.

Art. 21—Any provisions that may be contrary to or incompatible with those contained in the present law are hereby abrogated.

4. *Social, Economic, and Youth Programs*

DURING THE first couple of years of Fascist rule, while Alberto De'
Stefani was Minister of Finance, the government generally pursued a
laissez-faire type of policy, returning the national life insurance program and the telephone system to private hands and giving tax advantages to bondholders and industrialists. In the spring of 1925 this began
to change as the government embarked on an increasingly interventionist kind of social and economic program. Count Giuseppe Volpi
took over the finance ministry, while Alfredo Rocco became a key
adviser to Mussolini in social and economic matters. Soon the Rocco
Labor Law and the Labor Charter (printed in Chapter 3) gave tangible
evidence of the new philosophy.

Some of the initial social legislation was conceived as a sop to the
workers who had lost their right to strike. This would appear to be the
case with one of the earliest programs, the much publicized National
Institution for Leisure Time (Opera Nazionale Dopolavoro), which
was designed to provide workers with opportunities for playing bil-
liards, engaging in sports, going on cheap excursions, and other activities. Hitler's Germany was to introduce a similar program, Strength
through Joy (Kraft durch Freude). By 1940 membership in the Italian
Dopolavoro reached 4,612,294. The decree establishing this organization on May 1, 1925, follows.

Law Creating the Dopolavoro Organization
(May 1, 1925)

Art. 1: The Opera Nazionale Dopolavoro [National Institution
for Leisure Time] is established in Rome with these aims:

(a) To provide healthy and profitable leisure-time activity for
the workers by means of institutions that develop their physical,
intellectual, and moral qualities;

(b) To promote the development of these institutions by providing them with necessary support and raising them to the legal
status of *Ente Morale*.[1]

SOURCE: Royal Decree-Law No. 582, May 1, 1925, published in
Gazzetta Ufficiale del Regno, No. 846 (May 14, 1925). My
translation.

1. *I.e.*, an incorporated educational or charitable body.—*Ed.*

(c) To co-ordinate all such associations and to equip them for propaganda purposes and other common aims and interests;

(d) To publicize the advantages of these institutions, and to make provisions for improving the qualities of life of the working classes;

(e) To award certificates of merit to those members who have proved themselves to be particularly deserving, or who have shown noteworthy proficiency and activity in promoting the aims and objects of the organization. . . .

Art. 5: The administration of the Opera Nazionale Dopolavoro is entrusted to the President, the Administrative Council, and the Executive Committee. . . .

Art. 6: The Council of the Opera Nazionale Dopolavoro is appointed by royal decree, upon proposal of the Head of the Government. . . . The President of the Council . . . is appointed by royal decree upon proposal of the Head of the Government. . . .

Art. 12: The Opera Nazionale Dopolavoro is under the control of the Ministry of National Economy. . . .

Another social program to be initiated in 1925 was an agency devoted to the protection of pregnant mothers and needy, orphaned, or emotionally disturbed children. While it no doubt did useful work, it found itself hard put to cope with the additional problems brought on during the 1930's when Mussolini deliberately called for a higher birth rate ("Win the battle of motherhood!") in order to provide manpower for his armies and national expansion. Christmas Day of 1933 was to be proclaimed the "Day of Mother and Child," and mothers who could bear fourteen to nineteen children were personally received by the *Duce* and given copies of Pius XI's *Casti connubi.* The decree-law of December 10, 1925, establishing the National Institution for Maternity and Child Welfare follows.

Law Creating the National Organization for Maternity and Child Welfare
(December 10, 1925)

Art. 1: An *Ente Morale* [*i.e.,* an incorporated educational or charitable body] is founded in Rome under the name of National Institution for Maternity and Child Welfare. . . . The Institution

SOURCE: Decree-Law of December 10, 1925, reprinted in Benito Mussolini, *Fascism: Doctrine and Institutions* (Rome: "Ardita," 1935), pp. 251–264 *passim.*

is placed under the control of the Minister for the Interior, who shall approve the budget and the accounts.

Art. 2: The Institution is governed by a central Council composed of 27 members as follows: two senators and two deputies appointed by each Chamber for the duration of the legislature, and 23 members appointed by royal decree upon proposal of the Minister for the Interior. . . . Members appointed by royal decree remain in office four years and may be reappointed. . . .

Art. 4: The Institution, directly or in co-operation with its provincial or communal organs in the measure provided by regulations, attends to the protection of pregnant women; of deserted mothers; of mothers in need; of needy children up to their fifth year; of children who are physically and psychically abnormal; of adolescents who are materially and morally deserted, or who are addicted to vice or delinquency, up to the age of eighteen. Through provisions of this nature the Institution co-operates in the work already being done in other ways to protect mothers and children, and gives support to existing enterprises.

The Institution helps to spread the knowledge of scientific methods of prenatal hygiene and the care of children in their own or in public homes; organizes dispensaries to help pregnant women and attends to their health conditions with special regard to syphilis; organizes schools of puericulture and popular courses on hygiene for mothers and children; by agreement with Provincial Administrations and Institutions for the diseases of children, the Institution shall also enforce laws and regulations for the protection of mothers and children; and shall promote the amendment of existing measures when this is necessary for the physical and moral training of the children.

Art. 5: The Institution is vested with powers of control over all public and private institutions for maternity and child welfare. . . .

Art. 6: In carrying out its task of co-ordination the Institution is empowered to:

(a) Found institutions for the protection of maternity, create funds in aid of mothers, open homes for needy and deserted women who are nursing their children, and other institutions to protect maternity and children, where the existing forms of relief are inadequate to fill local requirements;

(b) Subsidize institutions which are not sufficiently provided with funds;

(c) Co-ordinate all public and private institutions for assistance to mothers and children, directing their activity in view of filling the most pressing local needs, and if necessary, revising their constitution and regulations, insofar as this is allowed for by existing laws.

Art. 7: The Institution is provided with the following funds: (1) a yearly contribution of 8,000,000 lire from the Minister for the Interior . . . ; (2) funds appropriated for the assistance of indigent children on the budget of certain institutes . . . ; (3) a percentage on the net profits of the "Monti di Pietà" [government-controlled pawnbroking establishments]; (4) a percentage on the [annual] net profits [of certain banks]; (5) one-fourth of the communal tax on the sojourn of travellers . . . ; (6) membership dues; (7) legacies, donations, oblations or subsidies made directly. . . .

In a speech at Pesaro in August, 1926, Mussolini announced the revaluation of the currency. The lira was stabilized at the so-called *quota novanta* (*i.e.*, 90 lire would equal one British pound sterling, whereas in 1921 the rate had been 100 lire to the pound). This new *lira di Pesaro* proved to be overvalued, thus making it hard for Italy to export her goods and contributing to the deflationary spiral that pushed the country into the Depression a good two years ahead of the Wall Street crash. Not until 1936 did Mussolini devalue the currency.

Meanwhile, unemployment trebled between 1926 and 1930. By 1932 some 1,150,000 were unemployed in a nation of 42,000,000 and at least one-half of the total labor force was *underemployed*. The *Duce*'s response was to introduce a 12 per cent wage cut for public employees, which only added to the deflationary trend.

As the storms of the Depression buffeted Italy, the government began to talk about the virtues of national self-sufficiency, especially in food production. Strutting before the newsreel cameramen, Mussolini would bare his torso in the harvest fields and call for winning the "battle of grain." He also stressed the need for draining the Pontine marshes and bringing marginal lands into cultivation. From 1925 to 1935 he managed to cut the country's wheat imports by 75 per cent, but in those same years per capita consumption of wheat declined 21 per cent. In other words, while he was winning the "battle," Italians were actually losing the grain. As a policy, autarky proved more successful in the industrial than in the agricultural sector, for it was easier to convince industrialists of the advantages of a cartel than to satisfy absentee landlords about the benefits of intensive cultivation of crops which the party judged necessary. Mussolini's program to raise protective tariffs led to foreign retaliation, so that by 1932 Italian exports were only 40 per cent of what they had been in 1929. During the Depression foreign tourists no longer could come in great numbers, a fact that further aggravated the imbalance of payments.

Though Mussolini lauded the virtues of rural life, he did almost nothing in the way of agrarian reform, apart from draining a few marshes (preferably those closest to Rome). The great latifundia were left untouched. Tenant farmers, sharecroppers, and migrant workers continued to eke out a living, and the legal status of the *mezzadri* (sharecroppers) was lowered to that of ordinary workers in the social hierarchy of the corporative state. Between 1926 and 1934 the real wages of farm workers declined between 50 and 70 per cent. When Fascism was overthrown in 1943 Italy had fewer peasant-owned farms than before. Only a small portion of the rural population that wanted to migrate to the cities was actually permitted to do so by the regime. In this way the quasi-feudal agrarian system was propped up for another generation. Serious land reform and release of surplus agricultural farm hands had to await the advent of the Republic.

In industry the worst phase of the Depression was around 1932, with textiles, a basic feature of Italy's economic life, the hardest hit. Throughout the years of economic crisis the country saw an increasing monopolistic tendency in industry, the "big fish" eating the "little fish" with the government's blessing. Monopolistic industries rigged prices, set production quotas, and generally behaved in cartel-like fashion. In January, 1933, the government organized the Institute for Industrial Reconstruction (IRI), a holding company that resembled somewhat the Reconstruction Finance Corporation in the United States. The IRI provided subsidies to salvage banks and big businesses, with the result that by 1940 the government held a 20 per cent interest in Italian industries. Thus state capitalism was encouraged by Fascism and became especially conspicuous in such categories as shipbuilding and aviation industries and petroleum production. Cynics scoffed that Fascism "socialized" the losses of businessmen while dividing the profits among a small number.

In October, 1934, the government reduced the work week to forty hours in order to spread out employment but did not increase the hourly pay; thus workers took a net loss in income. Real wages in Italy fell from 111.8 in 1925 (1913 = 100) to 100.5 in 1938. They were much lower than wage levels in France, Germany, or Britain. No effort was made to raise purchasing power as a means of combating the Depression, and Keynesian-type economics remained a mystery. In winter months the PNF's National Solidarity program administered a dole that was funded by contributions from employers and ordinary citizens. During the bad winter of 1934–35 it amounted to fifty *centesimi* a day, the equivalent of about five cents. (In Britain the daily dole was about five times as much, while in New York City it was ten times greater.) On the other hand, Mussolini's Italy did spend considerable sums on highway construction and certain kinds of public works. All sorts of governmental buildings—prefectures, post offices, and party headquarters—were constructed, generally in a massive, unappealing style.

With the advent of the Ethiopian War in 1935 a new chapter in the economic history of Fascism began. By shunting the unemployed into the armed forces, Mussolini managed to cut unemployment by some 300,000 during 1935–36. The first year of the Ethiopian conflict and the initial phase of the League of Nations-imposed sanctions had the effect of stimulating the Italian economy, but after 1936 the war produced severe strains. The nation clearly could not sustain a prolonged military effort. Nevertheless, Mussolini dispatched Fascist Militiamen and other troops to help Franco in the Spanish Civil War after July, 1936; they remained there until the spring of 1939. Immediately thereafter came the war in Albania. Little wonder that by 1936 the budget was badly out of balance and the government had to devalue the lira. It also had to increase its revenues, imposing death taxes and levying forced loans. Registration of bonds was required again for purposes of taxation. By 1937 it was reported that the cost of living had increased 20 per cent above the previous year. Meanwhile, there was growing evidence of outright corruption in high places and ubiquitous inefficiency in the bureaucracy. An ever increasing number of financiers and industrialists began to lose confidence in Mussolini's ability.

By 1938 another distinct shift in the government's social and economic attitude was apparent. Radical Fascists gained the upper hand and argued in favor of a more "proletarian" attitude against "plutocratic capitalism." Achille Starace, the coarse and doctrinaire secretary of the PNF in this period, was conspicuous in this regard. He persuaded Mussolini to join him in the denunciation of top hats, spats, and butterfly collars. Hierarchs were also ordered not to use starch in the collars of their black shirts, to stay out of night clubs, to stop drinking real coffee, and to quit riding in first-class railway accommodations.

Genuine economic growth during the years of Fascism was quite small. Whereas in 1925 the national income was 115.1 billion lire, in 1938 it had risen to only 138.2 billion lire (measured in the same 1938 prices). On a per capita basis this meant that in 1925 one earned 2,923 lire and in 1938 but 3,201 lire.

Fascism loved to extol the virtues of youth. The party's marching anthem was "Giovinezza" (Youth), which competed with the monarchy's "Marcia reale." Like the Communist party in Soviet Russia, Mussolini's PNF quickly saw the importance of inculcating its ideology among the youth and of organizing a variety of youth groups that would serve to train young people in national service and qualify them for eventual membership in the party. For children under the age of eight there was the Order of the Wolf, while those between eight and thirteen could join the Balilla organization, named for a legendary boy-hero who inspired nationalistic demonstrations in the eighteenth century by hurling rocks at some Austrian police. Its symbols were the musket and the book, and it successfully rivaled the Boy Scouts and Catholic youth organizations. Boys between the ages of fourteen and eighteen could go into the Avanguardisti, while those aged nineteen to twenty-one could belong to the Young Fascists, which had separate sections for boys and girls. After age twenty-one one was eligible to seek admission to the party.

Following is the decree establishing the Balilla youth organization for physical and moral training, headed by Renato Ricci until 1937.

Law Creating the Balilla Youth Organization
(April 3, 1926)

ART. I: An *Ente Morale*[2] is founded in Rome under the name of *Opera Nazionale Balilla*, for the moral and physical training of the young.

This institution is placed under the control of the Head of the Government, Prime Minister.[3]

ART. II: Children of either sex are entitled to assistance provided for in the present law, until the age of eighteen. . . .

ART. III: The institution achieves its ends through the organizations of the *Balilla* and *Avanguardisti*.

The organization of *Avanguardisti* shall more especially attend to the training of the young in preparation for military service.

ART. IV: Children from the age of eight to fourteen belong to the organization of the *Balilla*, children from fourteen to eighteen to the organization of the *Avanguardisti*. . . .

ART. VI: With regard to military service, young men who have belonged to the corps of *Avanguardisti* for a term of four years and have received a certificate of competence upon leaving the corps, may benefit by privileges granted by existing laws to young men who have followed courses of pre-military training. . . .

ART. VII: In order to complete the activity carried out by the corps of *Balilla* and *Avanguardisti*, the National Balilla Institution is empowered to:

1. found institutions for the assistance of youth, or promote their foundation;

2. subsidize institutions not provided with sufficient funds, if their object be similar to that of the National Balilla Institution;

3. promote the reform of the statutes and regulations of institu-

SOURCE: Law No. 2247 of April 3, 1926, reprinted in Benito Mussolini, *Fascism: Doctrine and Institutions* (Rome: "Ardita," 1935), pp. 264–270 *passim*.

2. An incorporated educational or charitable body.—*Ed.*

3. In November, 1929, it was placed under the control of the Ministry of National Education.—*Ed.*

tions empowered to award scholarships, so that examinations for the award be made compulsory and that, in cases of equal merit, preference be given to children and youths belonging to the corps of *Balilla* and *Avanguardisti.* . . .

ART. IX: The Institution is provided with the following funds:

1. membership dues;

2. legacies, oblations, donations or subsidies made to the National Balilla Institution;

3. a yearly contribution of one million lire from the Minister of the Interior.

ART. X: The National Balilla Institution is governed by a Central Council composed of a president, a vice-president and twenty-three councilors, appointed by royal decree upon proposal of the Head of the Government, Prime Minister.

The president is chosen from among officers of the Militia ranking not below *console generale* (on active service or in the special reserve) upon the advice of the General Commandant of the Militia. The president and vice-president remain in office four years and may be reappointed.

Members of the Central Council are: two representatives of the Ministry of the Interior, one of whom is appointed by the Bureau of Public Health; a representative for each of the following Ministries: Finance, War, Navy, Air Force, Education, National Economy, designated by their respective Ministers; a Militia officer of superior rank designated by the General Commandant of the Militia; a representative of the sporting federations designated by the Italian Olympic Committee, and a representative of the *Dopolavoro* institution.

Other members of the Council shall be chosen from among persons especially competent in studies connected with the moral and physical training of the young. . . .

ART. XII: A Provincial Committee may be formed in each Province, composed of a president and ten councilors. . . .

ART. XIV: A Communal Committee may be formed in each Commune, composed of a president and of as many councilors as shall be decided by the Provincial Committee, in proportion to the population of the Commune, with the approval of the Executive Board of the National Balilla Institution.

Members of the Communal Committee are chosen by the Provincial Committee preferably from among persons residing in the Commune. In Communes which possess secondary schools and bodies of the Militia, a teacher of the local school and the officer commanding the local Militia body are *ex-officio* members of the Committee.

Committees hold their meetings in premises provided free of charge by the Commune.

Members of the Central Committee may be withdrawn at any moment by the Head of the Government, Prime Minister, upon the proposal of the President, when they fail to carry out the task assigned to them. . . .

ABSTRACTS OF REGULATIONS
FOR ENFORCEMENT OF THE ABOVE LAW

ART. I: The Militia of *Avanguardisti* and *Balilla* is intended to give moral and physical training to the young, in order to make them worthy of the new standard of Italian life. . . .

ART. III: The recruiting of *Avanguardisti* and *Balilla*, within the age limits specified by the law, is voluntary.

In order to be allowed to join the organization, children require the consent of their parents or guardians. After their sixteenth year of age they shall also provide a certificate of good conduct. Admission is not limited in number.

ART. IV: The corps of *Avanguardisti* and *Balilla* are organized on military lines. They shall march by three.

Bodies are formed as follows: *Squadron,* eleven boys and a leader; *Manipulum,* three *squadrons; Centurium,* three *manipula; Cohort,* three *centuria; Legion,* three *cohorts.*

In places where the number of *cohorts* is over three but under six a single *legion* is formed. . . .

ART. X: In order to achieve the ends specified in the law, and in Art. I of the present regulations, the *Balilla* institution shall:

1. teach the young the spirit of discipline and of military training, and give them:

2. premilitary training;

3. physical training through gymnastics and sports;

4. spiritual and cultural training;

5. professional and vocational training;

6. religious teaching.

SOURCE: Royal Decree No. 6, January 9, 1927, reprinted in Benito Mussolini, *Fascism: Doctrine and Institutions* (Rome: "Ardita," 1935), pp. 270–275 *passim.*

ART. XI: Discipline means respect and obedience to military commanders and to persons who are entrusted with the civil and military training of the *Avanguardisti*.

The first rank of the hierarchy is the *capo-squadra*, chosen from among the *Avanguardisti;* he shall be looked upon as a comrade whose advice and example are to be followed.

Leaders ranking higher than *capo-squadra* have the same rank as officers of the Militia and shall be looked to by the *Avanguardisti* as their natural educators and instructors.

ART. XII: Breaches of discipline on the part of *Avanguardisti* are punished as follows: (a) oral reprimand, when the breach is merely negligence in performing duties;

(b) written reprimand to be sent to parents or guardians when the charge is continued negligence, or serious disobedience;

(c) suspension for a period ranging from one to three months for infringement of rules of good manners, or in cases of continued bad conduct;

(d) expulsion in cases which appear incorrigible and would set bad examples.

Expulsion entails the loss of all privileges of assistance and relief offered by the Institution to its members.

Oral reprimand is pronounced by leaders higher in rank than *capo-squadra;* written reprimand is made by the officer highest in rank in the Commune; suspension is ordered by the Communal Committee and expulsion by the Provincial Committee. . . .

ART. XXVII: Physical training through gymnastics and sport is given according to the official program for the secondary schools of the Kingdom. It is supplemented by excursions, camping, games, etc. Those who attend to the planning of these schemes should bear in mind that physical training also influences the spiritual education of the young.

Therefore the *Avanguardisti* and Militia are intended to train the young to appreciate beauty and strength, since intellectual life can only develop fully in a healthy and vigorous body. . . .

ART. XXX: The National Balilla Institution shall also train the conscience and minds of these boys, since they are destined to become the Fascist men of the future, from whose ranks national leaders will be selected.

The National Balilla Institution is highly qualified to carry out this task, since it has control over large groups of the young, whose minds are readily formed by proper care and education.

ART. XXXI: In order to achieve this end the National Institution may found schools for cultural training and centers of study and propaganda.

The doctrine of Fascism, its logical development and its historical signifiance, shall be taught in these schools. . . .

ART. XXXVIII: Religious instruction shall consist in the teaching of Catholic ethics, Christian doctrine, the Old Testament and the Gospels, and shall be imparted in such hours as specified in Article XL. The form of worship is that practiced by the Roman Catholic Church. . . .

In 1937, as a result of a feud between PNF Secretary Starace and Renato Ricci, who headed Balilla, the latter organization was abolished and Ricci dismissed. In its place emerged the Italian Youth of the Lictors (Gioventú Italiana del Littorio, GIL) as the co-ordinating organization for all the youth forces of the regime except the Fascist University Groups (GUF), which remained separate though also under strict party control. GUF also directed the School of Fascist Mysticism at Milan, one of the party's principal leadership schools. By 1940 some 8,500,000 youth belonged to GIL, while GUF enrolled more than 100,000. The following decree established GIL.

Law Creating Italian Youth of the Lictors
(October 27, 1937)

Art. 1—The Gioventú Italiana del Littorio, which is the unitary and totalitarian organization of all the youth forces of the Fascist Regime, is hereby established within the framework of the National Fascist Party, under the direct supervision of the Secretary of the National Fascist Party, Minister Secretary of State, who is the General Commandant of the organization.

The Gioventú Italiana del Litttorio has as its motto: "Believe! Obey! Fight!"

Art. 2—The Undersecretariat of State for Physical and Youth Education, which was attached to the Ministry of National Education by Royal Decree No. 1661 of September 12, 1929-VI, is hereby abolished.

SOURCE: Royal Decree-Law No. 1839, October 27, 1937, reprinted in Alberto Aquarone (ed.), *L'organizzazione dello stato totalitario* (Turin: Giulio Einaudi Editore, 1965), Appendix 60, pp. 561–562. By permission of Giulio Einaudi Editore. My translation.

The Opera Nazionale Balilla, which was established by Law No. 2247 of April 3, 1926-IV, is hereby absorbed by the Gioventú Italiana del Littorio.

The powers that were conferred by laws and regulations upon the president of the Opera Nazionale Balilla and the Ministry of National Education as regards the Opera Nazionale Balilla are hereby conferred upon the Secretary of the National Fascist Party, Minister Secretary of State, General Commandant of the Gioventú Italiana del Littorio.

The institutions, schools, academies, and colleges belonging to the Opera Nazionale Balilla are hereby transferred to the Gioventú Italiana del Littorio in their present actual and legal status.

All assets and liabilities of the Opera Nazionale Balilla and of the Fasci Giovanili di Combattimento, as well as real estate which is owned by the National Fascist Party and assigned for the purpose of providing Fascist youth with barracks and summer camp facilities, are hereby transferred to Gioventú Italiana del Littorio.

Art. 3—The Secretary of the National Fascist Party, Minister Secretary of State, is empowered by virtue of his title as General Commandant to issue regulations regarding the organization of the Gioventú Italiana del Littorio and its operation in the Kingdom, in Italian East Africa, Libya, and the Italian islands of the Aegean Sea.

Art. 4—Young people of both sexes between the ages of six and twenty-one who are presently enrolled in such organizations as the Young Fascists, Avanguardisti, Balilla, Sons of the Wolf, Piccole Italiane, Giovani Italiane, and Giovani Fasciste henceforth belong to the Gioventú Italiana del Littorio.

Young people who are enrolled in the organization of the Gioventú Italiana del Littorio are bound by the following oath: "In the name of God and of Italy, I swear to carry out the orders of the *Duce* and to serve with all my strength, and if necessary with my very blood, the Cause of the Fascist Revolution."

Art. 5—The tasks carried out by the Gioventú Italiana del Littorio in behalf of the youth are the following:

(a) Training of a spiritual, athletic, and premilitary type;

(b) Teaching of physical education in the elementary and middle schools, in accordance with programs to be worked out in conjunction with the Ministry of National Education;

(c) Establishing and operating courses, schools, colleges, and academies that are consonant with the aims of the Gioventú Italiana del Littorio;

(d) Providing of assistance of various kinds—chiefly through camps, recreational facilities, and educational support, but also by any other means that may be arranged by the Secretary of the National Fascist Party, Minister Secretary of State, General Commandant.

(e) Organizing trips and cruises.

The Gioventú Italiana del Littorio is further empowered to establish and encourage the establishment of scholarships and arrange for their distribution. . . .

In the regimentation of Italian youth the regime copied not only the Communist example of Soviet Russia but the Biblical Ten Commandments. Two versions of this Fascist "Decalogue," dated respectively 1934 and 1938, follow.

The Fascist Decalogue

I: 1934

1. Know that the Fascist and in particular the soldier, must not believe in perpetual peace.

2. Days of imprisonment are always deserved.

3. The nation serves even as a sentinel over a can of petrol.

4. A companion must be a brother, first because he lives with you, and secondly because he thinks like you.

5. The rifle and cartridge belt, and the rest, are confided to you not to rust in leisure, but to be preserved in war.

6. Do not ever say "The Government will pay . . ." because it is *you* who pay; and the Government is that which you willed to have and for which you put on a uniform.

7. Discipline is the soul of armies; without it there are no soldiers, only confusion and defeat.

8. Mussolini is always right.

9. For a volunteer there are no extenuating circumstances when he is disobedient.

SOURCE: Reprinted from *The Political and Social Doctrines of Contemporary Europe*, ed. by Michael Oakeshott (Cambridge University Press, 1941), pp. 180–1. By permission of the Cambridge University Press.

10. One thing must be dear to you above all: the life of the Duce.

II: 1938

1. Remember that those who fell for the revolution and for the empire march at the head of your columns.

2. Your comrade is your brother. He lives with you, thinks with you, and is at your side in the battle.

3. Service to Italy can be rendered at all times, in all places, and by every means. It can be paid with toil and also with blood.

4. The enemy of Fascism is your enemy. Give him no quarter.

5. Discipline is the sunshine of armies. It prepares and illuminates the victory.

6. He who advances to the attack with decision has victory already in his grasp.

7. Conscious and complete obedience is the virtue of the Legionary.

8. There do not exist things important and things unimportant. There is only duty.

9. The Fascist revolution has depended in the past and still depends on the bayonets of its Legionaries.

10. Mussolini is always right.

Mussolini's first Minister of National Education from 1922 to 1924 was Giovanni Gentile, the neo-Hegelian philosopher who was to compose in 1925 the *Manifesto of the Fascist Intellectuals* referred to in Chapter 2. Mussolini was rather indifferent to Gentile's educational reforms of 1923 which gave universities somewhat more autonomy, allowed considerable freedom to private schools, and stressed the infusion of philosophy into almost every facet of the curriculum (and in history in particular).

In the latter part of the 1920's various Fascist institutes were founded—e.g., the National Fascist Institute of Culture in Rome, with Gentile as its president; the Fascist University of Bologna; the Fascist-oriented Faculty of Political Science at Perugia; a new Fascist Italian Academy (1927), supposed to rival the Académie Française and to co-ordinate all work in the arts and sciences. Its sixty "immortals" were chosen by Mussolini and decked out with fine ostrich feathers. Gioacchino Volpe, the leading Fascist historian of the Risorgimento era, was secretary. Among the other notables were D'Annunzio and Guglielmo Marconi.

Elementary education expanded during the Fascist era (but it would have done so anyway). Illiteracy figures continued to decline (but at a slower rate). Efforts to "fascisticize" the Italian educational system persisted and met with some success at the elementary and intermediate school levels, though more in the category of athletic and extracurricular activities than in substantive courses, except for the peculiarly vulnerable disciplines of history, economics, and political science. Some of the Fascist innovations had merit so long as they were not carried to excess—for example, increased attention to physical education. Despite occasional pressure against law faculties and professors in the fields of history and the social sciences, academic freedom generally survived pretty well in the universities. But in August, 1931, the dictatorship interfered drastically with academic· freedom when it required every university professor to subscribe to the following oath.

Fascist Loyalty Oath Imposed upon Professors
(November 1, 1931)

Art. 18—Both regular professors (*professori di ruolo*) and temporary professors (*professori incaricati*) are required to take the following oath:

"I swear to be loyal to the King, to his royal successors, to the Fascist Regime, to observe loyally the Constitution and the other laws of the State, to exercise the profession of teacher and to carry out all academic duties with the aim of training upright and hardworking citizens who are devoted to the fatherland and to the Fascist Regime. I swear that I neither belong to nor shall belong to associations or parties whose activities do not harmonize with the duties of my profession."

Some 1,200 university professors ('the overwhelming majority) subscribed to the Fascist loyalty oath, much to the joy of Gentile, who exulted, "The undisciplined intellectual disappears from our midst."[4] Probably most professors did so in order to avoid the financial ruin they faced if they lost their posts in the middle of the Depression. Some, of course, were either indifferent or felt that the oath would not hamper presentation of subject matter in their own fields. Certain ones adhered because the Vatican indicated its approval, explaining that an oath "to the Fascist regime" was the equivalent of the expression "Government of the State."[5] Only about a dozen refused to join in this *trahison des clercs* and declared flatly that the oath was a violation of both academic and political freedoms. They included some of Italy's most internationally renowned savants (*e.g.*, Gaetano De Sanctis,

SOURCE: Decree-Law of August 28, 1931, "Dispositions Regarding Higher Education," published in *Gazzetta Ufficiale* (Oct. 8, 1931) and effective as of November 1, 1931. My translation.

4. Quoted in Daniel Binchy, *Church and State in Fascist Italy* (London: Oxford University Press, 1941), p. 465.

5. *L'Osservatore Romano* (Dec. 4, 1931), cited in *ibid.*, p. 465.

Lionello Venturi, and Giuseppe A. Borgese). Similar oaths were required in October, 1934, of members of the venerable and prestigious Accademia dei Lincei; in that case there were ten nonjurors.

From the time of the Gentile educational reforms of 1923, and especially in the mid-1930's, the PNF was interfering almost constantly with the work of the Ministry of National Education in an effort to achieve the party's goal of a school system that would be profoundly Fascist both in spirit and in form. Textbooks in the elementary schools were filled with such slogans as "Mussolini ha sempre ragione" (Mussolini is always right). Aping the Jacobins of the French Revolution, the Fascists began to use a "revolutionary" Fascist calendar, with Roman numerals marking the years since October 30, 1922. When the GIL was created in 1937 it insisted on close collaboration with the schools and arranged special athletic events on Saturdays (*sabato fascista*), summer camps, and programs of party indoctrination. The culmination of this effort to educate a "new Italian man" occurred on February 15, 1939, when the Grand Council approved the Fascist School Charter, drawn up by Giuseppe Bottai, an idealistic young Catholic Fascist hierarch who had recently become Minister of National Education. In contrast to the thirty aphorisms of the Labor Charter of 1927, to which it was often compared, the School Charter contained twenty-nine points. It conceived of scholastic obligation as "national service," in the execution of which the schools, GIL, and GUF (Fascist University Groups) would work in closest harmony. Membership in GIL now became obligatory for every student. The influence of the Nazis' labor-service program (Arbeitsdienst) was apparent in Article 5. The hostility toward co-education was also clear. Because of Italy's entry into World War II sixteen months later, only a few provisions of the charter were implemented; among these was Article 26, which, in effect, established state control over the last private and parochial schools. Bottai's School Charter is an important statement of the educational goals of Italian Fascism. Fortunately, the universities and intermediate schools managed to maintain pretty high standards in spite of frequent Fascist interference.

The Fascist School Charter
(February 15, 1939)

Principles, Goals, and Methods of the Fascist School

I.—In the moral, political, and economic unity of the Italian nation which is realized integrally in the Fascist State, the schools—which

source: Approved by the Fascist Grand Council, February 15, 1939. Printed in Ministero dell'Educazione Nazionale, *Dalla Riforma Gentile alla Carta della Scuola* (Rome, 1941). My translation.

provide the essential foundation for the solidarity among all the social forces from the family to the corporations and the Party—shape the human and political conscience of the new generations.

By means of study conceived as forming a mature mind, the Fascist schools bring into reality the principle of popular culture that finds inspiration in the eternal values of the Italian race and its civilization. And, through work, this principle is engrafted in the actual crafts, arts, professions, sciences, and military life.

II.—Under the Fascist order, the periods for scholastic and political education coincide. The schools, GIL, and GUF together form a single instrument of Fascist education. The duty to attend them constitutes the scholastic service, to which all citizens are bound from early age to that of twenty-one years. This service consists in attending the schools and GIL from the fourth to the fourteenth year; it continues in the GIL until the twenty-first year for those who no longer go to school. University students must belong to the GUF. A personal record book, similar to the worker's employment booklet, will attest to the fulfillment of scholastic service; and both will be taken into account in the evaluation of the individuals in offices and other type of work.

III.—Studies will be arranged in accordance with the actual physical and intellectual abilities of young people; these studies will aim at their moral and cultural training, and at their political and military preparation, in harmony with the goals of the GIL. The only criterion for admitting young people to studies and allowing them to go on in the schools is that given by individual talents and capabilities. The state colleges will guarantee that capable but poor people shall be able to continue their studies.

IV.—Physical education, which is provided in the schools by the GIL, will encourage and favor the gradual growth and physical strengthening of the young people, as well as their psychical progress. The technique of such training shall aim at harmonious development, efficiency, high moral standards, self-assurance, and a strong sense of discipline and duty.

In the university system the GUF shall supervise the athletic and military training of the young people.

V.—Work—which is protected by the State in all its forms, whether intellectual, manual, or technical, as a social duty—contributes, together with studies and physical training, toward shaping character and intelligence.

Manual work shall have its place in the programs of all the

schools, from the elementary to the highest. Special periods of work are to be organized and directed by the school authorities in the workshops, fields, and on the sea, so that the social and productive consciousness that is characteristic of the corporative system may be developed.

VI.—Study, physical exercises, and manual work provide the schools with the means for testing talent. The main tasks of the schools are to provide cultural and professional orientation so that men capable of facing the actual problems of scientific research and production may be trained according to reason and needs.

The principle of selection must go on continuously in the schools, so that the special functions and responsibilities of the various types of schools may be safeguarded.

VII.—There is a natural solidarity between family and schools; they collaborate intimately and uninterruptedly to the end of educating and orienting youth. Parents and relatives participate in the life of the schools and learn there to know the common aims and methods which help to strengthen children and young people on the path of the traditional religion and destiny in Italy.

Structure of the Fascist Schools

VIII.—The Italian schools are characterized by the following "orders":

(a) Elementary, consisting of:
   1. Nursery school (*scuola materna*), two years;
   2. Elementary school, three years;
   3. Labor school, two years;
   4. Artisan school, three years.
(b) Intermediate, consisting of:
   1. Middle school (*scuola media*), three years;
   2. Professional school, three years;
   3. Technical school, two years.
(c) Superior, consisting of:
   1. Classical lyceum, five years;
   2. Scientific lyceum, five years;
   3. Teacher-training institute, five years;
   4. Technical-commercial institute, five years;
   5. Institute for agricultural, industrial, land surveying, and nautical skills, four years.

(d) University, consisting of:
1. Faculties of jurisprudence, political science, economics, and commerce;
2. Faculties of letters and philosophy, and of teacher training;
3. Faculties of medicine and surgery, and of veterinary medicine;
4. Faculties of mathematical, physical, and natural sciences, of statistical, demographic, and actuarial sciences;
5. Faculty of pharmacy;
6. Faculties of engineering, mining engineering, and industrial chemistry;
7. Faculty of architecture;
8. Faculty of agriculture;
9. Schools for special purposes.

The courses of study leading to academic degrees shall last from four to six years. Under exceptional circumstances certain courses of study may be of shorter duration.

In addition to the regular teaching institutes in each faculty, there may also be established for graduate students specialized courses and schools.

Special "orders" of study and training include the following:

(a) Institutes for art instruction, consisting of:
1. Beginners' course in art, three years;
2. School of art, five years;
3. Institute of art, eight years;
4. Teacher-training course for design and applied art, two years;
5. Art lyceum, five years;
6. Academy of art, four years;
7. Conservatory of music, from six to ten years;
8. Academy of dramatic art, three years.

(b) Institutes for the instruction of women, consisting of:
1. Women's institute, three years;
2. Women's teacher training, two years.

(c) Courses for training skilled workers. . . .

The Elementary Order

IX.—[Describes the structure and functions of the nursery school (ages four to six), elementary school (ages six to nine), and labor school (ages nine to eleven).]

X.—The artisan school trains pupils from ages eleven to fourteen in the labor traditions of the Italian family. . . .

The Intermediate Order

XI.—The middle school, attended jointly by all those who intend to pursue studies on the superior order, inculcates the first essentials of humanistic culture for young people from the age of eleven to fourteen, according to a rigorous principle of selection. . . . In its programs, which are inspired by the most modern didactic principles, the teaching of Latin is the means for moral and mental training. Labor here will assume the form and method of productive labor.

XII.—The professional school is designed for young men from the age of eleven to fourteen who intend to prepare for the kinds of work typical of the great centers. . . . Labor, scientifically organized, has a preponderant part here.

XIII.—The technical school, lasting two years, complements the professional school by preparing students specifically for lesser positions and specialized work in the great industrial, commercial, and agricultural enterprises.

The Superior Order

XIV.—The classical lyceum, five years in length, integrates the teaching of ancient languages and literature with that of modern languages and literature, and perpetuates and revives the high humanistic tradition of our studies. . . . Scientific instruction will be included to the degree that this corresponds with the aims of the school.

XV.—The scientific lyceum, five years in length, associates classical traditions with the values of present-day life in the formation of a modern humanism. Scientific instruction, conducted with rigorous methodological order, is designed to develop habits of scientific and technical research; and, by means of labor, to bring about their practical application. Literary instruction will be carried out by methods that are appropriate to the goals of this school.

XVI.—The teacher-training institute, five years in length, prepares people to teach children. Its character is humanistic and professional combined. . . . A year of practice teaching [follows] four years of classroom work. . . .

XVII.—The technical-commercial institute, five years in length, looks after the training of young people for office work in public and private management. . . .

XVIII.—The professional institutes, four years in length, are divided into four types: the training of experts in the fields of agriculture, industry, land surveying, and nautical skills. . . .

THE UNIVERSITY ORDER

XIX.—The university's goal is to promote the progress of science in an order of high political and moral responsibility and to provide the necessary scientific training for carrying out professional work. Courses at the level of the graduate school will be strictly scientific. . . . Athletic and military training and labor service will also contribute to the education of the youth.

THE ORDER FOR INSTRUCTION IN THE ARTS

XX.—The figurative-art institutes bring intimately together in their programs the techniques of the applied arts and the principles of pure art. . . .

THE ORDER FOR GIRLS' SCHOOLS

XXI.—The destination and social mission of women, which are quite distinct in Fascist life, have as their foundation different and special educational institutes. The transformation of the coeducational schools will be brought about over a period of time as the new directions of feminine work become defined in the corporative order. The Order for Girls' Schools . . . will prepare [girls] spiritually for home management and for teaching in the nursery schools.

COURSES FOR TRAINING SKILLED WORKERS

XXII.—The courses for the training of skilled workers and the improvement of their skills have the aim of providing and enlarging the technical and productive capacity of the labor force with respect to the needs of the national economy in the sectors of agriculture, industry, commerce, credit, and insurance. The professional associations, one of whose principal duties is to provide specialized instruction for their personnel, will take steps directly to this end by means of appropriate agencies and under the over-all supervision of the Ministries of National Education and of Corporations. Courses for workers may also be instituted by the PNF and dependent organizations, by the Commissariat for War Production, by the Ministry of Agriculture and Forests, and other agencies.

TEACHERS

XXIII.—The training of teachers is the subject of special care and provisions. Vocational training, theoretical knowledge, and clarity of expression, whereby knowledge is acquired and transmitted, will be brought together and refined in experimental didactical centers, in educational laboratories and museums, in methodological institutes attached to the major universities, and in apprenticeship courses for the training of teaching assistants.

The method of competition for teaching positions will be determined according to the type of school, discipline, and location. . . .

EXAMINATIONS

XXIV.—In each order of schools those pupils who show sufficient achievement will be promoted to the classes above them. [This] is determined by the over-all judgment given in each subject by the instructors at the end of the term. At the completion of each course of study in the elementary, intermediate, superior, artistic, and girls' orders, the pupils must take a comprehensive examination (*esame di licenza*). The comprehensive examination in the superior order is a state examination, administered by a committee made up of the instructors from the particular school and with participation of two representatives from the Ministry. . . .

XXV.—[Describes the manner of promotion from one grade to another.]

THE NATIONAL AGENCY FOR INTERMEDIATE AND SUPERIOR EDUCATION

XXVI.—The National Agency for Intermediate and Superior Education, which is the agency for promoting, co-ordinating, and controlling all of the nonstate schools in these two orders, has the task of stimulating private initiative as well as that of the communes, provinces, and other bodies; of promoting the creation of schools that will respond to particular economic and cultural needs, restrain the migration of students into the cities, and ensure that these private and nonstate entities emulate the state schools in a salutary manner.

TEXTBOOKS

XXVII.—The State will provide appropriate textbooks for all of the schools in the elementary order. The textbooks of the intermediate and superior orders that provide the direct and immediate subject matter of their courses of study may not be printed without the prior approval of either the manuscript or the proofs by the Ministry of National Education.

THE SCHOOL YEAR

XXVIII.—The school year and the academic year are composed of periods of classes alternating with periods of vacation. During the vacation periods labor service will be assigned.

School hours may not exceed twenty-four per week in any school except in the university order and in the order for instruction in the arts. . . .

EDCUATIONAL ASSISTANCE

XXIX.—Measures for providing educational assistance will fulfill on the level of political and social solidarity the intimate collaboration that exists between the Party and the school.

5. Fascism, the Catholic Church, and the Jews

ONE OF the epochal events of the Fascist regime, and certainly its most enduring legacy, was the signing of the Lateran Pacts with the Holy See in 1929. These agreements were received enthusiastically by a large segment of the population who were relieved that after half a century of acrimony between Church and State, peace had at last been achieved, thanks to the Vatican's recognition of the unified Italian Kingdom. As has already been mentioned, Mussolini began to backtrack from his youthful anticlericalism even before the March on Rome, and his first speech as Prime Minister ended with an invocation for divine assistance. The Church, far more alarmed by political extremism on the left than on the right, made friendly overtures toward Mussolini's regime in 1923 by disavowing the anti-Fascist stance of Luigi Sturzo, secretary of the Catholic Popular party. Resigning his post, Sturzo went into exile, and the party rapidly disintegrated. His friend and associate, Alcide De Gasperi, was to be arrested by the Fascists and spend several months in jail in 1927 before papal intercession gained his release. He worked inconspicuously in the Vatican library for the next sixteen years.

Meanwhile Mussolini pushed ahead with plans to win over the Vatican. By agreeing to restore the crucifix to schools and courtrooms and to schedule Masses for public functions (to say nothing of his campaign against the Masonic Lodge), the *Duce* paved the way for the appointment in February, 1925, of a committee of laymen to review legislation affecting ecclesiastical affairs. Working quietly, this group presented a report at year's end. At the same time secret negotiations got under way outside Parliament to solve the "Roman Question." Despite occasional tension—such as the dispute between the Balilla youth organization and the 100,000 Catholic Boy Scouts (Esploratori Cattolici), which was resolved by virtually disbanding the latter in 1928—these negotiations went ahead fairly smoothly under the supervision of Cardinal Secretary of State Gasparri, Marchese Eugenio Pacelli, and Pius XI himself. Some of the final sessions took place at night in Mussolini's residence. At last the momentous agreements, which included a political treaty settling the Roman Question, a religious concordat, and a financial convention, were signed on February 11, 1929, by Cardinal Gasparri and Mussolini in the Lateran Palace. Seminarists intoning the "Te Deum" competed with Militiamen on the square in front who shrieked the Fascist cry "Eia, alalà!" Important provisions of the political treaty and the concordat are printed below.

Treaty Between the Holy See and Italy (February 11, 1929; Effective June 7, 1929)

. . . *Art. 1*—Italy recognizes and reaffirms the principle set forth in Art. 1 of the Constitution of the Kingdom of Italy of March 4, 1848, whereby the Roman Catholic and Apostolic Religion is the sole religion of the State.

Art. 2—Italy recognizes the sovereignty of the Holy See in the field of international relations as an attribute that pertains to the very nature of the Holy See, in conformity with its traditions and with the demands of its mission in the world.

Art. 3—Italy recognizes full possession and exclusive and absolute power and sovereign jurisdiction of the Holy See over the Vatican, as at present constituted, with all its appurtenances and endowments. Thus the Vatican City is established for the special purposes and with the provisions laid down in the present Treaty. The confines of the Vatican City are indicated on a plan which constitutes the first appendix to the present Treaty of which it forms an integral part. . . .

Art. 4—The sovereignty and exclusive jurisdiction which Italy recognizes on the part of the Holy See with regard to the State of the Vatican implies that there can be no interference on the part of the Italian Government therein, nor any other authority than that of the Holy See. . . .

Art. 6—Italy undertakes to furnish through agreement with the agencies concerned, assurances to the Vatican City of an adequate water supply within the territory.

It will also provide for communication with the Italian State Railways by constructing a railroad station within the Vatican City. . . .

It will provide moreover for the linking up, directly with other States also, of the telegraph, telephone, radio-telegraph, radio-telephone and postal services within the Vatican City. . . .

Art. 8—Italy, considering the person of the Sovereign Pontiff as sacred and inviolable, declares that any and every attempt against

SOURCE: *Treaty and Concordat Between the Holy See and Italy: Official Documents* (Washington: National Catholic Welfare Conference, 1929), pp. 37–51 *passim.* English translation of the official Italian text reprinted by courtesy of the United States Catholic Conference, Washington, D.C.

him, as well as any incitement to commit such, to be punishable by the same penalties as attempts against the person of the King or incitement to commit the same.

Public offenses or insults committed in Italian territory against the person of the Sovereign Pontiff, whether by deed or by spoken or written word, are punishable by the same penalties as similar offenses and injuries against the person of the King.

Art. 9—In conformity with the provisions of international law, all persons having a fixed residence within the State of the Vatican are subject to the sovereignty of the Holy See. . . .

Art. 10—Dignitaries of the Church and persons attached to the Pontifical Court, who will be designated in a list to be agreed upon by the High Contracting Parties, even when not citizens of the State of the Vatican, shall always and in every case, so far as Italy is concerned, be exempt from military service, from jury duty and from all services of a personal character. . . .

Ecclesiastics who, in the performance of the duties of their office, are occupied in the execution of the acts of the Holy See shall not be subjected on account of such execution to any hindrance, investigation or molestation on the part of the Italian authorities.

Every foreigner invested with ecclesiastical office in Rome shall enjoy the same personal guarantees as belong to Italian citizens by virtue of the laws of the Kingdom of Italy.

Art. 11—The central corporate entities of the Catholic Church are exempt from all interference on the part of the Italian State (except for the provisions of Italian law concerning the acquisitions of moral entities[1]) and also from expropriation with regard to real estate.

Art. 12—Italy recognizes the right of the Holy See to send and to receive diplomatic representatives according to the general provisions of international law. . . .

Art. 17—Contributions of whatever kind due to the Holy See from the other central organizations of the Catholic Church and from the organizations directly managed by the Holy See, even outside of Rome, as also those due to dignitaries, functionaries and employees, even when not fixed, beginning with the first of January, 1929, shall be exempt in Italian territory from any tax whatsoever on the part of the State or of any other entity. . . .

---

1. *I.e.*, incorporated charitable or educational bodies.—*Ed.*

Art. 19—Diplomatic representatives and envoys of the Holy See, diplomatic representatives and envoys of foreign nations to the Holy See, and Dignitaries of the Church coming from abroad directly to the State of the Vatican, if provided with passports issued by the countries from which they come and viséed by papal representatives abroad, may without any other formality proceed through Italian territory to the State of the Vatican. The same procedure will apply to these persons when, provided with a regular papal passport, they leave the State of the Vatican for abroad.

Art. 20—Merchandise coming from abroad and consigned to the State of the Vatican, or to institutions or offices of the Holy See which are located outside thereof, shall always be admitted at any point on the Italian frontier or at any port of the Kingdom to pass through Italian territory with full exemption from custom duties and intercommunal taxes. . . .

Art. 22—At the request of the Holy See and on delegation of power, which may be given by the Holy See either in single cases or permanently, Italy will provide within her own territory for the punishment of crimes committed within the State of the Vatican. When, however, an individual who has committed a crime therein takes refuge in Italian territory, he shall be dealt with forthwith according to the provisions of Italian law.

The Holy See will hand over to the Italian State individuals who have fled within the State of the Vatican charged with acts committed in Italian territory which are considered criminal by the laws of both States. . . .

Art. 23—For the execution within the Kingdom of Italy of sentences pronounced by tribunals of the State of the Vatican the principles of international law will be applied.

On the other hand, sentences and decisions pronounced by ecclesiastical authorities, which have to do with ecclesiastical or religious persons in spiritual or disciplinary matters, and which are officially communicated to the civil authorities, will have full juridical efficacy immediately in Italy even so far as the civil effects are concerned.

Art. 24—With regard to the sovereignty pertaining to it in the field of international relations, the Holy See declares that it wishes to remain and will remain extraneous to all temporal disputes between nations, and to international congresses convoked for the settlement of such disputes, unless the contending parties make a joint appeal to its mission of peace; nevertheless, it reserves the right in every case to exercise its moral and spiritual power.

In consequence of this declaration, the State of the Vatican will always and in every case be considered neutral and inviolable territory. . . .

Art. 26—The Holy See maintains that with the agreements signed today adequate assurance is guaranteed as far as is necessary for the said Holy See to provide, with due liberty and independence, for the pastoral regime of the Diocese of Rome and of the Catholic Church in Italy and in the world. The Holy See declares the "Roman Question" definitively and irrevocably settled and, therefore, eliminated; and recognizes the Kingdom of Italy under the dynasty of the House of Savoy with Rome as the Capital of the Italian State.

Italy, in turn, recognizes the State of the Vatican under the sovereignty of the Supreme Pontiff.

The Law of May 13, 1871, No. 214, is abrogated, as well as any other decree or decision contrary to the present Treaty.

Art. 27—The present Treaty will be submitted to the Sovereign Pontiff and to the King of Italy for ratification within four months from the date of signing and will become effective immediately on the exchange of ratifications.

Rome, February 11, 1929.

Signed: PIETRO Cardinale GASPARRI.

Signed: BENITO MUSSOLINI.

Concordat Between the Holy See and Italy
(*February 11, 1929*)

Art. 1—Italy, according to the terms of Art. 1 of the Treaty, guarantees to the Catholic Church free exercise of spiritual power, free and public exercise of worship, as well as jurisdiction in ecclesiastical matters, in conformity with the provisions of the present Concordat; and, where it shall be necessary for the carrying out of their spiritual ministry, grants to ecclesiastics protection on the part of its authorities.

SOURCE: *Treaty and Concordat Between the Holy See and Italy: Official Documents* (Washington: National Catholic Welfare Conference, 1929), pp. 59–82 *passim*. English translation of the official Italian text reprinted by courtesy of the United States Catholic Conference, Washington, D.C.

In consideration of the sacred character of the Eternal City, episcopal see of the Sovereign Pontiff, center of the Catholic world, and goal of pilgrimages, the Italian Government will take precautions to prevent the occurrence in Rome of everything that might be contrary to this sacred character.

Art. 2—The Holy See may communicate and correspond freely with the Bishops, the clergy and the whole Catholic world, without any interference on the part of the Italian Government.

Bishops, likewise, in everything that concerns their pastoral office, may communicate and correspond freely with their clergy and with all the Faithful. . . .

Art. 3—Students in theology, those preparing for the priesthood who are in the last two years of study preliminary to theology, and novices in religious institutes may, on their own request, put off from year to year, up to the age of twenty-six, the fulfillment of the obligations of military service.

Ordained clerics (*in sacris*) and religious who have taken their vows are exempt from military service except in case of general mobilization. . . .

However, even when general mobilization is ordered, priests who are entrusted with the care of souls are exempt from the obligation of answering to the call. . . .

Art. 4—Ecclesiastics and religious are exempt from jury duty.

Art. 5—No ecclesiastic may be employed or remain in the employment or service of the Italian State or of any of the public departments subordinate to the same without the express permission of his diocesan Bishop.

The revocation of this permission deprives the ecclesiastic of power to continue exercising the duty of office assumed.

In any case apostate priests or those who have incurred censure cannot be employed or retained in a teaching post, or in an office or an employment in which they are brought into immediate contact with the public. . . .

Art. 7—Ecclesiastics may not be requested by magistrates or other authorities to give information regarding persons or matters which may have come to their knowledge through the exercise of their sacred ministry. . . .

Art. 9—As a general rule, buildings open for worship are exempt from confiscation or occupation. . . .

Except in cases of urgent necessity, the police cannot in the exercise of their duties enter buildings used for worship without having given previous notice to the proper ecclesiastical authority. . . .

Art. 11—The State recognizes the holy days established by the Church. . . .

Art. 19—The selection of Archbishops and Bishops pertains to the Holy See. Before proceeding to the [appointment] of an Archbishop, a Bishop, or a Coadjutor with the right of succession, the Holy See will communicate the name of the person chosen to the Italian Government in order to be sure that the latter has no objection from a political standpoint. . . .

Art. 20—Bishops before taking possession of their dioceses shall take an oath of loyalty at the hands of the Head of the State according to the following formula:

"Before God on the Holy Gospels, I swear and promise, as becomes a Bishop, loyalty to the Italian State. I swear and promise to respect, and to make my clergy respect, the King and the Government established according to the constitutional laws of the State. I swear and promise, moreover, that I shall not participate in any agreement or take part in any discussion that might be injurious to the Italian State or detrimental to public order and that I shall not permit my clergy to take part in such. Being mindful of the welfare and of the interests of the Italian State, I shall endeavor to ward off any danger that may threaten it."

Art. 21—The awarding of ecclesiastical benefices pertains to ecclesiastical authority.

The competent ecclesiastical authority will communicate confidentially to the Italian Government the names of those who are to be invested with parochial benefices, and the investiture can have no effect until after thirty days from the date of the said communication. . . .

Art. 22—Ecclesiastics who are not Italian citizens cannot be appointed to Italian benefices. Moreover, the Bishops of the dioceses and the rectors of parishes must speak Italian. . . .

Art. 24—The *Exequatur*, the royal *Placet* and all imperial or royal appointments in the matter of filling benefices and ecclesiastical offices in the whole of Italy are abolished. . . .

Art. 28—In order that their consciences may be at ease, the Holy See will grant full condonation to all those who hold ecclesiastical property as a result of the Italian laws by which the patrimony of the Church was dispersed. . . .

Art. 29—The Italian State will reconsider its legislation dealing with matters ecclesiastical, for the purpose of changing and reorganizing it so as to bring it into harmony with the principles envisaged by the Treaty made with the Holy See and by the present Concordat. . . .

Art. 30—The management, both ordinary and extraordinary, of property belonging to any ecclesiastical institute or religious association whatsoever will be carried out under the supervision and control of the proper Church authorities without any interference on the part of the Italian State and without the obligation of converting the real estate into cash. . . .

Art. 34—The Italian State, desirous of restoring to the institution of marriage which is the foundation of the family, the dignity that belongs to it according to the Catholic traditions of its people, recognizes the civil effects of the sacrament of matrimony as administered according to the regulations of the Canon Law.

The banns of marriage as defined above will be published both in the parish church and in the city- or town-hall.

Immediately after the celebration of a marriage, the parish priest will explain to the married couple the civil effects of the marriage, reading the articles of the Civil Code which have to do with the rights and duties of husbands and wives and will make a record of the ceremony. Within five days he will send a complete copy of this record to the municipal building in order that it may be transcribed in the register of the civil authorities.

Questions having to do with the nullification of marriage and with the dispensation of a marriage "ratum et non consummatum" are reserved to the jurisdiction of ecclesiastical tribunals and courts. . . .

As regards cases of personal separation, the Holy See is willing that the same shall be judged by the civil judicial authority.

Art. 35—For the schools of secondary education maintained by ecclesiastical or religious organizations, the policy of state examinations remains in force, the candidates from these schools taking the examinations on exactly the same conditions as are prescribed for the candidates from schools maintained by the institutions of the Government.

Art. 36—Italy considers the teaching of Christian doctrine, according to the form handed down by Catholic tradition, as the foundation and capstone of public education. Therefore, Italy agrees that the religious instruction now given in the public elementary school shall be further developed in the secondary schools according to a program to be agreed upon by the Holy See and the State.

This instruction is to be given by teachers and professors who are priests or religious approved by ecclesiastical authority and who will be aided by lay teachers and professors holding for this purpose proper certificates of fitness and capacity, these certificates to be issued by the diocesan Bishop.

Revocation of the certificate by the Bishop immediately deprives the individual of the right to teach.

No texts will be adopted for this religious instruction in the public schools except such as are approved by ecclesiastical authority.

Art. 37—The directors of state associations for physical education, for premilitary instruction, as well as the directors of the Avanguardisti and the Balilla, in order to facilitate the religious instruction and care of the youth entrusted to their charge, will so arrange their programs that they will not interfere with the young people's fulfillment of their religious duties on Sundays and holy days of obligation.

The officials of the public schools will make similar provisions in the matter of arranging the classes to be held on holy days. . . .

Art. 43—The Italian State recognizes the auxiliary organizations of the "Azione Cattolica Italiana" inasmuch as these, according to the regulations of the Holy See, carry on their activities independently of all political parties and under the immediate direction of the Hierarchy of the Church for the teaching and practice of Catholic principles.

The Holy See takes occasion on the signing of the present Concordat to renew its prohibition to all the ecclesiastics and religious to enroll or take part in any political party.

Art. 44—If, in the future, any difficulty should arise with regard to the interpretation of the present Concordat, the Holy See and Italy will proceed with mutual understanding to an amicable solution.

Art. 45—The present Concordat will be effective upon the exchange of ratifications simultaneously with the Treaty made by the two High Contracting Parties by which the "Roman Question" is eliminated. . . .

Mussolini's star soared throughout the Catholic world. Humble Italian peasants shed their customary indifference for public affairs long enough to flock to church to pray for the pontiff who had "given back God to Italy and Italy to God." The reconciliation doubtless contributed to the *Duce*'s top-heavy triumph in the plebiscite of March 24, 1929. But news of the agreements shocked those laic foes of the dictatorship who had clung to the hope that the Church might throw its moral weight to their side of the struggle, or at least remain neutral. To them it seemed as if Pius XI overstepped himself on February 13, 1929, when he referred glowingly to the *Duce* as "a man . . . whom Providence has caused us to meet." During the spring, objections to ratification mounted from lay groups, while at the same time both the dictatorship and the Vatican indulged in harsh polemics, much to the bewilderment of outsiders.

The fears of a good many Fascists and other nationalists that the King would become the "Pope's altar boy," and the converse fears of Catholics that the Pope might end up the "King's chaplain" (to use Mussolini's flippant phrases) led to sharp, even brutal clarification by the *Duce* of the meaning of the pacts. On May 13 in a long speech in the new, hand-picked Chamber of Deputies he claimed state control over all education of youth. Finally he boasted of the "ethical character" of the Italian State, which "is Catholic but also Fascist, indeed above all else exclusively and essentially Fascist."[2]

The Pope lost no time in flatly rejecting many of these claims. He declared himself "intransigent about the Church's rights in the field of education," and he noted pointedly that "education for conquest" could only lead "to general conflagration." Harsh rebuttals and counterrebuttals were hurled by the spokesmen of the rival authoritarian institutions. On June 6, the eve of the date fixed for the exchange of ratifications, the Vatican published a long letter from the Pope to Cardinal Gasparri in which he refuted many of the interpretations set forth by Mussolini. The Holy Father had the better of the argument, and Mussolini was wise enough to recognize this. Next day, swallowing his irritation, he drove to the Vatican to exchange ratifications in a ceremony that was not only correct but even amicable.

Most Catholics seemed to console themselves with the hope that the *Duce*'s intentions were honorable and that, on balance, the Church had achieved most of its aims. As a result, civil authorities acceded to the desires of churchmen whenever these did not flout the interests of Fascism; by the same token, ecclesiastical authorities usually gave their *nihil obstat* to the works of Mussolini and prudently glossed over all but the most blatantly un-Christian aspects of Fascist doctrine and practice. Yet the liberal Irish Catholic scholar Daniel A. Binchy was correct when he wrote that the experiences with Fascist Italy and Nazi Germany during the 1930's eventually "led Pius XI, although by temperament inclined to sympathize with authoritarian government, to

2. Benito Mussolini, *Scritti e discorsi (1929–1931)* (Milan: Hoepli, 1934), VII, 34 ff.

recognize in modern dictatorships the most formidable danger to Christianity in our time."[3]

The basic difference between the would-be totalitarian Fascist state and the authoritarian Roman Catholic Church was clearly revealed in an acrimonious dispute that simmered along from 1929 until it erupted violently in the spring of 1931 over the status of the Catholic lay organization Azione Cattolica (Catholic Action). This new dispute was far more vehement than the one terminated by the Lateran Pacts. Catholic Action had become prominent in Italy once more when the Popular party disintegrated. In 1929 it possessed in Italy some 250 diocesan committees, 4,000 men's sections, and 5,000 Catholic youth and university clubs. Determined to control all mass organizations, Mussolini was extremely jealous of Catholic Action, which in many rural areas was stronger than his PNF. He therefore sought a pretext to eliminate it, even though Article 43 of the Concordat grudgingly recognized its independence. Among other things, he suddenly accused it in the spring of 1931 of harboring leaders of the outlawed Popular party and of carrying on social work in competition with Fascist syndical and welfare programs. There was some truth to these charges, for Catholic Action, though in no sense an organ of the Populars, did include within its ranks a great many veterans of the disbanded party, and its membership swelled considerably after 1929—a development that annoyed the *Duce*. Ramifications of the dispute extended into the university and youth organizations. The newly created Fascist University Groups (GUF) attacked the Italian Catholic University Federation (FUCI), and on May 30 the government suppressed the latter.

Meanwhile, the Vatican newspaper *L'Osservatore Romano* skirmished with Mussolini's *Popolo d'Italia* and chronicled many incidents in which the dictatorship had interfered forcibly with Catholic associations, seizing their publications, illegally "inspecting" them, and encouraging violence against individual members. Pius XI's growing displeasure with Fascist totalitarianism became more evident in public statements, including the encyclical *Quadragesimo anno*, issued on May 15, 1931, the fortieth anniversary of Leo XIII's *Rerum novarum*. In it he expressed grave fears about not only Marxism and unbridled laissez-faire capitalism but also the "exclusively bureaucratic and political character" of the new Fascist syndical and corporative organizations which risked "serving particular political aims rather than contributing to the initiation of a better social order." The encyclical made clear, however, that the Church's own system of corporativism was acceptable. *Quadragesimo anno* was to carry much weight with Portugal's dictator, Salazar, and other Catholic advocates of clerico-corporativist regimes. Key excerpts from this encyclical follow.

3. *Church and State in Fascist Italy* (London: Oxford University Press, 1941), pp. 219–220.

The Church and the Fascist-Type
Corporative State: Quadragesimo anno
(*May 15, 1931*)

81. Now this is the primary duty of the state and of all good citizens: to abolish conflict between classes with divergent interests, and thus foster and promote harmony between the various ranks of society.

82. The aim of social legislation must therefore be the re-establishment of vocational groups. . . .

85. . . . In these associations the common interests of the whole group must predominate; and among these interests the most important is the directing of the activities of the group to the common good. Regarding cases in which interests of employers and employees call for special care and protection against opposing interests, separate deliberation will take place in their respective assemblies and separate votes will be taken as the matter may require.

86. It is hardly necessary to note that what Leo XIII taught concerning the form of political government can, in due measure, be applied also to vocational groups. Here, too, men may choose whatever form they please, provided that both justice and the common good be taken into account. . . .

91. Within recent times, as all are aware, a special syndical and corporative organization has been inaugurated which, in view of the subject of the present Encyclical, demands of Us some mention and opportune comment.

92. The state here grants legal recognition to the syndicate or union, and thereby confers on it some of the features of a monopoly, for in virtue of this recognition, it alone can represent respec-

SOURCE: *Quadragesimo anno*, May 15, 1931, Encyclical Letter of His Holiness Pius XI on Reconstructing the Social Order and Perfecting It Conformably to the Precepts of the Gospel, in Commemoration of the Fortieth Anniversary of the Encyclical *Rerum novarum*, printed in Oswald von Nell-Breuning, S.J., *Reorganization of Social Economy: The Social Encyclicals Developed and Explained* (Milwaukee: Bruce Publ. Co., 1936–37), pp. 423–426 *passim*. Reproduced by permission of Bruce Publishing Company.

tively workingmen and employers, and it alone can conclude labor contracts and labor agreements. Affiliation to the syndicate is optional for everyone; but in this sense only can the syndical organization be said to be free, since the contribution to the union and other special taxes are obligatory for all who belong to a given branch, whether workingmen or employers, and the labor-contracts drawn up by the legal syndicate are likewise obligatory. It is true that it has been authoritatively declared that the legal syndicate does not exclude the existence of unrecognized trade associations.

93. The corporations are composed of representatives of the unions of workingmen and employers of the same trade or profession, and as true and genuine organs and institutions of the state, they direct and co-ordinate the activities of the unions in all matters of common interest.

94. Strikes and lockouts are forbidden. If the contending parties cannot come to an agreement, public authority intervenes.

95. Little reflection is required to perceive the advantage of the institution thus summarily described: peaceful collaboration of the classes, repression of socialist organizations and efforts, the moderating influence of a special ministry.

But in order to overlook nothing in a matter of such importance, and in the light of the general principles stated above, as well as of that which We are now about to formulate, We feel bound to add that to Our knowledge there are some who fear that the state is substituting itself in the place of private initiative, instead of limiting to necessary and sufficient help and assistance. It is feared that the new syndical and corporative institution possesses an excessively bureaucratic and political character, and that, notwithstanding the general advantages referred to above, it risks serving particular political aims rather than contributing to the initiation of a better social order.

96. We believe that to attain this last-named lofty purpose for the true and permanent advantage of the commonwealth, there is need before and above all else of the blessing of God, and, in the second place, of the co-operation of all men of good will. We believe, moreover, as a necessary consequence, that the end intended will be the more certainly attained, the greater the contribution furnished by men of technical, commercial, and social competence, and, more still, by Catholic principles and their application. We look for this contribution, not only to Catholic Action

(which has no intention of displaying any strictly syndical or political activities), but to Our sons, whom Catholic Action imbues with these principles and trains for the Apostolate under the guidance and direction of the Church, of the Church, We say, which in the above-mentioned sphere, as in all others where moral questions are discussed and regulated, cannot forget or neglect its mandate as custodian and teacher, given it by God. . . .

The growing friction between Pius XI and Mussolini's regime reached its climax on June 29, 1931, when the pontiff issued the encyclical *Non abbiamo bisogno* ("We have no need"), written in vigorous Italian rather than in Latin in order to emphasize its urgency. He took elaborate precautions to evade Fascist postal censorship; indeed, Mgr. Francis Spellman of New York flew several hundred copies directly from Vatican City to Paris. The text came out in newspapers abroad before Italians read it on July 5 in *L'Osservatore Romano* (which, incidentally, went on sale in the kiosks five hours earlier than usual and thus escaped confiscation until the issue was almost exhausted). The effect was electrifying. The Pope had flatly rejected the charge that Catholic Action leaders were chiefly directors of the defunct Popular party, and he complained bitterly about the Fascists' manner of dissolving Catholic organizations.

Pius XI on Catholic Action:
Non abbiamo bisogno
(June 29, 1931)

We must needs speak to you, Venerable Brethren, about events which have recently occurred in this, Our Episcopal City of Rome, and throughout Italy, that is to say, in the very territory of which We are Primate—events which have had such a vast and such a strong repercussion everywhere, conspicuously so in all of the dioceses of Italy and throughout the Catholic World.

These occurrences are summarized in a very few and very sad words. There has been an attempt made to strike unto death that which was and that which always will be dearest to Our heart as Father and as Shepherd of Souls; and We can, We even must,

SOURCE: "Encyclical of Pope Pius XI on Catholic Action," in *Sixteen Encyclicals of His Holiness Pope Pius XI, 1926–1937* (Washington, D. C.: National Catholic Welfare Conference, 1938), pp. 1, 7–8, 15, 21–22, 24–25, 27, 30–31. Reprinted by courtesy of the United States Catholic Conference, Washington, D.C.

subjoin "and the way in which it was done offends Us still more." . . .

Already on several occasions, Venerable Brethren, in the most solemn and explicit manner and assuming entire responsibility for what We were saying, We have protested against the campaign of false and unjust accusations which preceded the disbanding of the associations of the young people and of the university students affiliated with Catholic Action. It was a disbanding which was carried out in a way and with the use of tactics which would give the impression that action was being taken against a vast and dangerous organization of criminals. And the proceedings were directed against young men and young women who are certainly some of the best among the good and concerning whom We are happy and paternally proud to pay them tribute still once more. It is noteworthy that even among the officers of the law charged to carry out these orders of suppression, there were many who were ill at ease and showed by their expressions and courtesies that they were almost asking pardon for doing that which they had been commanded. We have appreciated the delicate feelings of these officers, and We have reserved for them a special blessing.

However, in sad contrast to the manner of acting of these officials, there were how many acts of mistreatment and of violence, extending even to the striking of blows and the drawing of blood! How many insults in the press, how many injurious words and acts against things and persons, not excluding Ourself, preceded, accompanied and followed the carrying into effect of this lightning-like police order which very frequently, either through ignorance or malicious zeal, was extended to include associations and organizations not contemplated in the orders of the superiors, such as the oratories of the little ones and the sodalities of the Children of Mary. And all of this sad accompaniment of irreverences and of violences took place in the presence of and with the participation of members of a political party some of whom were in uniform, and was carried into effect with such a unison of action throughout all Italy and with such a passive acquiescence on the part of the civil authorities and the police as to make one necessarily think of some uniform directions received from some high authority. It is very easy to admit, and it was also equally easy to have foreseen, that the limits of these directions could and would have almost necessarily been exceeded. . . . We cannot—We,

Church, religious, faithful Catholics (and not alone We)—We cannot be grateful to one who, after putting out of existence socialism and anti-religious organizations (Our enemies and not alone Ours), has permitted them to be so generally readmitted, as all see and deplore, and has made them even more strong and dangerous inasmuch as they are now hidden and also protected by their new uniform. . . .

And here We find Ourselves in the presence of a contract between authentic affirmations on the one hand and not less authentic facts on the other hand, which reveal, without the slightest possibility of doubt, the proposal, already in great part actually put into effect, to monopolize completely the young, from the tenderest years up to manhood and womanhood, and all for the exclusive advantage of a party, of a regime based on ideology which clearly resolves itself into a true and real pagan worship of the state, which is no less in contrast with the natural rights of the family than it is in contradiction to the supernatural rights of the Church. To propose and promote such a monopoly, to persecute for this reason Catholic Action, as has been done for some time more or less openly or under cover, to reach this end by striking Catholic Action in the way that has recently occurred, is truly and actually to prevent children from going to Jesus Christ, since it impedes them from going to His Church and even arrives at the point of snatching them with violence from the bosom of both, because where the Church is, there is Jesus Christ. . . .

A conception of the state which makes the young generations belong entirely to it without any exception from the tenderest years up to adult life cannot be reconciled by a Catholic with the Catholic doctrine nor can it be reconciled with the natural right of the family. It is not possible for a Catholic to reconcile with Catholic doctrine the pretense that the Church and the Pope must limit themselves to the external practices of religion, such as Mass and the Sacraments, and then to say that the rest of education belongs to the state. . . .

With everything that We have said up to the present, We have not said that We wished to condemn the party as such. We have intended to point out and to condemn that much in the program and in the action of the party which We have seen and have understood to be contrary to Catholic doctrine and the Catholic practice and therefore irreconcilable with the name and with the profession of Catholics. And in doing this, We have fulfilled a precious duty of Our Episcopal ministry toward Our dear sons who are members of the party, so that they can rest tranquil with the proper consciences of Catholics.

We believe, then, that We have thus at the same time accomplished a good work for the party itself, because what interest and success can the party have in a Catholic country like Italy in maintaining in its program ideas and maxims and practices which cannot be reconciled with a Catholic conscience? . . .

You Bishops of Italy know that no mortal man—not even the head of a state or of a government—but the Holy Ghost—has placed you there in places which Peter assigned to you to rule the Church of God. These and so many other holy and sublime things that concern you, Venerable Brethren, are evidently ignored or forgotten by him who thinks of you and calls you, Bishops of Italy, "Officials of the State," from which the very formula of the oath, which it is necessary for you to make to the sovereign, clearly distinguishes and separates you, for the oath especially states, "as is convenient for a Catholic bishop." . . .

Everything is definitely promised in answer to prayer. . . .

And since from so many prayers We must hope for everything, and since everything is possible to that God Who has promised everything in answer to prayer, We have confident hope that He will illumine minds to Truth and turn wills to Good, so that the Church of God, which wishes nothing from the state that belongs to the competence of the state, will cease to be asked for that which is the Church's competence—the education and the Christian formation of youth—and this not through human favor, but by Divine mandate, and that which therefore she always asks and will always ask with an insistence and an intransigeance which cannot cease or waver because it does not come from human desire or design, or from human ideas, changeable in different times and places and circumstances, but from the Divine and inviolable disposition.

On July 9, 1931, the Fascist party declared that participation in Catholic Action was incompatible with party membership; whereupon thousands resigned from the religious society. On the other side of the ledger, many Catholic Actionists turned in their PNF cards. The two organizations sparred for another month or so before reaching a shaky truce on September 2. This came in the wake of discreet negotiations by Fr. Pietro Tacchi-Venturi, S.J., and after Mussolini agreed to shove aside two of his most vocal critics of Catholic Action (PNF Secretary Giovanni Giuriati and Carlo Scorza). The *Duce* was disturbed by foreign criticism too and had no desire to bring about an Italian *Kulturkampf*.

The chief terms of the compromise were that Catholic Action was to be diocesan (not national) in character and under direct control of the bishops (rather than under officers elected by the members), who would not select its officers from among those who had belonged to "parties hostile to the regime"; that the professional sections were to have no syndical functions; and that youth organizations were to stay out of sports. Superficially it seemed as if the dictatorship had triumphed, but the Church could console itself that despite decentralization, the society survived and remained independent. Both parties greeted the settlement with unfeigned relief. To demonstrate his satisfaction, Mussolini paid an official call to the Holy Father on the third anniversary of the Lateran Pacts; they conversed for more than an hour. Next month he had the coveted Collar of the Annunciation bestowed upon Eugenio Cardinal Pacelli (the future Pius XII).

Anti-Semitism did not become a doctrinal part of Italian Fascism until 1938. In earlier years Mussolini had often expressed disgust for Hitler's racism, and certainly numerous Jews had been conspicuous in the Fascist party from the outset. Nor was anti-Semitism a feature of Italian life in general in modern times. The 56,000 native members of Italy's 26 autonomous Jewish "communities" in 1937 were well assimilated in the nation's public and cultural life. The arrival of several thousand refugees from Germany, Austria, and Czechoslovakia in the late 1930's scarcely posed a problem.

What, then, were the reasons for the sudden about-face by Mussolini? To some extent, the new racist program may have been stimulated by a measure of "Social Darwinism" that was expressed by certain propagandists during the conquest of Ethiopia. But the chief consideration was Italy's growing ideological tie with Nazi Germany after the announcement of the Axis in the autumn of 1936 and Germany's annexation of Austria early in 1938, which brought Hitler's Reich to the Brenner Pass. Prodded by such racist fanatics as Giuseppe Preziosi and Roberto Farinacci, Mussolini gave the go-ahead to racism in Italy on July 14, 1938, when a curious "Manifesto of the Racist Scientists" was published in the newspapers, setting forth ten allegedly scientific bases for an "Aryan" racial policy in Italy. It was backed by an anonymous group of university professors. Blatantly anti-Semitic propaganda now began to be published in a new periodical, *Difesa della razza* (Defense of the Race). The text of the racist manifesto follows:

Manifesto of the Racist Scientists
(July 14, 1938)

1. *Human races exist.* That human races exist is no longer an abstraction in our mind, but corresponds to a phenomenal and material reality that is perceptible through our senses. Almost always this reality is represented by imposing masses of millions of men possessing similar inherited physical and psychological characteristics that will be passed on to the next generation. To say that human races exists does not mean, a priori, that there are superior and inferior human races, but only that there are different human races.

2. *Great races and little races exist.* One must not only admit the existence of major, systematic groups commonly called races and categorized by certain characteristics; one must also admit the existence of minor, systematic groups (as, for example, the Nordics, the Mediterraneans, the Dinarics, etc.), characterized by a larger number of common features. From the biological standpoint, these groups constitute true races, the existence of which is self-evident.

3. *The concept of race is a purely biological one.* It is therefore based on considerations other than the concepts of peoples and nations, which are founded essentially on historic, linguistic, and religious considerations. However, the root of differences among peoples and nations is to be found in differences of race. If Italians differ from Frenchmen, Germans, Turks, Greeks, etc., this is not just because they possess a different language and different history, but because their racial development is different. There have been shifting relationships among the different races that from very ancient times have produced the various peoples. Thus, in some instances, one race has exercised absolute dominion over others; in some instances they have all become harmoniously fused; and in other instances there continue to be different races that are entirely unamalgamated.

4. *The people of present-day Italy are of Aryan origin and their*

SOURCE: Published in *Il Giornale d'Italia* (Rome) and other Italian newspapers, July 14, 1938, and reprinted in the appendix of Renzo De Felice, *Storia degli ebrei italiani sotto il fascismo* (Turin: Giulio Einaudi Editore, 1961), pp. 611–612. By permission of Giulio Einaudi Editore. My translation.

civilization is Aryan. The people of Aryan civilization have inhabited our peninsula for several millennia. Very little has endured
of the civilization of the pre-Aryan peoples. The origin of present-
day Italians can be traced back primarily to elements of those same
races that have constituted and still constitute the perennially living
tissue of Europe.

5. *It is a legend that great masses of men were transplanted in
historic times.* After the invasion of the Lombards, Italy experienced no other significant influx of people capable of influencing
the racial physiognomy of the nation. From this fact we may draw
the conclusion that, whereas the racial composition of other European nations has varied notably even in modern times, the racial
composition of present-day Italy, if examined in broad outline, is
the same as it was a thousand years ago. Thus, the absolute majority of our present 44 million Italians are descendants of families
that have been inhabiting Italy for a millennium.

6. *A pure "Italian race" is already in existence.* This pronouncement does not rest on a confusion of the biological concept of race
with the historic and linguistic concept of people and nations, but
on the very pure blood tie that unites present-day Italians with the
generations that have inhabited Italy for thousands of years. This
ancient purity of blood is the Italian nation's greatest title of
nobility.

7. *It is time for Italians frankly to proclaim themselves to be
racists.* It is on the basis of racism that all the work of the Regime
in Italy has thus far been accomplished. In the speeches of the
Head of the Government there have always been very frequent
references to the concepts of race. The question of racism in Italy
must be considered from a strictly biological standpoint, with no
philosophical or religious overtones. The concept of racism in Italy
must be essentially Italian, and its thrust is Aryan and Nordic. This
does not mean, however, the introduction into Italy of theories of
German racism as they now exist, nor does it mean that Italians and
Scandinavians are the same thing. It means only that Italians should
recognize a physical, and especially a psychological, model of the
human race, a model that because of its purely European characteristics is entirely different from all the non-European races. This
means elevating the Italians to an ideal plane so that they will have
greater self-consciousness and responsibility.

8. *It is necessary to draw a neat distinction between the Mediterraneans of Europe (Western) on the one hand, and Orientals*

and Africans on the other. One must regard as most dangerous those theories that argue in favor of an African origin for several European peoples, and that would include even the Semitic and Hamitic peoples in one common Mediterranean race by postulating relations and ideological sympathies that are absolutely inadmissible.

9. *The Jews do not belong to the Italian race.* In general, nothing has remained of the Semites who during the course of the centuries landed on the sacred soil of our fatherland. Even the Arab occupation of Sicily has left nothing apart from the memory of certain names; and, in any case, the process of assimilation was always very rapid in Italy. The Jews represent the only people that have never been assimilated in Italy, and that is because they are made up of non-European racial elements, entirely different from the elements that gave rise to the Italians.

10. *The purely European physical and psychological character-istics of the Italians must not be altered in any way.* Marriage is admissible only within the context of the European races; and in these cases one cannot speak of outright hybridism, as these races belong to a common stock that differs only in certain character-istics while being quite the same in a great many others. The purely European character of the Italians will become altered if crossed with any non-European race whatsoever that serves as a trans-mitter of any civilization differing from the Aryans' millenary civilization.

Fascist Italy's sudden shift toward anti-Semitism brought on a new clash with Pius XI. In 1937 the pontiff had issued the encyclical *Mit brennender Sorge,* expressing deep sorrow over Hitler's racist pro-gram, and on occasion he had expressed relief that Italy was engaging in no persecution of this kind. One can imagine his dismay, then, when he read the racist manifesto of July 14, 1938. He censured these heresies immediately and unequivocally. Anti-Semitism, by its denial of the Fatherhood of God and the brotherhood of man, struck at the very roots of Christianity. "If there is anything worse than the various theories of racialism and nationalism, it is the spirit that dictates them," he declared on July 21. Then he infuriated Mussolini by taunting him over adopting policies that deliberately imitated Nazi Germany and were in direct violation of the noblest traditions of the Roman Empire which he supposedly was anxious to restore. The *Duce* was even more furibund when the Pope bluntly explained to Belgian pilgrims on September 3, "Spiritually we are Jews."[4] Mussolini's police sought to

4. Daniel Binchy, *Church and State in Fascist Italy* (London: Oxford University Press, 1941), pp. 615–617.

confiscate several issues of *L'Osservatore Romano* and the Jesuit periodical *Civiltà Cattolica* in the midst of these recriminations. Then, on September 18, in a speech in Trieste, Mussolini made a vigorous pronouncement on the Jewish question.

Mussolini's Defense of Racist Policy
(*Trieste, September 18, 1938*)

. . . With respect to domestic affairs, the burning question of the moment is the racial problem. In this sphere, too, we shall adopt the necessary solutions. Those who try to make out that we have simply imitated, or worse, that we have been obedient to suggestions, are poor fools whom we don't know whether to pity or despise.

The racial problem has not broken out suddenly, as is thought by those people who are accustomed to sudden awakenings because they are used to long, sluggish slumbers. It is related to our conquest of the Empire; for history teaches that empires are won by arms, but held by prestige. And prestige demands a clear-cut racial consciousness which is based not only on difference but on the most definite superiority.

The Jewish problem is thus merely one aspect of this phenomenon. Our position has been determined by these incontestable considerations of fact. In spite of our policy, world Jewry for the last sixteen years has been an irreconcilable enemy of Fascism. In Italy our policy has resulted in a veritable race on the part of Semitic elements to assault our ship of state.

Nevertheless, Jews possessing Italian citizenship who have attained indisputable military or civil merits in the eyes of Italy and the regime will find understanding and justice. As for the others, a policy of segregation will be followed.

In the end, the world will perhaps be more astonished by our generosity than by our rigor; unless the Jews both abroad and here at home, and especially their new and unexpected friends who defend them from too many professorial positions, compel us to change our course radically. . . .

Despite some resistance within the Fascist Grand Council from Giuseppe Bottai, a decree-law for the "Defense of the Italian Race" was announced on November 17, 1938.

SOURCE: *Il Popolo d'Italia* (Milan), No. 261 (Sept. 19, 1938). My translation.

Provisions for the Defense of the Italian Race
(*November 17, 1938*)

CHAPTER ONE: PROVISIONS RELATING TO MARRIAGES

Art. 1—Marriage of an Italian citizen of Aryan race to a person belonging to another race is prohibited.

Marriage contracted in violation of such prohibition is null and void.

Art. 2—In view of the prohibition set forth in Art. 1, the marriage of an Italian citizen to a person of foreign nationality shall require the prior consent of the Minister of Interior.

Violators are subject to imprisonment up to three months and a fine of up to 10,000 lire.

Art. 3—In view of the prohibition set forth in Art. 1, employees of the civil and military administrations of the State, of the various organizations of the National Fascist Party or those controlled by it, of the administration of the provinces, communes, parastatal bodies, syndical associations, and related agencies may not contract marriage with persons of foreign nationality.

Except when the gravity of the case requires the application of the penalties set forth in Art. 2, violation of the above-mentioned prohibition will result in the loss of one's post of employment and of seniority.

Art. 4—With respect to the application of Articles 2 and 3, non-native-born Italians shall not be considered foreigners.

Art. 5—Upon a request to issue marriage banns, the official of the civil state is required to ascertain, independently of the statements of the parties involved, the racial and citizenship status of both applicants.

Under the circumstances envisaged in Art. 1, he shall proceed neither to issue marriage banns nor to perform the marriage.

Any official of the civil state who violates the provision of the present article may be punished by a fine ranging from 500 to 5,000 lire.

Art. 6—A marriage performed in violation of Art. 1 shall have no

SOURCE: Royal Decree-Law No. 1728, November 17, 1938-XVII, published in *Gazzetta Ufficiale*, No. 264 (Nov. 19, 1938). My translation.

civil legality, and therefore shall not be entered in the public registers. . . .

Violators may be punished by a fine ranging from 500 to 5,000 lire.

Art. 7—The official of the civil state who has proceeded to transcribe the relative documents pertaining to a marriage performed in violation of the provisions set forth in Art. 2 is required to make an immediate report of this fact to the competent authorities.

CHAPTER TWO: ON MEMBERS OF THE JEWISH RACE

Art. 8—For all legal purposes:

(a) A person is a member of the Jewish race if born of parents both of whom are of the Jewish race, even if he belongs to a religion other than Judaism;

(b) A person shall be considered to be a member of the Jewish race if he is born of parents one of whom is of the Jewish race and the other of foreign nationality;

(c) A person shall be considered to be a member of the Jewish race if born of a mother of the Jewish race and of an unknown father;

(d) A person shall be considered to be a member of the Jewish race if he subscribes to the Jewish religion, even if he is born of parents of Italian nationality and only one of them is of the Jewish race; or if he is in any way enrolled as a member of a Jewish community; or if he has in any other fashion made manifestations of Jewishness.

A person born of parents of Italian nationality only one of whom is of the Jewish race, and who belonged to a religion other than Judaism as of October 1, 1938-XVI, is not to be considered to be of the Jewish race.

Art. 9—Membership in the Jewish race must be declared and entered in the public registers. All extracts from these registers and relative certificates which pertain to members of the Jewish race must make explicit mention of such entry. Similar mention must be included in the documents pertaining to exemptions or authorizations by the public authorities.

Violators of the provisions of the present article are to be punished by a fine of up to 2,000 lire.

Art. 10—Italian citizens of the Jewish race may not:

(a) Render military service in time of either peace or war;

(b) Exercise the functions of tutor or custodian of minors or handicapped persons not of the Jewish race;

(c) Be owners or managers in any fashion of enterprises that are declared to be related to the national defense . . . ; or of enterprises of any nature that employ more than one hundred people; nor be assigned managerial functions in said enterprise, nor assume in any manner the offices of administrator or auditor;

(d) Be the owners of lands which altogether have an appraised valuation in excess of 5,000 lire;

(e) Be owners of urban buildings which altogether have a tax value greater than 20,000 lire. Buildings for which a schedule of taxes has not been prepared will have this established on the basis of investigations carried out for the purpose of applying the extraordinary tax on real estate property as set forth in Royal Decree-Law No. 1743 of October 5, 1936-XIV.

On the proposal of the Minister of Finance and with the concurrence of the Ministers of Interior, Grace and Justice, Corporations, and Foreign Exchange, a royal decree will specify the regulations for carrying out the provisions set forth above in letters (c), (d), and (e).

Art. 11—A parent who is of the Jewish race may be deprived of his parental authority over his children if they belong to a different religion from Judaism and if it is shown that he is imparting to them an education that does not correspond to their religious principles or to national ends.

Art. 12—Members of the Jewish race may not employ Italian citizens of the Aryan race in their own households as servants.

Violators are to be punished by a fine of from 1,000 to 5,000 lire.

Art. 13—The following agencies may not employ persons of the Jewish race:

(a) Civil and military administrations of the State;

(b) The National Fascist Party and the organizations subordinate to it or under its control;

(c) The administrations of provinces, communes, public institutions of assistance and welfare, and those incorporated bodies, institutes, and enterprises, including those of transportation, administered or supported with the help of the provinces, communes, public institutions of assistance and welfare, or their trusts;

(d) The administrations of municipal enterprises;

(e) The administrations of parastatal incorporated entities, however they may be formed or labeled, of National *Opere*, of the various syndical associations and collateral bodies, and, in general, of all incorporated bodies and institutes of public law, even those with autonomous structures, which are subject to either inspection or control by the State, or to whose maintenance the State provides contributions of a continuing sort;

(f) The administrations of those enterprises auxiliary or directly subordinate to the incorporated entities referred to in letter (e) above; or those which derive from it in major degree the necessary means for attaining their specific goals; or corporations whose capital is provided at least in half by State participation;

(g) The administrations of banks of national scope;

(h) The administrations of the private insurance companies.

Art. 14—The Minister of Interior, upon documented request of the interested parties, may in individual cases declare the provisions of Articles 10 and 11, as well as letter (h) of Article 13, inapplicable in the cases of:

(a) Members of families of those who fell in the Libyan War, the World War, the Ethiopian War, and the Spanish Civil War, and of those who fell in the Fascist cause;

(b) Persons who meet one of the following conditions:

1. Persons who were mutilated, disabled, or wounded, war volunteers, and recipients of decorations for valor in the Libyan War, World War, Ethiopian War, and Spanish Civil War;

2. Combatants in the Libyan War, World War, Ethiopan War, and Spanish Civil War who have received at least the War Cross for Merit;

3. Persons who were mutilated, disabled, or wounded in the Fascist cause;

4. Members of the National Fascist Party in the years 1919, 1920, 1921, 1922, and the second half of 1924;

5. Fiumean legionaries;

6. Persons who have earned exceptional recognition, as determined by Art. 16.

In the cases envisaged under letter (b) above, the benefit may also be extended to members of the family of the persons listed thereunder, even if they are deceased.

The interested parties may request that the decision handed down by the Minister of Interior be entered in the public registers.

The decision of the Minister of Interior is not subject to any gravamen, either of an administrative or of a jurisdictional nature.

Art. 15—With respect to the application of Art. 14, in addition to the spouse, a family shall be considered to include ancestors and descendants up to the second degree.

Art. 16—In order to evaluate the special merits referred to above in Art. 14, (b), number (6), there shall be established in the Ministry of Interior a committee made up of the Undersecretary of State for Interior (who will preside), a Vice-Secretary of the National Fascist Party, and the Chief of Staff of the Volunteer Militia of National Security.

Art. 17—Foreign Jews may not establish permanent residence in the Kingdom, Libya, or Aegean possessions.

CHAPTER THREE: TEMPORARY AND FINAL PROVISIONS

Art. 18—For a period of three months from the time the present decree goes into effect, the Minister of Interior is empowered, after consulting the appropriate administration, to exempt in special cases from the prohibition set forth in Art. 3 those employees who intend to contract marriage with a foreigner of the Aryan race.

Art. 19—With respect to the application of Art. 9, whoever finds himself in the conditions set forth under Art. 8 must report this to the office of the civil state of the commune of residence within 90 days from the date the present decree goes into effect.

Whoever fails to fulfill such obligation within the prescribed time, or furnishes inexact or incomplete data, will be punished by imprisonment up to one month and a fine of up to 3,000 lire.

Art. 20—Employees of the agencies mentioned in Art. 13 who are members of the Jewish race shall be discharged from service within a space of three months from the date the present decree goes into effect.

Art. 21—Regular employees of the State who are discharged from service in accordance with Art. 20 are permitted to claim the retirement benefits due them. . . .

Art. 22—Insofar as they are applicable, the provisions referred to in Art. 21 are extended to the incorporated entities mentioned in Art. 13, letters (b), (c), (d), (e), (f), (g), and (h). . . .

Art. 23—No matter how they were made, all concessions of Italian citizenship to foreign Jews after January 1, 1919, are revoked in every way.

Art. 24—Foreign Jews and those to whom Art. 23 applies who began their sojourn in the Kingdom, Libya, or the Aegean possessions after January 1, 1919, must leave the territory . . . by March 12, 1939-XVII. . . .

Art. 25—The provisions in Art. 24 shall not apply to Jews of foreign nationality who, prior to October 1, 1938-XVI:

    (a) were over sixty-five years of age;

    (b) contracted marriage with persons of Italian citizenship. . . .

Art. 26—The questions relative to the application of the present decree will be resolved in individual cases by the Minister of Interior after consulting those Ministers who may also be affected and receiving the prior opinion of a committee appointed by him. . . .

Art. 27—Nothing new is introduced with regard to public worship and activities by Jewish communities according to existing laws, except for modifications that may become necessary in order to coordinate these laws with the provisions of the present decree.

Art. 28—Any disposition that is contrary to . . . the present decree is hereby abrogated.

Art. 29—The Government of the King is authorized to issue the necessary provisions for the execution of the present decree. . . .

On November 15 another decree-law provided for the exclusion of all persons of the Jewish race from "any office or employment in schools of any kind or grade" attended by Italian students. An analogous measure applied to Jewish membership in educational and academic associations, and to enrollment in schools "attended by Italian students." An exception was made, however, for "students of the Jewish race who professed the Catholic religion": these could be registered in Catholic-sponsored elementary and secondary schools. Moreover, Jewish congregations could establish their own elementary and secondary schools, and Jews were permitted to be enrolled in "universities or institutes of higher education of the Kingdom . . . on a temporary basis." On December 22 a decree-law called for the dismissal of all Jews from the Italian armed forces and the Fascist Militia. But a touch of humanity permitted officers and noncommissioned officers who were so dismissed to retain their uniforms; the officers could also continue to use the title of their rank. In addition, certain provisions were made for pensions. Finally, over the protest of Pius XI, who announced that it was a violation of the Lateran Pacts, Mussolini forbade marriage between Jews and Gentiles. At least in comparison to those who found themselves under the Nazi heel, the Jews in Italy managed to get along tolerably well until 1943, thanks to the good will of most of the citizenry and the discreet assistance given by the Church. After the Nazis seized control of northern Italy in September,

1943, however, the plight of the Jews became desperate. Some 9,000 lost their lives from then until the liberation in 1945.

We know from the diary of Mussolini's son-in-law and Foreign Minister, Count Ciano, that because of the renewed tension with the Vatican, Fascist circles were worried about a speech Pius XI planned to deliver on February 11, 1939. Unhappily, the pontiff died the day before. The *Duce* tried in vain to obtain a copy of the undelivered speech. Twenty years went by before it was made public. Actually there was nothing explosive in it, but it openly deplored the persecution of the Church in Germany and contained some barbed references to Mussolini's regime. The speech advised Italian bishops to "note well not to forget that very often there are observers or informers (you can call them spies and you will be telling the truth) who, because of their own zeal, or for a task entrusted to them, listen to you in order to denounce you although, of course, they have not understood the slightest thing you have said, and if need be, will have understood the opposite."[5]

On March 2, 1939, Cardinal Pacelli was elected Pope, as Pius XII. Of aristocratic birth and manner, the new pontiff was a Roman of the Romans, far more suave and cautious than either his predecessor or his still more forthright successor, John XXIII. He made it clear that he intended to follow a more conciliatory policy toward Germany and Italy than had Pius XI. He forestalled a new clash with Mussolini in the spring of 1939 by bringing the terms of the Catholic Action compromise to their logical conclusion—abolishing the last vestiges of curial supervision and substituting a three-man commission composed of members of the diocesan hierarchy.

During and after the Second World War Pius XII took pride in being called the "Pope of Peace." Unquestionably he tried to prevent war in 1939, and failing that, to keep Italy neutral. But to do this he was prepared to renew the appeasement policies that had characterized diplomacy in the pre-Munich era. More recently Pius XII has come to be criticized as the "Pope of Silence" as regards the apportionment of responsibility for the war. For many years he had displayed considerable sympathy for the Italian variety of fascism—in contrast to his unbending hostility to the Communist dictatorship in Russsia and his irritation with Hitler's rule in Germany. But in the course of the conflict, and especially after the turn of the military tide against the Axis, Pius XII became visibly disenchanted with Mussolini's regime. For several months before the *coup d'état* of July 25, 1943, the Vatican sought to build up the "dyarchy" by showing good will to the House of Savoy. In the new era that was emerging, Mussolini's type of regime no longer served the needs of the Church. The Vatican's twenty-year flirtation with Fascism would be relegated to the archives of papal history; for the foreseeable future Christian Democracy would serve as the Church's political arm in Italy.

5. See Charles F. Delzell, "Pius XII, Italy, and the Outbreak of War," *Journal of Contemporary History*, II, 4 (1967), 137–161.

6. The Day of the Lion

"BETTER TO live for one day as a lion than a thousand years as a lamb!" the *Duce* cried out to his Blackshirts in September, 1935. By that year aggressive militarism and an activist foreign policy had become the most obvious features of Fascism.

Mussolini had come to power with an ultranationalist program that called for an end to the allegedly shabby treatment that Italy had suffered at the peace table. Yet in the 1920's, with the notable exception of his high-handed bombardment of the Greek island of Corfu in 1923, Mussolini's foreign policy was relatively moderate. Old-line professional diplomats ran the Foreign Office for the first three years, though Mussolini held the ministerial portfolio personally from 1922 until September, 1929. In 1924 he reached an accommodation of sorts with Yugoslavia over Fiume. That same year Italy was among the first countries to establish "correct" diplomatic relations with the Soviet Union, despite the *Duce's* undisguised intentions to suppress the Italian Communist party. With France there was always considerable jealousy over naval strength and resentment of France's security arrangements with the Little Entente countries of east-central Europe and with Poland. Moreover, Mussolini was greatly annoyed by France's friendly reception of Italian anti-Fascist refugees, who made Paris their principal center.[1] In 1925 he joined Britain as a guarantor of the Locarno agreements, which stabilized the western frontier of Germany. Whereas Mussolini manifested a somewhat ambivalent attitude toward Weimar Germany, he became openly sympathetic in the late 1920's to the "revisionist" aims of the other defeated countries, Hungary, Bulgaria, and Austria. In the case of the latter state Mussolini subsidized the Heimwehr (Home Defense Units), which under Prince Ernst von Starhemberg became increasingly fascist in ideology.

A new phase of Italian foreign policy began in 1930. Although relinquishing the Ministry of Foreign Affairs from September, 1929, until July, 1932, to Dino Grandi, Mussolini did not intend to give up control over policy. In a speech in Rome in 1930 on the anniversary of the Fascist advent to power, he declared that the struggle had moved beyond the confines of Italy to the world arena. He called for re-armament ("So long as guns exist they will be more beautiful than pretty . . . words"), for revision of treaties, and "peaceful" expansion toward the Danubian basin.

Soon he was talking explicitly about "Fascism for export." Within

1. Regarding the two decades of anti-Fascist activities by the opposition at home and abroad, see Charles F. Delzell, *Mussolini's Enemies: The Italian Anti-Fascist Resistance* (Princeton: Princeton University Press, 1961).

another decade "all Europe will be Fascist." In 1932 the *Duce* told a crowd in Milan, "The twentieth century will be the century of Fascism"; for a third time in history Italy will direct human civilization. Henceforth the Fascists provided secret subsidies to numerous fascistic movements abroad. Feeling that Grandi was too docile to co-ordinate this kind of policy, Mussolini took back for himself the Foreign Ministry in July, 1932, and gave Grandi an ambassadorial assignment in London. Mussolini remained Foreign Minister until 1936, when he handed it over to his ambitious son-in-law, Count Galeazzo Ciano. Meanwhile he took command of the Ministry of War in July, 1933, and in November added the portfolios of Navy and Air. Thus he personally controlled all the service ministries.

Hitler came to power in Germany at the end of January, 1933. Though there had been some ideological links, the two dictators had not yet met personally. Italy was still joined to Britain and France in the Locarno pacts; moreover, she still favored keeping Austria out of Germany's control. In the spring of 1933 Mussolini proposed a Four-Power Pact with Britain, France, and Germany, his idea being that they could co-operate as a consortium in deciding Europe's political problems. But France was not happy with the idea, and the agreement was never ratified. Its only significance was that it showed the *Duce's* desire to have Italy play a big role.

On March 18, 1934, Mussolini delivered an important speech in Rome wherein he openly proclaimed Fascism to be a "universal phenomenon" and then went on to discuss Italy's relations with her neighbors.

Fascism a Universal Phenomenon
(*March 18, 1934*)

COMRADES! Today marks the second quinquennial assembly of the regime. . . .

In the period since 1929 Fascism has changed from an Italian phenomenon into a universal phenomenon. . . .

This is neither the place nor the time for a detailed examination of our international relations. My quick "tour of the horizon" will be limited to those states with which we have common boundaries, and to problems of a rather general character.

Our relations with Switzerland are more than cordial. A treaty

SOURCE: Speech by Benito Mussolini in Rome's Teatro Reale dell' Opera on March 18, 1934, the occasion of the Quinquennial Assembly of the Regime. *Popolo d'Italia* (Rome), No. 67 (Mar. 20, 1934), reprinted in *Opera Omnia di Benito Mussolini*, ed. by Edoardo and Duilio Susmel (Florence: La Fenice, 1958), Vol. 26, pp. 185–193 *passim*. My translation.

of friendship signed in 1924 will lapse next September, and we are
ready to renew it for the same period of time.

After the war we followed a friendly policy with Austria, based
on the defense of her integrity and independence. For a long time
we were alone in doing this; but when the situation assumed a
dramatic quality, others joined us. We intend to continue along
this line of policy. Austria is aware that she can count on us for the
defense of her independence as a sovereign state and that we shall
spare no effort to improve the condition of her people.

Our relations with Yugoslavia are normal—that is to say, diplo-
matically correct. It is possible to improve them because the economic relations between our two countries are complementary.
The problem of Italo-Yugoslav relations should be faced only
when the necessary prerequisites for its solution have been clarified.

Our relations with France have improved from a general standpoint, but reality impels me to emphasize that not one of the large
and small problems that have been on the agenda during the past
fifteen years has neared a solution. Nevertheless, a *rapprochement*
along moral lines has been brought about, and as regards some of
the most important questions concerning Europe, this is a favorable
element that we hope may lead to further developments.

During the last few days the President of the Council of Hungary and the Chancellor of the Austrian Republic were the guests
of the Italian Government. The protocols we signed show what
has been accomplished. It is unnecessary to strain their interpretation. Friendly relations exist among Italy, Austria, and Hungary,
and since the war these have acquired greater justification and
foundation. Hungary, isolated and deprived even of the territories
that are absolutely Magyar, found in Italy a sense of comprehen-
sion and solidarity that is not just of recent origin and that has
clearly been expressed in many aspects of our foreign policy.
Hungary pleads for "justice" and the fulfillment of the promises
solemnly made during the period of the treaties. Italy has supported and continues to support this plea. The Hungarians are a
strong people who deserve to have, and will have, a better destiny.
The protocols, signed a few days ago in Rome, which lay down
the conditions for closer collaboration among Italy, Austria, and
Hungary, do not exclude further amplifications and more extensive
collaboration with other states. It is a question of breaking loose
from the realm of phrases and finally and resolutely entering into
the realm of facts.

The problems of a general character concern first of all the League of Nations. The need for reform has almost universally been accepted. It is clear that the proposed reform should be undertaken after the conclusion of the Disarmament Conference, because if the conference fails, the reform of the League of Nations will no longer be necessary and it will be enough to record its death. That the Disarmament Conference will fail, at least as regards its original important objectives, is generally agreed. (In fact, this is the only kind of peaceful agreement that has been reached.) The states that are now armed will not disarm, while those that are not armed will be able to arm themselves to a greater or lesser degree for defensive purposes. The Italian Memorandum has torn off the mask that concealed this problem in its crude reality. If the armed states refuse to disarm, they will not be abiding by the fifth section of the Versailles Treaty, and they cannot logically oppose the practical application of that parity of rights which was recognized for Germany in December, 1932. There is no other alternative. It is a pure illusion, perhaps already confirmed by facts, to pretend that a people like the Germans can be kept eternally disarmed—unless one is going to make it his objective to use force to prevent the eventual rearmament of Germany. But this game would involve one supreme stake: war—viz., the lives of millions of men and the destiny of Europe. We have put forward the proposal that Germany, without further endless evasions, should be allowed to arm to the degree that she requests as far as effectives and defensive matériel are concerned, and that she should also sign a convention along the lines proposed in the Italian Memorandum, in order that among both the large and the small powers of Europe an atmosphere of understanding may be re-established, for without this, Europe is doomed to decline. . . .

This hurried survey of foreign policy should be linked, and I do so immediately and logically, with Italy's military problem. Assigning highest priority to financial retrenchment and making use of the credit balances of the budget which resulted from the unusual situation of 1928, the Fascist Government has considerably reduced military estimates for both last year and next year. But we cannot go any further. Never at any time—and especially today, on account of the paralysis of the so-called Conference on unattainable Disarmament—was there such a categorical and imperative duty for a nation that must remain alive to keep strong—and even more so in the case of Italy, which must calmly develop the internal, renovating work of the Revolution. It is necessary to be militarily strong, not for aggressive purpose but in order to be able to cope with any emergency. . . .

The military power of a state and the future and safety of a nation are linked to the demographical problem, and this poses a serious problem for all countries of the white race, including our own. I must reaffirm once again, and in the most peremptory manner—and it will not be the last time either—that numbers are the indispensable prerequisite for leadership. Without numerical superiority everything declines, crumbles away, and dies. . . . The notion that an increase of population brings about a condition of poverty is so idiotic that it does not even deserve the honor of rebuttal. . . .

The historical objectives of Italy have two names: Asia and Africa. South and east are the cardinal points that should excite the interest and determination of Italians. There is little or nothing to do toward the north, and the same is true toward the west, whether it be Europe or overseas. These two objectives of ours are justified by geography and history. Of all the large Western powers of Europe, Italy is the nearest to Africa and to Asia. A few hours by sea and much less by air are enough to link up Italy with Africa and with Asia. Let nobody misunderstand the meaning of this century-old task that I assign to the present and to the future Italian generations. It is not a question of territorial conquests—and this should be heard by everyone, both near and far—but a natural expansion that should lead to collaboration between Italy and the people of Africa, between Italy and the Near East and the Middle East. . . .

The aim we have in mind is the development and exploitation of the still-countless resources of these two continents—and especially Africa—and of bringing these areas more closely into the orbit of world civilization. Italy is in a position to accomplish this task. Her location in the Mediterranean, which is resuming its historic role of uniting the East to the West, confers this right and binds Italy to this obligation. We do not intend to claim either monopolies or privileges, but we do claim and we intend to make clear that those countries who arrived ahead of us, those who are satisfied and those who are conservative, should not try to block on every side the spiritual, political, and economic expansion of Fascist Italy. . . .

Anti-Fascism has ceased to exist. . . . But there is one danger that can threaten the Regime, and this may be represented by what is commonly called the "bourgeois spirit"—that is to say, a spirit of satisfaction and adjustment, a tendency toward skepticism, compromise, an easy life and advancement. . . . I do not exclude the existence of the bourgeois temperament, but I deny that those who have it can be Fascists. The creed of the Fascist is heroism, that of the bourgeois is egoism. There is only one remedy against this danger, the principle of continual revolution. . . .

The fourth great historical epoch of the Italian people—which future historians will label the Epoch of the Blackshirts—has already begun. This epoch will see integral Fascists—that is to say, those who are born, reared, and spend their lives in our climate, and who are endowed with those virtues that confer upon a people the privilege of leadership in the world. . . .

Despite the *Duce*'s talk about the "universality" of Fascism, his efforts to organize a kind of Fascist "International" at a congress in Montreux, Switzerland, in December, 1934, proved stillborn. Now that Hitler was in power, a new fascistic Mecca had begun to supplant the old shrine at Rome.

For a brief period in 1934 Mussolini acted as the principal champion of Austrian independence in the face of a threat from Hitler's Nazis. Ever since 1928 Mussolini had sought to make Austria an Italian satellite. He had backed at first Prince Starhemberg's Heimwehr movement, and later the dictatorship of Chancellor Engelbert Dollfuss. The *Duce* was entertaining Frau Dollfuss in Italy when Austrian Nazis suddenly murdered her husband in his office in Vienna on July 25, 1934. After two days of fighting, the Nazis called off their *Putsch* when it was learned that Mussolini had ordered Italian troops to the Brenner Pass and that France and Czechoslovakia might also take action. Hitler thereupon sought to disown any connection with the conspiracy.

In the wake of that crisis Mussolini met with French and British leaders in April, 1935, at the town of Stresa on Lake Maggiore.

The Stresa Conference
(April 11–14, 1935)

JOINT RESOLUTION OF THE STRESA CONFERENCE, APRIL 14, 1935

The Representatives of the Governments of Italy, France, and the United Kingdom have examined at Stresa the general European situation in the light of the results of the exchanges of views which have taken place in recent weeks, of the decision taken on March

SOURCE: British White Paper, Cmd. 4880.

16 by the German Government,[2] and of the information obtained by British Ministers during the visits recently paid by them to several European capitals. Having considered the bearing of this situation on the policy defined in the arrangements reached respectively in Rome and in London, they found themselves in complete agreement on the various matters discussed.

1. They agreed upon a common line of conduct to be pursued in the course of the discussion of the request presented to the Council of the League of Nations by the French Government.[3]

2. The information which they have received has confirmed their view that the negotiations should be pursued for the development which is desired in security in Eastern Europe.

3. The Representatives of the three Governments examined afresh the Austrian situation.

They confirmed the Anglo-Franco-Italian declarations of February 17 and September 27, 1934, in which the three Governments recognized that the necessity of maintaining the independence and integrity of Austria would continue to inspire their common policy. . . .

4. As regards the proposed Air Pact for Western Europe, the Representatives of the three Governments confirmed the principles and procedure that should be followed as envisaged in the London *communiqué* of February 3, and agreed to continue actively the study of the question with a view to the drafting of a pact between the five Powers mentioned in the London *communiqué* and of any bilateral agreements which might accompany it.

5. In approaching the problem of armaments, the Representatives of the three Powers recalled that the London *communiqué* envisaged an agreement to be freely negotiated with Germany to take the place of the relevant clauses of Part V of the Treaty of Versailles, and took into careful and anxious consideration the recent action of the German Government and the report furnished by Sir John Simon of his conversations with the German Chancellor on this subject.

It was regretfully recognized that the method of unilateral repudiation adopted by the German Government, at a moment

2. On that date Hitler denounced the disarmament provisions of the Treaty of Versailles and announced a program of compulsory military service in Germany. *Ed.*

3. On March 20, 1935, the French Government had called for an extraordinary meeting of the Council of the League. *Ed.*

when steps were being taken to promote a freely-negotiated settlement of the question of armaments, had undermined public confidence in the security of a peaceful order. . . .

6. The Representatives of the three Governments took into consideration the desire expressed by the States, whose military status was respectively determined by the Treaties of Saint-Germain, Trianon, and Neuilly, to obtain the revision of this status. . . . They agreed to recommend the other States concerned to examine this question with a view to its settlement by mutual agreement within the framework of general and regional guarantees of security.

ANGLO-ITALIAN DECLARATION, APRIL 14, 1935

. . . The Representatives of Italy and of the United Kingdom, the Powers which participate in the Treaty of Locarno only in the capacity of guarantors, formally reaffirm all their obligations under that Treaty, and declare their intention, should the need arise, faithfully to fulfil them. . . .

FINAL DECLARATION OF THE STRESA CONFERENCE, APRIL 14, 1935

The three Powers, the object of whose policy is the collective maintenance of peace within the framework of the League of Nations, find themselves in complete agreement in opposing, by all practicable means, any unilateral repudiation of treaties which may endanger the peace of Europe, and will act in close and cordial collaboration for this purpose.

The Stresa Front collapsed within a few months, partly because the Anglo-German naval agreement of June, 1935, was negotiated behind the backs of France and Italy, and partly because Britain insisted on a policy of economic sanctions by the League of Nations to punish Italy for invading Ethiopia. Italy's consequent isolation in the war against Ethiopia was to be of major importance in inducing Mussolini to seek the friendship of Hitler's Germany by sacrificing Austria to the *Führer*. Henceforth the *Duce* showed almost total lack of restraint in matters of foreign policy.

A clash at the oasis of Wal Wal near the border of Italian Somaliland in September, 1934, signaled the start of the Ethiopian crisis, though Mussolini had decided early in 1933 that he would soon undertake a war of conquest. His primary motive was the naked desire for imperialist expansion in the only place that was still available. He sought to justify his war with arguments that the African territory would provide Italy with important raw materials and markets, an outlet for her burgeoning population, and enable her to spread the blessings of Roman civilization and religion; moreover, it would be justified revenge for the defeat Italy had suffered at Adowa in 1896.

In January, 1935, Mussolini was, in effect, given a green light by France's Foreign Minister Pierre Laval, who was anxious to retain Italian friendship in the face of the growing German danger. As a gesture of good will Laval turned over some surplus Sahara wasteland to be added to the sands of Italian Libya. Britain's Conservative government under Stanley Baldwin preferred to straddle the problem. On the one hand, he wished to uphold the Covenant of the League of Nations and preserve the independence of Ethiopia; on the other, he wished to appease Mussolini. Matters were brought to a head on October 2, 1935, when the *Duce* stepped out on the balcony of Rome's Palazzo Venezia to proclaim all-out war against Ethiopia.

Mussolini Launches the War in Ethiopia
(October 2, 1935)

Blackshirts of the Revolution, men and women of all Italy, Italians scattered throughout the world, across the mountains and across the oceans, listen!

A solemn hour is about to strike in the history of the fatherland. Twenty million men are at this moment gathered in the piazzas throughout the whole of Italy. Never in the history of mankind has there been seen a more gigantic demonstration. Twenty million men: a single heart, a single will, a single decision. This demonstration is meant to show and it does show to the world that the identity between Italy and Fascism is perfect, absolute, and unchangeable. Only brains weakened by puerile illusions or benumbed in a crass ignorance can think the contrary, because they do not know what this Italy of 1935, this Italy of the thirteenth year of the Fascist era is.

For many months the wheel of destiny, under the impulse of our calm determination, has been moving toward the goal. In these last hours the rhythm has become faster and cannot now be halted. Not only is an army marching toward its objectives, but 44,000,-

SOURCE: Speech of Mussolini from the balcony of Palazzo Venezia in Rome, October 2, 1935. Printed in *Popolo d'Italia* (Rome), No. 236 (Oct. 3, 1935); reprinted in *Opera Omnia di Benito Mussolini*, ed. by Edoardo and Duilio Susmel (Florence: La Fenice, 1959), Vol. 27, pp. 158–160. My translation.

000 Italians are marching in unison with this army, because there is an attempt to commit against them the blackest of all injustices, to rob them of a place in the sun.

When in 1915 Italy united its lot with those of the Allies, how many shouts of admiration and how many promises! But after the common victory, to which Italy had brought the supreme contribution of 670,000 dead, 400,000 disabled, and 1,000,000 wounded, when it came to sitting around the table of the stingy peace, to us were left only the crumbs from the sumptuous colonial booty of others. For thirteen years we have been patient while a ring was being tightened ever more rigidly about us to suffocate our overflowing vitality. With Ethiopia we have been patient for forty years. Now, that's enough!

At the League of Nations, instead of recognizing the just rights of Italy, they talk of sanctions. Now, until there is proof to the contrary, I refuse to believe that the true and generous people of France can associate themselves with sanctions against Italy. The 6,000 dead of Bligny, who perished in a heroic attack which drew admiration even from the enemy, would turn in their graves. Until there is proof to the contrary, I refuse to believe that the true people of Great Britain want to spill blood and push Europe on the road to catastrophe in order to defend an African country universally stamped as a barbarous country and unworthy of taking its place with civilized peoples.

To sanctions of an economic character we shall reply with our discipline, with our sobriety, and with our spirit of sacrifice. To sanctions of a military character we shall reply with orders of a military character. To acts of war we shall reply with acts of war.

Let nobody delude himself that he can deflect us without first having to defeat us. A people which is proud of its name and its future cannot adopt a different attitude. But let it be said once again in the most categorical manner, as a sacred pledge which I take at this moment before all the Italians who are listening to me, that we shall do everything possible to avoid a colonial conflict assuming the character and bearing of a European conflict. This may be the wish of those who see in a new war revenge for fallen temples, but it cannot be our wish.

Never more than in this historic epoch has the Italian people revealed the force of its spirit and the power of its character. And it is against this people to which humanity owes the greatest of its conquests, it is against this people of heroes, poets, artists, navigators, and administrators that they dare to speak of sanctions.

Proletarian and Fascist Italy, Italy of Vittorio Veneto and of the Revolution! To your feet! Let the cry of your decision fill the heavens and be a comfort to the soldiers who are about to fight in Africa, and let it be a spur to our friends, and a warning to our enemies in all parts of the world—a cry of justice and a cry of victory!

After much agonizing debate and under the prodding of Britain's chief spokesman at Geneva, Anthony Eden, the Assembly of the League of Nations voted to condemn Italy as the aggressor (only Austria, Hungary, and Albania supported Italy). But afraid of taking all-out measures against Mussolini lest such action lead to World War II, the Baldwin government proposed only partial and mild economic measures under Article 16 of the Covenant, as the following resolution made clear. Neither petroleum, steel billets, nor pig iron was included in the list of items prohibited to Italy.

League of Nations Sanctions Against Italy
(October 11–19, 1935)

(a) PROPOSAL I, adopted by the Co-ordination Committee, October 11, 1935.

EXPORT OF ARMS, AMMUNITION, AND IMPLEMENTS OF WAR

With a view to facilitating for the Governments of the Members of the League of Nations the execution of their obligations under Article 16 of the Covenant, the following measures should be taken forthwith:

1. The Governments of the Members of the League of Nations which are enforcing at the moment measures to prohibit or restrict the exportation, re-exportation, or transit of arms, munitions, and implements of war to Ethiopia will annul these measures immediately.

2. . . . prohibit immediately the exportation, re-exportation, or transit to Italy or Italian possessions of arms, munitions, and implements of war enumerated in the attached list.

SOURCE: Sanctions Resolutions adopted by the Co-ordination Committee, First Session, October 11–19, 1935. *League of Nations Official Journal,* Special Supplement No. 145, pp. 14–27 *passim;* British White Paper, Cmd. 5071.

3. . . . take such steps as may be necessary to secure that arms, munitions, and implements of war enumerated in the attached list, exported to countries other than Italy, will not be re-exported directly or indirectly to Italy or to Italian possessions.

4. The measures provided for in paragraphs 2 and 3 are to apply to contracts in process of execution.

Each Government is requested to inform the committee through the Secretary-General of the League within the shortest possible time of the measures which it has taken in conformity with the above provisions. . . .

(b) PROPOSAL II, adopted by the Co-ordination Committee, October 14, 1935.

FINANCIAL MEASURES

. . . The Governments of the Members of the League of Nations will forthwith take all measures necessary to render impossible the following operations:

1. All loans to or for the Italian Government and all subscriptions to loans issued in Italy or elsewhere by or for the Italian Government;

2. All banking or other credits to or for the Italian Government . . . ;

3. All loans to or for any public authority, person, or corporation in Italian territory . . . ;

4. All banking or other credits to or for any public authority, person or corporation in Italian territory . . . ;

5. All issues of shares or other capital flotations for any public authority, person, or corporation in Italian territory . . . ;

6. The Governments will take all measures necessary to render impossible the transactions mentioned in paragraphs 1–5 whether effected directly or through intermediaries of whatsoever nationality. . . .

(c) PROPOSAL III, adopted by the Co-ordination Committee, October 19, 1935.

PROHIBITION OF IMPORTATION OF ITALIAN GOODS

. . . 1. The Governments of the Members of the League of Nations will prohibit the importation into their territories of all goods (other than gold or silver bullion and coin) consigned from

or grown, produced, or manufactured in Italy or Italian possessions, from whatever place arriving;

2. Goods grown or produced in Italy or Italian possessions
which have been subjected to some process in another country, and
goods manufactured partly in Italy or Italian possessions and partly
in another country will be considered as falling within the scope of
the prohibition unless 25 per cent. or more of the value of the
goods at the time when they left the place from which they were
last consigned is attributable to processes undergone since the
goods last left Italy or Italian possessions;

3. Goods, the subject of existing contracts, will not be excepted
from the prohibition;

4. Goods *en route* at the time of imposition of the prohibition
will be excepted from its operation . . . ;

5. Personal belongings of travellers from Italy or Italian possessions may also be excepted from its operation. . . .

(d) PROPOSAL IV, adopted by the Co-ordination Committee, October 19, 1935.

EMBARGO ON CERTAIN EXPORTS TO ITALY

. . . 1. The Governments of the Members of the League of
Nations will extend the application of paragraph 2 of Proposal No.
I of the Co-ordination Committee to the following articles as
regards their exportation and re-exportation to Italy and Italian
possessions, which will accordingly be prohibited:

(a) Horses, mules, donkeys, camels, and all other transport
animals;

(b) Rubber;

(c) Bauxite, aluminium and alumina (aluminium oxide), iron
ore, and scrap iron;

Chromium, manganese, nickel, titanium, tungsten, vanadium,
their ores and ferro-alloys (and also ferro-molybdenum, ferro-
silicon, ferro-silico-manganese, and ferro-silico-manganese aluminium);

Tin and tin-ore.

List (c) above includes all crude forms of the minerals and
metals mentioned and their ores, scrap, and alloys; . . .

The British-sponsored sanctions policy infuriated virtually all Italians
and brought to a sudden end the era of friendship between England

and Italy that had dated from the Risorgimento. On November 16, 1935, the eve of the application of the sanctions policy, the Fascist Grand Council adopted the following resolution.

The Fascist Grand Council's Resolution
(November 16, 1935)

The Fascist Grand Council, assembled on the eve of the application of the so-called sanctions against Italy, considers November 18, 1935, as a date of ignominy and iniquity in the history of the world; it denounces the sanctions, never before applied, as a plan to suffocate the Italian people economically and as a vain effort to humiliate it, in order to prevent it from realizing its ideals and defending its very justification for life.

The Fascist Grand Council praises the exemplary calm and the tenacious discipline with which the Italian people shows itself fully aware of the historic import of the present events, and invites it to meet the sanctions with the most implacable resistance, mobilizing, through the organs of the regime, all the moral energies and material resources of the nation; it invites Italians to hang flags outside their homes for twenty-four hours during Monday, November 18; it summons to Rome on December 1 the 94 provincial women's committees of mothers and widows of those who fell in the Great War, in order to co-ordinate and intensify the resistance in which a supremely important part is assigned to the women of Italy; it orders a stone record of the siege to be sculptured on the buildings of the Italian communes, so that the enormous injustice perpetrated against Italy, to which the civilization of all continents owes so much, may remain on record through the centuries; it sends the expression of its sympathy to those States which, by refusing to adhere to sanctions, have aided the cause of peace and interpreted the spirit of the peoples.

The Fascist Grand Council is convinced that the coming test will reveal to the world the Roman virtue of the Italian people in the Year XIV of the Fascist era.

SOURCE: Resolution of the Fascist Grand Council, November 16, 1935, published in *Il Popolo d'Italia* (Rome), No. 281 (Nov. 17, 1935); reprinted in *Opera Omnia di Benito Mussolini*, ed. by Edoardo and Duilio Susmel (Florence: La Fenice, 1959), Vol. 27, p. 183. My translation.

In Italy Mussolini sought to pose as leader of a "war . . . of the poor, the disinherited, the proletariat [against a] front of conservatism, selfishness and hypocrisy." Hypocrisy there was, for in December, 1935, in the midst of the sanctions imbroglio, British Foreign Secretary Sir Samuel Hoare and French Premier Laval secretly concocted a deal that would have allowed Mussolini to obtain more than two-thirds of Ethiopia (more than he had thus far conquered), leaving Ethiopia with only a narrow corridor to the Red Sea.

When news of the Hoare-Laval pact soon leaked out, it inflicted a lethal blow to the League. In France indignation was so great that the Laval government fell, while in Britain widespread anger finally forced Baldwin to ask for Hoare's resignation. Thereafter, Eden, the anti-Italian apostle of collective security, became Foreign Secretary. Belatedly he tried to get oil added to the sanctions list and was on the verge of success in March, 1936, when suddenly Hitler occupied the Rhineland, diverting everyone's attention from Ethiopia. Meanwhile, Emperor Haile Selassie had to flee from his capital as Italian forces under Emilio DeBono and Pietro Badoglio poured in from the north while others under Rodolfo Graziani invaded from the south.

At last on May 9, 1936, Mussolini, in another balcony harangue, proclaimed victory and gave King Victor Emmanuel III the additional title of Emperor of Ethiopia. Soon that conquered state was consolidated administratively with Eritrea and Italian Somaliland as "Italian East Africa." For a few weeks Mussolini was at the pinnacle of his popularity at home.

Mussolini Proclaims Victory in Ethiopia
(May 9, 1936)

Officers, noncommissioned officers, soldiers of all the armed forces of the State in Africa and in Italy, Blackshirts of the Revolution, Italian men and women in the fatherland and throughout the world, listen!

With the decisions that you will learn within a few moments, decisions acclaimed by the Fascist Grand Council, a great event is accomplished. The fate of Ethiopia is sealed today, the ninth of May, in the fourteenth year of the Fascist era.

Our gleaming sword has cut all the knots, and the African victory will remain in the history of the fatherland complete and

SOURCE: Speech of Benito Mussolini from the balcony of Palazzo Venezia in Rome on May 9, 1936, printed in *Il Popolo d'Italia* (Rome), No. 131 (May 10, 1936); reprinted in *Opera Omnia di Benito Mussolini*, ed. by Edoardo and Duilio Susmel (Florence: La Fenice, 1959), Vol. 27, pp. 268–269. My translation.

pure, a victory such as the legionaries who have fallen and those who survive dreamed of and willed. Italy has her empire at last—a Fascist empire because it bears the indestructible symbols of the will and of the power of the Roman lictors, because this is the goal that for fourteen years spurred on the exuberant and disciplined energies of the young and dashing generations of Italy. An empire of peace, because Italy desires peace, for herself and for all men, and she decides upon war only when it is forced upon her by imperious, irrepressible necessities of life. An empire of civilization and of humanity for all the peoples of Ethiopia. That is in the tradition of Rome, which, after victory, associated the different peoples with her own destiny.

Here is the law, O Italians, which closes one period of our history and opens up another like a vast pass that looks out on all the possibilities of the future:

(1) The territories and the peoples that belonged to the Empire of Ethiopia are placed under the full and complete sovereignty of the Kingdom of Italy.

(2) The title of Emperor of Ethiopia has been assumed for himself and his successors by the King of Italy.

Officers, noncommissioned officers, soldiers of all the armed forces of the State in Africa and in Italy, Blackshirts, Italian men and women!

The Italian people has created the empire with its blood. It will fertilize it with its labor and will defend it with its arms against anybody whomsoever. In this supreme certainty, legionaries, raise up on high your insignia, your weapons, and your hearts, to salute after fifteen centuries the reappearance of the empire upon the fateful hills of Rome.

Will you be worthy of it? [*The crowd erupts in shouts of* "Yes!"]

This answering cry is as a sacred oath that binds you before God and before men for life and for death. Blackshirts, legionaries, the salute to the King!

Mussolini's triumph went to his head; an impressionable victim of an exaggerated case of *Ducismo*, he became overconfident of future victories as well.

During the last two months of the Ethiopian War, Mussolini toyed between restoring a semblance of good relations with Britain and France or shifting over to Germany. In April and May the *Duce* and Ambassador Grandi in London seemed to lean toward the former strategy (which was also favored by Britain's new King Edward VIII). But by June, Mussolini and his newly appointed Foreign Minister, Count Ciano, decided in favor of Hitler. A mixture of envy for the *Führer*, combined with resentment toward the British, was responsible. Evidence of the new policy was provided that month when Mussolini advised Austria's Chancellor Kurt von Schuschnigg (who had succeeded the murdered Dollfuss) to seek an understanding with Hitler. The *Duce* sensed that the internal situation in Austria had shifted against him during the preceding year or two. The fascism that was to triumph in Austria was to be the German, not the Italian, variety.

The process of Italo-German *rapprochement* was hastened by the events of the Spanish Civil War, which broke out in the middle of July, 1936. At once Mussolini furnished aerial support to General Francisco Franco's rebels and eventually dispatched 70,000 Italian "volunteers" (mostly members of the Fascist Militia) to assist them in the field. For the *Duce* a victory by Franco would mean another significant advance for the "universal doctrine" of fascism, further encirclement of France, and a possibility of driving the British from Gibraltar, thereby converting the Mediterranean into "Mare Nostrum." He even had visions of acquiring the Balearic Islands. Germany also sent aid to Franco, though not to the extent that Italy did.[4]

Thus it was hardly surprising that Foreign Minister Ciano headed to Germany in October, 1936, for talks with Hitler. Since Austria was no longer a bone of contention, the two Fascist powers could announce their future co-operation. This Mussolini did on November 1 in Milan's great cathedral square.

Mussolini's Announcement of the Rome-Berlin Axis
(Milan, November 1, 1936)

. . . A great country during these last few days has earned extensive sympathy from the masses of Italian people. I allude to Germany.

The meeting at Berlin resulted in an agreement between the two countries on certain questions, some of which are particularly interesting in these days. But these agreements, which have been included in special statements and duly signed—this vertical line between Rome and Berlin is not a partition, but rather an axis around which all the European states animated by the will to collaboration and peace can also collaborate. Germany, although

SOURCE: *Il Popolo d'Italia* (Milan), No. 303 (Nov. 2, 1936). My translation.

4. Regarding the Spanish Civil War, see especially Part II.

surrounded and solicited, did not adhere to sanctions. With the Agreement of July 11 [between Austria and Germany] an element of dissension between Berlin and Rome disappeared, and I may remind you that even before the Berlin meeting Germany had practically recognized the Empire of Rome.

It is not a matter for surprise that today we hoist the flag of anti-Bolshevism. For this is our old flag; we were born under that sign; we have waged war against that enemy and we conquered him by means of our sacrifices and our blood. . . .

In September, 1937, Mussolini crossed the Alps for his first trip to the German capital and his second personal visit with Chancellor Hitler (whom he had first met in Venice in June, 1934). The state visit was a triumphal progress from Munich to Berlin and was climaxed on the Maifeld, where Hitler assembled an enormous crowd of 800,000. Wearing his own newly designed uniform, the *Duce* addressed the vast assembly in German, but a sudden torrential rainstorm reduced the carefully prepared text almost to a sodden rag as he tried to read it faster and faster, to the great confusion of the crowd. Even so, Mussolini, if not the Germans, came away from the meeting in a state of exaltation and henceforth was under the spell of the *Führer*.

Mussolini Reaffirms the Rome-Berlin Axis
(Berlin, September 28, 1937)

Comrades! The visit that I am paying to Germany and her *Führer*, and the speech that I am about to make, represent an important point in the life of our two nations and also in my own. The demonstrations with which I have been received have deeply moved me. My visit should not be measured by the same standard as the usual diplomatic-political visits, and the fact that I have come to Germany today does not mean that I shall be traveling somewhere else tomorrow.

I have come among you not merely as Head of the Italian Government but above all in my capacity as the head of a national revolution, which thereby wishes to give proof of its close connection with your revolution. Although the course of the two revolutions may have been somewhat different, the goal they have sought and reached is the same: the unity and greatness of the people.

Fascism and Nazism are two manifestations of that parallelism of

SOURCE: *Il Popolo d'Italia* (Milan), No. 271 (Sept. 29, 1937). My translation.

historic positions that links the life of our nations, which have achieved unification in the same century and by the same actions.

There are no secret intentions hidden behind my visit to Germany. Nothing will be planned here to divide a Europe which is already divided enough. The solemn confirmation of the fact and stability of the Rome-Berlin Axis is not directed against other states. We National Socialists and Fascists want peace, and we shall always be ready to work for peace, a true and fruitful peace which does not ignore, but solves, the questions that arise from the inter-relationships of peoples. To the whole world, which is asking tensely what the result of this meeting will be, war or peace, the *Führer* and I can answer with a loud voice: Peace!

Just as Fascism has for fifteen years given Italy outwardly and spiritually a new countenance, so also has your revolution given Germany a new countenance—new, even though it is based, as in Italy, on the loftiest and most imperishable traditions that are compatible with the necessities of modern life. I wanted to see for myself this countenance of the New Germany. And, on seeing it, I am now more than ever convinced that this New Germany—in her strength, her justifiable pride, and her desire for peace—is a basic element of European life.

I believe that the reason for much misunderstanding and distrust among nations is that those responsible are not aware of the new reality which is emerging. The life of nations, like that of individuals, is not something that is fixed once for all, but is subject to a constant process of change. To judge a nation on the basis of figures and descriptions or of writings of twenty or fifty years ago is a mistake which may prove fatal. This mistake is often committed against Italy. If the national revolutions of Germany and Italy were better known, many prejudices would disappear and many points of conflict would lose their justification.

We have in common many elements of our *Weltanschauung*. Not only have National Socialism and Fascism everywhere the same enemies, in the service of the same master—the Third International—but they have many conceptions of life and history in common. Both believe in will as the determining power in the life of nations and the driving force of their history, and therefore they reject the teachings of so-called historical materialism and its political and philosophical by-products.

Both glorify work, in its innumerable forms, as the sign of human nobility. Both are based on the young people, whom we train to discipline, courage, resistance, love of the fatherland, and contempt for easy living.

The resurrected Roman Empire is the work of this new spirit with which Italy is inspired. The German rebirth is also the work of a spiritual force, of faith in an idea, in which at first only one man believed—then a handful of pioneers and martyrs, then a minority, and finally an entire nation.

Germany and Italy follow the same goal in the sphere of economic autarky. Without economic independence the political independence of a nation is doubtful, and a nation of great military power may become the victim of an economic blockade. We experienced this danger in all its immediacy when fifty-two states, assembled in Geneva, decided upon criminal economic sanctions against Italy. Those sanctions were carried out with extreme rigor but did not attain their object, and even gave Fascist Italy an opportunity of proving her powers of resistance to the world.

In spite of all the pressure put upon her, Germany did not take part in the sanctions. We shall never forget this. On that occasion there appeared, for the first time, and in the clearest manner, the existence of a necessary solidarity between Nazi Germany and Fascist Italy. What the world now knows as the Rome-Berlin Axis was born in the autumn of 1935, and has worked in the last two years for the ever stronger *rapprochement* of our two peoples to each other, as for the growing political strengthening of the peace of Europe.

Fascism has its ethics, to which it intends to remain true, and these ethics are identical with my own moral code: to speak clearly and openly and, when one has a friend, to march with him to the end.

All of the arguments advanced by our enemies are untrue. Neither in Germany nor in Italy is there a dictatorship, but rather organizations and forces which serve the people. No regime, in any part of the world, has the approval of the people to the same extent as the regimes of Germany and Italy. The greatest and the most authentic democracies in the world today are the German and Italian.

In other countries, under cover of the "inviolable rights of man," policy is governed by the forces of money, of capital, of secret societies, and of political groups in strife with one another. In Germany and Italy no private force can, in any way, influence the policy of the state.

This community of Italo-German ideas has found its expression in the struggle against Bolshevism, the modern form of the darkest Byzantine arbitrary force, that unbelievable exploitation of the credulity of the lower classes, that government of famine, bloodshed, and slavery. Ever since the War, Fascism has fought with utmost energy against this form of human degeneration which lives on lies; it has fought with words and with arms. For when words are not enough, and when threatening circumstances demand, arms must be taken up.

We have acted in this way in Spain, where thousands of Italian Fascist volunteers have fallen to save Western civilization, a civilization which may still experience a rebirth if it turns its back upon the false and lying gods of Geneva and Moscow and draws nearer to the luminous truths of our revolution.

Comrades, my speech is almost finished. Outside our own frontiers we and you are not making propaganda in the banal sense of the word in order to gain converts. We believe that truth itself possesses enough power to penetrate everywhere and that it will ultimately be victorious. The Europe of tomorrow will be Fascist by the logical force of circumstances and not by our propaganda.

It is twenty years since your great *Führer* shouted to the masses the rousing cry which was to become the war cry of the entire German people: *"Deutschland, erwache!"* [Germany, awake!]

Germany has awakened. The Third Reich has come into being.

I don't know whether or when Europe will awaken, as was said at the Nuremberg Party Congress; for secret, but to us well enough known, forces are at work to turn a civil war into a world conflagration. What is important is that our two great nations—who together comprise an imposing, ever growing mass of 115 million people—stand together in a single, unshatterable determination. And today's gigantic demonstration is giving proof of this to the world.

Less than two months later, in the protocol printed below, Fascist Italy acceded to the Anti-Comintern Pact signed by Germany and Japan the year before. This was a clear indication of their antipathy for Soviet Russia.

Italy's Accession to the Anti-Comintern Pact
(*Protocol Signed in Rome, November 6, 1937*)

The Government of the German Reich, the Italian Government, and the Imperial Japanese Government.

Considering that the Communist International continues constantly to endanger the civilized world in the West and East, and disturbs and destroys its peace and order,

Convinced that close co-operation between all States interested in maintaining peace and order can alone diminish and remove this danger,

Considering that Italy, which since the beginning of the Fascist Government has combated this danger with inflexible determination and has eradicated the Communist International in its territory, has decided to take its place against the common enemy side by side with Germany and Japan who, for their part, are animated by the same desire to guard against the Communist International,

Have agreed as follows, in accordance with article II of the Agreement against the Communist International concluded on November 25, 1936, in Berlin between Germany and Japan.

Art. 1: Italy accedes to the Agreement against the Communist International together with the additional Protocol, concluded between Germany and Japan on November 25, 1936, a copy of which is annexed.

Art. 2: The three Powers signing the present Protocol agree that Italy shall be considered as an original signatory of the Agreement and additional Protocol mentioned in the preceding article, the signature of the present Protocol being equivalent to the signature of the original text of the said Agreement and additional Protocol.

Art. 3: The present Protocol is considered as an integral part of the above-mentioned Agreement and additional Protocol.

Art. 4: The present Protocol is drawn up in the German, Italian, and Japanese languages, each text being regarded as an original. It comes into force on the date of signature. . . .

Done in triplicate at Rome, November 6, 1937—in the XVI year

source: Document No. 17, *Documents on German Foreign Policy, 1918–1945*, Series D (Washington, D.C.: Department of State, 1956) I, 26–27.

of the Fascist era, i.e., November 6 of the 12th year of the Showa
period.

/s/ JOACHIM VON RIBBENTROP

CIANO

M. HOTTA

In March, 1938, Mussolini gave his approval to Hitler's sudden annexation of Austria. "Tell Mussolini I will never forget him for this!" was
the grateful and almost hysterical response of the *Führer*.[5] Henceforth the balance of power in the Danubian basin began to shift in
favor of Germany. Italy was rapidly to become enslaved to the Reich.

Two months later Hitler visited Florence, Naples, and Rome. He
was unhappy to spend so much time with King Victor Emmanuel, as
protocol required of a visiting head of state. When he learned of
Hitler's annoyance, Mussolini consoled the German foreign minister:
"Tell the *Führer* to be patient; I have had to be for sixteen years!"[6]

The month of September saw Hitler's demands against Czechoslovakia come to a head. At the desperate request of British Prime
Minister Chamberlain, Mussolini persuaded Hitler to agree to a four-
power conference at Munich. This was the *Duce*'s greatest hour in
diplomacy; he was the only one of the Big Four able to converse in all
the languages. In Italy there were delirious cries of relief that Munich
had "saved" the world from war.

During the winter of 1938–39 both the British and the French
sought to woo Italy back into their fold, but they could not agree on
the bait. Mussolini remained contemptuous of their efforts. France is a
nation "ruined by alcohol, syphilis, and journalism," he told Ciano.
Early in 1939 he was encouraging Italian Irredentists to shout for
"Nice, Corsica, Tunis!"

Hitler tore up the Munich agreement and seized the rest of Czechoslovakia in March, 1939. Belatedly the British and French realized that
their policy of appeasement was not working. They now proceeded to
make a commitment to Poland and halfheartedly sought Stalin's cooperation.

Annoyed by Hitler's failure to keep him fully informed of impending German moves, Mussolini responded in kind by suddenly invading
Albania on Good Friday (April 7). The war was quite unnecessary,
for Albania was already an Italian vassal. The plans for the invasion
had long been prepared, but the final decision was made on the spur of
the moment by Mussolini and Ciano. The announcement apparently
met with some faint opposition from Victor Emmanuel, but he
quickly gave in. Albania's King Zog, his American-born queen, and

5. Quoted in Alan Bullock, *Hitler: A Study in Tyranny* (rev. ed.; New
York: Harper & Row, 1964), p. 431.

6. Quoted in Luigi Salvatorelli and Giovanni Mira, *Storia del Fascismo*
(Rome: Edizioni Novissima, 1953), p. 831.

newborn child fled by donkey over the mountains into Greece. The war soon ended in Italian victory but destroyed what was left of the confidence Italy had earlier tried to inspire among the Balkan countries.

In May, 1939, Hitler's Foreign Minister Joachim von Ribbentrop came to Milan to tighten the Axis into a full-fledged alliance. An American newspaperman reported that Ribbentrop did not get a friendly reception from the Milanese, a story that greatly incensed Mussolini. By telephone he instructed Ciano to counteract this impression by concluding as quickly as possible a formal military alliance. The youthful and none too clever Foreign Minister was caught unprepared; he did not have a detailed draft treaty available. But Ribbentrop did; it was the German text that was adopted with minor amendments. By the terms of this "Pact of Steel" between "two regimes," Italy found herself pledged to support Germany even in a war of aggression.

"Pact of Steel" Between Germany and Italy
(May 22, 1939)

The German Chancellor and His Majesty the King of Italy and Albania, Emperor of Ethiopia, deem that the time has come to strengthen the close relationship of friendship and homogeneity, existing between National Socialist Germany and Fascist Italy, by a solemn Pact.

Now that a safe bridge for mutual aid and assistance has been established by the common frontier between Germany and Italy fixed for all time, both Governments reaffirm the policy, the principles and objectives of which have already been agreed upon by them, and which has proved successful, both for promoting the interests of the two countries and also for safeguarding peace in Europe.

Firmly united by the inner affinity between their ideologies and the comprehensive solidarity of their interests, the German and Italian nations are resolved in future also to act side by side and with united forces to secure their living space and to maintain peace.

Following this path, marked out for them by history, Germany and Italy intend, in the midst of a world of unrest and disintegration, to serve the task of safeguarding the foundations of European civilization. . . .

SOURCE: Document No. 426, in *Documents on German Foreign Policy, 1918–1945*, Series D (Washington, D.C.: Department of State, 1956), VI, 561–564.

Art. 1—The High Contracting Parties will remain in continuous contact with each other in order to reach an understanding on all questions affecting their common interests or the general European situation.

Art. 2—Should the common interests of the High Contracting Parties be endangered by international events of any kind whatsoever, they will immediately enter into consultations on the measures to be taken for the protection of these interests.

Should the security or other vital interests of one of the High Contracting Parties be threatened from without, the other High Contracting Party will afford the threatened Party full political and diplomatic support in order to remove this threat.

Art. 3—If, contrary to the wishes and hopes of the High Contracting Parties, it should happen that one of them became involved in warlike complications with another Power or Powers, the other High Contracting Party would immediately come to its assistance as an ally and support it with all its military forces on land, at sea and in the air.

Art. 4—In order to ensure in specific cases the speedy execution of the obligations of alliance undertaken under Article 3, the Governments of the two High Contracting Parties will further intensify their collaboration in the military field, and in the field of war economy.

In the same way the two Governments will remain in continuous consultation also on other measures necessary for the practical execution of the provisions of this Pact.

For the purposes indicated in paragraphs 1 and 2 above, the two Governments will set up commissions which will be under the direction of the two Foreign Ministers.

Art. 5—The High Contracting Parties undertake even now that, in the event of war waged jointly, they will conclude an armistice and peace only in full agreement with each other.

Art. 6—The two High Contracting Parties are aware of the significance that attaches to their common relations with Powers friendly to them. They are resolved to maintain these relations in the future also and together to shape them in accordance with the common interests which form the bonds between them and these Powers.

Art. 7—This Pact shall enter into force immediately upon signature. The two High Contracting Parties are agreed in laying down that its first term of validity shall be for ten years. In good time before the expiry of this period, they will reach agreement on the extension of the validity of the Pact.

In witness whereon the Plenipotentiaries have signed this Pact and affixed thereto their seals.

Done in duplicate in the German and the Italian languages, both texts being equally authoritative.

Berlin, May 22, 1939, in the XVIIth year of the Fascist era.

/S/ JOACHIM V. RIBBENTROP   GALEAZZO CIANO

SECRET ADDITIONAL PROTOCOL TO THE PACT OF FRIENDSHIP AND ALLIANCE BETWEEN GERMANY AND ITALY[7]

At the time of signature of the Pact of Friendship and Alliance, both Parties have reached agreement on the following points:

1. The two Foreign Ministers will reach agreement as quickly as possible on the organization, headquarters and working methods of the commissions for military questions and questions of war economy to be set up under their direction as provided for in Article IV of the Pact.

2. In execution of Article IV, paragraph 2, of the Pact the two Foreign Ministers will as quickly as possible take all necessary steps to ensure continuous collaboration in the fields of the press, information and propaganda in accordance with the spirit and aims of the Pact.

For this purpose each of the two Foreign Ministers will assign to his country's Embassy, in the capital of the other, one or more specially qualified experts who, in direct collaboration with the Foreign Ministry there, will continually consult on the steps which are suitable for promoting the policy of the Axis and counteracting the policy of opposing Powers in the fields of the press, information and propaganda.

Berlin, May 22, 1939—in the XVIIth year of the Fascist Era.

/S/ JOACHIM V. RIBBENTROP   GALEAZZO CIANO

The Italians had gained the erroneous impression that Hitler would not take action for at least another three years. Mussolini also thought of the pact chiefly as a way of increasing Italy's bargaining power with

---

7. The signed original of this secret protocol in the German Foreign Ministry archives was, like the pact, printed with the German and Italian texts on alternate pages. It was not bound with the rest of the pact, but inserted loose in the volume.—*Ed.*

France. Before the Pact of Steel was finally signed in Berlin on May 22, however, the *Duce* came to his senses sufficiently to warn Hitler that Italy would not be ready for war until 1943. Hitler had no intention of being bound by Mussolini's timetable; the very next day, without bothering to inform Rome, he told his generals to prepare for war against Poland "at the earliest favorable moment."

On August 11 when Ciano conferred with Hitler at Salzburg he suddenly realized the imminence of war. From then on the Italian Foreign Minister had second thoughts about Hitler and began to doubt the judgment of his father-in-law. The Italian government learned of Hitler's Pact of Neutrality and Nonaggression with Stalin only two days before it was signed in Moscow on August 23, 1939. Flabbergasted, Ciano conferred with the *Duce* and instructed officials to prepare documents setting forth reasons why Italy could not go to war at this juncture. On August 26 a deliberately long list of requests for economic and military aid was dispatched to Berlin. "It's enough to kill a bull, if a bull could read," Ciano wrote in his diary. Next day Mussolini sent the following message to Hitler regarding Italy's situation.

Mussolini's Message to Hitler
Regarding Italian Support
(August 27, 1939)

FUEHRER: I reply to your letter[8] delivered to me by the Ambassador. The world does not and will not know before the outbreak of hostilities what the attitude of Italy is, and will learn instead that Italy has concentrated her forces towards the frontiers of the great democracies. On the French frontiers I have actually concentrated seventeen divisions, plus twenty-seven Alpini battalions, plus the frontier guards. Two new divisions are proceeding to Libya—a weak point in our strategic dispositions—and these will bring up the number of metropolitan divisions to *six*, plus four of Libyan Arabs. These measures are more than a demonstration; they will leave the French and British in a state of uncertainty, and will confront them with a disposition of forces at least equal to theirs.

I see you are convinced that an immediate intervention by me in

SOURCE: Document No. 350, *Documents on German Foreign Policy, 1918–1945*, Series D (1937–1945) (Washington, D.C.: Department of State, 1956), VII, 353–354. Transmitted in cipher by telephone to the Italian Embassy in Berlin at 4:30 P.M., August 27, 1939.

8. See Doc. No. 341 in *ibid.*, dated 12:10 A.M., August 27, 1939, and delivered to Mussolini at 9 A.M. that day. It requested most of the things referred to in Mussolini's reply.—*Ed.*

the first phase of the conflict, especially if—as you say, and as is right—you will not be taking the initiative on the Western Front, thereby bringing upon Italy the mass of Franco-British troops and exhausting the limited Italian resources, might have serious repercussions on the development of the war for you as well.

All that can be done from the psychological point of view to underline Italian-German solidarity will be intensified by press, radio, cinema and thorough propaganda.

I am prepared to send you the greatest possible number of workers for your industries and agriculture compatible with my present and prospective mobilization measures.

It is my desire to keep in closest contact with you, Fuehrer, in order to co-ordinate the action of our two countries and make it conform—in every field—to the requirements which will result from the course of events.

MUSSOLINI

On September 1, the same day that Hitler launched the invasion of Poland, he sent Mussolini the following telegram which, at German insistence, was not made public for some time:

Hitler's Message to Mussolini
(September 1, 1939)

DUCE: I thank you most cordially for the diplomatic and political support which you have been giving recently to Germany and her just cause. I am convinced that we can carry out the task imposed upon us with the military forces of Germany. I do not therefore expect to need Italy's military support in these circumstances. I also thank you, Duce, for everything which you will do in future for the common cause of Fascism and National Socialism.

ADOLF HITLER

Mussolini was allowed to stay on the sidelines for a few months, and he announced Italy's status as that of "nonbelligerency" rather than pure

SOURCE: Document No. 500, *Documents on German Foreign Policy, 1918–1945*, Series D (1937–1945), Vol. VII (Washington, D.C.: Department of State, 1956), p. 483. It would appear that this telegram was sent in response to a personal message from Mussolini to Hitler, conveyed through Ambassador Attolico early that morning. *Ed.*

"neutrality." All through the ensuing winter the Vatican put great pressure on Italy to stay out of the war. At Christmas an unprecedented exchange of visits by the Pope and the House of Savoy took place; Pius XII was doing his best to strengthen the "dyarchy" and encourage the King to resist any move toward war.

On March 18, 1940, the *Duce* conferred with Hitler at the Brenner. On that occasion he cast aside all discretion and told the *Führer* that Italy would indeed join in the conflict but would have to decide the date. In a subsequent memorandum of March 31 to the King, Mussolini explained that it would be "a war parallel to that of Germany to obtain our objectives, which can be summed up in this phrase: liberty on the seas; a window on the ocean."[9]

Learning of this development and of the impending German blitzkrieg in the West, the Pope dispatched warnings to the Low Countries, and after their invasion he sent telegrams expressing his sorrow at their being overrun. This precipitated a new clash with the Fascist regime. Mussolini's envoy to the Holy See delivered a protest in person, whereupon Pius XII raised his voice: "Whatever may happen, We have absolutely nothing to be ashamed of, and We do not even fear deportation to a concentration camp!"[10]

But the efforts of the Vatican to keep Italy at peace failed. Seeing Hitler's legions quickly overrun France, Mussolini was determined to join the kill. Without bothering to inform the Fascist Grand Council, and with no opposition from the King, the *Duce* summoned a vast throng to the square in front of his Palazzo Venezia balcony on June 10, 1940, to hear the following announcement.

Mussolini's Speech Declaring War
 (June 10, 1940)

Fighters on the land, on the sea, and in the air! Blackshirts of the Revolution and the Legions! Men and women of Italy, of the Empire, and of the Kingdom of Albania! Listen!

An hour that has been marked out by destiny is sounding in the sky above our fatherland! [*Lively acclaim.*] The hour of irrevocable decisions! The declaration of war has already been handed [*acclamations, loud shouts of* "War! War!"] to the ambassadors of Great Britain and France. We are going onto the battlefield against

SOURCE: *Il Popolo d'Italia* (Milan), XXVII, 163 (June 11, 1940). My translation.

9. *I Documenti diplomatici italiani, Nona serie (1939–1943)*, III (Rome: Istituto Poligrafico dello Stato, 1958), 576–578.

10. Secrétairerie d'Etat de sa Sainteté, *Actes et documents du Saint Siège relatifs à la Seconde Guerre Mondiale*, ed. by Pierre Blet, Angelo Martini, Burkhart Schneider, Tome I: *Le Saint Siège et la guerre en Europe: Mars 1939–Août 1940* (Vatican City, 1965), pp. 453–455.

the plutocratic and reactionary democracies of the West who at every stage have hindered the march and have often threatened the very existence of the Italian people.

Several lustrums of our most recent history can be summarized in these words: promises, threats, blackmail, and at the end—to crown it all—the ignoble siege carried out by fifty-two states of the League of Nations.

Our conscience is entirely tranquil. [*Applause.*] Along with you, the entire world is witness to the fact that our Italy of the Lictors has done everything that was humanly possible to forestall the storm that is now engulfing Europe; but everything was in vain.

It would have been enough if the treaties had been revised and modified in accordance with the changing needs in the life of nations rather than being considered as untouchable for all eternity. It would have been enough if the stupid policy of guarantees, which turned out to be especially deadly to those who accepted them, had not been undertaken. It would have been enough if the proposal which the *Führer* made on October 6 of last year at the end of the Polish campaign had not been rejected.

But all of that now belongs to the past. If today we have decided to face the risks and sacrifices of a war, it is because honor, our interests, and our future firmly demand it, since a great people is truly such only if it holds sacred its obligations and does not evade the supreme tests that determine the course of history.

After having solved the problem of our land frontiers, we are taking up arms in order to establish our maritime frontiers. We want to break the territorial and military chains that are strangling us in our own sea. A nation of 45 million souls is not truly free unless it has free access to the ocean.

This gigantic struggle is only one phase of the logical development of our revolution; it is the struggle of peoples who though poor are rich in workers versus exploiters who cling fiercely to their monopoly of all the earth's wealth and gold; it is the struggle of young and fertile peoples against sterile ones who stand on the verge of decline; it is the struggle between two centuries and two ideas.

Now that the die has been cast and our determination has resulted in burning our ships behind us, I solemnly declare that Italy does not intend to drag into the conflict any of the other peoples who border it on either land or sea. Switzerland, Yugoslavia,

Greece, Turkey, Egypt: take note of these words of mine. It is up to them, and only to them, if these words will be scrupulously maintained.

Italians! In a memorable meeting that took place in Berlin, I said that according to the laws of Fascist morality, whenever one has a friend, he stands by him to the end. ["Duce! Duce! Duce!"] We have done that, and we shall do it with Germany, with her people, and with her marvelous armed forces.

On the eve of this event of century-long importance, we turn our thoughts to His Majesty the King and Emperor [*the crowd erupts in great applause at the mention of the House of Savoy*], who, as always, has interpreted the spirit of the fatherland. And we salute by acclamation the *Führer*, leader of our great ally, Germany! [*The people applaud at length at the mention of Hitler.*]

Proletarian and Fascist Italy, strong, proud, and united as never before, is on her feet! [*The crowd shouts with a single voice: "Yes!"*] We have but one categorical and obligatory watchword for everyone. Already it has soared across the Alps to the Indian Ocean and has stirred our hearts: Victory! [*The people erupt in very loud applause.*] And we shall win, in order that we may at last give a long period of peace with justice to Italy, to Europe, and to the world.

People of Italy! Rush to arms, and show your tenacity, your courage, your valor!

Despite the fact that he himself had been personally in charge of the service ministries since 1933, Mussolini led his country into the war quite unprepared. The Italian Army could not get across the French frontier until June 21, a day before the armistice terms were signed by Germany. Mussolini, who had hoped to obtain Nice, Savoy, Corsica, Djibouti, and perhaps even Tunisia, was treated contemptuously by the Germans and permitted (in the Franco-Italian armistice of June 24) to acquire only the border town of Mentone and the Red Sea port of Djibouti.

After more or less giving up the idea of invading England, Hitler instructed his Foreign Minister to sign a Three-Power Pact with Italy and Japan on September 27, 1940. It called for a "New Order" in both Europe and Greater East Asia. Article 3 bound them to assist one another in case any of them were "attacked by a power at present not involved in the European War or in the Sino-Japanese Conflict." Clearly the United States was such a power. Soviet Russia was specifically excluded by Article 5, though the Kremlin may well have had some doubts as to the candor of that promise.

Three-Power Pact of Germany, Italy, and Japan
(September 27, 1940)

The Governments of Germany, Italy and Japan, considering it as the condition precedent of any lasting peace that all nations of the world be given each its own proper place, have decided to stand by and co-operate with one another in regard to their efforts in Greater East Asia and the regions of Europe respectively wherein it is their prime purpose to establish and maintain a new order of things calculated to promote mutual prosperity and welfare of the peoples concerned.

Furthermore it is the desire of the three Governments to extend co-operation to such nations in other spheres of the world as may be inclined to put forth endeavours along lines similar to their own, in order that their ultimate aspirations for world peace may thus be realized. Accordingly the Governments of Germany, Italy and Japan have agreed as follows:

Art. 1—Japan recognizes and respects the leadership of Germany and Italy in the establishment of a new order in Europe.

Art. 2—Germany and Italy recognize and respect the leadership of Japan in the establishment of a new order in Greater East Asia.

Art. 3—Germany, Italy and Japan agree to co-operate in their efforts on the aforesaid lines. They further undertake to assist one another with all political, economic and military means when one of the three Contracting Parties is attacked by a power at present not involved in the European War or in the Sino-Japanese Conflict.

Art. 4—With a view to implementing the present Pact, Joint Technical Commissions the members of which are to be appointed by the respective Governments of Germany, Italy and Japan will meet without delay.

Art. 5—Germany, Italy and Japan affirm that the aforesaid terms do not in any way affect the political status which exists at present as between each of the three Contracting Parties and Soviet Russia.

Art. 6—The present Pact shall come into effect immediately upon

SOURCE: Document No. 118, *Documents on German Foreign Policy, 1918–1945*, Series D (1937–1945) (Washington, D.C.: Dept. of State, 1960), XI, 204–205. The original text was drawn up in English.

signature and shall remain in force for ten years from the date of its coming into force.

At proper time before the expiration of the said term the High Contracting Parties shall, at the request of any one of them, enter into negotiations for its renewal.

In faith whereof, the Undersigned, duly authorized by their respective Governments, have signed this Pact and have affixed hereto their Seals.

Done in triplicate at Berlin, the 27th day of September 1940—in the XVIIIth year of the Fascist Era—, corresponding to the 27th day of the 9th month of the 15th year of Showa.

/s/ JOACHIM V. RIBBENTROP

CIANO

KURUSU

By August, 1940, Italy's war machine was functioning a little better. Mussolini's men managed to capture British Somaliland (the first English colony to be stolen in a century). The *Duce* at the same time asked Hitler to let Italian pilots share in the "honor" of bombing London. Next month still other Italian forces, led by General Graziani, moved from Libya some 70 miles into Egypt. Despite the critical needs of the Battle of Britain, Prime Minister Churchill dispatched two badly needed divisions to Suez. By late autumn General Wavell was able to launch a counterattack that drove the Italians westward some 500 miles, halfway across Libya, with the loss of 130,000 prisoners of war—so many that British army dispatches described them in terms of so many acres.

Meanwhile, Mussolini was determined to spread the banner of Fascist Italy in another sector. Egged on by Ciano, he ordered the invasion of Greece on October 28, 1940, the anniversary of the March on Rome. He informed Hitler only on the day it occurred. The Italian ultimatum was cast in the following terms.

The Italian Ultimatum to Greece
(October 28, 1940)

The Italian Government has repeatedly noted how, in the course of the present conflict, the Greek Government assumed and maintained an attitude which was contrary not only with that of

SOURCE: Associated Press version, *New York Times* (Oct. 29, 1940), p. 4. The Italian Minister to Greece (Grazzi) delivered the ultimatum to General Metaxas at 3 A.M., October 28. The ultimatum expired at 6 A.M.

formal, peaceful, good neighborly relations between two nations but also with the precise duties which were incumbent on the Greek Government in view of its status as a neutral country.

On various occasions the Italian Government has found it necessary to urge the Greek Government to observe these duties and to protest against their systematic violation, particularly serious since the Greek Government permitted its territorial waters, its coasts and its ports to be used by the British fleet in the course of its war operations, aided in supplying the British air forces and permitted organization of a military information service in the Greek archipelago to Italy's damage.

The Greek Government was perfectly aware of these facts, which several times formed the basis of diplomatic representations on the part of Italy to which the Greek Government, which should have taken consideration of the grave consequences of its attitude, failed to respond with any measure for the protection of its own neutrality, but, instead, intensified its activities favoring the British armed forces and its cooperation with Italy's enemies.

The Italian Government has proof that this cooperation was foreseen by the Greek Government and was regulated by understandings of a military, naval, and aeronautical character. The Italian Government does not refer only to the British guarantee accepted by Greece as a part of the program of action against Italy's security but also to explicit, precise engagements undertaken by the Greek Government to put at the disposal of powers at war with Italy important strategic positions on Greek territory, including air bases in [Thessaly] and Macedonia designed for attack on Albanian territory.

In this connection the Italian Government must remind the Greek Government of the provocative activities carried out against the Albanian nation, together with the terroristic policy it has adopted toward the people of Ciamuria and the persistent efforts to create disorders beyond its frontiers.

For these reasons, also, the Italian Government has accepted the necessity, even though futilely, of calling the attention of the Greek Government to the inevitable consequences of its policy toward Italy. This no longer can be tolerated by Italy.

Greek neutrality has been tending continuously toward a mere shadow. Responsibility for this situation lies primarily on the shoulders of Great Britain and its aim to involve ever more countries in war.

But now it is obvious that the policy of the Greek Government has been and is directed toward transforming Greek territory, or at least permitting Greek territory to be transformed, into a base for war operations against Italy.

This could only lead to armed conflict between Italy and Greece, which the Italian Government has every intention of avoiding.

The Italian Government, therefore, has reached the decision to ask the Greek Government, as a guarantee of Greek neutrality and as a guarantee of Italian security, for permission to occupy with its own armed forces several strategic points in Greek territory for the duration of the present conflict with Great Britain.[11]

The Italian Government asks the Greek Government not to oppose this occupation and not to obstruct the free passage of the troops carrying it out.

These troops do not come as enemies of the Greek people and the Italian Government does not in any way intend that the temporary occupation of several strategic points, dictated by special necessities of a purely defensive character, should compromise Greek sovereignty and independence.

The Italian Government asks that the Greek Government give immediate orders to military authorities that this occupation may take place in a peaceful manner. Wherever the Italian troops may meet resistance this resistance will be broken by armed force, and the Greek Government would have the responsibility for the resulting consequences.

The war in Greece went badly for the Italians, who were halted within three weeks and pushed back into Albania. In November Mussolini sought to make General Badoglio his scapegoat and relieved him of command. (Badoglio was to get his revenge on July 25, 1943.) By December Mussolini was in the embarrassing situation of having to beg Hitler for assistance. The Germans, however, were unable to send

11. On May 6, 1941, Anthony Eden, the British Foreign Secretary, said to the House of Commons: ". . . In the early morning, at 3:00 o'clock, the Italian Minister called on General Metaxas and presented him with an ultimatum, which, he said, would come into force at 6:00. The ultimatum contained this clause:—that Italy demanded certain bases in Greece. General Metaxas said, 'What bases?' The Italian Minister said that he did not know. Those were the cynical conditions in which the first attack on Greece was made, before even the ultimatum expired, and those were the conditions in which our guarantee first came into effect." (*Parliamentary Debates*, House of Commons, 5th series, Vol. 371, col. 733.)

troops to the Balkans until the spring of 1941. The necessity of cleaning up that peninsula before invading Russia caused Hitler to lose five precious weeks—enough to prevent him from capturing Moscow in the first year of the war and, in effect, making his eventual defeat almost inevitable.

Italy's armed forces performed poorly almost everywhere. On November 11, 1940, British sea and air power in the Mediterranean knocked out three Italian capital ships at their Taranto base at the cost of only two British planes and one pilot killed. Not content with that, other British naval units struck the Italian fleet off Cape Matapan on March 28–29, 1941, sinking three cruisers and two destroyers, and a few weeks later another squadron bombarded Genoa in daylight. By that spring the British had driven the Italians completely out of East Africa and reinstated Emperor Haile Selassie on his throne.

In June 1941 Mussolini joined Hitler in the invasion of Stalin's Russia. "We cannot count less than Slovakia. . . . The destiny of Italy is intimately bound up with that of Germany," he told the Italian commander.[12] And following the Japanese attack on Pearl Harbor in December, both Axis powers declared war on the United States—once again without opposition from the King and with no consultation of the Grand Council.

By 1942 the situation was much worse. Hitler dispatched General Erwin Rommel to fill the breach in Libya. His forces advanced that summer from Tobruk into Egypt, and Mussolini crossed the Mediterranean in anticipation of a victory parade in Cairo. But El Alamein was as far as the Axis forces could get. The *Duce* had to sneak back to Rome. In October the British launched an attack from El Alamein that carried them triumphantly all the way to Tunisia, while the next month Anglo-American troops landed in Morocco and Algeria. At the same time the Red Army bitterly counterattacked at Stalingrad. Thus the turning point of the war had been reached. Physically ill, the *Duce* was rapidly losing prestige and power at home. All of his enemies began to come out of hiding. In vain he tried to persuade Hitler to make peace with Russia and concentrate his efforts against the "Anglo-Saxons." Ciano dreamed of organizing an Italo-Balkan peace bloc against Germany. Never was there any co-ordinated military planning between the two Axis powers—in contrast to the efficiency of the Anglo-American Joint Chiefs of Staff.

---

12. Quoted in F. W. Deakin, *The Brutal Friendship: Mussolini, Hitler and the Fall of Italian Fascism* (New York: Harper & Row, 1962), pp. 15–16.

7. *Monarchist* Coup d'État and *Republican Fascism*

THE UNENDING series of military debacles abroad and the increasingly heavy Allied aerial bombardment of the homeland led to profound defeatism among the Italian people. The breakdown of the transportation system and the economy, along with the obvious poor health of the *Duce* and his unwillingness to eliminate corruption in high places, all served to augment the nation's despair. In February, 1943, Mussolini tried to stem some of the criticism by "changing the guard" in his Council of Ministers. Ciano was dismissed from the Foreign Office and sent as ambassador to the Holy See; already he was conspiring with certain party hierarchs to unseat his father-in-law. In March, 1943, a great wave of strikes broke out in Turin and Milan, the first to take place in Italy since the advent of the dictatorship. Communist infiltrators did their best to impart an antiwar and political aura to them.

Within weeks three parallel and sometimes interlocking conspiracies gained momentum. On the one hand, high Army leaders plotted to replace the *Duce* with someone like Marshal Pietro Badoglio. Dissident Fascist officials were anxious to put the government in the hands of such men as Ciano, Grandi, and Bottai. Spokesmen of the clandestine anti-Fascist parties hoped to restore free political institutions and end the war; Ivanoe Bonomi, an elderly ex-premier, was their titular leader. All of these groups tried to persuade the King to take action and use the regular Army to checkmate the Fascist Militia. But he remained as silent and indecisive as he had been in 1922, in 1924, and in 1940.

The successful Allied invasion of Sicily on July 10, 1943, accelerated the political unrest; it was clear that the peninsula would be next. On the nineteenth Mussolini and top Army leaders conferred with Hitler at Feltre in Venetia. The military men made it clear to the *Duce* that without vast military aid from Germany, Italy could not stay in the war. But Mussolini was not capable of standing up to Hitler, who contended that Germany could not divert such large-scale assistance. On the same day hundreds of Allied planes bombed Rome's railway yards. The terrifying raid made a profound impression on the citizenry and at last frightened the King to the point of deciding to take action. Mussolini meanwhile had bowed to pressure from PNF leaders and scheduled a meeting of the Fascist Grand Council for the evening of July 24—its first gathering since 1939. At what turned out to be an all-night session, the *Duce* was confronted by a determined intraparty revolt. Led by Ciano, Grandi, Bottai and others, 19 of the 26 hierarchs expressed their lack of confidence in Mussolini and turned to the King. Following is the text of the Grandi resolution:

Dino Grandi's Resolution at the Fascist Grand Council
(Palazzo Venezia, Rome, July 24–25, 1943)

THE GRAND Council, meeting at this hour of supreme trial, turns its thoughts first of all to the heroic fighting men of every Service who, side by side with the proud people of Sicily, in whom the single faith of the Italian nation shines most brightly, are renewing the noble traditions of hardy valor and indomitable spirit of self-sacrifice of our glorious Armed Forces;

Having examined the internal and international situation and the political and military conduct of the war,

It proclaims the sacred duty of all Italians to defend at whatever cost the unity, independence, and liberty of our fatherland, the fruits of the sacrifices and efforts of four generations, embracing the period from the Risorgimento to the present day, and the life and future of the Italian people.

It affirms the necessity for the moral and material unity of all Italians in this grave and decisive hour for the destiny of our country.

It declares that to this end it is necessary to revive forthwith all the offices of State and to assign to the Crown, the Grand Council, the Government, Parliament, and the Corporations the duties and responsibilities prescribed by our statutory and constitutional laws.

It invites the Head of the Government to request His Majesty the King—toward whom the heart of all the nation turns with loyalty and confidence—to assume, for the honor and the salvation of our fatherland, not only the effective command of the Armed Forces, on land, sea, and in the air, in accordance with Article 5 of the *Statuto* of the Realm, but also that supreme power of decision which our laws ascribe to him, and which, throughout the nation's history, has ever been the glorious heritage of our august dynasty of Savoy.

The Grand Council adjourned about 2:30 A.M., Sunday, July 25. At noon Mussolini requested to be received in special audience by the King at 5 P.M. He arrived at the monarch's residence bearing documents designed to prove that the Council's vote was merely advisory.

SOURCE: Benito Mussolini, *Storia di un anno* (*Il tempo del bastone e della carota*), 2d ed. (Milan: Mondadori, 1944), pp. 83–84. My translation.

But Victor Emmanuel had decided to exploit the Council's action and regard it as a perfectly constitutional vote of nonconfidence. The twenty-minute audience ended when the King informed the *Capo del Governo* that he had decided to appoint Marshal Badoglio in his stead. The *Duce* remonstrated; finally he murmured, "Then everything is finished." The King promised the ex-dictator protection for himself and family. As Mussolini stepped out of the royal villa, a captain of the carabinieri moved forward and suggested he climb into a waiting police ambulance to avoid a "hostile crowd." Falling into this trap, Mussolini was driven to a nearby police barracks, not yet aware he was under arrest. At 10:45 P.M. the Rome radio announced tersely the replacement of Mussolini and then broadcast two proclamations, one signed by the King, the other by Badoglio. The latter proclamation follows.

Marshal Badoglio's Continuation of the War
(July 25, 1943)

Italians! By order of His Majesty the King and Emperor, I assume the military government of the country with plenary powers.

The war continues. Although severely stricken in its invaded provinces, in its destroyed cities, Italy remains loyal to its plighted word, in proud defense of its thousand-year-long traditions.

Let all ranks close around His Majesty the King and Emperor, who is the living image of the fatherland and an example for everyone.

The charge given me is clear and precise. It will be scrupulously executed; and whoever deludes himself into thinking that he can impede its normal development, or attempts to disturb the public order, will be struck down inexorably.

Long live Italy! Long live the King!

[signed]   PIETRO BADOGLIO
Marshal of Italy

Caught unawares and bemused by the action of the Grand Council, the Fascist Militia (MVSN) made no effort to resist the action of the King and Badoglio.

The conspirators had the dual intention of removing Mussolini from power and breaking away from Germany, but events quickly revealed they had no rational plan for co-ordinating the two problems. They had achieved the first without making coherent preparations for the latter. Instead of clear-eyed, stouthearted statesmen, Italy found herself

SOURCE: *Il Messaggero* (Rome), July 26, 1943. My translation.

led by mediocre, superannuated Machiavellians—seventy-two-year-old Badoglio and seventy-four-year-old Victor Emmanuel III.

During the ensuing "45 days" of royal-military dictatorship in Rome, the Germans were not at all fooled by Badoglio's pledge, "The war continues." Hitler rapidly found the troops he had asserted at Feltre were unavailable, and sent them pouring over the Brenner. The Badoglio government miscalculated fatally in assuming that Italy could sidestep the Allies' "unconditional surrender" formula and negotiate a *volte-face*. The Allies, for their part, were unduly distrustful of the Italians and did not realize how weak they actually were in the face of the German build-up. Much precious time was lost before the armistice was signed in Sicily on September 3 and proclaimed over the radio by Badoglio the evening of the eighth, just as General Eisenhower's invasion forces were approaching the beachhead at Salerno.

Marshal Badoglio's Proclamation of the Armistice
(September 8, 1943)

The Stefani News Agency communicates under date of yesterday, September 8:

The Head of the Government, Marshal of Italy Badoglio, made the following announcement over the radio this evening at 19:45 hours:

"The Italian Government, having recognized the impossibility of continuing the unequal struggle against the overwhelming power of the adversary, and with the intention of sparing the Nation from further and graver disasters, has requested an armistice from General Eisenhower, Commander-in-Chief of the Anglo-American Allied Forces.

"The request has been accepted.

"Consequently, every act of hostility against the Anglo-American forces must cease on the part of Italian forces in every location. They shall react, however, to possible attacks coming from any other source."

September 8, 1943, marked the beginning of a new era in Italian history, the war of national liberation. Expecting the Germans to seize Rome at any moment, the King and Badoglio fled in panic that night, leaving no clear instructions as to who was to take charge. They made their way to Brindisi on the heel of the Italian boot; there they anxiously awaited the arrival of British advance units. For the next twenty months Italy was divided in two parts: the Allies in control of the

SOURCE: *Il Messaggero* (Rome), September 9, 1943. My translation.

south, with the King's government as their puppets; the Germans in control of the north, with the rescued Mussolini as their creature.

One of the first things the Allies demanded of the royal government was the signing of the so-called Long Armistice to supplement the Short Armistice of September 3. The latter had omitted reference to "unconditional surrender" and had restricted itself to military clauses; the Long Armistice contained political and economic strictures, and in its original version mentioned "unconditional surrender." After remonstrances from Badoglio, the Allies eventually agreed to modify some of this terminology, and Eisenhower tactfully handed him a letter clarifying that the terms would be attenuated to the degree that Italy "worked her passage" (Churchill's phrase) by helping in the war against Germany. Despite these revisions there was no doubt that the Allies controlled the destiny of the Italian people in the liberated zones. As matters turned out, several clauses of the Long Armistice were never implemented. Yet many misunderstandings continued, and there were enough highhanded Allied actions to persuade many Italians to credit the wildest rumors.

Instrument of Surrender of Italy
(Malta, September 29, 1943)

Whereas in consequence of an armistice dated September 3rd, 1943, between the United States and the United Kingdom Government on the one hand and the Italian Government on the other hand, hostilities were suspended between Italy and the United Nations on certain terms of a military nature;

And whereas in addition to those terms it was also provided in the said Armistice that the Italian Government bound themselves to comply with other conditions of a political, economic and financial nature to be transmitted later; . . .

1. (A) The Italian Land, Sea and Air Forces wherever located, hereby surrender unconditionally.

(B) Italian participation in the war in all Theaters will cease immediately. . . .

2. The Italian Supreme Command will give full information concerning the disposition and condition of all Italian Land, Sea and Air Forces, wherever they are situated and of all such forces of Italy's Allies as are situated in Italian or Italian occupied territory.

SOURCE: U.S. Department of State, Treaties and Other International Acts, Series 1604, Armistice with Italy, 1943 (Washington, D.C.: Government Printing Office, 1947), pp. 3–4, 7–12 passim.

3. . . . The Italian Supreme Command will take the necessary measures to insure Law and Order, and to use its available armed forces to insure prompt and exact compliance with all the provisions of the present instrument. . . .

4. Italian Land, Sea and Air Forces will within the periods to be laid down by the United Nations withdraw from all areas outside Italian territory notified to the Italian Government by the United Nations and proceed to areas to be specified by the United Nations. . . .

18. The forces of the United Nations will require to occupy certain parts of Italian territory. . . .

22. The Italian Government and people will abstain from all action detrimental to the interests of the United Nations and will carry out promptly and efficiently all orders given by the United Nations.

23. The Italian Government will make available such Italian currency as the United Nations may require. . . .

25. (A) Relations with countries at war with any of the United Nations, or occupied by any such country, will be broken off. . . .

26. Italian subjects will pending further instructions be prevented from leaving Italian territory except as authorized by the Allied Commander-in-Chief and will not in any event take service with any of the countries or in any of the territories referred to in article 25 (A) nor will they proceed to any place for the purpose of undertaking work for any such country. Those at present so serving or working will be recalled as directed by the Allied Commander-in-Chief. . . .

29. BENITO MUSSOLINI, his Chief Fascist associates and all persons suspected of having committed war crimes or analogous offences whose names appear on lists to be communicated by the United Nations will forthwith be apprehended and surrendered into the hands of the United Nations. Any instructions given by the United Nations for this purpose will be complied with.

30. All Fascist organizations, including all branches of the Fascist Militia (MVSN), the Secret Police (OVRA), all Fascist youth organizations will insofar as this is not already accomplished be disbanded in accordance with the directions of the Allied Commander-in-Chief. The Italian Government will comply with all such further directions as the United Nations may give for abolition of Fascist institutions, the dismissal and internment of Fascist

personnel, the control of Fascist funds, the suppression of Fascist ideology and teaching.

31. All Italian laws involving discrimination on grounds of race, color, creed or political opinions will insofar as this is not already accomplished be rescinded, and persons detained on such grounds will, as directed by the United Nations, be released and relieved from all legal disabilities to which they have been subjected. The Italian Government will comply with all such further directions as the Allied Commander-in-Chief may give for repeal of Fascist legislation and removal of any disabilities or prohibitions resulting therefrom.

32. (A) Prisoners of war belonging to the forces of or specified by the United Nations and any nationals of the United Nations, including Abyssinian subjects, confined, interned, or otherwise under restraint in Italian or Italian-occupied territory will not be removed and will forthwith be handed over to representatives of the United Nations. . . .

(B) Persons of whatever nationality who have been placed under restriction, detention or sentence (including sentences in absentia) on account of their dealings or sympathies with the United Nations will be released under the direction of the United Nations and relieved from all legal disabilities to which they have been subjected. . . .

37. There will be appointed a Control Commission representative of the United Nations charged with regulating and executing this instrument under the orders and general directions of the Allied Commander-in-Chief. . . .

43. The present instrument shall enter into force at once. It will remain in operation until superseded by any other arrangements or until the voting into force of the peace treaty with Italy. . . .

Signed at Malta on the 29th day of September, 1943.

/s/ Badoglio
Marshal PIETRO BADOGLIO
Head of the Italian Government

/s/ Dwight D. Eisenhower
DWIGHT D. EISENHOWER
General, United States Army,
Commander-in-Chief, Allied Force

In the face of unrelenting Allied pressure, Victor Emmanuel at last consented to declare war on Germany on October 13, 1943. The Allies thereupon recognized Italy not as an ally but as a "co-belligerent." After much backing and filling, the Anglo-Americans eventually equipped and trained an Italian Corps of Liberation and sent it into battle in the final stages of the war.

Meeting in Moscow during the last part of October, 1943, the Foreign Ministers of the Allied "Big Three" agreed upon an important tripartite declaration calling for "negative and positive" measures to stimulate the growth of Italian democracy. Because of British pressure, no mention at all was made of the House of Savoy, though the question of what to do with the monarchical institution that had been so intimately bound up with the Fascist regime had become a burning issue in Italy.

Tripartite Declaration of Moscow Regarding Italy ### *(October 30, 1943)*

The Foreign Secretaries of the United States of America, the United Kingdom and the Soviet Union have established that their three Governments are in complete agreement that Allied policy towards Italy must be based upon the fundamental principle that Fascism and all its evil influences and emanations shall be utterly destroyed and that the Italian people shall be given every opportunity to establish governmental and other institutions based upon democratic principles.

The Foreign Secretaries of the United States of America and the United Kingdom declare that the action of their Governments from the inception of the invasion of Italian territory, in so far as paramount military requirements have permitted, has been based upon this policy.

In the furtherance of this policy in the future the Foreign Secretaries of the three Governments are agreed that the following measures are important and should be put into effect:—

1. It is essential that the Italian Government should be made more democratic by the introduction of representatives of those sections of the Italian people who have always opposed Fascism.

SOURCE: Annex 4 to the Protocols of the Conference, in U.S. Department of State, *Foreign Relations of the United States, Diplomatic Papers, 1943*, Vol. I: *General* (Washington: U.S. Government Printing Office, 1963), pp. 759–760.

2. Freedom of speech, of religious worship, of political belief, of the press and of public meeting shall be restored in full measure to the Italian people, who shall also be entitled to form anti-Fascist political groups.

3. All institutions and organizations created by the Fascist regime shall be suppressed.

4. All Fascist or pro-Fascist elements shall be removed from the administration and from the institutions and organizations of a public character.

5. All political prisoners of the Fascist regime shall be released and accorded a full amnesty.

6. Democratic organs of local government shall be created.

7. Fascist chiefs and other persons known or suspected to be war criminals shall be arrested and handed over to justice.

In making this declaration the three Foreign Secretaries recognize that so long as active military operations continue in Italy the time at which it is possible to give full effect to the principles set out above will be determined by the Commander-in-Chief on the basis of instructions received through the Combined Chiefs of Staff. The three Governments parties to this declaration will at the request of any one of them consult on this matter.

It is further understood that nothing in this resolution is to operate against the right of the Italian people ultimately to choose their own form of government.

The resurgent anti-Fascist parties formed a Committee of National Liberation in September, 1943. Most of the left-wing parties insisted on the abdication of Victor Emmanuel and the abolition of the monarchy as the prerequisite for political renovation and wholehearted Italian participation in the war effort. All through the winter of 1943–44 they refused to accept posts in the government of the King and Badoglio. In the spring, however, the situation changed in a sensational manner. Palmiro Togliatti, the Communist party leader who had spent years in exile in Moscow, returned to Italy and promptly announced that the Communists were ready to enter the Badoglio government and concentrate on winning the war. The Anglo-Americans realized that it would not do if only the Communists entered the government. In order to make it possible for the other parties to join in a coalition government, the British reluctantly agreed with the Americans that pressure must be put on the King to withdraw from public life. At last they forced him to issue a statement on April 12, 1944, promising to step aside as soon as Rome should be liberated.

King Victor Emmanuel III's Announcement of Withdrawal
(April 12, 1944)

The Italian people know that I have always been at their side in difficult times and happy ones. They know that eight months ago I put an end to the Fascist regime and brought Italy, notwithstanding every danger and risk, to the side of the United Nations in the struggle for liberation against Nazism.

The Italian Navy, Air Force and Army, obedient to my call, during the past eight months have been fighting undauntedly against the enemy, shoulder to shoulder with the Allied forces. The Italian contribution to victory is and shall ever be more great. The day will come when, our deep wounds healed, we shall once more take our place as a free people among free nations.

Putting into effect what I have suggested to the Allied authorities and to my Government, I have decided to withdraw from public affairs by appointing my son, the Prince of Piedmont, Lieutenant General of the Realm. This appointment will become effective by a formal transfer of power on the day on which the Allied troops enter Rome. This decision, which I and my family firmly believe furthers national unity, is final and irrevocable.

Rome was finally freed on June 4. The next day the King announced the transfer of power to his son, Prince Humbert, as Lieutenant General of the Realm. Premier Badoglio was also compelled to step down in the face of opposition from parties in the Committee of National Liberation. He was succeeded by Ivanoe Bonomi, the elderly chairman of the Rome committee. Bonomi retained the premiership until the Germans were evicted from northern Italy in May, 1945.

After the liberation of Rome the process of purging the country of the remnants of Fascism accelerated markedly. Count Carlo Sforza, a distinguished diplomat of the pre-Fascist era and one of the most prestigious of the returning exiles, drafted the following purge law. Proclaimed on July 27, 1944, it provided the basis for *epurazione*.

SOURCE: *New York Times*, April 12, 1944.

The Sforza Purge Law Regarding Fascist Crimes
(*July 27, 1944*)

THE FUNDAMENTAL LAW REGARDING FASCIST CRIMES
TITLE I: PUNISHMENT OF CRIMES

Art. 1: All penal regulations that were designed to safeguard institutions and political organs created by Fascism are hereby abrogated.

Sentences previously pronounced on the basis of such regulations are hereby annulled.

Art. 2: Those members of the Fascist Government and those Fascist hierarchs who are found guilty of having annulled constitutional guarantees and destroyed the freedom of the people, of having created the Fascist regime, and of having compromised and betrayed the fate of the nation, thereby leading it to the present catastrophe, shall be punished by life imprisonment, and by death in cases of the gravest responsibility.

They shall be tried by a High Court of Justice, composed of a president and eight members, to be appointed by the Council of Ministers from high magistrates who are either in active service or in retirement, and from other distinguished persons of unimpeachable rectitude.

Art. 3: Those who are found guilty of having organized Fascist squads which carried out acts of violence or destruction, and those who promoted or led the insurrection of October 28, 1922, shall be punished in accordance with Article 120 of the Penal Code of 1889.

Those who promoted or led the *coup d'état* of January 3, 1925, and those who thereafter by relevant acts contributed to the maintenance of the Fascist regime in power shall be punished in accordance with Article 118 of the same code.

Whoever is guilty of committing other crimes for Fascist motives, or who has taken advantage of the political situation created by Fascism, shall be punished in accordance with the laws that were in effect at the time.

SOURCE: Legislative Decree-Law No. 159 of the Lieutenant Generalcy. Printed in Tommaso Fortunio, *La legislazione definitiva sulle sanzioni contro il fascismo* (Rome: Nuove Edizioni Jus, 1946), pp. 44–46. My translation.

Art. 4: The crimes that are covered in the preceding article shall be judged, in accordance with their respective jurisdiction, by the Courts of Assize, the Tribunals, and the praetors.

The Courts of Assize shall consist of two magistrates, as prescribed by the Unified Text of legislative regulations defining the structure of the Courts of Assize, and by five peoples' judges to be chosen by lot from apposite lists of citizens of irreproachable moral and political conduct.

Art. 5: Whoever in the period since September 8, 1943, has committed or shall commit any criminal act of disloyalty toward the State and its military defense, or by any form whatsoever of intelligence, correspondence, or collaboration with the German invader lends the enemy comfort or assistance, shall be punished in accordance with the regulations of the Millitary Penal Code for time of war.

The penalties prescribed for military personnel shall also apply to nonmilitary personnel.

Military personnel shall be tried by military tribunals; nonmilitary personnel by civilian courts.

Art. 6: No one who is guilty of the crimes set forth in the present decree and who has gone unpunished because of the continuing existence of the Fascist regime may invoke in his own behalf the statute of limitations.

In the same manner, amnesties and indulgences that may have been granted after October 28, 1922, shall not apply to crimes set forth in the present decree, and if they have already been so applied, the relevant declaratory documents are hereby rescinded.

The High Commissioner is hereby empowered to propose the revocation of sovereign acts of clemency that may have been granted hitherto.

Sentences pronounced for such crimes may be declared to be juridically nonexistent if such decisions were influenced by a state of moral coercion created by Fascism. Pronouncement in this regard shall be entrusted to a section of the Supreme Court of Cassation, as designated by the Minister Keeper of the Seals.

The dispositions of the present article shall not apply to those crimes that are punishable by imprisonment for less than a maximum period of three years.

Art. 7: For crimes envisaged under the present title, the penalty of imprisonment may be reduced by up to one-fourth, while the death penalty and life imprisonment penalty may be replaced by imprisonment for a period of not less than five years under the following circumstances:

(a) If the guilty party assumed a hostile position with respect to Fascism prior to the outbreak of the present war;

(b) If he has participated actively in the struggle against the Germans.

If the broad, extenuating circumstances envisaged by the Penal Code of 1889 should be found to exist, the penalties of death and life imprisonment may be replaced by a period of imprisonment for thirty years, and the other penalties may be reduced by one-sixth.

The guilty party may be declared exempt from punishment if he has particularly distinguished himself with acts of valor during the struggle against the Germans.

Art. 8: Whoever, for Fascist motives or in order to take advantage of the political situation created by Fascism, has committed acts of particular gravity which though perhaps falling short of criminal acts are nevertheless contrary to the norms of rectitude and political probity, shall be subject to temporary exclusion from public office and even to deprivation of his political rights for a period not to exceed ten years.

The provisions envisaged by the present article shall be applied by Provincial Committees presided over by a magistrate and composed of two other members chosen by lot from the peoples' judges referred to in Article 4.

As regards members of the Legislative Assemblies or of agencies or institutes that by their votes or actions contributed to the maintenance of the Fascist regime and to making possible the war, their dismissal from their posts shall be decided by the High Court referred to in Article 2; and this shall be without prejudice to the sanctions set forth in the present decree insofar as these are applicable.

Art. 9: Without prejudice to penal action, the property of those citizens who have betrayed the fatherland by spontaneously and actively placing themselves at the service of the German invaders shall be confiscated to the advantage of the State.

In the case of penal action, confiscation shall be prounounced by whatever judiciary authority hands down the sentence. In other cases, it shall be pronounced by the competent tribunal for the territory, upon request of the High Commissioner.

Art. 10: The dispositions of the Code of Penal Procedure, insofar as they are applicable, shall be valid for anything that is not covered in the present title.

By autumn, however, the purge ground almost to a halt in the face of bureaucratic foot-dragging and a veto expressly imposed by Churchill to prevent Sforza (who was vigorously antimonarchist) from being given a cabinet position. Premier Bonomi was thus forced to restructure his government in December, 1944, without the participation of either the Socialist or Action parties, both of which were thoroughly angered by Churchill's interference. As a kind of political miasma settled over Rome, the eyes of Italians began to turn, hopefully or fearfully as the case might be, toward the Po Valley, where a powerful Resistance force was preparing to launch its liberation offensive against the Germans and their Fascist collaborators.

Mussolini was a prisoner atop the Gran Sasso in the Apennines when the armistice was announced on September 8, 1943. In the confusion that occurred when the King and Badoglio fled from Rome, Hitler was able to send Captain Otto Skorzeny and some ninety paratroopers in gliders to swoop down and rescue the former dictator like a second Andromeda. The sickly *Duce* was flown to Germany, where in humiliation he confronted the *Führer.* The old Axis relationship was finished; henceforth it was, at best, a "brutal friendship." When the *Duce* intimated that he thought his own career had run its course, Hitler snapped that if he wished to return to Italy he must head a pro-Nazi government and place the "traitors of July 25" on trial. If Mussolini had refused, Hitler would have turned to someone even more Germanophile, like Roberto Farinacci. Powerless, the *Duce* listened apathetically to the harangue and acquiesced. Later Hitler sought to cheer him by alluding to "secret weapons" that would assure ultimate victory, and he referred him to his own quack physician for treatment. The latter, according to Joseph Goebbels, found Mussolini suffering from circulatory trouble and disordered bowels, "the typical ailment of a modern revolutionary politician."[1]

Quickly Hitler shunted Mussolini to Munich to broadcast a message to his fellow countrymen. Somehow the old spellbinder mustered the requisite quota of bombast on September 18 as he appealed to faithful Blackshirts to renew Axis solidarity, regroup Italian armed forces around the Fascist Militia, purge the "royalist betrayers" of the regime, and destroy the "parasitical plutocracy" so that labor could now become the "indestructible basis of the state."

1. Louis P. Lochner (ed.), *The Goebbels Diaries, 1942–1943* (Garden City: Doubleday, 1948), p. 470.

Mussolini's Denunciation of the House of Savoy
(September 18, 1943)

Blackshirts! Italian men and women! After a long silence my voice reaches you again, and I am sure that you recognize it. It is the voice that has summoned you on difficult occasions and that has celebrated with you the triumphant days of our fatherland. I waited a few days before addressing you because, after a period of moral isolation, it was necessary for me to re-establish contact with the world.

Long speeches are inappropriate on the radio, and in order to be brief, I shall begin with July 25, the day in which the most incredible of all the adventures of my adventurous life took place. . . . [At this point Mussolini described at length his experiences since July 25, 1943.]

While we recognize our responsibilities, we wish also to set forth clearly those of others, beginning with the Chief of State, who, having exposed himself but failing to abdicate—as the majority of Italians had expected he would—can and must be called directly to account. It is his dynasty which throughout the war—a war which the King himself declared—has been the principal agent of defeatism and of anti-German propaganda. His lack of interest regarding the course of the war, and his prudent and not always so prudent mental reservations have lent themselves to all kinds of profit by the enemy. As for the heir to the throne [Crown Prince Humbert], although he asked to take command of the armies of the south, he has never appeared on the battlefield. Now I am more than ever convinced that the House of Savoy intended to prepare and organize the *coup d'état*, even in its smallest details, with Badoglio as an accomplice and executor, and with the complicity also of certain pusillanimous and shirking generals and certain cowardly Fascist elements. There can be no doubt but that the King authorized armistice negotiations right after my arrest, negotiations that perhaps were already under way between the dynasties of Rome and London. It was the King who advised his accomplices to trick Germany in the vilest way, even denying that negotiations were in progress after they had been concluded. It is the dynastic establish-

SOURCE: Radio address from Munich. Printed in *Il Corriere della Sera* (Milan), September 19, 1943. My translation.

ment which planned and carried out the demolition of Fascism, the very Fascism that twenty years ago had saved it. . . .

In view of all these facts, it is not the regime that betrayed the monarchy, but rather the monarchy that betrayed the regime. . . . When a monarchy fails in its duties, it loses all reasons for further existence. As for our traditions, they are far more republican than they are monarchist. The unity and independence of Italy were desired more by the republican current and its purest and greatest apostle, Giuseppe Mazzini, than they were by the monarchists. The State that we wish to erect will be national and social in the highest sense of the word—that is to say, it will be Fascist by going back to our origins.

While waiting for the movement to develop until it becomes irresistible, our postulates shall be the following:

1. Take up arms once more alongside Germany, Japan, and the other allies. Only blood can cancel such a shameful page from the history of the fatherland.

2. Set about reorganizing without delay our armed forces around the Militia formations. . . .

3. Eliminate the traitors and particularly those who until 9:30 P.M. of July 25 were members of the Party—and in some cases for many years—and who have joined the ranks of the enemy.

4. Annihilate the parasitic plutocracies, and finally make of labor the object of our economy and the indestructible foundation of the State. . . .

Farmers, laborers, and white-collar workers! The State that will emerge from this gigantic ordeal will be yours, and as such you will defend it against anyone who dreams of an impossible return to the past.

Our will, our courage, our faith will restore to Italy its good face, its future, its possibility for life, and its place in the world. More than just a hope, this must be a supreme certainty for all of you.

Long live Italy! Long live the Republican Fascist Party!

Soon Mussolini and other top Fascists were sent back to northern Italy to organize an "Italian Social Republic." Its capital was to be situated at the resort town of Salò on the shore of Lake Garda, close to the German communications line over the Brenner, so that Mussolini and his entourage could be kept under close surveillance by SS General

Karl Wolff and Ambassador Rudolf Rahn. Knowing that he had lost the support of most of the upper and middle classes, Mussolini desperately sought to ingratiate himself with the northern working groups. To this end, he refurbished some of the slogans he had expressed in his socialistic youth; he also did his best to blame the corruption of the regime's final years on profiteering "plutocrats" and minions of the monarchy.

The signal was given to fanatic Militiamen to organize a brand-new Partito Fascista Repubblicano (PFR); Alessandro Pavolini became its secretary. This new Republican Fascist party held its first (and only) congress in Verona in mid-November, 1943. There Mussolini unwrapped a demagogic, eighteen-point manifesto that sought to undercut Communist appeal to the working masses and at the same time not alienate completely whatever support he could still elicit from the propertied and lower-middle-class groups who in the past had loomed so large in the political sociology of Fascism. In some respects the Verona manifesto harked back to Mussolini's pre-World War I Marxian views and to the 1919 republican edition of "Fascism of the first hour."

The Verona Manifesto of
Mussolini's Italian Social Republic
(November 14, 1943)

In its first national report, the Fascist Republican Party:

Lifts its thoughts to those who have sacrificed their lives for republican Fascism on the battlefronts, in the piazzas of the cities and villages, in the limestone pits of Istria and Dalmatia, and who should be added to the ranks of the martyrs of our Revolution, and to the phalanx of all those men who have died for Italy.

It regards continuation of the war alongside Germany and Japan until final victory, and the speedy reconstruction of our Armed Forces which will serve alongside the valorous soldiers of the *Führer*, as goals that tower above everything else in importance and urgency.

It takes note of the decrees instituting the Extraordinary Tribunals, whereby party members will carry out their unbending determination to administer exemplary justice; and, inspired by Mussolini's stimulus and accomplishments, it enunciates the following programmatic directives for Party actions:

SOURCE: Printed in Attilio Tamaro, *Due anni di storia, 1943–1945*, II (Rome: Tosi, 1949), 249–252. My translation.

With Respect to Domestic Constitutional Matters

1. A Constituent Assembly must be convened. As the sovereign power of popular origin, it shall declare an end to the Monarchy, solemnly condemn the traitorous and fugitive last King, proclaim the Social Republic, and appoint its Head.

2. The Constituent Assembly shall be composed of representatives of all the syndical associations and all the administrative districts, and it shall include representatives of the occupied provinces by means of delegations from those evacuees and refugees who are in liberated territory. It shall likewise include representatives of the combatants and the prisoners of war by means of the repatriation of disabled personnel; representatives of Italians abroad; of the courts, of the universities, and of every other body or institution whose participation will contribute to making the Constituent Assembly a synthesis of all the worthy elements of the Nation.

3. The Republican Constituent Assembly must ensure to citizens, soldiers, workers, and taxpayers the rights to check up on and make responsible criticism of the actions of the various public administrations.

Every five years citizens shall be called upon to vote on the appointment of the Head of the Republic.

No citizens who is arrested *in flagrante* or for preventive reasons may be held more than seven days without an order from the judiciary authority, and an order from the judiciary authority shall also be required for searches in domiciles.

In the exercise of their duties the courts shall act with complete freedom.

4. Both the negative electoral experience that Italy has already gone through and the partially negative experience of a method of nomination that proved to be too rigidly hierarchical make it necessary to find a solution that will reconcile opposing needs. A mixed system seems to be most advisable—for example, popular election of the representatives in the Chamber, and appointment of ministers by action of the Head of the Republic and the Government; and elections of the Fascio in the Party, save for ratification and appointment of the National Directory by action of the *Duce*.

5. There must be only one organization that shall have the task of training people for political activity.

The Party, which is an order of fighters and believers, must become an organism of absolute political purity, worthy of being the custodian of the Revolutionary Idea.

Membership in the party shall not be necessary for any employment or task.

6. The religion of the Republic shall be the apostolic Roman Catholic one. Every other cult that does not violate the law shall be respected.

7. All those who belong to the Jewish race are foreigners. For the duration of the war they shall be regarded as being of enemy nationality.

In Foreign Policy

8. The essential goal of the Republic's foreign policy must be the unity, independence, and territorial integrity of the fatherland within the maritime and Alpine boundaries that were laid out by nature, by the sacrifice of blood, and by history—boundaries which are threatened by the enemy through invasion and through the promises made by London to refugee governments.

Another essential goal shall consist of demanding recognition of the need for living space that is indispensable for a population of 45 million in an area that is insufficient to feed them.

Such a policy, moreover, shall be carried out through the establishment of a "European Community," based on a federation of all those nations which accept the following principles:

(a) Elimination from our continent of the centuries-old British intrigues;

(b) Abolition of the internal capitalistic system, and struggle against the world plutocracies;

(c) Development of the natural resources of Africa for the benefit of both European peoples and the natives, and with absolute respect for those people who—like the Egyptian Muslims in particular—are already organized in civic groupings.

In Social Matters

9. The Basis of the Social Republic and its primary object shall be manual, technical, and intellectual labor in all of its manifestations.

10. Private property, which is the fruit of labor and of individual savings and the integration of the human personality, shall be guaranteed by the State.

11. In the national economy the State's sphere of action shall embrace everything that because of its dimensions or functions lies outside the private sector and falls within the collective interest.

Public utilities and, as a rule, munitions industries must be managed by the State through government-controlled agencies.

12. In every enterprise (industrial, private, state, or government-regulated) representatives of technicians and workers shall work closely together (and with full knowledge on the part of management) in the establishment of fair wages and in the equitable distribution of profits to provide reserve funds, rewards for capital investment, and profit sharing by the workers themselves.

In certain enterprises this may take place by extending the prerogatives of existing factory shop-steward committees; in others, by replacing administrative committees with management committees composed of technicians and workers along with a representative of the State; and in still others, by means of para-syndical co-operatives.

13. In agriculture, the proprietor's right of private initiative shall be restricted whenever there is evidence of an absence of such initiative.

The expropriation of uncultivated lands and of badly managed farms may lead either to subdivision of these lands among the day workers in such a way as to transform them into private farmers, or to the establishment of co-operative farms of a para-syndical or para-statal type, depending on the specific agricultural economic need.

This is, in any case, already anticipated by existing legislation, and the Party and syndical organizations are providing the necessary impetus for the implementation thereof.

14. The right of private farmers, artisans, professional people, and artists to carry on productive work for their individual families and other groupings shall be fully recognized, save for their obligation to deliver to collection depots those quantities of produce that are set forth by law, and to be checked as to the accuracy of such deliveries.

15. Since housing is not only a right of property but a right to property, the Party is inscribing in its program the creation of a National Agency for People's Housing, which shall take over the existing Institute, broaden its activity to the utmost, and supervise the providing of housing to workers' families in every category either by means of outright construction of new residences or by gradual renovation of existing ones.

With respect thereto, the general principle is hereby affirmed that rental payments shall constitute legal title of acquisition as soon as the investor's capital has been reimbursed in just measure.

This agency shall requisition and distribute unused premises and shall undertake temporary construction as its first task in resolving the problems brought about by wartime destruction.

16. The fact that a worker is enrolled by the authorities in an occupational syndicate shall not prevent his being transferred to another syndicate if he should have the requisite qualifications. The syndicates shall be combined in a single confederation that shall include all workers, technicians, and professional men but shall exclude those proprietors who are neither directors nor technicians. It shall be entitled the General Confederation of Labor, Technology, and the Arts.

Employees of state industrial enterprises and of public utilities shall form occupational syndicates in the same manner as every other worker. All the imposing social security measures that have been put into effect by the Fascist Regime during the past twenty years shall remain in effect. The Charter of Labor provided the consecration of this program both in word and in spirit and shall be the point of departure for further progress.

17. With regard to one of our most urgent current problems, the Party believes that there must be no delay in instituting a program of fair wages for the workers, to be achieved through agreements that set up minimum national standards, and also through prompt local readjustments. This is even more urgent for low-income and medium-income employees of both state and private enterprises. In order for this measure to be effective and not turn out to be harmful in the final analysis for all concerned, it will be necessary that a portion of wages and salaries shall be paid in the form of commodities, to be distributed at officially established prices through co-operatives, factory commissaries, and an expanded "Provvida" agency. Any store found guilty of violations shall be requisitioned and placed under either para-statal or co-operative forms of management.

Only in this way can there be stabilization of prices and monetary values, and purification of market operations.

As for the black market, it is imperative that speculators—who are on the same moral level with traitors and defeatists—shall be brought within the jurisdiction of the Extraordinary Tribunals and made subject to the death penalty.

18. By means of this preamble to the work of the Constituent Assembly, the Party is demonstrating that not only is it moving toward the people, it is staying with the people. The Italian people, for their part, must realize that there is only one way for them to

safeguard the achievements of yesterday, today, and tomorrow—
and that is by hurling back the enslaving invasion of the Anglo-
American plutocracies, who have shown in a thousand clear ways
that they intend to make even more difficult and miserable the lives
of Italians.

There is only one way to attain all of our social goals: Fight!
Work! Win!

On January 13, 1944, the Italian Social Republic announced the
"Premise for a New Italian Economic Structure." Socialization, this
document explained, would occur wherever necessary for national self-
sufficiency and in those sectors concerned with production of raw
materials, energy, and indispensable services. In these the state would
be financier and administrator, issuing bonds to reimburse the present
investors. Workers would share in the management of both national-
ized and private enterprises. Publicly financed ones would be run by a
management council elected by all the workers, clerks, and technicians; privately financed enterprises would be run by councils in which
the workers would be equally represented with the stockholders. In
private shops, or where there was a single boss with at least fifty
workers, a three-member advisory council of workers, clerks, and
technicians would be instituted. Additional regulations set forth responsibilities of the factory head and methods for his removal.

The neo-Fascists sought to preserve and utilize the factory shop-
steward committees or "internal commissions" (which the Socialists
and Communists had re-established during Badoglio's "45 days") but
to put their own men in control of them. The left-wing parties quickly
disavowed such perverted committees and organized in their place new
underground "agitation committees." The Social Republic proved to
be as unsuccessful in achieving its socio-economic and political goals as
in recruiting voluntary military support. Actual socialization never got
beyond a few tentative beginnings, and the much discussed Constituent
Assembly never met.

The brutality of the neo-Fascist regime was made evident to everyone by the Verona purge trial of January 8–10, 1944, at which
Mussolini, under pressure from Berlin, had his own son-in-law and
several other hierarchs found guilty and shot for their "traitorous"
action at the Fascist Grand Council meeting of July 24/25, 1943.

Meanwhile, in myriad ways the great majority of people in the
north made it clear they were surfeited with Mussolini's opportunistic
rhetoric and the dregs of society who followed him about in these last
months. Anxiously awaiting the arrival of liberation forces from the
south, thousands of northerners who were in danger of being con-
scripted into Nazi-Fascist military units and felt they had nothing to
lose joined the Armed Resistance which was developing in the mountains and later in the cities, chiefly under the aegis of the Committees
of National Liberation. If caught by the enemy, as thousands of
resisters were, they could expect no mercy.

Hopes were high that the summer of 1944 would bring emancipation to the north. Rome had been liberated in June, and Florence in August. But thereafter the polyglot Allied forces, whose strength in Italy had been greatly sapped in order to carry out what proved to be an unnecessary invasion of southern France in August, 1944, bogged down in the rugged Apennines short of Bologna. The Nazi-Fascists carried out cruel combing operations against Resistance units that had organized free "republics" in many narrow valleys. When the patriots received word from Allied headquarters in November that it would be necessary to hibernate for the winter, a great wave of despair swept through their ranks. It was in the midst of this "letdown" on the part of the anti-Fascists that Mussolini left Salò and traveled to his old stronghold of Milan to deliver what turned out to be his last public address on December 16, 1944. It proved to be one of his best oratorical performances and aroused short-lived enthusiasm on the part of his audience in the Lirico Theater. The *Duce* set forth his version of the events of the preceding year and a half with skill and held out some olive branches to those who were not strictly Fascist. The "single party" upon which the Social Republic was founded must be preserved, he said, but alongside it might exist other groups with the right of responsible, constructive criticism within the framework of the neo-Fascist regime.

Mussolini's Last Public Address
(Milan, December 16, 1944)

Comrades! Dear comrades of Milan! I shall dispense with any preamble and enter immediately into the heart of the subject matter of my speech.

At sixteen months' distance from the tremendous date of the unconditional surrender, imposed and accepted according to the democratic and criminal formula of Casablanca, the evaluation of events poses once more for us these questions: Who is guilty of betrayal? Who has suffered or is suffering the consequences of this treachery? . . .

The unconditional surrender announced on September 8 was desired by the Monarchy, by Court circles, by the plutocratic currents of the Italian bourgeoisie, by certain clerical forces, combined for the occasion with Masonic ones, and by the General Staffs which no longer believed in victory and which were headed by Badoglio. As early as . . . May 15, the ex-King wrote in his diary (which has recently come into our possession) that we must "disengage" from the German alliance. Beyond a shadow of doubt,

SOURCE: *Il Corriere della Sera* (Milan), December 17, 1944. My translation.

it was the ex-King who ordered the surrender, and Badoglio who carried it out. But in order to get to September 8, there first had to be a July 25—viz., the *coup d'état* and the change of regime.

The justification for the surrender—viz., the impossibility of continuing the war—was denied forty days later, on October 13, when war was declared against Germany. That declaration was no mere symbolic act. From that time on there has been collaboration between Badoglio's Italy and the Allies, carried on behind the lines by labor units; while the fleet, which had been built in its entirety by Fascism, passed completely into the hands of the enemy and immediately began to operate with the enemy fleets. Thus, it was not peace, but rather continuation of the war by means of so-called co-belligerency. It was not peace, but rather the transformation of the entire territory of the nation into one immense battlefield—and that is to say, one immense field of ruins. It was not peace, but rather the now predicted participation of Italian ships and troops in the war against Japan.

From all of this it is clear that those who have suffered the consequences of the betrayal are, first of all, the Italian people. It can be declared that the Italian people did not commit treason toward the German ally. Except for a few sporadic instances, Army units melted away without offering any resistance to orders coming from the German commands to disarm. Many Army units that were located away from the fatherland, and many Air Corps units, rallied at once to the side of the German forces—and this was true of tens of thousands of men. All the formations of the Militia, except for one battalion in Corsica, went over—every last man of them—to the side of the Germans. . . .

. . . While a portion of the Italian people accepted the surrender as a result of either irresponsibility or exhaustion, another portion lined up at once alongside Germany. It is time to tell our Italian, German, and Japanese comrades that the contribution made by Republican Italy to the common cause since September, 1943— and despite the temporary reduction in size of the Republic's territory—has been far greater than is commonly believed.

For obvious reasons, I cannot go into detailed statistics of the total contribution made by Italy in both the economic and the military sectors. Our collaboration with the Reich in soldiers and workers is represented by this figure: 786,000 men on September 30 [1944]. This fact is incontrovertible, since it comes from German sources. One should add to this the formerly interned military personnel—that is to say, several hundred thousand men involved in Germany's productive process—and other tens of thousands of Italians who already were in the Reich, where they had gone in recent years as free laborers in the factories and fields. In the face of this evidence, Italians who live in the territory of the Social Republic have the right, once and for all, to raise their heads and demand that their effort be fairly judged in a comradely manner by all members of the Tripartite Pact. . . .

On September 15 [1943], the National Fascist Party became the Fascist Republican Party. At that time there was no dearth of sick and opportunistic elements—perhaps they were in a state of mental confusion—who wondered if it would not have been wiser to eliminate the word "Fascism," and to place the accent exclusively on the word "Republic." I rejected then, just as I would reject today, that useless and cowardly suggestion.

It would have been both cowardliness and an error to lower our banner which had been consecrated by so much blood, and to allow those ideas that are serving today as the password in the intercontinental struggle to circulate almost as though they were contraband. By treating this as a matter of expediency, we would have suffered the consequences and been discredited in the eyes of the enemy and especially in our own midst.

Thus by continuing to call ourselves Fascists, as we shall always do, and by dedicating ourselves to the cause of Fascism as we have done since 1919 until the present, we have given, in the wake of recent events, a new thrust to action in both the political and the social fields. Actually, more than a new thrust; one might better say, a return to original positions. It is a matter of historical record that prior to 1922 Fascism had republican tendencies, and the reasons why the insurrection of 1922 spared the Monarchy have been explained.

From the social standpoint, the program of Republican Fascism is but the logical continuation of the program of 1919—of the achievements of the splendid years that took place between the announcement of the Labor Charter and the conquest of the empire. Nature does not operate by leaps; and economics even less so.

It was necessary first to build a foundation of syndical legislation and corporative bodies before we could take the subsequent step toward socialization. Even at the first meeting of the Council of Ministers on September 27, 1943, I declared that "the Republic would be unitary in the political field and decentralized in the administrative one, and that it would have a very pronounced social content in order to resolve the social question in at least its most glaring aspects, and in order to stabilize the status, function, and responsibility of labor in a truly modern national society."

In that same meeting, I carried out the first step designed to achieve the broadest possible national harmony, by announcing that the Government excluded the possibility of any rigorous measures against anti-Fascist elements.

In October I drafted and revised what is known in Italian political history as the Manifesto of Verona, which set forth in several well-defined points the program not only of the Party but of the Republic. That took place on November 15, just two months after the reconstitution of the Fascist Republican Party.

That Manifesto of the National Assembly of the Fascist Republican Party—after offering a salute to those who have sacrificed their lives for the Fascist cause, and reaffirming as its supreme goal the continuation of the struggle alongside the powers of the Tripartite Alliance, and the reconstruction of the Armed Forces— set forth its eighteen-point program.

Let us look now at what has been done, what has not been done, and above all why it has not been done.

The Manifesto began by demanding the convocation of a Constituent Assembly. This has not been summoned, and it will not be until after the war. I tell you with the utmost frankness that I found it superfluous to convene a Constituent Assembly when the territorial extent of the Republic, in view of the course of military operations, cannot in any way be regarded as definitive. It seemed to me premature to create a proper legal state with fully developed institutions when there were no armed forces to defend it. A state that does not have armed forces available is anything but a state.

In the Manifesto it was said that no citizen can be held more than seven days without an order from the judiciary authority. That has not always occurred. The reasons are to be found in the multiplicity of our own police agencies and those of our ally, as well as in the activity of the outlaws who have sought to shift these problems to the level of civil war based on reprisals and counter-reprisals. Anti-Fascists have sought to play up certain episodes and have distorted the facts with their usual false generalizations. But I must say in the most explicit way possible that such methods deeply disgust me, even if they are employed only occasionally. The State, as such, cannot adopt methods that degrade it. For centuries people have talked about the law of retaliation. Well, it must be a law and not a more or less personal and arbitrary action. . . .

Since the Party is in the process of becoming an "order of fighters" through the creation of the Black Brigades, the Verona postulate has the character of an inviolable and sacred pledge. In that same Article V which states that a Party membership card is not a prerequisite for any employment or post, a solution was given to the problem that I shall label collaboration with other elements in governing the Republic. In my telegram dated March 10 of the Year XXII [1944] to the heads of provinces, that formula was used again and better defined. As a result, any discussion of a multiparty system is completely inappropriate.

In the course of history, among the various forms in which the republic has developed as a political institution among different peoples, there have been many republics of a totalitarian type— that is to say, with just one party. I shall not mention the most totalitarian of them, that of the Soviets, but I shall recall one that enjoys the sympathies of the high bonzes of the democratic gospel—the Turkish Republic, which rests on a single party, that of the people, and on a single youth organization, the Turkish Hearth.

At a certain point in Italy's historical evolution it may develop that there will be fruitful results if, alongside the single Party that is responsible for the overall direction of the State, there may be other groups present which, as Article III of the Manifesto of Verona says, can exercise the right of review and responsible criticism of the actions of the public administration. Groups which, on the basis of their loyal, integral, and unreserved acceptance of the trinomial of Italy, Republic, and Socialization, would have the responsibility of examining the measures of the Government and of local agencies, of reviewing the methods of application of these measures, as well as the persons who are entrusted with public offices and who must be answerable in their work to the citizen in his composite role of soldier-worker-taxpayer.

The assembly of Verona set forth in Article VIII its postulates regarding foreign policy. It was solemnly affirmed that the essential goal of the Republic's foreign policy is "the unity, independence, and territorial integrity of the fatherland within the maritime and Alpine boundaries that were laid out by nature, by the sacrifice of blood, and by history."

As regards territorial unity, I refuse—because I know Sicily and our Sicilian brothers—to take seriously the so-called separatist movements of despicable mercenaries financed by the enemy. Perhaps this separatism has another motive—our Sicilian brothers may want to break away from Bonomi's Italy in order to join up with Republican Italy.

It is my profound conviction that as soon as the struggles are behind us and the phenomenon of outlawry is liquidated, the moral unity of Italians tomorrow will be infinitely stronger than it was yesterday, because it will have been cemented by exceptional sufferings that have not spared a single family. And when the soul of a people is saved through moral unity, its territorial integrity and its political independence are also saved.

At this point a word should be said about Europe and our conception thereof. I shall not linger over the question of what is Europe, of where it begins and where it ends from a geographical standpoint. Nor shall I speculate whether an attempt at unification today would have better success than previous ones. That would lead me too far astray. I shall say here only that the formation of a European community is desirable and perhaps even possible, but I must say very explicitly that we do not feel we are Italians because we are Europeans; rather we feel we are Europeans because we are Italians. The distinction is not just a subtlety; it is fundamental.

Just as the nation is the result of millions of families who possess their own physiognomy even though they also possess a national common denominator, so in the European community every nation must join as a well-defined entity in order to avoid letting the community itself sink into internationalism of a socialist stamp or vegetate in the generic, equivocal cosmopolitanism of Jewish and Masonic stamp.

While some points in the Verona program have been outstripped by a succession of military events, more concrete achievements have been realized in the economic and social field. Here the innovation has radical aspects. Points XI, XII, and XIII [of the Verona Manifesto] are fundamental. Set forth in the "Premise for a New Italian Economic Structure," they have found their practical application in the Law on Socialization. The interest aroused throughout the world has been truly great, and today in all quarters—even in that part of Italy dominated and tortured by the Anglo-Americans—every political program contains the demand for socialization.

Workers who at first were somewhat skeptical now understand the importance of it. Its implementation is in progress. Its rhythm would have been faster in other times. But the seed has been sown. Whatever happens, this seed is bound to germinate. It is the inauguration of that which eight years ago, here in Milan before 500,000 cheering people, I prophesied would be the "century of labor," in which the laborer would emerge from the economic and moral status of a wage earner to assume the role of a producer who is personally involved in the development of the nation's economy and prosperity.

Fascist socialization is the logical and rational solution that, on the one hand, avoids the bureaucratization of the economy through State totalitarianism and, on the other, overcomes the individualism of the liberal economic system which, though it proved to be a useful instrument for progress in the early phase of the capitalistic form of economics, is today no longer suitable in the face of new demands of a "social" character in the various national communities.

Through socialization, the best elements drawn from the ranks of the workers will be able to demonstrate their talents. I am determined to continue in this direction.

I have already entrusted two sectors to the various categories of laborers—viz., local administration and food distribution. These sectors, which are very important and especially so under present circumstances, are already completely in the hands of the workers. Now they must show, and I hope that they will show, their specific preparation and their civic-mindedness.

As you see, something has been accomplished during these twelve months, in the midst of incredible and growing difficulties brought about by objective circumstances of the war and blind opposition from those elements who have sold out to the foe. . . .

In very recent days the situation has improved. The fence-straddlers, those who were waiting on the side lines for the Anglo-Americans to come, are in decline. What has happened in Bonomi's Italy has brought them disillusionment. Everything that the Anglo-Americans promised them has turned out to be a miserable propagandistic trick. I think I am right when I declare that the people of the Po Valley not only do not want the arrival of the Anglo-Saxons; they scorn them. And they do not want to have anything to do with a government which—even though it has Togliatti as a vice-premier—would bring back to the north the reactionary, plutocratic, and dynastic forces—these latter already openly enjoying the protection of England. . . .

We intend to defend the Po Valley tooth and nail. [*Shouts of*

"Yes!"] We intend that the Po Valley shall remain republican while we wait for all of Italy to become republican. [*Enthusiastic shouts of* "Yes!" "All!"] If the day should ever come when the entire Po Valley is contaminated by the enemy, the destiny of the entire nation will be compromised. But I sense, I see, that tomorrow a form of armed and irresistible organization will arise that will render life practically impossible for the invaders. We should make out of the entire Po Valley a single Athens! [*The crowd erupts in unanimous shouts of approval:* "Yes! Yes!"]

From what I have told you, it is obvious that not only has the enemy coalition not won; it will not win. The monstrous alliance between plutocracy and Bolshevism was able to perpetrate its barbaric war like the execution of an enormous crime, and it has struck crowds of innocent people and destroyed what European civilization created over a span of twenty centuries. But it shall not succeed in destroying with its darkness the eternal spirit that built these monuments.

Our absolute faith in victory rests not on motives of a subjective or sentimental nature, but on positive and determined elements. If we were to doubt our victory, we should have to deny the existence of Him who rules, according to justice, the destinies of man.

When we as soldiers of the Republic re-establish contact with the Italians on the other side of the Apennines, we shall have the pleasant surprise of finding more Fascism there than we left behind. The disillusionment, the misery, the political and moral abjection are exploding not only in the old phrase, "We were better off . . . ," but in the revolts which from Palermo to Catania, and from Otranto to Rome itself, are creeping through every portion of "liberated" Italy.

The Italian people south of the Apennines have their spirits full of burning nostalgia. Enemy oppression on the one hand and the bestial persecution by the Government on the other cannot help but give nourishment to the Fascist movement. It was easy to erase the external symbols; to suppress the idea is impossible! [*The crowd shouts,* "Never!"]

The six anti-Fascist parties are bustling to proclaim that Fascism is dead, because they sense that it is alive. Millions of Italians are comparing yesterday with today; yesterday, when the banner of the fatherland was waving from the Alps to equatorial Somalia and Italians were one of the most respected peoples on earth.

There is no Italian who does not feel his heart beat faster at the sound of an African name, at the sound of a hymn that accompanied the legions from the Mediterranean to the Red Sea, at the sight of a colonial helmet. There are millions of Italians who from 1929 to 1939 lived through what can be called the epic poetry of the fatherland. These Italians still exist; they are suffering, and they still believe in and are ready to close ranks to resume the march in order to reconquer all that was lost and is today garrisoned between the dunes of Libya and the tropical fruit trees of Ethiopia by thousands and thousands of casualties, the flower of innumerable Italian families who have not forgotten and are unable to forget.

Already the signs signaling this resumption can be seen, especially here in this city of Milan, which is always in the forefront and warlike, and which the enemy has savagely struck but not in the least subdued.

Comrades! Dear Milanese comrades! It is Milan which must give, and shall give, the men, the arms, the will, and the signal of resurgence! [*Applause. . . .*]

Mussolini hoped that his reversion to some of the policies of "Fascism of the first hour" would underscore the differences between the Social Republic and the capitalistic southern kingdom which, according to him, was subservient to Allied "plutocracies." The first socialization of large industrial enterprises took place in February, 1945; in March the program was extended to many steel, chemical, paper, and printing establishments. Fiat, Montecatini, Alfa Romeo, and Acciaierie Lombarde were among the plants affected. Mussolini made no effort to resurrect the corporative state.

The *Duce*'s sudden renewal of interest in the proletariat met with skepticism from most workers, who knew well that for two decades Fascist economics had been geared far more to the well-being of property owners than to that of themselves. Resistance leaders quickly warned workers of the "colossal fraud" of "socialization" and often achieved resounding success. For example, when 32,676 Fiat employees in Turin were asked to vote in March on nominations for shop-steward committees and management councils, 31,450 abstained. There were 547 blank ballots, and 274 were nullified. Only 405 were valid.[2]

By late March most Fascist hierarchs sensed that Allied forces would break into the Po Valley at any time. Desperately hoping to stave off at least some of the retribution they could surely expect, they sought to dismantle some of the most vicious of their heterogeneous police

2. Raimondo Luraghi, *Il movimento operaio torinese durante la resistenza* (Turin, 1958), pp. 268–270.

forces. But it was too late to make the Italian people forget the terroristic aspects of the police state that had been operating alongside the Germans. The insurrection and liberation occurred before the "face lifting" could be finished.

On April 5 the Allies kicked off their final offensive. By April 14/15 they had blasted their way into the flatland sector between Imola and Bologna. On the twelfth the supreme organ of the Resistance, the Committee of National Liberation for Upper Italy (CLNAI), denounced as war criminals all members of the Fascist directorate and next day laid down guidelines for handling Nazi-Fascist prisoners.

Mussolini left Salò for Milan on the evening of April 18 and set up headquarters in the prefectural palace. He did not yet know that SS General Karl Wolff was trying to negotiate an armistice with Allied representatives in Switzerland. In Milan many schemes raced through his mind. One was an abortive effort to turn over political power to the Socialist and Action parties in an effort to split the Committee of National Liberation and save his own skin. The left-wing parties immediately turned him down. Then, through an emissary, he sought to win a guarantee from Resistance leaders that would allow him and his henchmen, and their families, to retreat from Milan into the northern Valtellina. The response to this was curt: if the *Duce* wished to surrender unconditionally, he must come to the CLNAI in the sole place that it considered to be neutral, the palace of the archbishop in Milan's Piazza Fontana. Only in that way might he gain assurance of a regular trial.

The insurrection in Milan, the nerve center of the Armed Resistance, took place between April 24 and 26. On the twenty-fifth the CLNAI agreed upon various decrees, one of which established special popular courts of assize, tribunals of war, and commissions of justice. By implication it ordered Mussolini's execution, for Article 5 stated:

> Members of the Fascist Government and the hierarchs of Fascism who are guilty of suppressing the constitutional guarantees, destroying popular liberties, creating the Fascist regime, compromising and betraying the fate of the country, and conducting it to the present catastrophe are to be punished with the penalty of death, and in less grave instances life-imprisonment.[3]

Those who organized Fascist squads that carried out deeds of violence and those who led the "insurrection" of October 28, 1922, were to be punished according to the Penal Code of 1889. Anyone guilty of crimes against the state since September 8, 1943, would be punished in accordance with the military laws of war in effect as of that time. The accused might defend himself if he could prove that he had prevented

3. The decree is cited in Franco Catalano, *Storia del CLNAI* (Bari: Laterza, 1956), pp. 413–419.

atrocities and destruction of national property. Or, if he had been forced to collaborate with the foe as a result of grave threats to his person or family, he could plead for leniency. Unquestionably this was stern. "If the Liberation had occurred a year earlier," one of the key CLNAI officials has observed, "the insurrectional movement would have shown much greater generosity. But the ferocious Nazi-Fascist repressions of the second half of 1944 had embittered the popular mind."[4]

At about 5 P.M. on April 25, Mussolini and a handful of his friends arrived at Cardinal Schuster's palace in Milan. An hour later CLNAI representatives appeared. Mussolini asked what dispositions they were ready to make. Their answer was still the terse formula "Unconditional surrender." The ensuing conversation brought out the fact that the Germans were negotiating with the Resistance and the Allies without having notified Mussolini. The *Duce* thereupon jumped up, sputtering, "Once too often Germany has stabbed Italy in the back! The Germans have always treated us like slaves." Then he asked to be excused so that he could speak with the German consul, promising to return by 8 P.M.

Instead, he and his retinue decided to flee in a motor caravan, heading for Switzerland. Unable to cross the border, he threw in his lot once more with the Germans, hiding himself in a truck in one of their convoys retreating up the western shore of Lake Como. On the twenty-seventh the convoy was halted at Musso by a partisan roadblock. Mussolini and his faithful camp follower, Claretta Petacci, as well as various other Fascists were soon recognized by the partisans and taken prisoner. The Germans were allowed to continue on their way. On the afternoon of the twenty-eighth, a Communist execution squad came up from Milan. Ordering Mussolini and Signorina Petacci suddenly to stand up before a garden wall in Giulino di Mezzegra, they fired a burst of bullets into the victims. Their bodies and those of some fifteen other Fascists were then hauled to Milan, the city that had seen the birth of Fascism. Early on Sunday morning, the twenty-ninth, the corpses of the *Duce*, wearing the uniform of a squadrist Militiaman, and his mistress were laid out and then strung up by their feet in a service station at Piazzale Loreto, the same square where a year before the German Command had publicly executed fifteen resisters. An infuriated mob repeatedly kicked and spat upon the swinging cadavers. After this lugubrious display, the corpses of Mussolini and his mistress were buried secretly near Milan. (Eventually in 1957 the *Duce*'s body was removed to the family vault in the cemetery of his home town of Predappio.) The CLNAI deemed it expedient on April 30 to take note of the violent and repulsive scene at Piazzale Loreto and issue a public statement that sought to put the affair into historic perspective.

4. Leo Valiani, *Tutte le strade conducono a Roma* (Florence, 1947), pp. 338–340.

The Execution of Mussolini

. . . The shooting of Mussolini and his accomplices, ordered by the CLNAI, is the necessary conclusion of a historical era which leaves our country still covered by material and moral scars, and the conclusion of an insurrectional struggle which signified for the fatherland the prerequisite for its rebirth and reconstruction. The Italian people could not begin a free and normal life—which Fascism for twenty years denied them—if the CLNAI had not timely demonstrated its iron decision to carry out a judgment which had already been pronounced by history.

Only at the price of this neat break with a shameful and criminal past could the people have the assurance that the CLNAI is determined to pursue with firmness the democratic renovation of the country. Only at this price can there and must there occur, in the forms of strictest legality, the necessary purging of the residues of Fascism at the end of the insurrectional phase.

Fascism itself is the only responsible element for the explosion of popular hate, which on this single occasion has gone to excesses, and which is understandable only in the climate willed and created by Mussolini.

The CLNAI, just as it has known how to conduct the insurrection—admirable for its democratic discipline, which infused into all the insurgents a sense of responsibility in this great historic hour—and just as it has known how, without hesitation, to render justice to those responsible for the ruin of the fatherland, intends that in the new epoch which is now opened to the free Italian people such excesses must not repeat themselves. . . .

The Committees of National Liberation redoubled their efforts to discipline the partisans and the citizenry and generally achieved good results. If there had been no CLN's to exercise authority, the situation could have been much worse. Soon "people's courts of assize" replaced the informal "military tribunals" of the first days. By June these were superseded by "extraordinary courts of assize," approved by the Allied Military Government. The number of Fascists and supposed Fascists who were killed in northern Italy during the insurrectionary period can only be guessed. In 1952 a Christian Democratic Minister of Interior reported to Parliament that the figure was 2,344. One investi-

SOURCE: Statement by the Committee of National Liberation for Upper Italy. Published in *La Libertà* (Milan), April 30, 1945. My translation.

gator who felt sympathy for the other side has estimated 40,000.[5] Probably the truth lay in between.

The Armed Resistance had mobilized at various times between September 8, 1943, and April 25, 1945, some 200,000 men and women. Of these, probably one fifth lost their lives. The over-all casualties of the northern patriots and of the Italian Corps of Liberation that was formed in the south compared favorably with those suffered by the Allies during the entire peninsular campaign. It was largely because of this "other Italy" that a people who had been dazed and demoralized in 1943 could by 1945 regain much of their self-esteem; it was also largely because of this "other Italy" that the nation could become a signatory to a peace treaty in 1947 that was far more generous than Italians could reasonably have expected in September, 1943.

The war had come to an end. So had Italian Fascism. As a matter of fact, Fascism had been moribund at least since 1941–42, when it became clear to the great majority of Italians that Mussolini's ideology and alliance with Hitler meant endless, senseless wars which the country had neither the resources for nor the desire to win. Those industrial, agrarian, military, clerical, and other "fellow travelers" who in earlier years had been happy to "use" Fascism to serve their own purposes quickly began to sever their links with the increasingly demagogic, "proletarian" latter-day Fascism, leaving only a hard core of fanatics to stand by the sickly *Duce* after 1943. A civil war was necessary to eliminate most of this final residue of militant Blackshirts.

Relatively little of what Mussolini regarded as his greatest achievements have endured, apart from the Lateran Pacts with the Church (which were maintained only with the help of Communist votes!), a system of highways, some public works, and certain facets of his social welfare system. The much-touted corporative state collapsed in July, 1943. Its only surviving traces are bits of largely unused machinery in such fields as collective bargaining, in which national and compulsory uniformities are now imposed in labor agreements and are made binding even on those who have not participated in their negotiation. There also continues to be frequent state intervention in the settlement of labor disputes. The Institute for Industrial Reconstruction (IRI), one of the Fascist innovations of the Depression era, has continued. So has the tendency toward greater state participation in many key industries. One must concede, too, that a good many other remnants of Fascist legislation, including that forbidding birth control, have lingered on the books, despite frequent efforts of alert critics to whittle away such anachronisms.

The House of Savoy, which under Victor Emmanuel III had so closely tied itself to the Fascist regime, could not regain its prestige even after the old man's abdication and the advent of young Humbert II as "King of the May" in 1946. A national referendum on June 2, 1946, rejected the monarchy by a vote of 12,717,923 to 10,710,284.

5. Carlo Simiani, *I giustiziati fascisti dell'aprile 1945* (Milan, 1949).

Rome and every province to the north voted solidly in favor of a republican form of government.

The same elections produced a Constituent Assembly that drew up a Constitution for the Italian Republic. It went into effect on January 1, 1948. Those left-wing parties which for a time had hoped that the Committees of National Liberation could be preserved and integrated into the political structure were disappointed. Instead, the pre-Fascist parliamentary and administrative system was largely restored, but with some noteworthy improvements. The Senate, for example, was to be elective rather than appointive, and provision was made for regional self-government instead of the excessively centralized pattern of pre-Fascist and Fascist days. Women gained full voting rights with men. Safeguards against a new dictatorship were to be found in a Supreme Constitutional Court (modeled on the American system), and a High Council of the Magistracy, as well as in a bill of rights (though some, like the "right to work"—a phrase borrowed from the Soviet Constitution of 1936 and signifying the right to "full employment"—were more in the nature of aspirations than reality). A National Economic and Labor Council and provisions for the use of the initiative and referendum have proved to be less significant features of the new constitutional system.

Deprived of her overseas possessions and most of her Slavic border minorities (though not her German-speaking population in the Alto Adige), the new Italy has repudiated Fascism's ultranationalism and has become instead one of the most vigorous advocates of European economic and political integration. As a result of this more enlightened policy and of massive financial assistance from the United States in the postwar years, Italy's standard of living and economy have reached new highs, though a great disparity remains between north and south. Whether or not the country can be equally successful in streamlining its ponderous bureaucracy and modernizing and expanding its educational system is less clear at this time.

Italy will long be confronted by serious social and political problems. Alienation runs deep in the Italian psyche. In a country where one fourth of the electorate votes Communist, where a much smaller but stubborn minority of monarchists and neo-Fascists continue their nostalgic dreams on the far right, and where the moderates are split along clerical and economic lines, there is no likelihood of "consensus politics." But if apathy and cynicism toward democratic, constitutional government do not once again get the better of the citizenry, the center-left political forces ought to be able to regroup and push ahead with the reforms that are required to strengthen and stabilize Italian democracy. Barring unforeseen international and economic crises, or the appearance of some new charismatic leader, it does not seem likely that the majority of Italians will easily turn again to the demagogic pattern of Mussolini's Fascism.

II

Fascism in Spain

---

8. The Falange Española

It was not until the early 1930's that authentically fascist movements appeared on the scene in Spain, a country that was beginning to move awkwardly from a feudalistic agrarian economy into the first stages of a semi-industrialized society. The emergence of various extremist movements of the radical right was brought about by the cumulative impact of several developments during the preceding decade. These included the Moroccan rebellion of the early 1920's and the resultant military dictatorship in Spain; the pervasive economic depression that began in 1929; the political ferment that overthrew King Alfonso XIII in April, 1931, and inaugurated the anticlerical Second Republic; and the growing schism within the Spanish revolutionary syndicalist movement. The latter current had attracted considerable support in Catalonia and other parts of Spain during the previous generation; and just as had already been the case in Italy, its left wing was now moving increasingly in the direction of Marxian communism, while its right wing was assuming a nationalistic and fascist-like posture.

A clear example of this effort to persuade anarcho-syndicalists to adopt a program of "national syndicalism" was to be seen in March, 1931. At that time Ramiro Ledesma Ramos, a young Castilian postal clerk and ex-student of the University of Madrid who had recently spent some time in Germany, where he was impressed by Hitler's National Socialist party (and even went so far as to affect Hitler's hair style), founded a short-lived, anti-Marxist weekly paper entitled *La Conquista del Estado* (The Conquest of the State). He called for the creation of "military-type teams without hypocrisy before the rifle's barrel."[1] Then, three months later, in Valladolid, a twenty-five-year-old man of rural background (and a paid organizer of the sugar-beet growers there), Onésimo Redondo Ortega, founded a somewhat similar group with a weekly newspaper, *Libertad*. Strongly clerical and anti-Semitic, Redondo also found much to admire in Hitler's youth movement, which he had observed at first hand at the University of

---

1. *Historia de la Cruzada Española,* ed. by Joaquín Arrarás (Madrid, 1939–43), Vol. III, p. 423.

Mannheim in 1930. Somehow he perceived the Nazi *Führer* as the embodiment of Christianity engaged in struggle with communism.

In September, 1931, Redondo and Ledesma combined their meager forces under the somewhat boastful title Juntas de Ofensiva Nacional-Sindicalista (Juntas for the National-Syndicalist Offensive). The members of the JONS (Jonsistas) belonged to the first revolutionary organization in Spain to bear the label of national syndicalism. Borrowing the red and black colors of the Anarchists and the yoked arrows of the Catholic Monarchs, they proclaimed a sixteen-point program that included such slogans as "Arriba!" and "España, Una, Grande y Libre!" They denounced separatism and class war; called for Spanish expansion into Gibraltar, Tangier, French Morocco, and Algeria; and demanded the elimination of foreign influences in Spain. Unlike Hitler, they assigned a high place to the Roman Catholic religion, which in their eyes seemed to have the same "racial" significance for Spain that "Aryan blood" did for Nazi Germany. But the Jonsistas made very little headway. By mid-1932 government hostility forced Redondo to flee to Portugal and his newspaper to cease publication.

Meanwhile, more othodox right-wing groups became politically active. In Navarre the ultraclerical, reactionary Comunión Tradicionalista of Carlist royalists, bitter enemies of the "illegitimate" Bourbon dynasty against whom they had fought a series of civil wars in the nineteenth century, organized a "traditionalist" militia known as the Requetés. These medievalist-minded warriors stressed the virtues of Catholic corporativism and perfervid regionalism.

Less hidebound but equally Catholic was the more broadly based CEDA, whose initials stood for Spanish Confederation of Autonomous Rightist Groups. Led by a middle-aged Salamanca lawyer, José María Gil Robles, the "Cedistas" were deeply influenced by the Jesuits and Catholic Action, a dedicated organization of the laity.

The CEDA brand of conservatism did not satisfy certain industrialists and financiers in Bilbao and other cities who preferred to offer financial encouragement to those who would promote a movement more akin to Mussolini's Fascism. Their eyes came to rest on José Antonio Primo de Rivera, the handsome, eldest son of the late General Miguel Primo de Rivera, who had headed a military dictatorship in Spain from 1923 until 1930 (in the wake of the army's setback in Morocco). Born in Andalusia in 1903, José Antonio was a restless, romantic young *marqués* who studied law but displayed equal interest in poetry and foreign languages. The elitist theories of José Ortega y Gasset and other contemporary conservative writers made a favorable impression upon him. While his philandering father headed the government, José Antonio was content to remain on the sidelines, but after the General's overthrow and death in 1930 the son turned increasingly to politics. He concluded that his father's regime had been too old-fashioned in its military and authoritarian garb. To be sure, King Alfonso XIII had referred to the General as "my Mussolini," and the General had expressed admiration for Mussolini's dictatorship and in

1926 had signed a treaty of friendship and arbitration with Italy. But his conservative Unión Patriótica stopped short of becoming a clear-cut fascist party. The son felt that his father had also failed to grasp the wisdom of building a governmental system that would rest on the political representation of national syndicates.

By early 1933 the aristocratic José Antonio was ready to organize an elitist movement that would seek to achieve radical political and economic reforms through what he called "totalitarian" means. He would employ the ideological watchwords of nationalism to arouse the idealism and enthusiasm of Spanish youth. Hitler's advent to power in Germany in January, 1933, further encouraged José Antonio to think that fascism was the wave of the future. Supported by Bilbao bankers and others, he gathered around him a handful of *señoritos* who decided to label their movement "F.E." and publish a weekly under that heading. The initials could be interpreted to stand for either "Fascismo Español" or "Falange Española" [Spanish Phalanx]. By the autumn of 1933 the latter signification was chosen in order to stress the autonomous nature of the Spanish movement and to avoid the kind of confrontation with Republican authorities that had resulted in the suppression of his newspaper *El Fascio* after one issue in March.

The official debut of this newest current of right-wing radicalism took place on Sunday afternoon, October 29, 1933, in Madrid's Teatro de la Comedia. José Antonio was the principal speaker before the well-dressed audience of some 2,000 middle-aged and young men, among whom was Ledesma. Additional thousands heard the speech by radio. In his address the poetic young Falangist denounced the liberal democratic system and criticized the socialists for mistakenly adopting a program based on materialism and class struggle. He called instead for the creation of an intensely nationalistic "movement" that would eliminate all political parties and organize a "totalitarian" state in Spain that would be based on families, municipalities, and professions. The movement must not shrink from violence, he declared, and it must seek to renew Spain's imperial grandeur, surrounding it with a religious aura. Many in his audience were disappointed that he did not deliver an unqualified diatribe against the Republic or set forth a summons for immediate dictatorship.

José Antonio Primo de Rivera
on the Foundation of the Spanish Falange
(*Comedia Theater, Madrid, October 29, 1933*)

No WHOLE paragraph of gratitude: simply, "Thank you," as befits our terse, military style.

When in March 1762 a man of ill omen called Jean Jacques

SOURCE: José Antonio Primo de Rivera, *The Spanish Answer* (selected and translated, with an introduction by Juan Macnab

Rousseau published *The Social Contract*, political truth ceased to be a permanent entity. In earlier, less shallow ages, States had historic missions to perform, and justice and truth were written upon their brows, and even upon the stars. Jean Jacques Rousseau came to inform us that justice and truth were not permanent categories of thought at all, but decisions of the will at any given moment.

Jean Jacques Rousseau supposed that each people as a whole possessed a soul of its own, higher in rank than each of our individual souls, and that this higher *ego* was endowed with an infallible will, capable at any given moment of defining justice and injustice, good and evil. This collective sovereign will was expressible only by suffrage—in which the majority conjecture prevailed over the minority one in guessing what the higher will might be. It follows that voting—the game of dropping little slips of paper into a ballot-box—had the power to tell us at any given moment whether there was a God or not, whether truth was true or false, and whether our country ought to go on existing or would be better advised to commit suicide.

As the liberal State followed this teaching faithfully, it ceased to be the resolute executor of the country's destinies and turned into a mere spectator of electoral struggles. The only thing that mattered to the liberal State was that a certain number of gentlemen should be seated at the voting tables, that the ballot should begin at eight and end at four, and that the ballot-boxes should not be broken— whereas to be broken is the noblest fate that can befall a ballot-box. Thereafter, the liberal State must serenely abide by whatever emerged from the ballot, as if it had no interest in the matter at all. In other words, the liberal rulers did not even believe in their own mission. They did not believe they were there for the performance of an honourable task, but that anyone who thought the reverse and intended to assail the State, by fair means or foul, has just as good a right to say so and to do so as the guardians of the State itself had to defend it.

Hence arose the democratic system, which is, first of all, the most ruinous possible system for the squandering of energy. A man

Calder, from the *Obras Completas de José Antonio Primo de Rivera*, ed. by Augustín del Rio Cisneros) (Madrid: Artes Gráficas Ibarra, S.A. [1964]), pp. 43–55. By kind permission of the Servicio Exterior, Delegación Nacional de la Sección Femenina, Falange Española Tradicionalista y de las J.O.N.S., Madrid.

endowed with gifts for the high function of governing, which is perhaps the noblest of all human functions, was obliged to devote eighty, ninety or ninety-five per cent of his energies to answering routine opposition criticism, to making election propaganda, to drowsing for hours on parliamentary benches, to flattering electors and enduring their impertinencies—because it was from them that he was going to get power—, to putting up with humiliation and indignities from those who, by very reason of the quasi-divine function of governing, were required to obey him; and then after all this, if he had an hour or two left after midnight or a few moments stolen from an uneasy repose, it was in that tiny period of spare time that the man endowed with gifts for governing was able to give serious thought to the basic functions of Government.

Later came the loss of the spiritual unity of peoples, for as the system worked by the achievement of majorities, anyone who set out to master the system had to obtain a majority of the votes. He had to obtain it, if necessary, by stealing votes from the other parties; and hence he must have no hesitation in calumniating them, in heaping the vilest obloquies upon them, in deliberately falsifying the truth, in not letting slip a single means of lying and vilification. Thus, although Fraternity was one of the postulates displayed on the title-page of the liberal State, there has never been a mode of collective life in which wronged men, in mutual enmity, have felt less fraternal than in the turbulent, unpleasant life of the liberal State.

Finally, the liberal State brought economic slavery, for the workmen were told, with tragic sarcasm: "You are free to work as you choose: no-one can force you to accept these conditions or those. However, as we are the rich, we offer you such conditions as we think fit. As free citizens, you are not obliged to accept them if you do not want to; but as poor citizens, if you do not accept the conditions we impose, you will die of starvation surrounded by the highest degree of liberal dignity." And so it came about that in the countries possessing the most superb parliaments and the finest democratic institutions, you had only to go a few hundred yards outside the luxury quarters of big cities in order to find yourself amid noisome slums, where workmen and their families lived huddled together in well-nigh subhuman conditions. In the country, a farm-labourer's hours were sunrise to sunset in the broiling heat, but owing to the free play of liberal economics he was lucky if in the course of a year he got eighty days' employment at three pesetas a day.

That is why socialism was born, and its birth was justified. We are not going to balk at any truth: the workmen were bound to defend themselves against that system, which gave them merely promises of rights, and took no pains to provide them with a fair living wage. Yet socialism, which was a legitimate reaction against that liberal enslavement, went astray in three ways: first, it accepted the materialist interpretation of life; secondly, it adopted an attitude of revenge; and thirdly, it proclaimed the dogma of the class war.

Socialism—above all the socialism constructed in the passionless frigidity of the study by the socialist apostles in whom the poor working men believed, and who have been shown up for what they really were by Alfonso García Valdecasas,[2]—socialism, thus understood, sees nothing in history but the play of economic forces; everything spiritual is suppressed, religion is the opium of the people, patriotism is a myth for the exploitation of the underdog. Socialism says all this. Nothing exists but production and economic organization. Workmen, therefore, must wring their souls well out, lest the least drop of spirituality should remain within them.

Socialism does not aspire to reestablish a social justice that has broken down through the faulty working of the liberal State; rather, it aims at reprisal. The further the injustice of the liberal system has gone in one direction, the further socialism seeks to carry its own injustice in the other.

Finally, socialism proclaims the monstrous dogma of class warfare. It proclaims the dogma that warfare between the classes is indispensable and occurs naturally in life, because there can never be any appeasing agent. Thus socialism, which started out as a just critique of economic liberalism, has brought us by a different route to the same pass as economic liberalism: disunity, hatred, separation, forgetfulness of every bond of brotherhood and solidarity between men.

Accordingly, when we, the men of our generation, look around us, we find a world in moral ruin, a world rent asunder by every kind of differences; and as regards what touches us most closely, we find a Spain in moral ruin, a Spain rent by every kind of hatred

2. A professor of law and rightist member of the Cortes (parliament), Valdecasas was one of the other two speakers at the Teatro de la Comedia that day. Julio Ruiz de Alda, a well-known aviator, was the third orator.— *Ed.*

and conflict. We have had to shed tears in the depth of our hearts when we have travelled through the villages of this wonderful country of Spain, those villages where you can still find people, beneath the humblest exterior, possessing a rustic gentility which never makes an extravagant gesture or uses a superfluous word; people who live in an outwardly dry way, on an apparently arid soil but one that astounds us by the fruitfulness that bursts forth triumphant in corn and vine. When we have been through those lands and seen those people, and known what sufferings they endure at the hands of petty local overlords, and how they are forgotten by every party group, divided, poisoned by underhand propaganda, we could not but apply to all those folk the words that the folk itself sang of the Cid, to see him roaming through the land of Castile in his banishment from Burgos:

"Ah God, what a good vassal, had he but a good lord!"

That is what we ourselves have found in this movement which starts today: the legitimate lord of Spain, but one like Saint Francis Borgia, a lord whom death cannot take from us. And for that, it must be a lord who is not at the same time a slave to an interest of group or class.

The movement of today—which is a movement and not a party, indeed you could almost call it an anti-party,—let all know from the outset that it is neither of the Right nor of the Left. For at bottom, Right means the aim of maintaining an economic organization even if it is unjust; and at bottom, Left means the desire to overthrow an economic organization, even if many good things should go by the board at the same time. Afterwards, these ideas are both decked out with a number of spiritual considerations. I declare to all who listen to us in good faith: all those spiritual considerations can find their place in our movement, but our movement will on no account bind its destiny to the group or class interest that lurks beneath the superficial distinction of Right and Left.

The Patria is a complete unity, wherein all individuals and all classes are integrated; the Patria cannot be in the hands of the strongest class or the best-organized party. The Patria is a transcendent synthesis, an individual synthesis, with ends of its own to achieve; and what we seek is that this movement of today, and the State which it brings forth, shall be the efficient, authoritarian instrument which serves that unchallengeable, permanent, irrevocable unity which is called the Patria.

And with that we already have the whole mainspring of our future actions and our present conduct, for we ourselves should be but one party the more, if we merely appeared in order to put forward a program of concrete solutions. Such programs have the advantage of never getting carried out. On the other hand, when you have a fixed attitude towards history and towards life, that attitude itself will provide the solution in any particular case, just as love tells us when we should quarrel and when we should embrace, though a genuine love has not the slightest "program" of either quarrels or embraces.

These are the things that are demanded by our complete sense of the Patria and of the State which is to serve the Patria:

That all the peoples of Spain, diverse as they are, shall feel themselves brought into harmony in one irrevocable unity of destiny.

That political parties shall disappear. Nobody was ever born a member of a political party; on the contrary, we are all born members of a family: we are all citizens of a Municipality: we all work at a job. These are our natural units: the family, the municipality and the profession; and if these are the realities of our lives, what need have we for the intermediate, pernicious instrument of political parties, which, in order to unite us in artificial groups, start by disuniting us in our genuine realities?

We want less liberal verbiage and more respect for the deep liberty of man. Man's liberty is respected only when he is regarded as the corporeal envelope of a soul capable of damnation or of salvation. Only when he is thus regarded can his liberty be said to be truly respected, and still more so if that liberty is combined, as we demand, in a system of authority, hierarchy and order.

We want all to feel they are members of a serious, complete community. In other words, there are clearly many kinds of tasks to be performed: some manual, some mental, others in the educational or social or cultural fields; but in a community such as we seek, let it be stated from the outset, there must be no passengers and no drones.

We want no song about individual rights of the kind that can never be enforced in the homes of the hungry. Instead, let every man, every member of the political community, simply by being a member of it, be given the means of earning a just and decent human livelihood by his work.

We want the religious spirit, which is the keystone in the finest arches of our history, to be respected and supported as it deserves; but that does not mean that the State should either interfere in functions which do not belong to it, or—as it used to do, possibly from motives other than those of authentic Religion—should share our functions which it is the State's job to perform for itself.

We want Spain resolutely to recover the universal sense of her own culture and history.

And we want one last thing. If in some cases this can only be achieved by violence, let us not balk at violence. Who has said—in speaking of "anything but violence"—that the supreme degree of the moral values consists in amiability? Who has said that when our feelings as human beings are outraged, it is our duty to be amiable? Dialectic, yes, as the first instrument of communication. But there is no dialectic admissible but that of the fist and the gun when the outrage is against justice or our native land.

These are the things we think about the future State which it is our job to build.

But our movement would not be fully understood if people believed that it was merely a mode of thinking; it is not a mode of thinking, it is a mode of being. We must not set before us political construction and architecture alone. We have to adopt, towards life as a whole and in each of our actions, an attitude that is human, profound and entire. That attitude is the spirit of service and sacrifice, the ascetic and military view of life. So let no one imagine that this is a recruiting-station for the provision of benefices; let no one imagine that we are assembled here to defend privileges. I only wish that this microphone could carry my voice into every working man's home, to tell them this: Yes, we do wear collars and ties. Yes, it would be possible for you to call us "señoritos." But we bring with us the will to fight for things which are of no interest to "señoritos" at all: we are here to fight, to get heavy but just sacrifices imposed on many people of our own classes, we are here to fight for a totalitarian State whose wealth shall reach the humble as well as the powerful. That is what we are like, because that is what the señoritos, the young gentlemen of Spain, always were like in history. That is how they achieved the real rank of señores, of gentlemen, because in distant lands, and in our own country too, they were able to face death and shoulder the harshest duties, for causes in which, as mere señoritos, they would have taken no interest at all.

I think the flag is hoisted. Now let us defend it cheerfully, poetically. In face of the advance of revolution, some people think that in order to unite everyone's wills the most watery solutions should be proposed, and that in their propaganda they ought to conceal everything that might arouse emotion or betray a thoroughgoing, energetic attitude. How wrong they are! Peoples have never been stirred by any but poets, and alas for him who, when faced with the poetry of destruction, cannot uplift the poetry of promise!

In a poetical movement, we will uplift this fervent yearning of Spain. Ours shall be the sacrifice, ours the renunciation, and ours will be the victory, a victory which—need I say it to you?—we are not going to win at the forthcoming election. At that election, vote whichever way you think least bad. But that is not where our Spain will come from, that is not our setting, that turbid, exhausted atmosphere, like a tavern at the end of a crapulous night. That is not where we belong. Yes, I believe I am to stand as a candidate; but I do so without faith and without respect, and I say that now, though it may lose me all my votes. I care nothing for that. We are not going to that place to squabble with the habitués over the insipid scraps of an unclean feast. Our place is outside, even if we may pass through the other on the way. Our place is in the open air, under the clear night sky, sword in hand and the stars above. Let the others go on with their revelries. We outside, in vigilance tense, fervent and secure, can already feel, in the glad quickening of our inward parts, the brightness of the dawn.

The first issue of the newspaper *Falange Española* appeared in December, 1933, and set forth the following basic points of the Falange.

Basic Points of the Falange
(*In* Falange Española, *December, 1933*)

The Spanish Falange firmly believes in Spain. Spain is not a territory, nor an aggregate of men and women. Spain is above all a unity of destiny; a historical fact, an entity, real in itself, which has performed world missions, and will have others still to perform.

SOURCE: From José Antonio Primo de Rivera, *The Spanish Answer* (selected and translated, with an introduction by Juan Macnab Calder, from the *Obras Completas de José Antonio*

Hence Spain exists, first, as something distinct from each of the individuals, classes and groups that compose her; secondly, as something higher than each of those individuals, classes and groups, or even than all of them put together.

Accordingly Spain, which exists as a distinct and higher reality, is bound to have ends of her own. These ends are: continued existence in unity, resurgence of internal vitality, and a preeminent share in the spiritual tasks of the world.

In the achievement of these ends, Spain is faced with a great obstacle. She is divided in three ways: by local separatisms, by the strife between political parties, and by class warfare.

Socialism ignores or forgets the reality of Spain. It is unaware that Spain is before all else a great unity of destiny. Separatists are interested in whether a region speaks a language of its own, or has racial features of its own, a climate of its own or special physical geography. But it can never be said too often that a nation is not a language, a race or a territory; it is a unity of destiny in the world order. That unity of destiny was and is called Spain.

Under the sign of Spain, and united in the world order, the peoples who compose Spain fulfilled their destiny. That spendid unity created a world, and nothing can justify breaking it up.

The political parties ignore the unity of Spain, because they envisage her from the viewpoint of a sectional interest. Some stand on the Right, others on the Left: to take that attitude towards Spain is to distort the truth. It is' like a one-eyed, sidelong view. That is not how things that are fair and bright should be looked at, but with both eyes, face on: not from a partial, party standpoint, which automatically distorts what it sees, but from the total standpoint of the Patria, which when regarded as a whole corrects our defects of vision.

Class warfare ignores the unity of the Patria, for it breaks up the idea of national production as a whole. In the state of class struggle, the employers set out to increase their earnings. The workmen do the same, and each in turn tyrannizes over the other. When there is not enough work to go round, the employers exploit the men;

Primo de Rivera, ed. by Augustín del Rio Cisneros) (Madrid: Artes Gráficas Ibarra, S.A., [1964]), pp. 59–68. By kind permission of the Servicio Exterior, Delegación Nacional de la Sección Femenina, Falange Española Tradicionalista y de las J.O.N.S., Madrid.

when there is a surplus, or when working-class organizations are very strong, the men exploit the employers. But neither workmen nor employers realize the truth, that they are both partners in the joint task of national production. Through not thinking of the national production but only of the interest or ambition of each class, both employers and workmen end by destroying and ruining each other.

If the struggle and decadence arise from our having lost the permanent idea of Spain, the remedy must lie in restoring it. We must again conceive of Spain as a self-existing reality, above differences between peoples, above party strife, above class struggle. Those who never lose sight of the higher reality of Spain will see all political problems in a clear light.

Some think of the State as a mere guardian of order, a spectator of the national life, which intervenes only when that order is disturbed, but has no firm belief in any particular idea. Others aim at dominating the State so as to use it, even to use it tyrannically, as an instrument of their group or class interests.

The Falange wants neither of those things: neither the indifferent State, the mere policeman, nor the class or group State. It wants a State which believes in the reality and high mission of Spain; a State which will serve that idea by assigning to each man, class and group the appropriate tasks, rights and sacrifices; a State of all Spaniards, that is, one that acts solely in view of that permanent idea of Spain, and never in subservience to class or party interests.

In order that the State may never belong to a party, political parties must be abolished.

Political parties arise as the result of a false political organization, namely the parliamentary system. In Parliament, a number of gentlemen say they represent those who elect them. But most of the electors have nothing in common with the elected: they do not come from the same families, or the same municipalities, or the same professional guilds. The only connexion between the people and those who say they represent the people is a number of pieces of paper dropped into a ballot-box every two or three years.

In order that this electoral machine may work, the life of towns and villages has to be feverishly stirred up every few years. The candidates shout, abuse one another, make impossible promises. The factions get excited, insult one another, murder one another. The most savage ill-will is whipped up during the election period. Hatreds are born, which may last for ever and make the life of the local community intolerable. But what do the victorious candidates care for the life of the villages? They go off to the capital, to display themselves in public, to get their names into the papers, to spend their time discussing complicated affairs which the villagers do not understand.

What need have the towns and villages of these intermediaries? To take part in the life of the nation, why should every man have to join a political party or vote for a party candidate? We are all born in a family; we all live in a municipality; we all have an occupation or profession. But nobody is born, or lives naturally, in a political party.

The political party is an artificial thing, which links us to people of other municipalities and other occupations with which we have nothing in common, while it separates us from our neighbours and fellow-workers with whom we really do live.

A genuine State, such as the Falange wants, will not be based on the sham of the political parties, nor on the Parliament which they engender. It will be founded on the authentic realities of life: the family, the municipality, and the guild or syndicate.

Thus the new State will have to recognize the integrity of the family as the social unit, the autonomy of the municipality as the territorial unit, and the guild, syndicate or professional association, as the genuine bases for the complete organization of the State.

The new State will not stand cruelly aloof from man's struggle to live, nor allow each class to take whatever steps it can to shake off the yoke of another class or to tyrannize over it. Since the new state belongs to all, it will regard as its own the ends of every group that composes it, and will watch over the interests of all as its own interests. The first purpose of wealth is to improve the living conditions of the many, not to sacrifice the many to the luxury and profit of the few.

Work is the best claim to civil dignity. Nothing can deserve more attention from the State than the dignity and welfare of workers. Thus it will consider that its first obligation, cost what it may, is to provide every man with work that will assure him not merely sustenance but a decent human livelihood. It will not do this as a charity, but as a duty. Hence neither the earnings of capital—today frequently unjust—nor the tasks· of labour will be determined by the interest or power of the class that may have the upper hand at any given moment, but by the overall interest of the national production and by the power of the State. The classes will not need to organize on a war footing in self-defence, because they will have the assurance that the State will unflinchingly safeguard their just interests.

But the syndicates and guilds will indeed have to organize—on a peace footing—because, though today shut out from public life by the artificial intervention of Parliament and the political parties, they will then become direct organs of the State.

In a word: the present situation of strife considers the classes as divided into two sides, with different and opposing interests; the new point of view considers all who contribute to production as interested in one and the same great common enterprise.

The Falange regards man as a combination of a body and a soul; that is, as capable of an eternal destiny and as the bearer of eternal values. Thus the maximum respect is paid to human dignity, to man's integrity and his freedom. But that profound freedom entitles nobody to undermine the foundations of public social life. It is not permissible that a whole people should be used as a field of experimentation by the audacity or extravagance of any individual. For all, the true freedom, which is achieved only by those who form part of a strong, free nation. For nobody, the freedom to disturb, to poison, to incite passions, to subvert the foundations of all lasting political organization. Those foundations are Authority, Hierarchy, and Order.

While the physical integrity of the individual is always sacred, it is not in itself sufficient to make him a participator in the public life of the nation. The individual's political status is justified only in so far as he performs a function in the national life. Only the incapacitated are exempt from this duty. Parasites, drones and those who seek to live as non-paying guests on the efforts of others will not be entitled to the slightest consideration in the new State.

The Falange cannot regard life as a mere interplay of economic factors. It rejects the materialist interpretation of history. The spiritual has been and is the mainspring in the life of men and peoples.

The preeminent aspect of the spiritual is the religious. No man can fail to ask himself the eternal questions about life and death, creation and the beyond. These questions cannot be answered with evasions: they demand affirmation or denial. Spain has always replied with the Catholic affirmation. The Catholic interpretation of life is, first of all, the true one; but historically, moreover, it is the Spanish one. By her sense of Catholicity, of Universality, Spain won unknown continents from the ocean and from barbarism. She won them in order to incorporate their inhabitants into a world enterprise of salvation. Accordingly, any reconstruction of Spain must be in a Catholic sense.

This does not mean that persecutions against non-Catholics are to arise again. The times of religious persecution are past. Neither does it mean that the State is going to take direct charge of functions which belong to the Church; nor that it will admit interferences or machinations of the Church which might harm the dignity of the State or the national integrity. It means that the new State will be informed by the Catholic religious spirit traditional in Spain, and will concord with the Church the considerations and protection which are her due.

The above is what the Spanish Falange wants. To obtain that, it proclaims a crusade to all Spaniards who desire the resurgence of a Spain that is great, free, just and genuine. Those who come to this crusade will have to prepare their minds for service and for sacrifice. They must regard life as a militia: discipline and danger, abnegation and renouncement of all vanity, envy, sloth and evil-speaking; and at the same time they will serve that spirit in a cheerful and sportsmanlike manner.

Violence can be lawful when used for an ideal that justifies it. Reason, justice and the Patria will be defended by force when they are attacked by force—or by guile. But the Falange will never use force as an instrument of oppression.

For example, it is a lie to announce to the workmen that a Fascist tyranny is approaching. All that the Falange signifies is union, eager fraternal cooperation, love.

The Spanish Falange, fired by a love, secure in a faith, will succeed in winning Spain for Spain, in the manner of a militia.

In Madrid on February 11, 1934, Ledesma's Jonsistas, who at this stage numbered some 300 and were composed chiefly of students and taxi drivers, decided to merge with José Antonio's 2,000 Falangists. For the next three years the movement was called the Falange Española de las Juntas de Ofensiva Nacional-Sindicalista, and each local unit was termed a Jons. The emblems, slogans, and national syndicalist ideology of the Jonsistas were taken over *in toto*. Leadership came from a jealous triumvirate composed of Ledesma, José Antonio, and the world-renowned aviator Julio Ruiz de Alda. José Antonio momentarily contented himself with supplying the enlarged movement with its literary and aesthetic overtones, but by October his group managed by a one-vote margin over the Ledesma faction in the National Council to elevate him to the position of *Jefe Nacional* (national leader). Thus, in a "democratic" way, a single leader was recognized. All the Falangists were required to take the following oath.

The Falangist Oath

I swear to give myself always to the service of Spain.

I swear to have no pride other than that of the fatherland and of the Falange and to live under the Falange in obedience and joy, impetuousness and patience, gallantry and silence.

I swear fidelity and submission to our leaders, honor to the memory of our dead, and imperturbable perseverance amid all vicissitudes.

I swear, wherever I may be, in order to obey or in order to command that I shall respect our Hierarchy from the first to the last rank.

I swear to reject and give no ear to any voice of either friend or foe who might weaken the spirit of the Falange.

I swear to preserve above all the idea of unity: unity among the lands of Spain, unity among the classes of Spain, unity within the individual man and among the men of Spain.

I swear to live in holy brotherhood with all members of the Falange and to lend every assistance and eliminate every difference whenever this holy brotherhood requests that I do so.

In November, 1934, the Falange adopted a Twenty-Seven-Point Program that was drawn up by Ledesma and given a laconic style by José Antonio. As had often been the case in Mussolini's Italy, doctrines were devised to rationalize what already had developed in practice. The manifesto set forth principles regarding national unity and empire, the latter point being left rather vague. Some Falangists implied that "empire" meant only cultural influence and diplomatic leadership, while others (including José Antonio in private conversations) expressed the hope of annexing Portugal. Point 6 proclaimed the State as the "totalitarian instrument to defend the integrity of the fatherland." The ninth paragraph called for "vertical" national syndicalism.[3] Other

SOURCE: Victor Fragoso del Toro (ed.), *La España de ayer: Recopilación de textos histórico-políticos*, I (Madrid: Editora Nacional, 1965), p. 380. By permission of the publisher. My translation.

3. In a speech at the Círculo Mercantil in Madrid on April 9, 1935, José Antonio made it clear that a single system of "vertical" national syndicates was preferable to Mussolini's "parallel" syndicates of employers and work-

points set forth the need for agrarian and industrial reforms, social justice and education. The most controversial item was Point 25 pertaining to the Church. Most of the Falangists of this period hoped to prevent the Church from encroaching upon the state's prerogatives. Point 27 forbade any further modification of the movement's label; but in the summer of 1937, as will be seen, Generalissimo Francisco Franco was to insist that the movement merge with the reactionary Carlist militia forces and add the word "Tradicionalista" to the title in Point 26, so that it would read: Falange Española Tradicionalista y de las Juntas Ofensivas Nacional-Sindicalistas. Point 27 thereupon was dropped. This revised version of 1937 is printed below.

The Twenty-Six-Point Program of the Falange
(1937)

NATION—UNITY—EMPIRE

1. We believe in the supreme reality of Spain. The strengthening, elevating, and magnifying of this reality is the urgent collective goal of all Spaniards. Individual, group, and class interests must inexorably give way in order to achieve this goal.

2. Spain has a single destiny in the world. Every conspiracy against this common unity is repulsive. Any kind of separatism is a crime which we shall not pardon.

The existing Constitution, to the degree that it encourages disintegration, weakens this common destiny of Spain. Therefore we demand its annulment in a thundering voice.

3. We have the determination to build an Empire. We affirm that Spain's historic fulfillment lies in Empire. We claim for Spain a pre-eminent position in Europe. We can tolerate neither international isolation nor foreign interference.

As regards the countries of Hispanic America, we favor unification of their culture, economic interests, and power. Spain will

SOURCE: Falange española tradicionalista y de las Juntas ofensivas nacional-sindicalistas, Vicesecretaría de Educación popular, *Fundamentos del Nuevo Estado* (Madrid: Ediciones de la Vicesecretaría de Educación Popular, 1943), pp. 5–10. My translation.

---

ers. "Vertical" syndicates will not require so bureaucratic a structure, he declared, and "will be able to function organically—in the way the Army does, for example—without any need for forming parallel committees of soldiers and officers." Quoted in Fragoso del Toro (ed.), *La España de ayer*, II (Madrid: Editora Nacional, 1965), p. 136. The unions of present-day Spain continue to be organized as "vertical syndicates."

continue to act as the spiritual axis of the Hispanic world as a sign of her pre-eminence in worldwide enterprises.

4. Our armed forces—on land, sea, and in the air—must be kept trained and sufficiently large to assure to Spain at all times its complete independence and a status in the world that befits it. We shall bestow upon our Armed Forces of land, sea, and air all the dignity they merit, and we shall cause their military conception of life to infuse every aspect of Spanish life.

5. Spain shall once more seek her glory and her wealth on the sea lanes. Spain must aspire to become a great maritime power, for reasons of both defense and commerce.

We demand for the fatherland equal status with others in maritime power and aerial routes.

State—Individual—Liberty

6. Our State will be a totalitarian instrument to defend the integrity of the fatherland. All Spaniards will participate in this through their various family, municipal, and syndical roles. There shall be no participation in it by political parties. We shall implacably abolish the system of political parties and all of their consequences—inorganic suffrage, representation of clashing groups, and a Parliament of the type that is all too well known.

7. Human dignity, integrity, and freedom are eternal, intangible values.

But one is not really free unless he is a part of a strong and free nation.

No one will be permitted to use his freedom against the nation, which is the bulwark of the fatherland's freedom. Rigorous discipline will prevent any attempt to envenom and disunite the Spanish people or to incite them against the destiny of the fatherland.

8. The National-Syndicalist State will permit all kinds of private initiative that are compatible with the collective interest, and it will also protect and encourage the profitable ones.

Economy—Labor—Class Struggle

9. Our conception of Spain in the economic realm is that of a gigantic syndicate of producers. We shall organize Spanish society corporatively through a system of vertical syndicates for the various fields of production, all working toward national economic unity.

10. We repudiate the capitalistic system which shows no understanding of the needs of the people, dehumanizes private property, and causes workers to be lumped together in a shapeless, miserable mass of people who are filled with desperation. Our spiritual and national conception of life also repudiates Marxism. We shall redirect the impetuousness of those working classes who today are led astray by Marxism, and we shall seek to bring them into direct participation in fulfilling the great task of the national State.

11. The National-Syndicalist State will not cruelly stand apart from man's economic struggles, nor watch impassively while the strongest class dominates the weakest. Our regime will eliminate the very roots of class struggle, because all who work together in production shall comprise one single organic entity. We reject and we shall prevent at all costs selfish interests from abusing others, and we shall halt anarchy in the field of labor relations.

12. The first duty of wealth—and our State shall so affirm—is to better the conditions of the people. It is intolerable that enormous masses of people should live wretchedly while a small number enjoy all kinds of luxuries.

13. The State will recognize private property as a legitimate means for achieving individual, family, and social goals, and will protect it against the abuses of large-scale finance capital, speculators, and money lenders.

14. We shall support the trend toward nationalization of banking services and, through a system of Corporations, the great public utilities.

15. All Spaniards have the right to work. Public agencies must of necessity provide support for those who find themselves in desperate straits.

As we proceed toward a totally new structure, we shall maintain and strengthen all the advantages that existing social legislation gives to workers.

16. Unless they are disabled, all Spaniards have the duty to work. The National-Syndicalist State will not give the slightest consideration to those who fail to perform some useful function and who try to live as drones at the expense of the labor of the majority of people.

LAND

17. We must, at all costs, raise the standard of living in the countryside, which is Spain's permanent source of food. To this

end, we demand an agreement that will bring to culmination without further delay the economic and social reforms of the agricultural sector.

18. Our program of economic reforms will enrich agricultural production by means of the following:

By assuring a minimum remuneration to all agricultural producers.

By demanding that there be restored to the countryside, in order to provide it with an adequate endowment, a portion of that which the rural population is paying to the cities for intellectual and commercial services.

By organizing a truly national system of agricultural credit which will lend money to farmers at low interest against the guarantee of their property and crops, and redeem them from usury and local tyrants.

By spreading education with respect to better methods of farming and sheep raising.

By ordering the rational utilization of lands in accordance with their suitability and with marketing possibilities.

By adjusting tariff policy in such a way as to protect agriculture and the livestock industry.

By accelerating reclamation projects. By rationalizing the units of cultivation, so as to eliminate wasted latifundia and uneconomic, miniscule plots.

19. Our program of social reforms in the field of agriculture will be achieved:

By redistributing arable land in such a way as to revive family farms and give energetic encouragement to the syndicalization of farm laborers.

By redeeming from misery those masses of people who presently are barely eking out a living on sterile land, and by transferring such people to new and arable lands.

20. We shall undertake a relentless campaign of reforestation and livestock breeding, and we shall punish severely those who resist it. We shall support the compulsory, temporary mobilization of all Spanish youth for this historic goal of rebuilding the national commonwealth.

21. The State may expropriate without indemnity lands of those owners who either acquired them or exploited them illegally.

22. It will be the primary goal of the National-Syndicalist State to rebuild the communal patrimonies of the towns.

NATIONAL EDUCATION—RELIGION

23. It shall be the essential mission of the State to attain by means of rigorous disciplining of education a strong, united national spirit, and to instill in the souls of future generations a sense of rejoicing and pride in the fatherland.

All men shall receive premilitary training to prepare them for the honor of being enlisted in the National and Popular Army of Spain.

24. Cultural life shall be organized so that no talent will be undeveloped because of insufficient economic means. All who merit it shall be assured ready access to a higher education.

25. Our Movement incorporates the Catholic meaning—of glorious tradition, and especially in Spain—of national reconstruction.

The Church and the State will co-ordinate their respective powers so as to permit no interference or activity that may impair the dignity of the State or national integrity.

NATIONAL REVOLUTION

26. The Falange Española Tradicionalista y de las JONS demands a new order, as set forth in the foregoing principles. In the face of the resistance from the present order, it calls for a revolution to implant this new order. Its method of procedure will be direct, bold, and combative. Life signifies the art and science of warfare (*milicia*) and must be lived with a spirit that is purified by service and sacrifice.

José Antonio's sensitivity to what was politically expedient was revealed late in 1934 when rumors spread that he would attend the International Fascist Congress in Montreux, Switzerland, promoted by the Italians. In a statement released to the press on December 18, he flatly denied this.

José Antonio's Statement Regarding the International
Fascist Congress
(December 18, 1934)

The news that José Antonio Primo de Rivera, Leader of the Falange Española de las JONS, is preparing to attend a certain International Fascist Congress that is to be held in Montreux is totally false. The Leader of the Falange was invited to attend; however, he flatly turned down the invitation in order to make clear the genuinely national character of the Movement, which has no intention of giving the appearance of possessing an international leadership.

Moreover, *the Falange Española de las JONS is not a fascist movement.*[4] It has certain similarities with fascism in the essential points that possess universal validity, but every day its own peculiar qualities are becoming clearer, and it is convinced that by pursuing this path it will achieve its most fruitful possibilities.

Although José Antonio refrained from employing the label "fascist" to describe his movement, he continued to display in his office an autographed photo of Mussolini, with whom he had conversed for half an hour in Rome in October, 1933, and during the Italo-Ethiopian War he stoutly defended the Italian cause. Yet this born aristocrat seems to have had no real personal respect for the *Duce*, and he told some friends that Mussolini had neither constructed a new juridical system nor achieved a revolution but had merely created a myth that the Spanish Falange could exploit to its own profit.[5] José Antonio's contacts with Nazism were somewhat less formal, confined chiefly to a brief vacation trip to Berlin in the spring of 1934. He was received by only minor officials. Although he seems to have been impressed by some of the economic and nationalist programs, his general reaction was negative.

In mid-January, 1935, José Antonio strengthened his position as "single Leader" of the Falange by persuading the party's Junta Política to expel Ledesma, who faded away into the labyrinth of the Spanish postal system until he was shot during the Civil War. José Antonio

SOURCE: Quoted in Fragoso del Toro (ed.), *La España de ayer*, II (Madrid: Editora Nacional, 1965), p. 79. By permission of the publisher. My translation.

4. Italics in the original.—*Ed.*
5. Stanley Payne, *The Falange: A History of Spanish Fascism* (Stanford: Stanford University Press, 1961), p. 77. Payne's book is the major study of the Falange.

then managed to get his own close friend, a lawyer named Raimundo Fernández Cuesta, appointed secretary general of the party. By this time the Falange had become a proper fascistic party, with the typical salute, and blue shirts as the uniform. The hierarchic structure of the party differentiated between "first-line" and "second-line" members. The former numbered only 5,000 at the beginning of 1935 and between 8,000 and 10,000 a year later. José Antonio, the *Jefe Nacional*, was also *Jefe de la Primera Línea*. Most of the first-line members belonged to the Blue Shirt Militia, which trained on Sundays and engaged in street fighting whenever this was deemed useful. José Antonio sought to maintain the Militia's poetic spirit by reading Kipling's "If" to them through a megaphone.[6] Two thirds of the party members were under the age of twenty-one, students making up the largest component, with professional men, white-collar workers, and some ordinary laborers also conspicuous. There was a very small women's section organized by José Antonio's sister Pilar. The Falangist hymn was "Face to the Sun," inspired by a poem by the Cuban Martí. On March 21, 1935, the first issue of the Falangist newspaper *Arriba!* appeared in Madrid.

Spain's worsening political crisis reached a new stage in the parliamentary elections of February 16, 1936. At that time a newly formed Spanish Popular Front coalition won political control, to the great alarm of rightist groups. In this election—the only one in which it participated—the Falange mustered 40,000 votes throughout the country; of these, 5,000 were obtained in Madrid (1.2 per cent of the total) and 4,000 in Valladolid (4 per cent of the total). José Antonio himself gained 7,000 votes in Cádiz but lost the seat he had held in the Cortes since 1933. Not a single Falangist was elected to the new Cortes. Thus the party was more isolated than ever. As street fighting intensified in Madrid, the Popular Front government suddenly outlawed the Falange on March 14 and arrested José Antonio, who was to spend the remaining few months of his life in jail.

In the spring of 1936 General Emilio Mola and other military men fomented plots against the Popular Front as word spread of new moves to grant political autonomy to the Basque country and other regions of Spain. By May they persuaded the underground Falangist Militia to help them against the workers' fighting groups. José Antonio was worried, however, lest the Falange be exploited as a tool and later discarded by the Army, as the following instructions issued from his prison cell in Alicante on June 24 made clear.

6. Hugh Thomas, "Spain," in S. J. Woolf (ed.), *European Fascism* (New York: Random House, 1968), p. 292.

José Antonio's Instructions from Prison
(June 24, 1936)

To All Territorial and Provincial Commands:
Urgent and Most Important

There has come to the attention of the *Jefe Nacional* the existence of numerous machinations in favor of more or less confused subversive movements in various provinces of Spain.

The majority of the leaders of our organization, as was to be expected, have kept headquarters informed of whatever projects they have undertaken, and have restricted themselves in the field of political action to carrying out instructions of their superior commands. However, some of them, carried away by an excess of zeal or by dangerous ingenuousness, have hastened to outline plans for local action and to compromise the participation of our comrades in certain political enterprises.

In most cases such action by comrades in the provinces has come about because they felt that the military status of those inviting them to conspire made them trustworthy. This makes it necessary to explain matters a bit more clearly.

The respect and esteem of the Falange for the Army has been proclaimed so often there is no need to reiterate it here. Ever since the announcement of the 27 Points we have said that it is our aspiration that a military conception of life, in the style of the Army, should infuse all Spanish existence. Moreover, on recent and memorable occasions, the Army has seen its dangers shared by our comrades.

However, admiration and profound respect for the Army as an essential organ of the fatherland does not mean that we must conform to every single idea, word, or project that any soldier or group of soldiers may profess, prefer, or cherish. Especially in the field of politics, the Falange—which detests flattery because it considers it the ultimate scorn for the one being flattered—regards itself as being no less qualified than the average soldier. The political training of soldiers is apt to be full of the noblest sort of

SOURCE: Text in Fragoso del Toro (ed.), *La España de ayer*, II (Madrid: Editora Nacional, 1965), pp. 398–401. By permission of the publisher. My translation.

ingenuousness. The isolation from politics that the Army has imposed on itself has generally had the effect of placing military men in a condition of dialectical defenselessness against the charlatans and ambitious elements within the parties. It is generally acknowledged that a mediocre politician can win much standing among soldiers by simply manipulating in a cynical way some of the most common qualities of military psychology.

For that reason, the political schemes of soldiers (excluding, of course, those elaborated by a handful of well-educated people in the Army) are not apt to be very relevant for the times. These schemes almost always start out with a basic error—that of believing that Spain's ills are the result of simple mismanagement of internal order, and that these can be corrected by handing over power to the above-mentioned charlatans who lack any conception of history, any genuine training, and any real desire to set the fatherland on the path to fulfillment of its destiny.

The participation of the Falange in any of these premature and ingenuous schemes would be a very grave undertaking and, even in case of victory, would bring about its complete demise. The reason for that is simply this: almost everyone who looks to the Falange for this kind of enterprise views the Falange not as a coherent body of doctrines nor as a force that intends to gain full control of the State, but simply as auxiliary shock troops, a kind of assault force, a youthful militia whose destiny tomorrow will be to pass in review before the supremely self-centered elements who have come to power.

Let all comrades consider up to what point it is offensive for the Falange to propose to take part as supernumeraries in a movement that does not intend to install the National-Syndicalist State or to launch the vast task of reconstructing the fatherland sketched out in our 27 Points but intends rather to reinstate a conservative, bourgeois mediocrity (of which Spain has experienced too many examples) that will only be adorned, for greater scorn, with the choreographic accompaniment of our Blue Shirts.

Since such a prospect certainly holds no attraction to any true militant, the present circular orders everyone in the most categorical and unmistakable terms to do the following:

1. No matter what position he holds in the hierarchy, every leader who is asked by a military or civilian element to take part in a conspiracy, uprising, or similar thing must confine himself to this response: "I cannot take part in anything, nor permit my comrades

to take part, in the absence of an express order from the central headquarters. Consequently, if the top leadership of the movement in question is interested in obtaining the help of the Falange, it must propose this directly to the *Jefe Nacional* and work out an understanding directly with him or with someone whom he has specifically designated."

2. No matter what position he holds in the hierarchy, any leader who agrees to local pacts with military or civilian groups without the express approval of the *Jefe Nacional* will be expelled from the Falange at once, and his expulsion will be publicized in every way possible.

3. As the *Jefe Nacional* insists on being personally assured of the fulfillment of this order, he instructs all territorial and provincial leaders with the greatest care to write to him in the provincial prison of Alicante, where he is now located, communicating to him their complete adherence to what is set forth in this circular and furnishing him with a detailed report of the towns to which JONS has transmitted this order. In directing such letters to the *Jefe Nacional*, the territorial and provincial leaders will not sign their own names but use only the name of their respective province or provinces.

4. A delay of more than five days in carrying out these instructions, counting from the date on which they are received, will be considered a grave offense against the duties of co-operation within the Movement.

What José Antonio feared was precisely what happened within a few months after General Francisco Franco and the Army gained the upper hand. In the meantime, José Antonio was convicted by a "people's court" and shot on November 20, 1936. Now that he was safely out of the way, he could be made the official martyr and patron saint of the emerging Franco dictatorship—a system which in all likelihood José Antonio would have opposed had he remained alive. After the Civil War the body of José Antonio was reinterred with ceremony in front of the high altar of Philip II's Escorial; and more recently it has been transferred to the "Valley of the Fallen" shrine in the Guadarrama mountains northwest of Madrid. Thus the cult of the "martyr" of the Spanish "Crusade" was given a new lease on life. On innumerable church walls in Spain are to be seen the commemorative words "José Antonio Presente."

9. The Civil War and Franco's Triumph

THE CIVIL War that broke out in the middle of July, 1936, was to drag on for almost three years, costing the lives of hundreds of thousands and producing all sorts of international repercussions. A day after the uprising of Army units in Spanish Morocco on July 17, one of the principal Army conspirators, General Francisco Franco, was flown in from the Canary Islands. His first decision was to take steps to obtain aerial transport planes from Italy and Germany so that he could move his 32,000 men across the Straits of Gibraltar. From northern Spain General Emilio Mola sent out similar pleas. Hitler's decision to aid the rebels was forthcoming on July 26; Mussolini's the next day. It was this decisive intervention by Germany and Italy that prevented the Republican government from quickly putting down the rebellion. Before the end of July German and Italian planes were facilitating the airlift to the mainland, and within six weeks all of southwestern Spain was taken. By September Franco's units were within 40 miles of Madrid.

But the capital remained under the control of the Republican (Loyalist) government, which hastily organized defenses with the help of workers' committees and militias. At first, not a single Communist was in the Loyalist government; liberal Republicans dominated it. But after September, 1936, when the left-wing Socialist, Francisco Largo Caballero, became premier, effective power tended to shift to his faction and to the Communists. "International brigades," made up of a broad spectrum of foreign anti-Fascist volunteers (including a good many Italians) but largely co-ordinated by the Comintern, soon appeared on Spanish battlefields. The Russians sent in numerous political advisers as well as some material and technical aid. By the spring of 1937 Communist forces also gained the upper hand in Barcelona over the autonomous Catalan republican government, hitherto controlled by the anarcho-syndicalists. The latter hated the Communists as bitterly as they did Franco's Insurgents, the Roman Catholic Church, and the capitalists.

Franco's Insurgents received even greater support from abroad than did the Republicans. For both Mussolini and Hitler (who had forged their Axis in October, 1936) there were obvious advantages to be gained by supporting Franco, as the following political analysis by the German ambassador in Rome made clear in the middle of December.

German and Italian Policy Toward the Spanish Civil War
(December 18, 1936)

. . . The interests of Germany and Italy in the Spanish troubles coincide to the extent that both countries are seeking to prevent a victory of Bolshevism in Spain or Catalonia. However, while Germany is not pursuing any immediate diplomatic interests in Spain beyond this, the efforts of Rome undoubtedly extend toward having Spain fall in line with its Mediterranean policy, or at least toward preventing political cooperation between Spain on the one hand and France and/or England on the other. The means used for this purpose are: immediate support of Franco; a foothold on the Balearic Islands, which will presumably not be evacuated voluntarily unless a central Spanish government friendly to Italy is set up; political commitment of Franco to Italy; and a close tie between Fascism and the new system of government to be established in Spain.

. . . In connection with the general policy indicated above, Germany has in my opinion every reason for being gratified if Italy continues to interest herself deeply in the Spanish affair. . . . The struggle for dominant political influence in Spain lays bare the natural opposition between Italy and France; at the same time the position of Italy as a power in the western Mediterranean comes into competition with that of Britain. All the more clearly will Italy recognize the advisability of confronting the Western powers shoulder to shoulder with Germany—particularly when considering the desirability of a future general understanding between Western and Central Europe on the basis of complete equality. In my opinion the guiding principle for us arising out of this situation is that we should let Italy take the lead in her Spanish policy. . . . Anyone who knows the Spaniards and Spanish conditions will regard with a good deal of skepticism and also concern for future German-Spanish relations (perhaps even for German-

SOURCE: Political Report of German Ambassador Hassell in Rome to German Foreign Ministry, December 18, 1936. Document 157 in *Documents on German Foreign Policy, 1918–1945,* Series D, Vol. III (Germany and Spanish Civil War, 1936–1939) (Washington, D.C.: Department of State, 1950), pp. 170–173 *passim.*

Italian cooperation) any attempt to transplant National Socialism to Spain with German methods and German personnel. It will be easier for Latin Fascism, which is politically more formalistic; a certain aversion to the Italians on the part of the Spaniards, and their resentment against foreign leadership in general, may prove to be a hindrance, but that is a matter for the Italians to cope with. . . .

By January, 1937, Mussolini dispatched some 44,000 Fascist "volunteers," co-ordinated by General Mario Roatta, to aid Franco. In the middle of March some of these Italian Fascists suffered a humiliating defeat at Guadalajara, some 30 miles northeast of Madrid, at the hands of Republican forces. Among the latter were a number of Italian anti-Fascist exiles who had formed a volunteer "Garibaldi" battalion. The psychological impact on Mussolini of this reversal was great. Not only did he decide to increase substantially the number of his troops in Spain; a few weeks later his agents assassinated Carlo Rosselli, the talented and highly articulate democratic socialist leader of the anti-Fascist émigré organization Justice and Liberty, who had rushed across the Pyrenees with the fighting slogan "Today in Spain, tomorrow in Italy!"[1]

At the same time that Mussolini's Italy was raising its stakes in the Spanish Civil War, Hitler's Germany was concluding a protocol with the Franco regime.

German-Nationalist Spain Protocol of March 20, 1937

PROTOCOL

136/73560–61

TOP SECRET   SALAMANCA, March 20, 1937.
                                                 zu Pol. I 1648g Rs.

The German Government and the Spanish Nationalist Government, convinced that the progressive development of the friendly relations existing between them serves the welfare of the German

SOURCE: Document 234 in *Documents on German Foreign Policy, 1918–1945*, Series D, Vol. III (Germany and Spanish Civil War, 1936–1939) (Washington, D.C.: Department of State, 1950), pp. 256–257.

1. See Charles F. Delzell, *Mussolini's Enemies: The Italian Anti-Fascist Resistance* (Princeton: Princeton University Press, 1961), Ch. IV.

and the Spanish peoples and will be an important factor for the maintenance of European peace, which is close to both their hearts, are agreed in their desire to lay down even now the guiding principles for their future relations, and for this purpose have come to an understanding on the following points:

1. Both Governments will constantly consult with one another on the measures necessary to defend their countries against the threatening dangers of Communism.

2. Both Governments will constantly maintain contact with one another in order to inform each other concerning questions of international policy which affect their joint interests.

3. Neither of the two Governments will participate in treaties or other agreements with third powers which are aimed either directly or indirectly against the other country.

4. In case one of the two countries should be attacked by a third power, the Government of the other country will avoid everything that might serve to the advantage of the attacker or the disadvantage of the attacked.

5. Both Governments are agreed in their desire to intensify the economic relations between their countries as much as possible. In this manner they reaffirm their purpose that the two countries shall henceforth cooperate with and supplement one another in economic matters in every way.

6. Both Governments will treat this protocol, which becomes effective at once, as secret until further notice. At the proper time, they will regulate their political, economic, and cultural relations in detail by special agreements in accordance with the principles laid down above.

Done in duplicate in the German and Spanish languages.

For the German Government:

For the Spanish Nationalist Government:

FAUPEL   FRANCISCO FRANCO

In the early autumn of 1936 Franco's rebels chose Salamanca to be the seat of their government, the "Junta de Defensa Nacional." Thus far the Falange had no official status with the Junta; it was simply an autonomous civilian force helping the rebel effort. Furthermore, it was virtually leaderless for several weeks, because the Republican government had arrested not only José Antonio Primo de Rivera but Fernández Cuesta and Ruiz de Alda, and had executed Ledesma. By this time Onésimo Redondo had also met a violent death. In desperation, the Falangist National Council met in Valladolid on September 4 to choose a successor to José Antonio. The choice fell on Manuel Hedilla, an ex-mechanic without formal education who had been a provincial leader in Santander. The new party *Jefe* established his headquarters alongside the Junta in Salamanca on October 1.

General Franco took a dim view of Hedilla and the other second-string Falangists, but by early 1937 he perceived the need for some kind of official ideology such as Falangism that would buttress the Army's unimaginative regime. He sensed too that the Army and he might reap political and military benefits if he gained control of both the Falange Blue Shirt militia (whose membership had swollen during the war to perhaps 126,000) and the 22,000-strong Requeté militia of the ultra-clerical, Carlist Traditionalists, dedicated foes of liberalism, Masonry, and the Jews. Franco's views in this regard were greatly reinforced by advice he received from his brother-in-law, Ramón Serrano Suñer, who arrived in Salamanca in March, 1937, after escaping from a Republican jail. Shrewdly political and much more fascistic-minded than Franco, Serrano Suñer was ambitious to take over the Falange and convert it into a "state party" that would do his bidding and at the same time be acceptable to the Army and the Church. He envisaged a "New State" that would be dominated by this single, authoritarian party and rest on the juridical and socio-economic base of corporativism.

By mid-April, 1937, it was clear to observers in Salamanca that a political crisis was imminent. Although both Nazi Germany and Fascist Italy felt closer ideologically to the Falange than to the old-fashioned Army types that surrounded General Franco, they preferred to hedge, as the following report of April 14 from the German ambassador in Salamanca shows.

German and Italian Policy Toward the Falange and General Franco
(April 14, 1937)

On April 11 [1937] I had a conference with General Franco lasting more than two hours, in the course of which he expressed his views on some questions of domestic policy, the future form of government, and the military situation.

Franco's starting point was that even before the outbreak of fighting the conviction had prevailed in wide circles in Spain that the country was not making any progress with the old parlia-

SOURCE: Letter of German Ambassador Faupel in Salamanca to German Foreign Ministry, April 14, 1937. Document 243 in *Documents on German Foreign Policy, 1918–1945*, Series D, Vol. III (German and Spanish Civil War, 1936–1939) (Washington, D.C.: Department of State, 1950), pp. 267–270 *passim.*

mentary system. The Falange, which in its ideas leaned heavily on the National Socialist and Fascist model, had only a year ago been very weak numerically. Only after the beginning of the Nationalist movement led by Franco had the Falange, with considerable assistance from Nationalist-minded officers, obtained a great number of adherents and thereby its present importance. But after the death of José Antonio Primo de Rivera, regarding whose death there is in Franco's opinion no doubt, the Falange lacked a real leader. Young Primo de Rivera, although he had as yet had little experience, had been a leader because of his intelligence and energy. His successor, [Manuel] Hedilla, was a completely honest person, but by no means equal to the demands imposed on the leader of the Falange. Hedilla was surrounded by a whole crowd of ambitious young persons who influenced him instead of being influenced and led by him.

As for the leaders of the monarchist parties, Franco spoke against [Manuel Fal Conde][2] in particular. . . .

Regarding his attitude toward the Falange and the monarchist parties, Franco told me that he wished to fuse these groups into one party, the leadership of which he himself would assume. To my objection that the leadership of a party would take up a very great deal of his time . . . , Franco replied that he, as head of the new unity party, intended to form a Junta, probably consisting of four representatives of the Falange and two representatives of the monarchist groups. The core of the unity party would be formed by the Falange, which had the soundest program and the greatest following in the country.

I discussed this development yesterday with our Landesgruppenleiter and the representation of the Fascio at the Italian Embassy; the latter, not inaccurately, described the situation in these words: "Franco is a leader without a party, the Falange a party without a leader." If in his attempt to bring the parties together Franco should meet with opposition from the Falange, we and the Italians are agreed that, in spite of all our inclination toward the Falange and its sound tendencies, we must support Franco, who after all intends to make the program of the Falange the basis of his internal policy. The realization of the most urgently needed social reforms is possible only with Franco, not in opposition to him.

I then directed the conversation with Franco to the rumor which

2. Leader of the Carlist Requetés.—*Ed.*

has been circulating here for several weeks regarding an impending regency. . . . Franco told me that for Spain the return to the monarchy was absolutely out of the question for the foreseeable future. . . .

When Falangist disorders in Salamanca presented him with a convenient pretext to intervene, Franco suddenly made the following speech from his balcony on the night of April 18. Paying lip service to the historic merits of both the Traditionalist and the Falangist forces, he called for the unification of their militias under his own leadership.

Franco's Call for Unification of the Fighting Forces (April 18, 1937)

In the sacred name of Spain, and in the name of all who through the centuries have died in behalf of a great, united, free, and universal Spain, I now address myself to our people:

We are confronted by a war that every day is taking on more of the character of a crusade, of a transcendental struggle of historic grandeur on the part of whole peoples and civilizations—a war in which Spain once again has been selected by history to serve as the field of tragedy and honor in order to bring peace to today's enraged world.

What started out on July 17 [1936] as our own civil war has today turned into a conflagration that is going to illuminate the future for centuries.

At this time, with a clear conscience and a firm sense of my mission in behalf of Spain and in accordance with the will of the Spanish fighters, I demand of everyone but one thing: Unity.

Unity, in order to bring the war speedily to an end; unity, in order to undertake the great new task of peace, crystallizing in the New Spain the thought and style of our National Revolution.

This unity which I call for in the name of Spain and in the sacred name of those who have given their lives for her does not mean a mere *conglomeration* of forces, or a governmental *concen-*

SOURCE: Falange española tradicionalista y de las Juntas ofensivas nacional-sindicalistas, Vicesecretaría de Educación Popular, *Fundamentos del Nuevo Estado* (Madrid: Ediciones de la Vicesecretaría de Educación Popular, 1943), pp. 11–18. My translation.

tration of political factions, or a *sacred union* of more or less patriotic type. There is nothing inorganic, fleeting, or temporary in what I am calling for.

I demand unity in our march toward a common goal—unity both internally and externally, both in faith and in doctrine, both as regards the forms to be manifested to the outside world and in those to be manifested to ourselves.

. . . The Movement that we are leading today is precisely that—a movement, not a program. And as such, it is in process of elaboration and subject to constant revision and improvement to the extent that is realistically possible. Far from being rigid or static, it is a flexible thing. As a movement, it has consisted of several stages.

The first of these we might label the ideal or normative. We are referring to all the centuries of struggle in behalf of the Spanish Reconquista, which sought to consolidate one unified, imperial Spain under the Catholic Monarchs, Charles V, and Philip II. That Spain, united for the purpose of defending and extending throughout the world a universal and Catholic idea, a Christian Empire, was the Spain which gave inspiration to so many other subsequent developments that sought to recover this sublime and perfect moment in our history.

The second chapter we shall call the historic or traditionalist one. How many sacrifices have been made during the eighteenth, nineteenth, and twentieth centuries to recover possessions that were lost along the paths marked out for us by the imperial, Catholic tradition of the fifteenth, sixteenth, and seventeenth centuries! Our greatest effort to revive that happy moment of Spain took place during the civil wars of the last century. And the clearest evidence of this is to be seen in the struggle of an ideal Spain (represented by the Carlists) against a bastard Spain, a Frenchified and Europeanized Spain of the liberals. The spiritual treasures of sixteenth-century Spain were kept alive and localized in the rugged terrain of Navarre.

And the third chapter is what we shall term the present or contemporary one. And it, in its turn, has contained a variety of sacred, heroic efforts toward unification, culminating in our own.

The first phase of this third chapter was the regime of Don Miguel Primo de Rivera—a period of transition between the Pronunciamiento of the nineteenth century and the organic conception of those movements that our present-day world labels "fascist" or "nationalist."

The second phase—which was extremely fruitful because it was dominated by young people who opened their pure eyes to the best in our past while remaining in the spiritual atmosphere of the present—saw the formation of the group known as the JONS (Juntas Ofensivas Nacional-Sindicalistas). And this was quickly broadened and integrated by fusion with the Falange Española. And leadership of this was assumed by the great national figure José Antonio Primo de Rivera, who continued thereby to give new vigor and contemporary relevance to his father's noble efforts, and also to influence other groups that were more or less related to Catholics and Monarchists . . . and motivated by noble and patriotic sentiments.

That was the status of our movement within the sacred tradition of Spain when July 17 [1936] erupted—a historic moment of fundamental importance, in which all these phases and personalities consolidated themselves for the joint struggle.

Above all, the Falange Española de las JONS, whose martyrs are no less holy and powerful than those of ancient times, has captured the support of masses of our young people. . . . From Navarre burst forth the movement that had been steadfastly mounting strength for more than two centuries—a Spanish tradition that was not in the least parochial or regional, but rather a universal, Hispanic, and imperial tradition which had been preserved amid those indestructible crags, waiting for the opportune moment to intervene and spread out, bringing with it an irrevocable faith in God and a deep love for our fatherland.

Other forces and elements that were represented in a variety of organizations and fighting forces (*Milicias*) also gave their support to the struggle.

All of these recruits for the Movement of July 17 (the decisive date in the final struggle of our history) are now enrolled in the military cadres of our glorious Army. And in the political and civic sector they are enrolled in comparable groups.

. . . We are determined, before God and the Spanish nation, to conclude rapidly this work of unification! A work of unification that our people have demanded of us, and a mission that God has entrusted to us.

To bring this to fruition, we intend to do two things. First, we shall maintain the spirit and style that the world demands of us in this hour and that the genius of our fatherland offers to us, struggling faithfully against all kinds of bastardy and *arribismo*. We need militiamen, soldiers of the faith, not politicasters or debaters.

Second, our heart and our will demand a resolute spirit among the fighting men at the front and the youth of Spain.

We do not want an old and corrupt Spain. We want a State in which the pure tradition and substance of our ideal Spanish past is manifested in new, vigorous, and heroic forms which the youth of today and tomorrow will bring to our people in this new imperial dawn.

And now let me address myself to those nations which because of shortsightedness and materialism sell out their press to the gold of the Reds and listen to the criminal propaganda broadcast by the Reds, traffic in the products of theft, and shake hands with robbers and assassins. Let me tell them that the greatest enemy of their empires, the greatest danger for their countries, no longer consists of those neighbors who once fought nobly against their frontiers, or those who are now reappearing in international life with unequaled power and demanding a place in the exploitation of the world. Now there is a greater danger that has come into existence —and this is destructive Bolshevism, Russian Communism, a revolution on the march—an enemy that, wherever it becomes entrenched, is hard to overthrow. It brings empires to disintegration, destroys civilizations, and creates those great human tragedies which, like the one in Spain, the world looks upon with indifference and shows no desire to understand.

Red propaganda invokes democracy, liberty of the people, and human fraternity, and charges Nationalist Spain with being an enemy of these principles. Against this purely verbal and formal democracy of the liberal State that everywhere is falling apart; against this liberal State with its fictions of parties, electoral laws, and balloting, its excess of formulas and conventions which, by confusing means with ends, overlook the true democratic substance; against these shams, we who have abandoned such doctrinaire concerns now propose instead an effective democracy that brings to the people what truly interests them—viz., a feeling that they are being governed by integral justice, not only as regards law and order but in social and economic matters; a sense of moral freedom in the service of a patriotic creed and an eternal ideal; and economic freedom, without which political freedom is just a mockery.

Liberalism's exploitation of Spaniards will now be replaced by a rational participation by everyone in the activities of the State, to be achieved through family, municipal, and functional groupings of a syndical sort.

We shall create justice and public order, without which human dignity is impossible. We shall form powerful armed forces on sea, land, and in the air that will conform to the heroic virtues that so often have been demonstrated by Spaniards. And we shall revive the classical university, which by continuing its glorious tradition and spirit, its doctrine and morals, will again provide light and guidance to the Spanish peoples.

This is the profile of the New State; this is what we made known to you in October of last year, and which we are going to bring about with firm step and no vacillation. This is what is common to the majority of Spaniards who are not poisoned by materialism or by Marxism. This is what figures in the creed of the Falange Española. This is what surrounds the spirit of our traditionalists. This is the common element of those people who, after burying a fallacious liberalism, have oriented their politics along the road of authoritarianism, increased patriotism, and social justice. This is what our Spanish history contains, a history that is so rich in effective freedoms set forth in its popular charters, statutory laws, and corporations.

This is what is treasured in the Catholic doctrine that is professed by the entire nation. . . .

Spaniards everywhere, lift up your hearts! Up with Spain!!! Long live Spain!!!

The next evening Franco and his henchmen inflicted the *coup de grâce*. A decree drawn up by Serrano Suñer proclaimed the unification of Falangists and Requetés as the official party of the Spanish "New State." The party label henceforth was Falange Española Tradicionalista y de las Juntas de Ofensiva Nacional-Sindicalista, more conveniently abbreviated to FET y de las JONS. Point 27 of the earlier program which had forbidden any such fusion was quietly dropped at this juncture.

Franco's Call for Unification of the Militias
(April 19, 1937)

. . . Efficient government . . . demands regimentation of both the individual and the collective activities of all Spaniards toward a common destiny.

SOURCE: *Boletín Oficial*, April 20, 1937; reprinted in Falange española tradicionalista y de las Juntas ofensivas nacional-sindica-

This truth, which the good sense of the Spanish people has perceived so clearly, is incompatible with the strife of parties and political organizations. . . .

Now that the war has reached an advanced stage and the hour of victory nears, it is urgent to undertake the great task of peace and to crystallize in the New State the thought and style of our National Revolution. . . .

The unification which I am demanding in the name of Spain and in the sacred name of those who have sacrificed their lives for it—both heroes and martyrs—and to whom we shall always look with fidelity, does not mean a conglomeration of forces or a mere governmental concentration, or a temporary union. . . . We must avoid the creation of an artificial party, but rather bring together all our recruits in such a way as to integrate and synthesize them into a single national political entity that will link State and Society and guarantee the political continuity and loyalty of the people to the State. . . .

In Spain, as in other countries where there are totalitarian regimes, traditional forces are now beginning to integrate themselves with new forces. The Falange Española has attracted masses of young people by its program, its new-style propaganda, and has provided a new political and heroic framework for the present and a promise of Spanish fulfillment in the future. The Requetés, in addition to possessing martial qualities, have served through the centuries as the sacred repository of the Spanish tradition and of Catholic spirituality, which have been the principal formative elements in our nationality—and whose eternal principles of morality and justice shall continue to inspire us. . . .

Because of all the foregoing,

I order that

Art. 1: The Falange Española and the Requetés, together with all their existing services and units, shall be integrated, under my leadership, into a single political entity of national character which henceforth shall be named the Falange Española Tradicionalista y de las JONS.

The principal mission of this organization (which shall stand

listas, Vicesecretaría de Educación Popular, *Fundamentos del Nuevo Estado* (Madrid: Ediciones de la Vicesecretaría de Educación Popular, 1943), pp. 18–23. My translation.

midway between our Society and State) is to communicate to the State the feelings of the people and to convey to it their thought as expressed in political and moral virtues, hierarchic service, and brotherhood.

Everyone who possesses a membership card in either the Falange Española or the Comunión Tradicionalista on the date of publication of this decree shall be regarded as an original and rightful member of the new organization, and other Spaniards who seek to join may do so after proper admission.

All other political organizations and parties are hereby dissolved.

Art. 2: The guiding organs of the new national political entity shall be the Chief of State (*Jefe del Estado*), a Secretariat or Political Junta, and the National Council.

It shall be the task of the Secretariat or the Political Junta to draw up the internal constitution of the body, the purpose of which shall be to assist the *Jefe* in preparing the organic structure of the State and to assist in every way the work of the government.

Half of its members (who will initiate its tasks) will be designated by the Chief of State; the other half will be elected by the National Council.

In a manner to be established by appropriate decrees, the National Council shall acquaint itself with whatever great national problems the Chief of State submits to it.

While steps are being completed for the definitive organization of the totalitarian New State, measures shall also be taken to satisfy the strong national yearnings of members of the Falange Española Tradicionalista y de las JONS to participate in the organisms and services of the State and impart new rhythm to them.

Art. 3: The fighting forces of the Falange Española and of the Requetés shall be fused into a single National Militia, but shall preserve their external emblems and banners. Other fighting forces that have won honor in the war shall also be incorporated therein.

The National Militia shall serve as an auxiliary of the Army.

The Chief of State shall be the Supreme Commander of the Militia. A general of the Army shall serve as the immediate commander, and he shall have two military assistants, who shall come respectively from the Militias of the Falange Española and the Requetés.

To preserve the purity of its style, two political counselors shall be named to the headquarters.

Done at Salamanca, the 19th of April, 1937.

In view of the military realities most rank-and-file Falangists prudently swore allegiance to Franco. But a number of balky party leaders, including Hedilla, refused and had to be arrested. Sentenced to solitary confinement and life imprisonment in the Canary Islands, Hedilla was transferred to Majorca after the war.

Falangism had become a tool of the military dictatorship. Power now rested securely in the hands of Franco, Serrano Suñer, and the military hierarchy, almost none of whom were old-line Falangists. Indeed, Franco stood much closer to the Spanish tradition of the *caudillo,* of the successful military leader and of old Miguel Primo de Rivera, then to the Falange. But the party could be used to checkmate monarchists, prelates, and bankers. In various interviews with correspondents in the summer and fall of 1937 Franco spoke of his intention of setting up a "totalitarian" state based upon a single-party movement. He kept open the possibility of a postwar monarchical restoration, but insisted that it would have to be a very different kind of monarchy from that which had collapsed in 1931. In reply to questions whether his new regime would resemble those in Italy and Germany, he answered affirmatively to the extent that Spain's New State would reinforce the principle of hierarchy, exalt patriotic love of country, practice social justice, and promote the well-being of both the middle and the working classes. At the same time, however, he stressed that Spain would not be blindly imitative, and he insisted that most of the modern formulas that characterize totalitarian regimes were already present in Spain's ancient traditions. All Spaniards would participate by means of the single totalitarian party in the municipal and syndical functioning of the New State.

On August 4, 1937, Franco gave his approval to the revised Statutes of the FET y de las JONS. Among the innovations were thirteen "special services," which tended to parallel the bureaucratic structure of the state and provide a measure of training for service therein. Party approval was necessary for appointments at the local and provincial levels of the bureaucracy. The statutes printed below bear the date July 31, 1939, and include a few changes in the functioning of the Jefatura Nacional that the conclusion of the war made possible.

Statutes of the Falange
Española Tradicionalista y de las JONS
(July 31, 1939)

In the Statutes of the Falange Española Tradicionalista y de las JONS that were approved by my decree of August 4, 1937, provision was included for making whatever modifications of the consti-

SOURCE: Decree by the Jefatura Nacional of July 31, 1939, printed in *Boletín Oficial* of August 4, 1939; reprinted in Falange española tradicionalista y de las Juntas ofensivas nacional-sindica-

tution and functioning of organs might be desirable at war's end and with the advent of peace. Together with some other changes that experience has suggested, I now proceed to approve the revised text of the above-mentioned Statutes. . . .

CHAPTER I: GENERAL REGULATIONS

Art. 1: The FET y de las JONS serves as the militant inspirational Movement and basis of the Spanish State. Through its determination and creed, it assumes the task of restoring to Spain a deep and indestructible sense of singleness of purpose and faith. Confident of its Catholic and imperial mission as the protagonist of History, it establishes the basis of an economic regime that will rise above interests of individuals, groups, and classes, and will foster the multiplication of goods for the service of State, Social Justice, and Christian personal freedom.

The FET y de las JONS provides the disciplined means whereby the people, united and orderly, are linked to the State, and the State inculcates upon the people the virtues of service, fraternity, and hierarchy.

For the attainment of all these goals and the heroic establishment of the State, it integrates into one single force the Comunión Tradicionalista (which stands as the guarantor of historic continuity) and the Falange Española de las JONS (which is the vocation, form, and style of the National Revolution).

The FET y de las JONS constitutes a permanent guardian of the eternal values of the fatherland that have been courageously defended in three civil wars, exalted by voice and blood of the new generation on October 29, 1934, and definitively redeemed by the Army and the popular Militia on the historic occasion of July 17, 1936.

Art. 2: The emblem of the FET y de las JONS shall consist of five intersecting arrows, with a yoke resting on the intersecting point.

Art. 3: The Movement constitutes one single legal personality with one single patrimony. Any authorization for the acquisition of properties shall be done for the benefit of this patrimony. . . .

---

listas, Vicesecretaría de Educación Popular, *Fundamentos del Nuevo Estado* (Madrid: Ediciones de la Vicesecretaría de Educación Popular, 1943), pp. 22–37 *passim.* My translation.

A special Regulation shall set forth the norms to govern the economic activities of the various organs of the FET y de las JONS.

Art. 4: The FET y de las JONS shall consist of the following elements and organs: (1) the members; (2) the local Falanges; (3) the Provincial Governing Bodies [Jefaturas]; (4) the Regional Inspectorates; (5) Services; (6) Militias and Syndicates; (7) National Inspectorates; (8) National Delegates; (9) General Secretary of the Movement; (10) Political Junta; (11) President of the Political Junta; (12) National Council; (13) the *Caudillo* or National Head of the Movement.

CHAPTER II: REGARDING MEMBERS

Art. 5: Members are divided into two categories—militants and adherents.

Militants are those who, in accepting resolutely the discipline of all organs of the Movement and declaring their willingness to consecrate themselves to the fulfillment of its ends, possess any of the following attributes:

(A) Those who belonged as of April 20, 1937, to one of the two integral forces of the Movement, or who have been admitted directly by the Political Junta prior to the publication of the Statutes that were approved by decree on August 4, 1937.

(B) The generals, *Jefes,* officials, and classes of the National Armed Forces of land, sea, and air who were either on duty or called into service during the war.

(C) Those who attain this status by personal decision of the *Caudillo* or by recommendation from the Provincial Jefaturas for reason of outstanding service to the National Cause, either in preparation for the Military Uprising or during the war.

(D) Those who attain this status by virtue of provisions in Art. 7.

Art. 6: Militants enjoy all the rights and obligations conferred upon them by the present statutes and regulations. An official booklet, approved by the Jefatura, will confirm their status.

Art. 7: Upon application, adherents may be admitted by the General Secretary, the provincial *Jefes,* and the local *Jefes.*

Adherents shall serve in the FET y de las JONS without any of the rights or status of members thereof. Prior to the expiration of five years, the appropriate provincial *Jefe* must decide clearly the status of the adherent, either raising him to the category of militant or excluding him from the Organization. An appeal from this decision may be made to the General Secretary.

Whenever an adherent demonstrates that he has given important service to the fatherland during the war, his status shall be decided within fifteen days. If the provincial *Jefe* does not then grant him the status of militant, the adherent may appeal to the General Secretary if endorsed by twelve militants or if the petition is accompanied by a statement from either the commander of the combat unit or the civil authorities.

Those who exercised political roles in the Central Administration prior to July 17, 1936, must make application directly to the General Secretary.

Art. 8: All members must subscribe to the formula of adherence and oath set forth by the National Jefatura of the Movement.

Members of the FET y de las JONS shall pay the specified progressive quota. . . .

CHAPTER III: REGARDING LOCAL ORGANIZATIONS

Art. 11: In order to constitute a local Falange, a minimum of twenty militant members and authorization from the provincial Jefatura are required. . . .

CHAPTER IV: REGARDING PROVINCIAL JEFATURAS AND REGIONAL INSPECTORATES

Art. 18: The *Caudillo* shall designate a Jefatura for each province, to be headed by only one militant.

These *Jefes*, who possess full authority and responsibility, shall have the responsibility of transmitting to the local Falanges in their provinces the decisions of the National *Jefe* of the Movement, and of seeing that these are fully carried out, and of inspecting the services of their geographical zone. . . .

CHAPTER V: REGARDING SERVICES

Art. 22: The National Jefatura of the Movement will create those services which it considers to be appropriate for the division of labor and the co-ordination of the energies of the FET y de las JONS in the work of national resurgence.

A delegate, freely appointed and dismissed by the national *Jefe*, shall head each National Service. Each service shall create whatever sections are necessary for the fulfillment of the National Syndicalist program.

Art. 23: Without prejudice to the powers bestowed upon the national *Jefe* by the preceding article, the following services shall exist: (1) External; (2) National Education; (3) Press and Propaganda; (4) Women's Section; (5) Social Work; (6) Syndicates; (7) Youth Organization; (8) Veterans' Organization; (9) Ex-Prisoners' Organization; (10) Justice and Rights; (11) Communication and Transportation; (12) Treasury and Administration; (13) Information and Investigation.

There shall also be a National Inspector of Education and Religious Assistance. . . .

Chapter VI: Regarding the Militia

Art. 27: Both in war and in peace the Militias represent the ardent spirit of the FET y de las JONS and its manly determination to serve the fatherland as a vigilant guardian of its principles against all domestic enemies. Not just a part of the Movement, it is the Movement itself and is involved in heroic military action in its behalf.

Art. 28: The Supreme Command of the Militias is held by the *Caudillo*, who may delegate his prerogatives to a *Jefe* who shall have direct responsibility.

The hierarchic structure of the Militias shall be set forth in a special Regulation.

Chapter VII: Regarding the Syndicates

Art. 29: The FET y de las JONS will create and maintain appropriate syndical organizations for regulating labor, production, and distribution. In each instance, the leaders of these organizations will come from the ranks of the Movement, and they will be co-ordinated and instructed by its Jefaturas in order to guarantee that the syndical organization conforms to the national interest and is infused with the ideals of the State.

Art. 30: The National Delegation of Syndicates will be entrusted to only one militant, and its internal organization shall be of vertical and hierarchical structure in the manner of a just, disciplined, and creative Army.

Chapter VIII: Regarding the Political Junta

Art. 31: The Political Junta, Delegation of the National Council and permanent organ of government of the FET y de las JONS, shall consist of a President who is freely appointed by the *Caudillo;* a Vice-President and ten National Councilors, five of whom are appointed by the Council upon recommendation of the *Caudillo,* and the other five appointed directly by the Council.

Vacancies that occur shall be filled by the *Caudillo* from members of the National Council. . . .

Art. 32: The duties of the Political Junta include:

1. The study and presentation of problems of interest to the broad advancement of the Movement.

2. The presentation to the national *Jefe* of those proposals and initiatives that he deems suitable in all respects.

3. Tendering advice to the national *Jefe* regarding whatever items he submits to them.

4. Examination of the budget and control of finances.

Whenever it is deemed necessary, the Political Junta may request oral or written information from any militant regarding matters in his competence.

Art. 33: The Junta shall meet at least once a month and whenever summoned by the national *Jefe* of the Movement or by its President.

Chapter IX: Regarding the National Council

Arts. 34 and 35:[3] The Council shall consist of: (1) The national *Jefe,* who is President thereof; (2) the Secretary General; (3) the Ministers; (4) the President of the Cortes; (5) the Vice-Secretary General; (6) the Vice-Secretaries of the Movement; (7) the *Jefe* in immediate command of the Militias; (8) the militants of the Movement who have occupied the positions of President and Vice-President of the Political Junta, Secretary General, and Vice-Secretary General of the FET y de las JONS; (9) the President of the Institute of Political Studies; (10) the National Delegates of the FET y de las JONS; (11) the provincial *Jefes* of the Move-

3. Modified and revised by Decree of November 23, 1942.

ment in Madrid, Barcelona, Valencia, Seville, Málaga, Bilbao, Saragossa, and Valladolid; (12) the militants whom the *Caudillo* designates because of merits or services, but not to exceed one hundred in number.

Vacancies may be filled freely at any time by the national *Jefe*. . . .

Art. 39: The National Council of the FET y de las JONS shall be acquainted with:

1. Basic policies regarding the structure of the Movement.
2. Basic policies regarding the structure of the State.
3. Guiding policies for syndical organization.
4. All great national questions that the *Jefe* of the Movement submits.
5. Great questions of an international nature.

The Council shall make recommendations whenever the *Jefe* of the Movement requests same.

Art. 40: The *Caudillo* shall secretly designate his successor, who will be proclaimed by the Council in case of his death.

Art. 41: The Council must meet every year on the seventeenth of July and whenever it is convened by the *Caudillo*. . . .

Chapter X: Regarding the General Secretary

Art. 43: The *Caudillo* shall freely appoint the General Secretary whose duties and powers are to:

1. Transmit all orders of the national *Jefe* and Political Junta to any of the organs of the Movement.
2. Inspect and direct, upon orders of the national *Jefe*, the work of the Provincial Jefaturas and Services.
3. Maintain discipline and propose to the Supreme Commander those measures which he regards as appropriate for the activity of the Movement but which do not transcend the competence of either the National Council or the Political Junta.
4. Maintain documentary order and consistency in the work of the FET y de las JONS.
5. Act as secretary at meetings of the National Council and the Political Junta, and carry out its decisions.
6. Participate as a Minister in the tasks of Government. . . .

Chapter XI: Regarding the President of the Political Junta

Art. 46: It is the function of the President of the Political Junta, who shall be freely appointed and dismissed by the national *Jefe*, to supervise the work of the Junta. . . .

Chapter XII: Regarding the National Jefe of the Movement

Art. 47: The national *Jefe* of the FET y de las JONS, who is Supreme *Caudillo* of the Movement, personifies all the values and all the honors thereof. As Author of the Historic Era wherein Spain is gaining the possibility of achieving its destiny and thereby the deepest aspirations of the Movement, the *Jefe* assumes in plenary fashion the most absolute authority.

The *Jefe* answers before God and before History.

Art. 48: It is the *Caudillo*'s right to designate his successor, who shall receive from him the same honors and obligations. The manner of succession, foreseen in the present Statutes, shall be regulated in its details by the National Council.

Chapter XIII: Regarding Revision and
Interpretation of the Statutes

Art. 49: These Statutes may be modified by the National Council upon recommendation of the national *Jefe*, but in urgent cases the *Jefe* may carry out this action by himself.

Their interpretation and doctrine shall always be in the power of the *Caudillo*, who is the only person who may determine the modalities of circumstance, rhythm, and timing for giving everlasting recognition to our Absent Ones, the builders and continuers of the Spanish Tradition, and to all those who have given their lives for the glory of Spain.

Additional disposition: The new National Council is approved by this Decree.

Done at Burgos, the 31st day of July, 1939, Year of the Victory.

FRANCISCO FRANCO.

When Fernández Cuesta arrived in rebel territory as a result of an exchange of prisoners in the fall of 1937, Franco decided to let him become party secretary again. But his authority in the Movement was never more than nominal, for Franco and Serrano Suñer always kept real power in their own hands. When the Generalissimo formed his first regular cabinet on January 30, 1938, he designated Serrano (scornfully called the *cuñadísimo,* or "most high brother-in-law" by his rivals) to be both Minister of Interior and *Jefe Nacional* for Press and Propaganda in the party. All the other ministerial posts were assigned to non-Falangists.

Meanwhile, the urgency of social and economic reforms in the New State was apparent. The German and Italian representatives in Salamanca had long pleaded with Franco to give attention to such matters. The Italian Fascists were especially anxious that he draw up a Charter of Labor along the lines Mussolini had followed in Italy in 1927. Before this document was completed, however, Franco's government announced the formation in January, 1938, of a Ministry of Syndical Organization, consisting of five national services: Syndicates; Jurisdiction and Housing of Labor; Social Security; Emigration; and Statistics. Provision was made for a Central Syndical Council of Co-ordination to superintend the work of national syndicalist centers in each province. Within a few months Labor Magistrates were also instituted to adjudicate disputes. Needless to say, appointments to all levels of this bureaucratic mechanism were tightly controlled from above. Furthermore, two important sectors—banking and agricultural production—were left outside the purview of the syndical structure. The former could look to the Ministry of Economics for protection, the latter to the Ministry of Agriculture. National syndicalism was never integrated with the legislative branch of government in Spain to the extent that it was in Italy, where Mussolini in 1939 finally converted the lower house of parliament into the Chamber of Fasces and of Corporations.

After lengthy consideration of three drafts, a Spanish Labor Charter was announced at last on March 9, 1938. Left-wing Falangists were not entirely pleased with the final version, which reflected a strongly paternalistic and regulatory attitude toward labor. The syndical structure that went into effect did not represent the workers but controlled them in the interests of the state and employers. This system contrasted markedly with the original Falangist theory which had looked upon the syndicates as dynamic revolutionary organisms to promote national economic reformation.

The Labor Charter
(March 9, 1938)

PREAMBLE

Reviving the Catholic tradition of social justice and the lofty sense of humanity that inspired the laws of the Empire, The State—

SOURCE: Decree of March 9, 1938, published in the *Boletín Oficial* of March 10, 1938, and in English translation by the Spanish

which is national by reason of being an instrument wholly at the service of the entire Nation, and syndical in so far as it represents a reaction against nineteenth century capitalism and communistic materialism—embarks upon the task of carrying out, with a disciplined constructive and soberly religious demeanor, the revolution that Spain is achieving to ensure that Spaniards may once more possess, for good and all, their Country, Bread and Justice.

To attain this end and at the same time put into practice the motto of the unity, greatness and freedom of Spain, it enters the social field with the determination that the common wealth shall be at the service of the Spanish people and that the country's economy shall be subordinated to that policy.

Basing itself on the postulate that Spain is one and indivisible as regards her destiny, it hereby declares its aim to make Spanish industry—in the fellowship of all its components—one and indivisible, so that it may minister to the needs of the country and uphold the instruments of its power.

The recently established Spanish State, in these declarations of what is to be the inspiration of its social and political economy, is putting faithfully into a concrete form the desires and demands of all who are fighting in the trenches and who compose, through their honor, valor and labor, the most progressive aristocracy of this era in the nation's history.

Be it known, therefore, to all Spaniards, who are united in sacrifice and in hope, that WE DECLARE:

I. WORK FOR ALL

Firstly. Work is man's participation in production by means of the willingly given exercise of his mental and manual abilities, according to his personal vocation, that he may live a more seemly and comfortable life whilst assisting in the development of the national economy.

Secondly. Work, being essentially personal and human, cannot be lowered to the merely material idea of a merchandise, nor be made the subject of any transaction incompatible with the self-respect of him who lends it.

Thirdly. The right to work is a consequence of the duty to do

---

Press Services, Ltd., 99 Regent St., London, W. 1, *The Labour Charter for Franco's Spain* (n.d.).

so that God demands of man for the fulfilment of his individual ends and the prosperity and greatness of his country.

Fourthly. The State values and exalts work—the fertile expression of man's creative spirit; and, as such, will protect it with all the force of the law, showing it the greatest consideration and making it compatible with other individual, family and social ends.

Fifthly. Work, being a social duty, will be universally demanded in some form or other of all Spaniards who are not cripples as it is deemed a tribute all must pay to the wealth of the country.

Sixthly. Work is one of the noblest attributes of rank and honor and is sufficient justification for demanding the assistance and guardianship of the State.

Seventhly. Service is that work which is given with heroism, disinterestedness and abnegation with the object of helping towards the supreme good which Spain represents.

Eighthly. All Spaniards have the right to work. The satisfaction of this right is one of the main concerns of the State.

II. Hours and Conditions of Work

Firstly. The State undertakes to exercise constant and effective action in defense of the worker, his living and his work. It will set proper limits to the working hours to prevent them being excessive and will grant labor every safeguard of a defensive and humanitarian order. It will specially prohibit night work for women and children, regulate home-work and free married women from the workship and the factory.

Secondly. The State will keep Sunday as a day of rest, as a sacred condition for the lending of labor.

Thirdly. Without loss of pay, and taking into account the technical requirements of the industry, the law will enforce the recognition of the religious holidays tradition demands, civil holidays which have been so declared and attendance at such ceremonies as the national leaders of the movement may ordain.

Fourthly. July 18th, the date of the beginning of the Glorious Rising, having been proclaimed a national holiday, will be celebrated as the Feast of Homage to Labor.

Fifthly. Every worker will have a right to paid yearly holidays in order to enjoy a deserved rest, and the necessary machinery to ensure the better fulfilment of this order will be prepared.

Sixthly. The requisite institutions will be created so that, in their leisure hours, the workers may have access to all means of culture, happiness, health, sport and volunteer training.

III. Remuneration and Security

Firstly. The minimum basis of payment for work shall be sufficient to provide the worker and his family with a worthy, moral living.

Secondly. Family subsidies will be established through suitable bodies.

Thirdly. The standard of living of the workers will be raised gradually and inflexibly in proportion as the higher interests of the nation permit.

Fourthly. The State will fix rules for regulating work, in accordance with which relations between workers and employers will be arranged. The principal contents of the said relations will be both the giving of labor and its remuneration and the reciprocal duty of loyalty, assistance and protection in the employers and faithfulness and obedience on the part of the workers.

Fifthly. Through the Guild the State will be at pains to learn whether economic and all kinds of conditions in which work is being done are fair to the workers.

Sixthly. The State will see to the security and continuity of work.

Seventhly. The employer shall inform his personnel of the progress of production sufficiently to strengthen their sense of responsibility in the same, and in the terms to be laid down by law.

IV. The Artisan

The artisan, who is a living heritage of a glorious guild past, will be fostered and efficiently protected, as being a complete embodiment of the human person in his work and representing a form of production equally distant from capitalist concentration and gregarious Marxism.

V. Agricultural Work

Firstly. Regulations for agricultural labor will be adapted to its special characteristics and the seasonal variations which Nature ordains.

Secondly. The State will pay special attention to the technical education of the agricultural producer, thus enabling him to perform all the work demanded by each unit of development.

Thirdly. The prices of the chief products will be regulated and fixed in such a way as to ensure a minimum profit in normal conditions to the agricultural employer, and consequently such as to make him pay his laborers wages that will enable them to improve their living conditions.

Fourthly. The aim will be pursued of giving every peasant family a small holding of family land sufficient for its own elementary needs and to provide work during periods of unemployment.

Fifthly. Rural life will be enhanced by the improvement of peasants' dwellings and of the sanitary condition of the villages and hamlets of Spain.

Sixthly. The State will guarantee to tenants continuity in cultivating their land by means of long term contracts to safeguard them against unjustified eviction and to ensure for them the extinction of debt for any improvements they may have made in the period. The State aspires to find ways and means to cause the land to pass, on fair terms, into the hands of those who work it directly.

VI. Toilers of the Sea

The State will look after the toilers of the sea with the utmost solicitude, giving them proper institutions to prevent depreciation of their wares and helping them to acquire the necessary equipment for carrying on their profession.

VII. Labor Magistracy

A new Labor Magistracy will be created based on the principle that this function of justice is a matter for the State.

VIII. Capital and its Role

Firstly. Capital is an instrument of production.

Secondly. The Enterprise (employer or Firm), as a producing unit, will arrange the members composing it in such a way that those of an instrumental nature shall be subordinate to those of a human category, and all alike to the common good.

Thirdly. The head of the Firm will take on himself its management, and be responsible to the State for the same.

Fourthly. After allotting a fair interest to capital, the profits of the Firm will be firstly applied to the reserves necessary for its sound position, the improvement of production and the betterment of working conditions and the living of the workers.

IX. CREDIT FOR DEVELOPMENT

Firstly. Credit will be so ordered that, besides attending to its task of developing the country's resources, it may assist in creating and supporting the small farmer, fisherman, industrialist and business man.

Secondly. Honorable conduct and confidence, based on skill in work, will comprise effective security for the granting of credit. The State will implacably suppress all forms of usury.

X. SOCIAL INSURANCE

Firstly. Savings will give the worker the certitude of being protected when in misfortune.

Secondly. There will be an increase in the social insurances against old age, disablement, maternity, work accidents, professional sicknesses, consumption and unemployment, the ultimate aim being the establishment of total insurance. A primary aim will be to devise means for providing a sufficient pension for superannuated workers.

XI. PROTECTION AND PRODUCTION

Firstly. National production constitutes an economic unit at the service of the Country. It is the duty of every Spaniard to defend, improve and increase it. All factors combining in production are subordinate to the supreme interest of the Nation.

Secondly. Individual or collective acts that in any way disturb normal production or attempt to do so, will be considered as crimes of treason against the Country.

Thirdly. Unjustifiable slackening in output will be the subject of appropriate punishment.

Fourthly. In general the State will not be a business concern, except to compensate for the absence of private initiative or when the higher interests of the nation so require it.

Fifthly. The State itself, or through the Guilds, will prevent all unfair competition in the field of production as well as such activities as obstruct the normal establishment or development of the national economy, but will encourage, on the other hand, all initiative that tends to its betterment.

Sixthly. The State recognizes private initiative as being a copious source for the economic life of the Nation.

XII. Property and the Family

Firstly. The State recognizes and protects private property as a natural means for fulfilling individual, family and social functions. All forms of property are subordinate to the supreme interests of the nation, whose interpreter is the State.

Secondly. The State assumes the task of multiplying and putting within the reach of all Spaniards those forms of property vitally bound up with the person, the family health, the ownership of land and the instruments or goods of labor for daily use.

Thirdly. It looks on the family as the prime natural unit and foundation of society and, at the same time, as a moral institution endowed with an inalienable right superior to any positive law. As a greater safeguard to its preservation and continuance, the immunity of family patrimony from attachment will be recognized.

XIII. Principles of the Organization

Firstly. The National Guild organization of the State finds its inspiration in the principles of Unity, Totality and Hierarchy.

Secondly. All factors of economy will be incorporated, by branches of production or services, in vertical Guilds. The liberal and technical professions will be similarly organized as the law may prescribe.

Thirdly. The vertical Guild is a corporation by public law, which is formed by combining into one single organism all elements that devote themselves to fulfilling the economic process within a certain service or branch of production, arranged in order of rank, under the direction of the State.

Fourthly. The officials of the Guilds will necessarily be chosen from the active members of the Spanish Traditionalist Phalanx [Falange].

Fifthly. The vertical Guild is an instrument at the service of the State through which it will chiefly carry out its economic policy. It is the duty of the Guild to know the problems of production and propose solutions subordinating them to the national interest. The vertical Guild may intervene through specialized bodies in the regulation, supervision and fulfilment of the conditions of work.

Sixthly. The vertical Guild may initiate and maintain bodies of investigation, moral, physical and professional education, savings and assistance, as well as other bodies of a social character of necessity to the elements of production.

Seventhly. It will establish employment bureaux to find work for the worker properly adapted to his ability and merits.

Eighthly. It is a duty of the Guilds to supply the State with exact data to work out the statistics of their production.

Ninthly. The law of Guild organization will decide the way in which the existing economic or professional associations shall be incorporated.

XIV. Protection of the Spanish Worker

The State will issue the opportune measures to be taken for protecting national labor in our territory; and through Labor Treaties, with other Powers, it will see to the protection of the professional position of Spanish workers residing abroad.

XV. Restoration of Spain

On the day of the promulgation of this Charter, Spain is engaged in a heroic military struggle, in which at the cost of heavy sacrifice she is saving the riches of the soul and the civilization of the world.

To the generosity of the Youth in arms and of Spain herself, national production with all its component factors must respond.

In this Charter of rights and duties we therefore set down as most urgent and necessary those of the elements of production which co-operate with their just and resolute contribution to the restoration of the soil of Spain and the foundations of her power.

XVI. Future of the Combatants

The State undertakes to incorporate in the posts of work, honor and command to which they have a right as Spaniards and which they have won like heroes, the young men who are fighting.

The FET y de las JONS was permitted to take over administration of social services in Spain through its Women's Section (Sección Femenina), a branch that had been established in 1934 by José Antonio's younger sister, Pilar. During the Civil War Falangist women helped the Army units in a variety of practical and cultural ways. By 1939 their membership had increased to more than half a million. After the end of hostilities Pilar reorganized the section on a permanent basis. Unmarried women were usually expected to spend six months in service, supervising more than one thousand youth centers and promoting health services, physical education, and the like.

Despite Franco's "shotgun marriage" of Falangists and Requetés, the two factions in the FET remained suspicious, and their youth groups never combined. The Carlists were unhappy to see the old-guard Falangist, Fernández Cuesta, given the secretaryship of the new party,[4] and they felt some reservations about the Ministry of Syndical Organization. On the other hand, they gained lasting satisfaction from the promulgation of clerical laws in 1938 that gave the Church complete educational rights, tied the state to Roman Catholicism, and rigidly circumscribed other religious groupings. Within a matter of a few weeks the Jesuits were fully reinstated in Spain, despite muttering from some Falangist quarters. The role of the Catholic Church was to be far more omnipresent in Franco's Spain than it was in Mussolini's Italy.

The police-state nature of Spain was quickly made clear by various decrees drawn up by Serrano Suñer, the Minister of Interior. For example, on April 22, 1938, the following law set forth strict censorship and regulation of the press.

Law Regarding the Press
(April 22, 1938)

. . . *Art. 1:* The State is responsible for the organization, supervision, and control of the national institution of the periodic press. It shall be the responsibility of the Ministry entrusted with the National Press Service to establish the appropriate regulations.

Art. 2: In the exercise of this function, the State shall:

1. Regulate the number and extent of periodical publications.
2. Intervene in the naming of the managerial personnel.
3. Regulate the profession of journalism.
4. Supervise the activity of the press.
5. Have the power of censorship. . . .
6. Take whatever measures are necessary on the basis of the principle set forth in Art. 1 of this law.

Art. 3: Should the exercise of the power mentioned first in the preceding article lead to property damage without there having

SOURCE: Published in *Boletín Oficial*, May 1, 1938; reprinted in Falange española tradicionalista y de las Juntas ofensivas nacional-sindicalistas, Vicesecretaría de Educación Popular, *Fundamentos del Nuevo Estado* (Madrid: Ediciones de la Vicesecretaría de Educación Popular, 1943), pp. 403–411 *passim.* My translation.

4. He held the post from December, 1937, until August, 1939, at which time Franco made him ambassador to Brazil.

been prior provocation by the injured party, the State shall arrange for proper reparation in a manner to be determined.

Art. 4: The above-mentioned functions shall be exercised by means of central and provincial agencies. The central agencies shall be the corresponding Ministry and the National Press Service.

In each province there shall be established a Press Service, dependent upon the National Service of the same name and subject to the respective Civil Government. . . .

Art. 8: The director of each periodical bears responsibility for it. He must be inscribed in the Official Register of Publishers, which will be maintained by the National Press Service, and to hold his position he must have the approval of the Ministry.

Art. 9: The publishing enterprise bears joint responsibility for the director's actions, whether of commission or omission. . . .

Art. 10: In the case of signed articles, the responsibility of the signer in no way exempts the director of the periodical from responsibility for publishing the article. . . .

Art. 20: The punishments for directors and enterprises to be decreed by the Ministry of Interior may range, according to the gravity of the case, among the following:

(a) Imposition of a fine.

(b) Dismissal of the director.

(c) Dismissal of the director, accompanied by the cancellation of his name in the Register of Publishers.

(d) Confiscation of the periodical.

Art. 21: The punishments set forth in the preceding article, except for the last named, shall be handed down by the Ministry.

The penalties set forth in sections (b) and (c) of the said article must be preceded by a hearing of the party involved.

An appeal against these may be made within fifteen days to the Head of the Government, who shall resolve the matter without further right of appeal.

Art. 22: Confiscation—which may take place only in cases of grave offense against the Regime and after repeated violation of condemned actions which clearly demonstrate backsliding on the part of the enterprise—shall be decided by the Head of the Government in a special decree that is not subject to appeal.

I decree the present Law, in Burgos, this 22nd day of April, 1938, the Second Triumphal Year.

FRANCISCO FRANCO   The Minister of the Interior,

RAMÓN SERRANO SUÑER

Both sides employed wholesale terrorism to maintain internal security during the Civil War. In the first months of the conflict the Republican forces got rid of their most conspicuous foes, who ranged from reactionaries to anarchists. Executions carried out by them almost certainly numbered in the tens of thousands, but as they steadily lost control of territory their purge slowed down markedly. For the Nationalists, on the other hand, the purge intensified as they seized control of more land. A minimum estimate of the political executions on the Nationalist side is 40,000 to 50,000; the true figure may well be double or triple that. Recent estimates put the number of deaths among Nationalist soldiers at about 70,000 out of approximately 1,000,-000 who were mobilized. Italians accounted for 2,000 of these fatalities, Germans 300, and Moorish mercenaries about 15,000. On the Republican side military deaths were more numerous, possibly exceeding 100,000. Of these perhaps 10 per cent were non-Spanish personnel, mostly in the International Brigades.

When the war came to an end on April 1, 1939, Franco's victory was total. No doubt it could be attributed as much to the internal friction and lack of efficiency that characterized the Popular Front government as to the military strength of Franco's forces. The *Caudillo*'s chief personal contribution had been to bring about and preserve political unity within his camp and to focus the energies of the Nationalists on attaining military victory. He managed to establish a Nationalist political community that was sufficiently broad and syncretistic to include all groups who were hostile to the Popular Front; and by not fully identifying himself with any specific political sector, Franco was able to act as arbiter over this hodgepodge of forces. Nevertheless, it was a dictatorship. And as Franco transferred his government to Madrid and extended his writ over the whole nation, he issued a series of orders that sharply reduced the possibility of effective opposition. The following decree of July 20, 1939, restricting meetings, manifestations, and public activities was typical.

Order Restricting Meetings,
Manifestations, and Public Activities
(*July 20, 1939*)

The hierarchic principles of the Regime have imposed the necessity of submitting to discipline and regulation certain types of initia-

SOURCE: Printed in *Boletín Oficial*, July 21, 1939; reprinted in Falange española tradicionalista y de las Juntas ofensivas nacional-sindicalistas, Vicesecretaría de Educación Popular, *Fundamentos del Nuevo Estado* (Madrid: Ediciones de la Vicesecretaría de Educación Popular, 1943), pp. 399–400. My translation.

tives, the timing and permission for which must be approved by the top political leadership of the State. To this end, and mindful of clarifying regulations handed down previously in this regard, the following rules shall be observed:

1. The holding of meetings and manifestations shall require authorization from the Minister of the Government. This must be requested in ample time, through the Civil Governor of the province, and must set forth the purpose of the action, the names of speakers who are supposed to speak, and the themes they are to discuss. The Civil Governors will forward these petitions to the Ministry with due information.

2. Exempted from the requirement of ministerial authorization are:

(a) Meetings held by legitimately established associations in accordance with their statutes, but this shall not prejudice the government's right to restrict the exercise of this right of association.

(b) Processions of the Catholic faith.

3. Such public acts as commemorations, inaugurations, dedications, homages, and analogous things also require ministerial authorization. . . .

A long-anticipated shake-up in the cabinet occurred on August 9, 1939, bringing the Falange even more tightly under the control of Franco, Serrano Suñer, and the Army generals. Serrano Suñer, who was the primary political genius of the regime, continued as Minister of Interior and also assumed the presidency of the FET Junta Política. Fernández Cuesta was relieved of the party secretaryship and appointed ambassador to Brazil. Brigadier General Muñoz Grandes was named Secretary General of the FET and director of the Militia, thereby preventing that force from becoming independent of the Army. The old military hierarchy was absolutely determined to forestall the emergence in the New Spain of any armed force comparable to the Nazi proletarian storm troopers (*Sturm Abteilung*) that Hitler had brutally purged on June 30, 1934.

The screws of the Spanish police state were still being tightened eleven months after the end of hostilities, as may be seen in a decree dated March 1, 1940, which outlawed Masonry and Communism. The latter ideology was given so loose a definition as to include not only Stalinists and Trotskyists but Anarchists as well.

Law Suppressing Masonry and Communism
(March 1, 1940)

Among the many factors that have exercised a pernicious influence and contributed to the decadence of Spain, mocking our healthy popular reactions and military heroism, perhaps none has been more important than the various secret societies and international forces of a clandestine type. Among these Masonry occupies the principal post, but there also figure on the fringes of public life a wide range of generally subversive organizations which, even if they fall short of being specifically secret societies, are nevertheless related to Masonry and borrow its methods, and which are assimilated and unified by Communism. . . .

Consequently, I order the following:

Art. 1: It shall be a crime, punishable according to the provisions of this law, to belong to Masonry, Communism, and other clandestine societies referred to in the following articles. The Government may add to said organizations whatever branches or auxiliary agencies it deems necessary and apply to them the provisions of this law as duly modified.

Art. 2: The above-mentioned organizations are dissolved and prohibited by law. Their properties are hereby declared confiscated and placed at the disposition of the responsible political authorities.

Art. 3: All propaganda that exalts the principles and pretended benefits of Masonry, Communism, or similar ideas that are hostile to religion, the fatherland and its basic institutions, and against social harmony, shall be punished by suppression of the periodicals or entities that subsidize them and by confiscation of their properties, and with the penalty of long imprisonment for the principal guilty person or persons and of shorter imprisonment for those who co-operated.

Art. 4: Masons are those who have entered into Masonry and have not been expelled therefrom, or have not denounced it or

SOURCE: *Boletín Oficial*, March 2, 1940; reprinted in Falange española tradicionalista y de las Juntas ofensivas nacional-sindicalistas, Vicesecretaría de Educación Popular, *Fundamentos del Nuevo Estado* (Madrid: Ediciones de la Vicesecretaría de Educación Popular, 1943), pp. 393–398 *passim*. My translation.

explicitly broken all ties therewith. . . . For the purpose of this law, the propagators, leaders, and active collaborators in Soviet, Trotskyite, Anarchist, and similar goals or propaganda are to be considered Communists. . . .

FRANCISCO FRANCO

A few months later the regime issued another decree designed to close what few loopholes remained. It prevented the formation of any association that fell outside certain tightly supervised categories.

Decree Regulating the Right of Association
(January 25, 1941)

The vigilance which the Public Authorities must maintain with respect to the so-called right of association requires that, until such time as there can be established definitive regulations of a wide-ranging nature, certain norms must be set up to supplant present deficiencies and clarify doubts that have arisen on the basis of legal texts whose force derived from constitutional principles that today have been abolished. . . .

Therefore, after deliberation by the Council of Ministers, I declare that:

Art. 1: Beginning with the publication of the present Decree in the *Boletín Oficial del Estado*, no associations may be formed without approval of the Ministry of Gobernación.

The following are exempted from this requirement:

1. Associations which have for their sole and exclusive object gain or profit, and which, for that reason, are regulated by provisions of Civil Law or Commercial Law.

2. Catholic associations that have exclusively religious aims.

3. Institutes or corporations that exist or function by virtue of special laws.

4. Co-operative associations registered with the Ministry of Labor.

SOURCE: *Boletín Oficial,* February 6, 1941; reprinted in Falange española tradicionalista y de las Juntas ofensivas nacional-sindicalistas, Vicesecretaría de Educación Popular, *Fundamentos del Nuevo Estado* (Madrid: Ediciones de la Vicesecretaría de Educación Popular, 1943), pp. 400–403 *passim.* My translation.

5. Associations subject to syndical legislation and to the discipline of the Falange Española Tradicionalista y de las JONS. . . .

FRANCISCO FRANCO

General Muñoz Grandes did not last long as Secretary General of the FET. His retirement was announced on March 15, 1940. No immediate successor was designated by Franco, who really had little need to name one, for Serrano Suñer continued to be the dominant figure in the party. The *Caudillo*'s brother-in-law added the post of Minister of Foreign Affairs to his already impressive list of responsibilities on October 16, 1940. This appointment enabled him to assist Franco in the delicate and difficult talks with Hitler a few weeks after Germany's stunning defeat of France.

The relationship between Nationalist Spain and Nazi Germany had been ostensibly cordial since the outbreak of the Civil War, but Hitler was less than happy with the way Franco seized control of the Falange, and he was even less pleased when Franco failed to pledge public support to Germany during the Munich crisis. By April, 1939, however, Spain had made amends to the extent to adhering to the Italo-German Anti-Comintern Pact. Moreover, at German insistence, a five-year Treaty of Friendship was signed at Burgos on March 31, 1939, by Ambassador Eberhard von Stohrer and the then Spanish foreign minister, General Gómez Jordana. By this pact the two countries promised to maintain constant touch with each other and also with Fascist Italy in order to exchange information regarding questions of international policy affecting their common interests. In case one of the two signatories became involved in warlike complications with a third party, the other promised to avoid any political, military, or economic action that might be disadvantageous to its partner.

German-Spanish Treaty of Friendship
(*Burgos, March 31, 1939*)

The German Chancellor
and
The Chief of the Spanish Government

In view of the community of interests of their Governments, the affinity of their political views, and the bonds of lively sympathy existing between their peoples,

filled with deep satisfaction over the fact that their friendly association has thus far proved so successful,

SOURCE: *Documents on German Foreign Policy, 1918–1945*, Series D, Vol. III (Germany and Spanish Civil War, 1936–1939) (Washington, D.C.: Department of State, 1950), Doc. 773, pp. 884–886.

and convinced that the development and consolidation of their mutual relations will serve the welfare of both peoples and, in addition, will constitute an important factor in the preservation of high spiritual values and the maintenance of the peace,

are agreed in their desire to affirm their common purposes through the conclusion of a treaty. . . .

ARTICLE 1

The High Contracting Parties will constantly maintain contact with each other in order to inform each other concerning questions of international policy affecting their common interests.

Should their common interests be jeopardized by international events of any kind, they will enter into consultation without delay regarding the measures to be taken to safeguard these interests.

ARTICLE 2

The High Contracting Parties are aware of the dangers facing their countries through the aspirations of the Communist International and will consult constantly as to measures that seem appropriate for combating them.

ARTICLE 3

In the event that the security or other vital interests of one of the High Contracting Parties should be externally threatened, the other High Contracting Party will grant the threatened party its diplomatic support in order to contribute to the best of its ability toward eliminating this threat.

ARTICLE 4

In view of the close friendship in which Germany as well as Spain is bound with Italy, both the High Contracting Parties will be mindful in the execution of the agreements made in articles 1 to 3 above of assuring also the collaboration of the Royal Italian Government.

ARTICLE 5

Neither of the High Contracting Parties will enter into treaties or other agreements of any kind with third powers which are aimed directly or indirectly against the other High Contracting Party.

The High Contracting Parties agree to inform each other regarding treaties and agreements affecting their common interests which they have previously concluded or will in the future conclude with third countries.

ARTICLE 6

In case one of the High Contracting Parties should become involved in warlike complications with a third power, the other High Contracting Party will avoid anything in the political, military, and economic fields that might be disadvantageous to its treaty partner or of advantage to its opponent.

ARTICLE 7

The High Contracting Parties will in special agreements arrange for measures which are calculated to promote the fostering of comradely relations and the exchange of practical military experience between their armed forces.

ARTICLE 8

Both High Contracting Parties shall make it their special concern to extend and promote their cultural relations. The implementation of this principle is reserved for special agreements.

ARTICLE 9

The High Contracting Parties are agreed in their desire to intensify economic relations between their countries as much as possible and affirm their intention of having Germany and Spain supplement each other and cooperate in economic matters in every way.

The implementation of these principles shall be reserved for special agreements.

ARTICLE 10

This treaty shall be ratified and the instruments of ratification shall be exchanged at Berlin as soon as possible.

The treaty shall remain in full force for a period of 5 years from the date of exchange of the instruments of ratification.

If 6 months before the expiration of the aforesaid period no notice of termination has been given, the treaty shall remain in force for 5 more years and in a like manner continue in the following periods of time.

In witness whereof the plenipotentiaries have signed this treaty. Done in duplicate in the German and Spanish languages at Burgos on March thirty-first, nineteen hundred and thirty-nine.

EBERHARD VON STOHRER

GÓMEZ JORDANA

There was closer affinity between Franco's regime and Mussolini's Italy than with Hitler's Germany if for no other reason than their common religious and Latin background. It was not surprising, therefore, that when Italian Foreign Minister Ciano visited Spain in 1939 he expressed enthusiasm at the way it was developing ideologically. He felt that Serrano Suñer was molding the Falange along the lines of the Italian Fascist party. Franco, for his part, supported Mussolini's last-minute efforts to dissuade Hitler from going to war with Poland.

When these efforts failed and World War II broke out, Franco quickly proclaimed Spanish neutrality. He knew well that after three years of bloodletting his country was in no shape to embark upon a new struggle. His sense of caution was strengthened, moreover, by the fact that a substantial number of Spanish officers expressed respect for the French Army and many upper-class Spaniards felt ties of friendship for England. In addition, Franco was influenced by the cautious attitude of the Portuguese government of Salazar, with which he held close bonds. (That semifascist regime had supported the Spanish Nationalists throughout the Civil War and had signed a treaty of friendship and nonaggression in March, 1939.) In September of that same year Salazar, who had healthy respect for British sea power, prudently adopted a policy of neutrality that was not unfriendly toward England.

During the so-called phony war in the winter of 1939–40 contacts between Madrid and Berlin were minimal. The situation changed sharply when the Germans launched their blitzkrieg into the Low Countries and defeated France in June, 1940. Very few Spanish military and political leaders were anxious to see Hitler's Germany achieve so decisive a victory as to gain complete domination of western Europe. The Spanish ambassador in Paris, who served as go-between for the French leaders in their armistice negotiations, tried to persuade the Germans not to station occupation forces throughout France. As things turned out, the Germans confined their direct control to northern and western France. Although the coastal zone of German occupation extended all the way to the border town of Hendaye on the Bay of Biscay, Hitler let the conservative Vichy regime control southeastern France, including most of the Pyrenees frontier.

This decisive shift in the European balance of power forced Spain to change her diplomatic position abruptly. Shifting from strict "neutrality" to "nonbelligerency" in favor of Hitler, she opened ports to German submarines and started talks with German military planners regarding the possibility of a combined assault against the British citadel of Gibraltar, the loss of which had been stirring Spanish resentment for more than two centuries. Falangist talk of imperialist expansion greatly intensified as the possibility of Spain's moving in on the overseas possessions of France in northwest Africa seemed suddenly within reach. Serrano Suñer, who for more than a year had been the chief architect of a policy of collaboration with the Axis, was elevated to the post of Foreign Minister in October, 1940. Not only did he sympathize ideologically with the Axis powers, he felt that it was imperative for Spain to negotiate the best possible deal with Hitler in order to safeguard her own future. But Franco was not willing to go as far as Hitler wanted him to go in assisting Germany in the struggle against Britain. Concerned always with Spain's self-interest and painfully aware of his country's economic weakness, Franco held Hitler at bay throughout a day of hard bargaining at Hendaye on October 23. While agreeing in principle to support the German effort against England, Franco made this hinge upon massive shipments of foodstuffs and weapons from the Reich, as well as upon German agreement to Spanish annexation of French Morocco and much of Algeria. Franco's demands so infuriated Hitler that he later growled to his aides that he would rather have all his teeth pulled than go through such haggling again. In the end, the *Führer* made a vague promise to ship Spain whatever was necessary. A secret protocol was signed by the respective foreign ministers providing for Spanish participation in the war, but implementation was left dependent on working out numerous details. Italy became a signatory to the pact too.

Italian-German-Spanish Secret Protocol
 (Hendaye, October 23, 1940)

The Italian, German, and Spanish Governments have agreed as follows:

1. The exchange of views between the Fuehrer of the German Reich and the Chief of the Spanish State, following conversations between the Duce and the Fuehrer and among the Foreign Ministers of the three countries in Rome and Berlin, has clarified the present position of the three countries toward each other as well as the questions implicit in waging the war and affecting general policy.

SOURCE: *Documents on German Foreign Policy, 1918–1945*, Series D (1937–1945) (Washington, D.C.: Department of State, 1960), XI, 466–467; *cf.* Document 221, n. 4, p. 377. The text of the Protocol is in the form modified by Ciano at Schönhof, where he met with Ribbentrop on November 3–4, 1940.

2. Spain declares her readiness to accede to the Tripartite Pact concluded September 27, 1940, among Italy, Germany, and Japan and for this purpose to sign, on a date to be set by the four Powers jointly, an appropriate protocol regarding the actual accession.

3. By the present Protocol Spain declares her accession to the Treaty of Friendship and Alliance between Italy and Germany and the related Secret Supplementary Protocol of May 22, 1939.

4. In fulfillment of her obligations as an ally, Spain will intervene in the present war of the Axis Powers against England after they have provided her with the military support necessary for her preparedness, at a time to be set by common agreement of the three Powers, taking into account military preparations to be decided upon. Germany will grant economic aid to Spain by supplying her with food and raw materials, so as to meet the needs of the Spanish people and the requirements of the war.

5. In addition to the reincorporation of Gibraltar into Spain the Axis Powers state that in principle they are ready to see to it, in accordance with a general settlement which is to be established in Africa and which must be put into effect in the peace treaties after the defeat of England—that Spain receives territories in Africa to the same extent as France can be compensated, by assigning to the latter other territories of equal value in Africa, but with German and Italian claims against France remaining unaffected. [Typewritten footnote on the document at this point reads: "The original text reads: 'thus protecting any German claims to be made against France,' and was corrected as above by the hand of his Excellency Minister Ciano."]

6. The present Protocol shall be strictly secret, and those present undertake to preserve its strict secrecy, unless by common agreement they decide to publish it.

Done in three original texts in the Italian, German, and Spanish languages.

For the Italian Government:	For the German Government:	For the Spanish Government:
G. CIANO	J. VON RIBBENTROP	R. SERRANO SUÑER

A few days after his talks with the Spanish officials at Hendaye and with the Vichy leaders, Marshal Pétain and Pierre Laval, at Montoire, Hitler traveled to Florence on October 28. There he reported to Mussolini on the nature of these conversations and discussed with the Duce the new problem of Greece—for on that very day Italy, somewhat to Hitler's annoyance, had dispatched an ultimatum to Athens that resulted in war. The excerpts from the document that follows set forth Hitler's views as to the best way of handling the interlocking problem of French Morocco, Gibraltar, and Spain.

Hitler-Mussolini Conference Regarding Vichy France,
Franco's Spain, and Greece
(Florence, October 28, 1940)

. . . [Hitler] then spoke about his conversation with Franco. The latter certainly had a stout heart, but only by an accident had he become Generalissimo and leader of the Spanish state. He was not a man who was up to the problem of the political and material development of his country. The Spaniards, moreover, seemed to have no feeling for the limits to their own strength and would be easily inclined to begin undertakings which they then could not carry through. In the negotiations with Germany they had, on the one hand, requested her to assume very concrete obligations, such as, for instance, the delivery of grain, gasoline, etc., but had always been very vague about what *they* would do. Thus they had, for example, reserved entirely for their own decision the important question of the time of Spain's entry into the war. If, on the other hand, they complained that nothing precise and concrete had been promised them in response to their colonial demands, this was so if only because in case such assurances became known, the danger of a secession of Morocco would be very great. Since Franco had declared, however, that he needed such assurances to justify to his people Spain's entry into the war, publication of these assurances was surely to be expected, and particularly because reticence was hardly one of the outstanding qualities of Spanish official quarters.

In this connection the Fuehrer repeated the promise already made to the Duce in the last conversation at the Brenner Pass [October 4, 1940], that he would on no account conclude peace with France if the claims of Italy were not completely satisfied. Naturally he could not give Spain such an assurance, for then Africa

source: Document 246, *Document on German Foreign Policy,* *1918–1945,* Series D (1937–1945) (Washington, D.C.: Department of State, 1960), XI, 420–421. The meeting took place in Florence's Palazzo Vecchio in the presence of German Foreign Minister Ribbentrop and Italian Foreign Minister Ciano.

would secede from France and it would take severe battles to reconquer it and to protect the Spanish Zone.

The Foreign Minister [Ribbentrop] then explained the technical development of the negotiations with the Spaniards and the present situation, and presented the Spanish text of the secret protocol, which the Spaniards had promised ultimately to sign. At the same time he described in particular the difficulties that Serrano Suñer had made with regard to point 5, that is, the formula envisaged for the solution of the colonial problem.

. . . In reply to a question by the Duce as to what should be done with Spain, the Fuehrer replied that the Spaniards claimed for themselves French Catalonia, a rectification of the Pyrenees frontier, Oran, French Morocco, enlargement of the territory of Rio de Oro to the twentieth degree of latitude and enlargement of Spanish Guinea. The Foreign Minister [Ribbentrop] observed that the Spanish demands were as unreasonable as the German and Italian demands were modest, and he referred again to the protocol which had been previously submitted and stressed its extremely confidential nature. Only six statesmen and their closest assistants knew of it. He then once more informed the Duce regarding the significance of the colonial formula in point 5 of the protocol and the difficulties that Serrano Suñer had made in this connection.

To a question from the Duce as to what the Spaniards should be given, the Fuehrer replied that they could not get any more than a substantial enlargement of Spanish Morocco. At the same time he stressed the fact that Germany had to have bases on the African coast and that he would prefer to lay claim to one of the islands off the coast of Africa for this purpose. If this were not possible, bases would have to be found on the African coast.

As far as Spanish accession to the Tripartite Pact and the German-Italian Alliance was concerned, it could not be announced until the military preparations for the protection of Spain were concluded. At a remark from the Duce to the effect that the announcement of possible agreements between Italy, Germany, and Spain might be very dangerous to Pétain's position, the Foreign Minister [Ribbentrop] again stressed the need for secrecy, but emphasized that if something should nevertheless leak out, it would be better if nothing too definite had been awarded the Spaniards and they had merely received vague promises. The Spaniards themselves had told him that because of their current food imports from the British Empire, they were perhaps even more interested than the Axis Powers in keeping it secret. They also knew that upon its becoming known that they had joined the Axis, Churchill would not hesitate to attempt the seizure of the Spanish islands and bases in the Atlantic.

To a question from the Duce as to the exact time of the intervention of the Spaniards in the military operations, the Fuehrer replied that Franco had been very vague here and had stated only that he would intervene when the military preparations were completed.

The Fuehrer then spoke again of Gibraltar and stated that, according to studies by German experts, the operation, if well prepared and executed with lightning speed, could go off well with very few troops and certain prospects of success. According to the Spaniards, they had already put the Canary Islands in a condition of defense. They could, moreover, be supported by heavy batteries, by dive bombers, long-range guns, and special troops.

To a question from the Duce as to whether it would not be well if the English found out that they could no longer put hope in Spain, the Fuehrer replied that, in his opinion, the announcement of Spain's joining the Axis must be postponed until it was absolutely certain that the English could not land in Spain and on the islands. The Duce mentioned in this connection that it would perhaps also be advantageous to the internal situation in Spain if the firm alignment with the Axis Powers could be announced. The Fuehrer then proposed that the three Foreign Ministers make all the preparations with Spain that were necessary for her entry into the war, as well as settle all other details still pending, and that a meeting then take place in Florence between the Fuehrer, the Duce, and Franco, at which the participation of Spain in the Tripartite Pact and the German-Italian Alliance could be announced with full publicity. . . .

As autumn gave way to winter the reluctance of Spain to enter the war increased. England had not collapsed in the face of the German aerial blitz, and Italy's invasion of Greece turned out to be a near-fiasco. Though German diplomats and military leaders did their best to talk Franco into joining actively in the war, they were met with one excuse after another by the wily Spaniard, who always kept his price high.

In the spring of 1941, in the wake of impressive German victories in Yugoslavia and Greece (where Hitler had come to the aid of Mussolini), Franco showed more interest in coming to terms with Hitler.

This was indicated by the addition of two Falangists to his cabinet and the appointment of José Luis de Arrese as Secretary General of the FET. But by this point Hitler had become less concerned with moves in the western Mediterranean and was instead focusing his attention on the imminent invasion of Russia, to take place on June 22.

The abrupt termination of Hitler's neutrality and nonaggression pact with Russia eliminated a major stumbling block to closer association between Germany and Franco's staunchly Catholic and anti-Communist regime. The early German victories on the eastern front suggested that Hitler would soon be master of all Europe. Though refraining from an outright declaration of war, Franco quickly announced that a "Blue Division" of 20,000 Falangist volunteers would fight alongside the Germans in northern Russia, defending "Christian Europe" from "Asiatic Communism." Upon learning of this, the jealous Mussolini, who had not been informed of the German-Spanish agreement, expressed his irritation to Count Ciano.[5]

Germany failed to knock out Russia before the end of 1941. What was worse, the Japanese attack on Pearl Harbor brought the United States into the war. Though Hitler was now anxious once more to enlist Spain's full participation in the war, Franco showed more reluctance than ever. Instead, he and Salazar formed an "Iberian Bloc" in February, 1942, to co-ordinate the foreign policies and safeguard the neutrality and independence of the two peninsular nations. This association became the most enduring aspect of Franco's foreign policy.

In the late summer of 1942 (coinciding with the German stalemate at Stalingrad and the American naval victories in the Pacific) Franco found it expedient to make a drastic shake-up in the political composition of his government. Since the very beginning of the dictatorship there had been hostility between Falangist extremists and the more conservative Army and royalist groups. The former were pro-Nazi, while the latter favored neutrality. A clash between Falangist and Carlist youths in Bilbao in August furnished Franco with the excuse to move. He removed Serrano Suñer as Foreign Minister, along with several of the latter's leading Falangist appointees, and for good measure dismissed two leading Army officers who had held the ministries of War and Interior. The political era of the *cuñadísimo* had come to an end. The dismissal of Serrano Suñer was widely interpreted as a shift away from the Axis by Franco. This it was to some degree. It was also an effort to improve the internal balance of the regime.

In November, 1942, American and British forces landed in French Morocco and Algeria. President Roosevelt gave prior assurances to Franco that he would not intervene against him if Spain made no hostile move against Allied forces in North Africa. Franco thereafter began to hedge with the Axis even more. Under Allied pressure he reduced the sale of tungsten and pyrites to the Central Powers.

5. *The Ciano Diaries, 1939–1943*, ed. by Hugh Gibson (Garden City: Doubleday, 1946), p. 370 (June 25, 1941).

Italy's overthrow of Mussolini and change of sides in the late summer of 1943 led to new internal pressures in Spain to "de-fascisticize" the Franco regime, lest Spain become the target of Allied intervention. On October 1 Franco referred to Spain's position as neutrality, not "nonbelligerency," and the Blue Division was withdrawn from Russia. Meanwhile, leading Spanish generals signed a carefully worded letter to Franco, reminding him of the way in which he had been chosen Generalissimo and asking if he did not agree that it was now appropriate to restore the monarchy. The *Caudillo* proceeded to talk to them individually, explaining that the American pledge of November, 1942, meant that his regime could feel secure, and that it would be unwise to restore the monarchy in the midst of such economic misery and uncertainty on the international scene. The Army leaders bowed to his arguments then and for the next two years. Thus Franco and his Movement were still seated firmly in the saddle when the war came to an end in May, 1945.

The defeat of Hitler's Germany signaled the end of the formally "fascistic" period of the Spanish dictatorship. As early as 1942 one could discern a tendency by Franco to minimize overt identification with Fascism and the Axis powers, and in the course of the next year his regime made a gesture in the direction of constitutionalism by restoring a national assembly, the Cortes, to represent heads of families, syndicates and professional associations, municipalities, the Falange, and the government. All candidates had to be either nominated or appointed by state organs, and the right to vote was tightly circumscribed. The Cortes was accorded the nominal right to approve new legislation, but all measures had to originate in the executive branch. Thus far the Cortest has never rejected a bill sent to it for approval.

Another step in the "liberalization" of the regime occurred in July, 1945, with the promulgation of a "Fuero de los Españoles," a kind of Spanish bill of rights. In principle it conceded most civil liberties, but in actual practice freedom of speech and dissent was negated by Article 33, which declared, "The exercise of the rights recognized [herein] may not attack the spiritual, national, and social unity of Spain."

At the same time Falangist influence and overt monarchist sentiment in the cabinet were reduced by a new shake-up. Arrese was dismissed from his post as Minister and Secretary General of the "Movement," as the FET had commonly come to be called, and his place was left vacant. Control of propaganda was transferred from the party to the Ministry of National Education. The outstretched-arm salute was also abolished. Several "neutral" technical specialists were brought in, and a strong appeal was made to Catholic opinion by the appointment of a leader of Catholic Action, Alberto Martín Artajo, to replace José Félix de Lequerica y Erquiza at the post of Foreign Minister. The amount of money provided for the Falange organization was cut significantly in 1945, and its leaders were advised to tone down their political propaganda. Greater emphasis was to be given to the allegedly "Catholic" nature of Falangism, and its earlier appeals to violence and imperialism were muted. Party ideologues even found, on occasion, nice things to say about liberal systems of government. National syndicalism, however, was to be preserved.

Franco was clearly anxious to eliminate insofar as possible pretexts for the victorious anti-Fascist Allies to intervene in the Iberian peninsula—a course of action which Soviet Russia in particular was advocating in 1945. Though President Harry Truman and Prime Minister Clement Attlee declined to go that far, they agreed with Premier Stalin at the Potsdam Conference on August 2 to bar the existing Spanish government from membership in the United Nations.

Ostracism of Franco's Spain by Potsdam Conference
(August 2, 1945)

. . . SECTION X [regarding admission to the United Nations] . . .

The three Governments feel bound, however, to make it clear that they for their part would not favor any application for membership put forward by the present Spanish Government, which, having been founded with the support of the Axis Powers, does not, in view of its origins, its nature, its record and its close association with the aggressor States, possess the qualifications necessary to justify such membership. . . .

In 1946 the United Nations voted formal censure of Franco's regime and advised members to withdraw their ambassadors from Madrid. By year's end France formally closed her border with Spain, so that the Iberian nation was left almost completely ostracized for some years except for the continuing friendship of Salazar's Portugal and Juan Perón's Argentina.

Spain's political developments since the end of World War II go beyond the scope of this study. It is enough to say here that as a result of both external and internal developments, the Generalissimo not only pulled through the immediate postwar crisis but was able to continue to rule his restive nation during the 1950's and 1960's. Most notable among those factors were the Cold War, which caused the United States to adopt a conciliatory policy toward Franco and eventually to facilitate Spain's entry into the United Nations, and the dictator's own skill in retaining the loyalty of both the Army and the Church while playing off the Monarchists against the Falangists.

After having promised several times to restore the monarchy, the seventy-six-year-old Franco at last proposed to his hand-picked Cortes on July 22, 1969, that Prince Juan Carlos de Borbón y Borbón, the thirty-one-year-old grandson of Alfonso XIII, be crowned upon the

SOURCE: Text in *New York Times*, August 3, 1945, p. 8.

retirement or death of the *Caudillo*. Thus Franco passed over Juan Carlos' relatively more liberal father, the long-exiled Don Juan, just as he ignored the two very conservative Carlist contenders, Prince Xavier de Borbón Parma and his son, Carlos Hugo. The Cortes gave its overwhelming approval to the nomination, whereupon Juan Carlos swore that he would be loyal to "His Excellency the Chief of State" (Franco), uphold "the Fundamental Laws," and give his "fidelity to the principles of the National Movement" (which is still the only legally permitted political organization in Spain and is strongly represented in the Cortes). By that action the King-designate pledged to perpetuate the regime that Generalissimo Franco had molded over a period of thirty-three years—a regime which in the autumn of 1969 seemed to be anxious to shed more of its Falangist coloration. Ironically, Franco chose the thirty-sixth anniversary of the founding of the Falange to announce widespread cabinet changes that appear to reduce the role of the Falangists in favor of men both from the "Opus Dei" organization of the Roman Catholic laity and from the ranks of rather liberal-minded "technocrats" who favor Spanish participation in the European Common Market. The announcement of these cabinet changes on October 29, 1969, set off clashes between the police and young Falangist demonstrators in front of Madrid's Teatro de la Comedia, where José Antonio had founded the Movement.

Only time will tell whether the political future of Spain will work out in the way that Franco desires.

III

Salazar's Portugal

10. The Clerico-Corporative Estado Novo

PORTUGAL WAS the first state in the Iberian peninsula to come under a semifascistic regime. Unlike Mussolini's Italy, however, the dictatorship did not come about through the triumph of a pre-existent fascist party. In the case of Portugal both the fascistic party and the Party-State came into being after the advent of the dictatorship. Although the Portuguese Party-State expressed respect and admiration for Mussolini's Italian dictatorship, it found most of its inspiration in the type of integral nationalism espoused by Charles Maurras's Action Française and in the clerico-corporativist philosophy set forth in the papal encyclicals of the nineteenth and twentieth centuries. The Portuguese authoritarian system was to serve as a model for at least some aspects of Franco's regime in Spain, Pétain's Vichy France, and Getulio Vargas's dictatorship in Brazil.

Despite the diminutive size of the homeland, Portugal has managed (albeit with increasing difficulty since the outbreak of colonial wars in 1961) to hang on to the fourth largest empire in the world. Prior to World War II industrialization was slight, and the nation's 7,700,000 people made their living chiefly by fishing and producing wine, cork, and olive oil. Illiteracy, which in the years of World War I characterized 65 per cent of the population, did not decline significantly until after the second world conflict; it is now less than 25 per cent. For centuries Portugal has benefited from commercial and security links with Britain.

In 1910 a revolution in Lisbon overthrew the liberal monarchy of the House of Coburg-Braganza and established an anticlerical republic which promptly separated Church and State along the lines followed in France five years earlier. Between 1910 and 1927 there were a score of attempts at revolution and some forty-three cabinets. Controversy over Portugal's decision to enter the war in 1916 on the side of the Entente added to the chronic political instability. In the peace settlement Portugal was given a scrap of German East Africa to add to Mozambique. But this did not prevent the republic from falling into disrepute as economic troubles mounted.

On May 28, 1926, the existing government was overthrown by an

Army movement led by General Manuel de Oliveira Gomes da Costa; Parliament was dissolved, and parties and trade unions were broken up. Two months later, however, General António Oscar de Fragoso Carmona deposed the ineffectual Gomes da Costa, who was allowed to go to the Azores in honorable exile. In February, 1927, insurrection against the military dictatorship broke out in Oporto and Lisbon. Officially described as "communist," it was inspired by intellectual reformers. After some heavy fighting it was suppressed.

At last in March, 1928, General Carmona was elected President of the Republic; he was to retain the position until his death in 1951. His first task was to find a financial expert who could straighten out the economy. The general turned to António de Oliveira Salazar, a professor of economics at the University of Coimbra. Born in 1889 at Santa Comba Dão in northern Portugal, Salazar was the son of a village innkeeper and peasant mother. He studied to become a priest, then turned to law, and finally switched to economics. Always a staunch Catholic, he studied closely the socio-economic philosophy set forth in *Rerum novarum* and other encyclicals of Pope Leo XIII and his successors—and most notably Pius XI's *Quadragesimo anno* of May, 1931. He also paid attention to the writings of such French Catholic sociologists as Frédéric LePlay, Albert de Mun, and René de la Tour du Pin. As a young man at Coimbra he was attracted by a movement preaching "Integralismo Lusitano," a nationalist movement influenced by and analogous to the Action Française of Charles Maurras. In 1921 Salazar was one of three on a Catholic Center party list to be elected to Parliament, but after attending the opening session he became so disgusted that he returned to his university post. On April 27, 1928, Salazar accepted President Carmona's invitation to become Minister of Finance but insisted on being granted extraordinary powers. Critics have often described Salazar as more of an accountant-bookkeeper than economist, and have argued that under his leadership the economic welfare of the people as a whole was held back. They do not deny, however, that his old-fashioned methods of strict accountancy and economy straightened out the financial muddle and eliminated some of the graft.

Before long this unmarried, frugal, and abstemious man became the dominant figure in Portugal. Aspiring to bring about a national revolution, he took a major step in that direction on July 30, 1930, when he announced the formation of the National Union (União Nacional). This was to be the only party permitted by the government. Some observers have likened it more to the political organization of Marshal Joseph Pilsudski in Poland than to Mussolini's Fascist party. It did not have to play a combative role in bringing Salazar to power; indeed, its first congress was not held until 1934, and its second was delayed until after World War II.

On July 5, 1932, Salazar was asked by President Carmona to assume the premiership; for all practical purposes he became dictator. Later he assumed for several years the posts of Minister of War and Minister of

Foreign Affairs as well. Salazar made no attempt to eliminate the figurehead Chief of State. Unlike Mussolini, Salazar never affected a uniform, and he made no effort to emulate the oratorical or charismatic qualities of the Italian *Duce*. He never left the country except on a very few occasions to cross the border into Spain to confer with General Franco; nor did he ever visit any of Portugal's vast overseas possessions. His political and economic ideas were set forth quietly over the radio and in the press. The following extracts from various pronouncements by the Portuguese dictator give some impression of his philosophy.

Political and Economic Doctrines of Salazar

STATE AND REGIMES

. . . *The State.* The State has the right to foster, harmonize and control all national activities, without destroying them, and its duty is to educate the youth in the love of their country, in discipline and those vigorous exercises which will prepare and incline it for a fruitful activity and for all that may be required of it by the honor and interests of the Nation. . . .

Power of the State. No one in Portugal would maintain the omnipotence of the State with regard to the mass of mankind, which is merely the raw material of great political achievements. No one here would think of regarding the State as the source of morality and justice without submitting its rules and decisions to the decrees of a higher justice. No one here would dare to proclaim might as the source of all right, without regard for individual conscience and the legitimate liberties of the citizen and the purpose inherent in the very existence of a man. . . .

State and Government. There can be no strong State without a strong Government.

The Sovereignty of the Nation. To take power out of the hands of party cliques; to place above all individual interests the interests of all, the interests of the nation; to keep the State from the clutches of audacious minorities but to maintain it in permanent touch with the needs and aspirations of the nation; to organize the

SOURCE: Excerpts from *Salazar, Prime Minister of Portugal, Says* . . . , a compendium of quotations published ca. 1940 in Lisbon by the Secretariat of National Propaganda, pp. 23–28, 47–48, 52–54, 57, 59–62 *passim*.

nation from top to bottom in all the different manifestations of its collective life, from the family to the administrative bodies and moral and economic corporations; to incorporate all this in the State, which will thus become its living expression: this is to make the sovereignty of the nation a real and living thing.

Regimes. All new regimes, lacking experience and even traditions, must be of slow and laborious growth. To apply new and different principles to old societies accustomed to live under another system, and especially with another spirit, is always a difficult task which even appears impossible to those who are in a hurry, and who feverishly demand that tomorrow's work should be done today. . . .

Three Fallacies. Many said: Let us abandon the common weal to political passion, to the whims of the greatest number—Life subordinated to politics—that was the Democratic formula. There were others who cried: Let us produce wealth without care or method so that everyone in the end shall benefit—economic values were held higher than those of life under the Liberal regime. Another group demanded: Let us divide among ourselves the present wealth and that which may be created in our time—Socialism subordinated economic life to social. The fallacy of these systems was amply demonstrated by the constant party warfare, the injustice of Liberal economic life, the devastation worked by Socialism. . . .

The Representative System. The families, the parishes, the townships, the corporations, which include all citizens, with their fundamental legal rights, are the bodies which compose the Nation, and, as such, must participate directly in the constitutions of the supreme organs of the State: this, more than any other, is the true expression of the representative system.

Parliaments. I foresee that parliaments in the future, even if they do not become purely political bodies, without any legislative character, will be obliged to approve only the general outlines of the more important laws, leaving to the Executive, as responsible for the work of administration, far wider powers than the controlling power which it at present possesses.

Corporative Chambers. The formula which seems best and which will perhaps be the formula of the future, is that the Government should legislate, in consultative collaboration with the Corporative Chambers, possibly with the assistance of a Council of legal experts. . . .

Newspapers. Newspapers are the spiritual food of the people, and, like all foods, must be controlled. . . .

POLITICAL ECONOMY

. . . *Political Economy.* We wish to advance towards a new political economy, working in harmony with human nature, under the authority of a strong State which will protect the higher interests of the Nation, its wealth and its labor, both from capitalist excesses and from destructive Bolshevism.

The State and Economy. One cannot hope to constitute a strong and well-balanced State without coordinating and developing the national economy, which today more than ever must form part of political organization. This is perhaps the greatest practical constitutional change that must be effected in all civilized nations. . . .

The State and Wealth. The State must not be the owner of the wealth of the nation nor allow itself to be corrupted by it. That it may be the supreme arbiter of all the interests of the nation it is imperative that it should not be a slave to any of them. . . .

Class Strife. We do not accept the strife of the productive classes as a historical fact nor as the principle underlying economic and social organization. The ultimate interests, both of individuals and groups, tend towards identity of national interests. But the immediate interests of workmen and employers, and sometimes of the workmen among themselves, often clash in actual life; all the more reason not to allow the discord to grow, all the more reason to reconcile opposing interests, to the advantage of both parties and with a view to normalize the economic life of the nation.

Communism. Communism is the synthesis of all the traditional revolts of matter against spirit, of barbarism against civilization. It is the "great heresy" of our age. . . .

Corporativism. Through corporative organization the economic life of the nation is an element of political organization. . . .

Syndicates. The professional syndicate is, through the homogeneity of interests within its sphere of production, the best basis for the organization of labor and the support, the fulcrum of the institutions which seek to raise and educate it and to protect it against injustice and adversity.

There can be no syndicate where there exists no corporative spirit, the consciousness of the value of labor in conjunction with production, an understanding of the necessity of cooperating with all the other factors with a view to the advancement of the economy of the nation. Where these qualities do not exist but only the spirit of class strife, there can be no true syndicate but only a revolutionary association using its strength in the service of disorder.

OUR NATIONALISM

Spirituality. From a civilization which is scientifically returning to barbarism we are irremissibly sundered by the spirituality which is the source, the soul, the life of our history. . . .

Portugal. It is a rare or unique thing in Europe and in all the world to be eight hundred years old, especially if the condition should be laid down that in the country in question the people, the nation, the State should have remained the same. Almost from the beginning, by the achievements of the first kings, our frontiers in the Iberian Peninsula were defined and fixed. Wars there were many, but there was no invasion or confusion of races or annexations of territory or changes of dynasty or alteration of frontiers: from first to last the leaders of the nation had the same Portuguese blood in their veins. . . .

Our Originality. One day it will be recognized that Portugal is governed by an original system, suitable to her history and geography, which are very different from all others; and we wish it might be understood that we have not eschewed the mistakes and vices of a false liberalism and a false democracy in order to fall into others which might be even worse, but rather to reorganize and strengthen the country in the principles of authority, of order, of the national traditions, reconciling these with those eternal truths which are, happily, the heritage of mankind and the crown of Christian civilization. . . .

The Nation. Nothing against the Nation, everything for the Nation.

Like a great family or a great concern, the nation, for the protection of its common interests and the attainment of its collective aims, requires a head to control it, a center of life and action.

The Nation cannot be identified with a political party, a party is not the same as the State, and the State in international life is not a subject but a collaborator and associate.

The man who becomes a nationalist belongs to no political party, no group or school: he makes use of materials according to their usefulness for the reconstruction of the country; his great, his only concern is that they should serve and become a part of the national system.

Nationalism. None of us, nationalists and lovers of our country, professes an aggressive nationalism of exclusiveness and hatred; rather, if we are attached to the idea of country, it is because our hearts and intellects instinctively tell us that the national sphere is still the best for the life and interests of humanity. . . .

There exist undoubtedly in the world political systems with which Portuguese nationalism has some resemblance and points of contact, most of which, indeed, are confined to the corporative idea; but in actual practice, and especially in the conception of the State and in the organization of the political and civil support of the Government, the differences are very marked.

We have not failed to consider every foreign experiment, every series of facts occurring in any part of the world, with a view to extracting useful lessons from them. But the chief source of our instruction, the source of the inspiration of the main lines of our political structure, has been our history and traditions, the temperament and, in a word, the actual life of the Portuguese. From this source we seek to draw what of the past remains or should remain living and fruitful, and from the present that which seems a sure gain and the aspirations that are rendered legitimate by the general progress and by a better understanding of justice.

Without misgiving we make Portuguese nationalism the indestructible basis of the New State; first, because it is the clearest lesson of our history; secondly, because it is an inestimable factor in social progress and education; thirdly, because we are a living example of how the spirit of patriotism, displayed by us on every continent, has served the cause of humanity.

The nationalism of the New State is not and can never be a doctrine of aggressive isolation, either of ideas or political theory, since, like all our history indeed, it has its roots in life and in friendly cooperation with other nations. We consider it as far removed from individualistic Liberalism, which had a foreign origin, and from the internationalism of the Left, as from all other theoretic or practical systems which have sprung up abroad in reaction to them. . . .

On February 22, 1933, Salazar's government promulgated a Constitution for what he now labeled the Portuguese New State (Estado Novo). Approved by a plebiscite on March 19, the Constitution went into effect on April 11. It provided for a Head of State (President of the Republic) elected directly for seven years;[1] a premier and council of ministers appointed by the President and responsible to him alone; a National Assembly elected by heads of families possessing a certain degree of education; a Corporative Chamber representing not only functional groupings (as in Italy) but also "moral," cultural, and other interests (eventually comprising twelve sections) and exercising advisory powers. Half the members of the National Assembly would be chosen by economic guilds or corporations; the other half would be elected by educated heads of families in geographical constituencies. Community of economic interests would be sought through the peaceful co-operation of all the forces of production; the guiding economic principle would be self-managed functional groupings that would seek to avoid the pitfalls of excessive state intervention, such as had occurred in Italy. Only one political party (the National Union) would be permitted. Until the end of World War II no opposition candidates presented themselves at elections to either the Presidency or the National Assembly. Private property would be preserved and ownership of small farms encouraged. There would be no free trade unions, and strikes and lockouts would be forbidden. Labor courts would adjudicate disputes. In general, the system curbed the working classes while leaving the employers substantially free to run their businesses as they wished. These latter points were spelled out in greater detail in the Statute of National Labor, proclaimed on September 23, 1933. Its 52 articles were modeled on the Italian Charter of Labor of 1927 (though not going quite as far in degree of state control) and on the papal encyclical *Quadragesimo anno* of 1931. Excerpts from the new Constitution of the Estado Novo follow.

Political Constitution of the Portuguese Republic (1933)

PART I: ON THE FUNDAMENTAL GUARANTEES

CHAPTER I: ON THE PORTUGUESE NATION

. . . *Art. 4.* The Portuguese nation is an independent State. Its sovereignty recognizes in the internal sphere morality and law as the only limitations; in the international field it recognizes only

SOURCE: Approved by the National Plebiscite of March 19, 1933, and brought into force on April 11, 1933. Certain amendments were made in 1935, 1936, 1937, 1938, 1945, and 1951. Quoted from *Political Constitution of the Portuguese Republic* (Lisbon: S.N.I., 1957), pp. 3–44 *passim.*

1. In 1959 direct election of the President was abolished. The powers of the Corporative Chamber were upgraded significantly by making it a substantial part of the electoral college that formally chose the President.

those limitations which are derived from conventions or treaties freely entered into, or from customary law freely accepted. It is the duty of the nation to co-operate with other states in preparing and adopting measures making for peace among people and for the progress of mankind.

Portugal advocates arbitration as a means of settling international disputes.

Art. 5. The Portuguese State is a unitary and corporative republic. . . .

Art. 6. It is the duty of the State:

I. To promote the unity and establish the juridical order of the nation by defining and enforcing respect for the rights and guarantees of morality, justice or the law, in the interest of the individual, of families, and local autonomous and public or private bodies;

II. To co-ordinate, stimulate and direct all social activities in order to promote a proper harmony of interests within the lawful subordination of private interests to the general good;

III. To strive to improve the conditions of the least favored social classes, endeavoring to secure for them a standard of living compatible with human dignity;

IV. To protect public health.

CHAPTER II: ON CITIZENS

. . . *Art. 8.* Portuguese citizens shall enjoy the following rights, liberties and individual guarantees: . . . [some 20 are enumerated]. . . .

Paragraph 1. The enumeration of the above rights and guarantees shall not exclude any others derived from the Constitution or the law, it being understood that citizens should always exercise them without injuring the rights of third parties, or damaging the interests of society or moral principles.

Paragraph 2. Special laws shall govern the exercise of the freedom of expression of opinion, education, meeting and of association. As regards the first item, they shall prevent, by precautionary or restrictive measures, the perversion of public opinion in its function as a social force. . . .

Paragraph 3. Imprisonment without formal charge is permitted in cases of *flagrante delictu* and in cases of the following actually committed, prevented or attempted crimes: those against the safety of the State; . . .

CHAPTER III: ON THE FAMILY

Art. 12. The State shall ensure the constitution and protection of the family as the source of preservation and development of the race, as the first basis of education, discipline and social harmony, and as the foundation of all political and administrative order through family grouping and representation in parish and on town councils. . . .

CHAPTER IV: ON CORPORATIVE BODIES

Art. 16. It is the duty of the State to authorize, unless otherwise provided by law to the contrary, all corporative, collective, intellectual or economic bodies, and to promote and assist their formation.

Art. 17. The principal aims of the corporative bodies, referred to in the preceding article, shall be scientific, literary or artistic, or physical training, relief, alms, or charity; technical improvement or solidarity of interests. . . .

CHAPTER V: ON THE FAMILY, CORPORATIVE ORGANIZATION AND AUTONOMOUS BODIES AS POLITICAL UNITS

Art. 19. It is the particular privilege of families to elect the parish councils.

This right is exercised by the head of the family.

Art. 20. In the corporative organization, all branches of the nation's activities shall be represented through their association in the corporative organizations, and it shall be their duty to participate in the election of town councils and provincial boards and the constitution of the Corporative Chamber.

Art. 21. Under the political organization of the State the parish councils shall elect the town councils which in turn shall elect the provincial boards. Local autonomous bodies shall be represented in the Corporative Chamber.

CHAPTER VI: ON PUBLIC OPINION

Art. 22. Public opinion is a fundamental part of the policy and administration of the country; it shall be the duty of the State to protect it against all those influences which distort it from the truth, justice, good administration, and the common weal.

Art. 23. The function of the press is of a public nature and for that reason it may not refuse to insert any official notices of normal dimensions on matters of national importance sent to it by the government.

CHAPTER VII: ON THE ADMINISTRATIVE ORDER

Art. 24. Civil servants are for the service of the community and not for that of any party or association of private interests; it is their duty to respect the authority of the State and cause others to do so. . . .

Art. 26. Planned interruption of public services or of those of interest to the community shall involve the dismissal of the offenders, without prejudice to any other liability at law. . . .

CHAPTER VIII: ON THE ECONOMIC AND SOCIAL ORDER

Art. 29. The economic organization of the nation must provide the maximum production and wealth for the benefit of society, and shall create a collective existence from which shall flow power to the State and justice to its citizens. . . .

Art. 31. It shall be the right and duty of the State to co-ordinate and control economic and social life with the following objects:

I. to establish a proper balance of the population, of professions, of occupations, of capital and of labor;

II. to protect the national economic system from agricultural, industrial and commercial ventures of a parasitic nature, or those incompatible with the higher interests of human life;

III. to secure the lowest price and the highest wage consistent with fair remuneration for other factors of production, by means of improved technical methods, services and credit;

IV. to develop the settlement of the national territories, to protect emigrants and to regulate emigration.

Art. 32. The State shall encourage those private economic activities which are the most profitable, relative costs being equal, but without detriment to the social benefit conferred and to the protection due to small home industries.

Art. 33. The State may only intervene directly in the management of private economic ventures when it has to finance them and for the purpose of securing a larger measure of social benefit than would otherwise be the case. . . .

Art. 34. The State shall promote the formation and development of the national corporative economic system, taking care to prevent any tendency among its constituent bodies to indulge in unrestricted competition with each other, contrary to their own proper aims and those of society, and shall encourage them to collaborate as members of the same community.

Art. 35. Property, capital and labor have a social function in the field of economic co-operation and common interest, and the law may determine the conditions of their use or exploitation in accordance with the community aim in view. . . .

Art. 37. Only economic corporations which are recognized by the State may conclude collective labor contracts, in accordance with the law, and those made without their intervention shall be null and void.

Art. 38. Disputes arising out of labor contracts shall be the concern of special tribunals.

Art. 39. In their economic relations with each other, neither capital nor labor shall be allowed to suspend operations with the object of imposing their respective claims. . . .

CHAPTER IX: ON EDUCATION, INSTRUCTION AND NATIONAL CULTURE

Art. 42. Education and instruction are obligatory and are the concern of the family and of public or private institutions in cooperation with the same.

Art. 43. The State shall officially maintain primary, secondary middle and high schools, and institutions for advanced education.

Paragraph 1. Elementary primary instruction is obligatory and may be given at home, or in private or state schools.

Paragraph 2. The arts and sciences shall be encouraged and their development, teaching and dissemination favored, provided that respect is maintained for the Constitution, the authorities and the co-ordinating functions of the State.

Paragraph 3. The instruction provided by the State, in addition to aiming at physical fitness and the improvement of intellectual faculties, has as its object the formation of character and of professional ability as well as the development of all moral and civic qualities, the former according to the traditional principles of the country and to Christian doctrine and morality.

Paragraph 4. No permission shall be required for the teaching of religion in private schools. . . .

CHAPTER X: ON THE RELATIONS OF THE STATE
WITH THE CATHOLIC CHURCH AND THE REGIME OF WORSHIP

Art. 45. The Catholic religion may be freely practiced, in public or in private, as the religion of the Portuguese Nation. The Catholic Church shall enjoy juridical personality and may organize itself in conformity with canon law and create thereunder associations or organizations, the juridical personality of which shall equally be recognized. The relationship between the State and the Catholic Church shall be one of separation, with diplomatic relations maintained between the Holy See and Portugal by means of reciprocal representation, and concordats or agreements entered into in the sphere of the Padroado (Patronage) and where other matters of common interest are, or need to be, regulated.

Art. 46. The State shall also ensure freedom of worship and organization for all other religious faiths practiced on Portuguese territory, their outward manifestations being regulated by law, and it may grant juridical personality to associations constituted in conformity with the creeds in question.

These provisions shall not apply to creeds incompatible with the life and physical integrity of the human person and with good behavior, or to the dissemination of doctrines contrary to the established social order. . . .

CHAPTER XII: ON NATIONAL DEFENSE

. . . *Art. 54.* Military service shall be general and compulsory. . . .

Art. 55. The law shall regulate the general organization of the nation in wartime in accordance with the principle of a nation in arms.

Art. 56. The State shall promote, encourage and assist civil institutions whose aim is to teach and discipline young persons in preparation for the fulfilment of their military and patriotic duties.

Art. 57. No citizen may hold or obtain employment from the State or local autonomous bodies unless he has fulfilled the duties to which he is liable under military law. . . .

PART II: ON THE POLITICAL ORGANIZATION OF THE STATE

CHAPTER I: ON SOVEREIGNTY

Art. 71. Sovereignty is vested in the nation; its representatives are the Head of the State, the National Assembly, the Government, and the Courts of Justice.

CHAPTER II: ON THE HEAD OF THE STATE

SECTION I: *On the election of the President of the Republic and of his Prerogatives*

Art. 72. The Chief of the State is the President of the Republic elected by the Nation.

Paragraph 1. The President is elected for a term of seven years. . . .

SECTION II: *On the Attributes of the President of the Republic*

. . . *Art. 82.* The acts of the President of the Republic must be countersigned by the President of the Council and by the appropriate Minister or Ministers; in default of this they shall be non-existent.

Counter-signatures are not required for:

 I. the appointment and dismissal of the Council of Ministers;

 II. messages addressed to the National Assembly;

 III. the message of resignation from office.

SECTION III: *On the Council of State*

Art. 83. The President of the Republic shall perform his functions in conjunction with the Council of State, composed of the following members:

 I. the President of the Council of Ministers;

 II. the President of the National Assembly;

 III. the President of the Corporative Chamber;

 IV. the President of the Supreme Court of Justice;

 V. the Procurator General of the Republic;

 VI. ten public men of outstanding ability, appointed for life by the Chief of State. . . .

CHAPTER III: ON THE NATIONAL ASSEMBLY AND THE CORPORATIVE
CHAMBER

SECTION I: *On the National Assembly*

Art. 85. The National Assembly shall be composed of one hundred and twenty Deputies, elected by the direct vote of the citizen electors, and its mandate will continue for a period of four years, which may not be prolonged save in the case of events which make the convocation of the electoral colleges impossible. . . .

Paragraph 2. Nobody may be a member of the National Assembly and of the Corporative Chamber at the same time. . . .

SECTION II: *On the members of the National Assembly*

Art. 89. . . .

Paragraph 2. The National Assembly may withdraw the mandates of those deputies who express opinions opposed to the existence of Portugal as an independent state, or who in any way instigate the violent overthrow of social and political order. . . .

SECTION III: *On the Attributes of the National Assembly*

Art. 91. The functions of the National Assembly are:

I. To make, interpret, suspend and revoke laws; . . .

SECTION IV: *On the activities of the National Assembly and of the promulgation of Laws and Orders*

Art. 94. The National Assembly shall be in session for a period of three months, beginning on November 25th of each year. . . .

Art. 95. The National Assembly shall meet in full session and its decisions shall be taken by absolute majority vote provided there is a quorum. . . .

Art. 97. The right to introduce legislation is vested equally in the government, and in any member of the National Assembly; . . .

Art. 98. Bills passed by the National Assembly shall be sent to the President of the Republic for promulgation as law within the fifteen days following. . . .

SECTION V: *On the Corporative Chamber*

Art. 102. There shall be a Corporative Chamber, equal in length of term with the National Assembly, composed of representatives of local autonomous bodies and social interests, the latter being those of an administrative, moral, cultural and economic order; the law shall designate those bodies on which such representation falls, the manner of their selection and the duration of their mandate. . . .

Art. 103. It is the duty of the Corporative Chamber to report and give its opinion on all proposals or draft bills and on all international conventions or treaties submitted to the National Assembly, before discussion thereof is commenced by the latter. . . .

Art. 104. The Corporative Chamber shall function in plenary sessions or in committees and sub-committees. . . .

CHAPTER IV: ON THE GOVERNMENT

Art. 107. The Government consists of the President of the Council of Ministers, who may conduct the affairs of one or more ministries, and the Ministers; . . .

Art. 108. The President of the Council shall be responsible to the President of the Republic for the general policy of the government and shall co-ordinate and direct the activities of all the Ministers, who shall be responsible to him politically for their acts.

Art. 109. It shall be the duty of the Government:

I. to countersign the acts of the President of the Republic;

II. to draw up decree-laws and, in cases of urgency, to approve international conventions and treaties;

III. to draw up decrees, regulations and instructions for the proper carrying out of laws;

IV. to superintend public administration as a whole. . . .

Art. 112. The Government depends exclusively upon possessing the confidence of the President of the Republic, and its continuance in office shall not depend upon the fate of its draft bills, or upon any vote of the National Assembly. . . .

Though calling itself "new," Salazar's authoritarian Estado Novo rested on the experience of Portugal's past. It did nothing to irritate the Army, the Church, or vested economic interests. Its institutions were intended to be in harmony with the principles of nationalism and clerico-corporative government. The Estado Novo fell short of deifying the state as "totalitarian," since it insisted that it must bow to the tenets of social justice and recognize that its powers were limited by a superior moral law. The actual implementation of the Estado Novo moved rather slowly; ostensibly it was encouraged to develop from below rather than be imposed from above.

Opposition to the regime persisted. One of the most significant rebellions occurred after the announcement of the Labor Charter of 1933. Led by the clandestine General Confederation of Labor and the Communists, it was harshly suppressed on January 18, 1934, and its leaders imprisoned. In 1937 there was an attempt to assassinate the dictator.

Meanwhile, the first elections under the new constitution were held on December 16, 1934. The small electorate was permitted to choose only candidates put forward by the National Union; no others were allowed on the ballot. The first National Assembly of the Estado Novo met on January 10, 1935. Next month President Carmona was elected for another term. He and his successors confirmed Dr. Salazar in the premiership for what turned out to be an uninterrupted 36 years.

When the Spanish Civil War broke out in July, 1936, Salazar sympathized at once with General Franco's Insurgents and ordered the strengthening of Portugal's armed forces. At the same time he substantially accelerated tendencies toward "fascistization" of the regime. Loyalty oaths were imposed on the civil service and the teachers. A 20,000-strong Portuguese Legion (Legião Portuguesa), with special air and naval "brigades" as well, was created as a militia for men over the age of eighteen. Trained by reserve officers, it was formally committed to a "heroic ethic," a "revolutionary mystique," and to the "defense of the spiritual patrimony of the Nation" as well as to the "defense of the corporative order." Contrary to some expectations, it was not dissolved at the end of World War II. About the same time a compulsory green-shirted State Youth Movement (Mocidade Portuguesa) was established, with a parallel organization for girls. At first it embraced the entire school and university population; later it was made compulsory only for those between the ages of seven and fourteen. The youth movement and the Portuguese Legion had their special uniforms and Roman salutes. Participation in the Mocidade and Legião was helpful to one's political advancement. Repressive police organizations also proliferated and eventually included such entities as the Guardia Nacional Republicana, the Policia de Segurança Publica, the Guardia Fiscal, and the dreaded secret International Police for the Defense of the State (PIDE).

During the Spanish Civil War, Portugal provided one of the main routes whereby supplies could reach Franco from Germany and elsewhere. This channel remained open until April, 1937, when the British government persuaded Salazar to permit the stationing of a British control along the frontier of Spain. By that time, however, Franco was able to get his foreign supplies directly through his own ports on the northern coast of Spain. The British did their best to preserve their traditional alliance with Portugal, for the latter had become of great strategic importance, situated as it was athwart the routes from Africa and the Mediterranean. As soon as Franco achieved victory in Spain, Salazar concluded a nonaggression pact with his regime (March 18, 1939), but in the next breath (May 22 and 26) reaffirmed the long-standing alliance with Britain. Portugal thus demonstrated her desire to maintain friendly relations with both the fascistic and the democratic powers.

In May, 1940, Salazar's government negotiated a concordat with the Holy See. The Roman Catholic Church was reconfirmed in its possession of most of the property it had held prior to the separation of Church and State in 1910. Religious instruction was restored to state schools, private church schools were allowed, and church marriages were to be recognized. On the other hand, divorce continued to be permissible in Portugal.

In the summer of 1940 after the German blitzkrieg destroyed the French Third Republic, Salazar was pleased to observe that Marshal Henri Philippe Pétain, the father figure of Vichy France, paid considerable attention to the Portuguese experience in designing the clerico-corporative institutions of his short-lived regime.

Some idea of Salazar's views with respect to the early phase of World War II may be discerned in the following extract from a dispatch sent to Berlin by the German minister in Lisbon in November, 1940, a few weeks after Hitler had conferred with Generalissimo Franco in an effort to persuade Spain to join the war on the side of the Axis.

*Salazar's Views of World War II as Reported by
the German Minister in Lisbon
(November 14, 1940)*

Minister President Salazar received me today for the first time since my return from my official journey[2] for a prolonged conversation. He acknowledged with admiration the description I gave him of German morale and stated that he had time and again received the same picture, lastly from Minister Nobre Guedes in Berlin. He considers Spain's territorial demands to be fully justified, but in repeating previous statements pointed out the unsatisfactory food situation of the country, which would be aggravated to catastrophic proportions by the anticipated English blockade, and which made it advisable to put off Spain's entry into the war as long as possible. He did not think that America would enter the war after Roosevelt's election and presumed that the present state, which he characterized ironically as *intervention pacifique*, would be maintained. He ruled out the possibility of American occupation of Portuguese islands, unless the front of the Axis Powers should be moved further westward. On the basis of the reports of the [Portuguese] Ambassador in London (group garbled), who is here now, he characterized England's will to resist as solid and not likely at this time to be broken by German air attacks alone, to which the population moreover had become adapted. He believes however that the continued weakening of the country as regards shipping space and port installations, is the decisive factor. A victory by England was in any event no longer possible. At the conclusion of the cordial conversation Salazar said that he was following our struggle with sympathy and expressed satisfaction that the two countries were linked by the same ideology.

As it turned out, Generalissimo Franco declined to declare war on any of the Allies, though he did agree to send a volunteer Falangist "Blue

SOURCE: Telegram, November 14, 1940, to German Foreign Office from Baron Oswald von Hoyningen-Huene, the German Minister in Lisbon, Document 332, printed in *Documents on German Foreign Policy, 1918–1945*, Series D (1937–1945) (Washington, D.C.: Department of State, 1960), XI, 571–572.

2. To Berlin, where he had reported to Ernst von Weizsaecker, State Secretary of the German Foreign Ministry.—*Ed.*

Division" to fight in Russia after June, 1941. And, as has been observed in Chapter 9, Franco and Salazar formed an "Iberian Bloc" in February, 1942, to co-ordinate their foreign policies and safeguard the neutrality and independence of their nations. Both countries were developing healthy respect for Anglo-American naval and air power, and Portugal had just lost her East Indian island of Timor to Japanese occupation. She was not to reoccupy it until October, 1945.

After the Italian *coup d'état* of July 25, 1943, overthrew Mussolini's Fascist regime, the new government of King Victor Emmanuel III and Marshal Pietro Badoglio made use of Lisbon as a secret meeting place to negotiate armistice terms with the Anglo-Americans. By the autumn of that year Salazar clearly recognized that the war had turned in favor of the Allies; thus, on October 13 he conceded to Britain the right to use Portuguese bases in the Azores for air and naval patrol of the North Atlantic. This privilege was shared by United States ships and planes. Salazar termed his new policy "collaborative neutrality."

When he learned of the death of Adolf Hitler at the end of April, 1945, Salazar dispatched a telegram of condolence to the new German chief of state, Admiral Karl Doenitz, whom Hitler had named for the post. But on May 6, just before Germany's capitulation, Portugal severed diplomatic relations with the Reich in the hope thereby of ingratiating herself with the triumphant Allies.

Salazar now began to muffle some of the more blatantly fascistic overtones in his propaganda line, and he made the Portuguese Legion less conspicuous. Governing in a slightly less authoritarian manner, he sometimes permitted opposition candidates to announce themselves—though in practice they were usually "persuaded" to withdraw their candidacies before the actual voting day. Despite such gestures toward the Western democracies (which in return agreed to let Portugal be an original signatory of the North Atlantic Treaty Organization in 1949), it was not until 1955 that Portugal could gain admittance to the United Nations.

The presidential election of 1958 marked the end of Salazar's "liberalization." That year General Humberto da Silva Delgado led a surprisingly strong opposition campaign for the presidency against Américo Deus Thomaz and received 23 per cent of the votes. Salazar reacted in January, 1959, by abolishing the system of direct elections for the presidency and substituting an electoral college wherein the Corporative Chamber, whose functions had been increased since the war, would play a substantial role. Seven years later General Delgado was found murdered just across the border in Spain.

Meanwhile, the year 1961 saw the beginning of protracted guerrilla warfare in Portugal's African colonies, a running sore which sapped what little vigor remained in Salazar's regime. Portugal became the target of much criticism from most of the members of the United Nations.

At last on September 27, 1968, an incapacitating stroke brought an end to Salazar's forty years of authoritarian rule.[3] President Deus Thomaz appointed Dr. Marcello Caetano to be Salazar's successor. A professor of law and former member of the cabinet, Caetano faced the difficult task of deciding how far he dared go in dismantling the harshest features of the clerico-corporativist dictatorship at home and its empire overseas without simultaneously arousing too much hostility from the Army, bankers, and other vested interests. After his first year in office it seemed fairly clear that Caetano intended to move slowly toward a semi-liberal regime. In the parliamentary elections of October 26, 1969, democratic oppositionists were allowed to put up candidates, though only the National Union enjoyed official sanction as a party. The voters gave a strong endorsement to Caetano, and one month later he announced the abolition of the secret political police (PIDE) which, under Salazar, had penetrated almost every sphere of public and private activity. If present trends continue, Portugal under Caetano may shift to a freer, growth-minded economic philosophy in contrast to Salazar's frugal, nationalistic policies. To what extent Portugal is ready to shed the remainder of her semifascistic political trappings remains to be seen.

3. Salazar died on July 27, 1970, without ever knowing that he had been replaced as Premier.—*Ed.*

Select Bibliography

General

CARSTEN, F. L. *The Rise of Fascism*. Berkeley: University of California, 1967.

DE FELICE, RENZO. *Le interpretazioni del fascismo*. Bari: Laterza, 1969.

LAQUEUR, WALTER, and GEORGE L. MOSSE (eds.). *International Fascism, 1920–1945* ("Journal of Contemporary History," No. 1). New York: Harper & Row, 1966.

LIPSET, SEYMOUR M. *Political Man: The Social Bases of Politics*. Garden City: Doubleday, 1960.

NOLTE, ERNST. *Die faschistischen Bewegungen: Die Krise des liberalen Systems und die Entwicklung der Faschismen*. Munich: Deutscher Taschenbuch-Verlag, 1966.

———. *Theorien über den Faschismus*. Cologne: Verlag Kiepenheuer & Witsch, 1967.

———. *Three Faces of Fascism: Action Française, Italian Fascism, National Socialism*. Trans. from German by Leila Vennewitz. New York: Holt, Rinehart & Winston, 1966.

ROGGER, HANS, and EUGEN WEBER (eds.). *The European Right: A Historical Profile*. Berkeley: University of California, 1965.

WEBER, EUGEN. *Varieties of Fascism*. Princeton: D. Van Nostrand, 1964.

WEISS, JOHN. *The Fascist Tradition: Radical Right-wing Extremism in Modern Europe*. New York: Harper & Row, 1967.

WOOLF, STUART J. (ed.). *European Fascism*. London: Weidenfeld & Nicolson, 1968.

Italy

ALATRI, PAOLO. *Le origini del fascismo*. Rome: Editori Riuniti, 1956.

AQUARONE, ALBERTO. *L'organizzazione dello stato totalitario*. Turin: Einaudi, 1965.

BAER, GEORGE W. *The Coming of the Italian-Ethiopian War*. Cambridge: Harvard University, 1967.

BINCHY, DANIEL A. *Church and State in Fascist Italy*. London: Oxford University, 1941.

BOTTAI, GIUSEPPE. *Vent'anni e un giorno, 24 luglio 1943*. Milan: Garzanti, 1949.

CASSELS, ALAN. *Fascist Italy*. New York: Thomas Y. Crowell, 1968.

———. *Mussolini's Early Diplomacy*. Princeton: Princeton University, 1970.

CASUCCI, COSTANZO (ed.). *Il Fascismo: Antologia di scritti critici*. Bologna: Il Mulino, 1961.

CHABOD, FEDERICO. *A History of Italian Fascism*. Trans. from Italian by Muriel Grindrod. London: Weidenfeld & Nicolson, 1963.

CHIURCO, GIORGIO A. *Storia della rivoluzione fascista*. 5 vols. Florence: Vallecchi, 1929.

CIANO, GALEAZZO. *The Ciano Diaries, 1939–1943*. Ed. by Hugh Gibson. Garden City: Doubleday, 1946.

———. *Diary, 1937–1938*. Ed. by Andreas Mayor. London: Methuen, 1952.

CLOUGH, SHEPARD B. *The Economic History of Modern Italy*. New York: Columbia University, 1964.

——— and SALVATORE SALADINO. *A History of Modern Italy: Documents, Reading and Commentary*. New York: Columbia University, 1968.

DEAKIN, F. W. *The Brutal Friendship: Mussolini, Hitler and the Fall of Italian Fascism*. New York: Harper & Row, 1962. Rev. ed., 2 vols. New York: Doubleday Anchor, 1966.

DE FELICE, RENZO. *Mussolini il rivoluzionario, 1883–1920*. Turin: Einaudi, 1965.

———. *Mussolini il fascista: Parte I: La conquista del potere, 1921–1925*. Turin: Einaudi, 1966.

———. *Mussolini il fascista: Parte II: L'organizzazione dello stato fascista, 1925–29*. Turin: Einaudi, 1969.

———. *Storia degli ebrei italiani sotto il fascismo*. Turin: Einaudi, 1961.

DEL GIUDICE, MAURO. *Cronistoria del processo Matteotti*. Palermo, 1954.

DELZELL, CHARLES F. *Mussolini's Enemies: The Italian Anti-Fascist Resistance*. Princeton: Princeton University, 1961. Reprinted, New York: Howard Fertig, 1971. Rev. Italian version, *I nemici di Mussolini*. Turin: Einaudi, 1966.

DI NOLFO, ENNIO. *Mussolini e la politica estera italiana, 1919–1933*. Padua, 1960.

Documenti diplomatici italiani. Settima Serie, 1922–1935; Ottava Serie, 1935–1939; Nona Serie, 1939–1943. Ministero degli Affari Esteri. Rome: Libreria dello Stato, 1957ff.

DORSO, GUIDO. *Mussolini alla conquista del potere*. Milan: Mondadori, 1961.

EINAUDI, MARIO. "Fascism," in *International Encyclopedia of the Social Sciences* (1968), V, 334–341.

Fascismo e antifascismo (1918–1948): Lezioni e testimonianze. 2 vols. Milan: Feltrinelli, 1963.

FERMI, LAURA. *Mussolini.* Chicago: University of Chicago, 1961.

FINER, HERMAN. *Mussolini's Italy.* London: Gollancz, 1935. Reprinted, New York: Grosset & Dunlap, 1965.

GAROSCI, ALDO. *Storia dei fuorusciti.* Bari: Laterza, 1953.

GERMINO, DANTE L. *The Italian Fascist Party in Power: A Study in Totalitarian Rule.* Minneapolis: University of Minnesota, 1959.

HALPERIN, S. WILLIAM. *Mussolini and Italian Fascism.* Princeton: D. Van Nostrand, 1964.

HUGHES, H. STUART. *The United States and Italy.* 2d rev. ed. Cambridge: Harvard University, 1965.

JEMOLO, ARTURO CARLO. *Chiesa e Stato in Italia dalla unificazione a Giovanni XXIII.* Turin: Einaudi, 1965.

KIRKPATRICK, IVONE. *Mussolini: A Study in Power.* New York: Hawthorn, 1964.

MACK SMITH, DENIS. *Italy: A Modern History.* New ed. revised and enlarged. Ann Arbor: University of Michigan, 1969.

MEGARO, GAUDENS. *Mussolini in the Making.* Boston: Houghton Mifflin, 1938. Reprinted, New York: Howard Fertig, 1967.

MINIO-PALUELLO, LORENZO. *Education in Fascist Italy.* London: Oxford University, 1946.

MONELLI, PAOLO. *Mussolini: An Intimate Life.* Trans. from Italian. London, 1953.

MUSSOLINI, BENITO. *Opera Omnia di Benito Mussolini.* Ed. by Edoardo and Duilio Susmel. 35 vols. Florence: La Fenice, 1951–62.

PERTICONE, GIACOMO. *La politica italiana nell'ultimo trentennio.* 3 vols. Rome: Edizioni Leonardo, 1945.

PINI, GIORGIO, and DUILIO SUSMEL. *Mussolini: L'uomo e l'opera.* 4 vols. 2d ed. Florence: La Fenice, 1957–58.

ROSENGARTEN, FRANK. *The Italian Anti-Fascist Press, 1919–1945.* Cleveland: Case-Western Reserve University, 1968.

ROSENSTOCK-FRANCK, LOUIS. *L'économie corporative fasciste en doctrine et en fait.* Paris: Librarie Universitaire J. Gamber, 1934.

ROSSI, ERNESTO. *I padroni del vapore.* Bari: Laterza, 1955.

SAITTA, ARMANDO. *Dal Fascismo alla resistenza: Profilo storico e documenti.* Florence: La Nuova Italia, 1961.

SALVATORELLI, LUIGI, and GIOVANNI MIRA. *Storia d'Italia nel periodo fascista.* 4th ed. Turin: Einaudi, 1962. Original edition, *Storia del Fascismo: L'Italia dal 1919 al 1945.* Rome: Novissima, 1952.

SALVEMINI, GAETANO. *Under the Axe of Fascism.* New York: Viking, 1936.

SCHMIDT, CARL T. *The Corporate State in Action: Italy under Fascism.* New York: Columbia University, 1939.

SCHNEIDER, HERBERT W. *Making the Fascist State.* New York: Oxford University, 1928.

SETON-WATSON, CHRISTOPHER. *Italy from Liberalism to Fascism, 1870–1925.* London: Methuen, 1967.

TAMARO, ATTILIO. *Due anni di storia, 1943–1945.* Rome: Tosi, 1949.

TASCA, ANGELO. *Nascita e avvento del fascismo: L'Italia dal 1918 al 1922.* Florence: La Nuova Italia, 1950. Original English edition under pseudonym, A. Rossi, *The Rise of Italian Fascism, 1918–1922.* London: Methuen, 1938. Reprinted, New York: Howard Fertig, 1966.

VIVARELLI, ROBERTO. *Il dopoguerra in Italia e l'avvento del fascismo (1918–1922).* Vol. I: *Dalla fine della guerra all'impresa di Fiume.* Naples: Istituto Italiano per gli Studi Storici, 1967.

WEBSTER, RICHARD A. *The Cross and the Fasces: Christian Democracy and Fascism in Italy.* Stanford: Stanford University, 1960.

WELK, WILLIAM G. *Fascist Economic Policy: An Analysis of Italy's Economic Experiment.* Cambridge: Harvard University, 1938.

WISKEMANN, ELIZABETH. *The Rome-Berlin Axis: A History of the Relations between Hitler and Mussolini.* London: Oxford University, 1949.

Spain

APARICIO, JUAN (ed.). *Antología: La conquista del estado.* Barcelona: Ediciones F. E., 1939.

ARRARÁS, JOAQUÍN (ed.). *Historia de la Cruzada española.* 8 vols. Madrid, 1939–43.

ARRESE, JOSÉ LUIS DE. *Escritos y discursos.* Madrid: Vicesecretaría de Educación Popular, 1943.

CARR, RAYMOND. *Spain, 1808–1939.* Oxford: Clarendon, 1966.

DETWILER, DONALD S. *Hilter, Franco und Gibraltar: Die Frage des spanischen Eintritts in den Zweiten Weltkrieg.* Wiesbaden: F. Steiner, 1962.

Documents on German Foreign Policy, 1918–1945. Series D (Germany and the Spanish Civil War, 1936–1939). Washington: Department of State, 1950ff.

DOUSSINAGUE, JOSÉ MARÍA. *España tenía razón (1939–1945).* Madrid, 1950.

Falange española tradicionalista y de las Juntas ofensivas nacional-sindicalistas, Vicesecretaría de Educación Popular. *Fundamentos del Nuevo Estado.* Madrid: Ediciones de la Vicesecretaría de Educación Popular, 1943.

FEIS, HERBERT. *The Spanish Story: Franco and the Nations at War*. New York: Knopf, 1948.

FERNÁNDEZ CUESTA, RAIMUNDO. *Intemperie, victoria y servicio: Discursos y escritos*. Madrid: Ediciones del Movimiento, 1951.

FRAGOSO DEL TORO, VICTOR. *La España de ayer: Recopilación de textos histórico-politicos*. 2 vols. Madrid: Editora Nacional, 1965.

JACKSON, GABRIEL. *Historian's Quest: A Twenty-Year Journey into the Spanish Mind*. New York: Knopf, 1969.

———. *The Spanish Republic and the Civil War, 1931–1939*. Princeton: Princeton University, 1965.

[LEDESMA RAMOS, RAMIRO.] *¿Fascismo en España? (Sus origines, su desarrollo, sus hombres)*, by Roberto Lanzas [pseud.]. Madrid: Ediciones "La Conquista del Estado," 1935.

LIVERMORE, HAROLD. *A History of Spain*. London: George Allen & Unwin, 1958.

LLOYD, ALAN. *Franco*. Garden City: Doubleday, 1969.

MARTIN, CLAUDE. *Franco, soldat et Chef d'État*. Paris, 1959.

NELLESSEN, BERND. *Die Verbotene Revolution: Aufstieg und Niedergang der Falange*. Hamburg: Leibniz, 1963.

PAYNE, STANLEY G. *The Falange: A History of Spanish Fascism*. Stanford: Stanford University, 1961.

———. "Falangism," in *International Encyclopedia of the Social Sciences* (1968), V, 288–292.

———. *Franco's Spain*. New York: Thomas Y. Crowell, 1967.

———. *Politics and the Military in Modern Spain*. Stanford: Stanford University, 1967.

PRIMO DE RIVERA, JOSÉ ANTONIO. *Obras completas*. Compiled and edited by Augustín del Rio Cisneros and Enrique Conde Gargollo. Madrid: "Diana," 1942.

———. *Textos inéditos y epistolario*. Madrid: Ediciones del Movimiento, 1956.

PUZZO, DANTE A. *Spain and the Great Powers, 1936–1941*. New York: Columbia University, 1962.

REDONDO, ONÉSIMO. *Obras completas*. 2 vols. Madrid: Publicaciones Españolas, 1954–55.

SERRANO SUÑER, RAMÓN. *Entre Hendaya y Gibraltar*. Mexico City, 1945.

SYDNOR, CHARLES W., JR. "Spanish-German Relations: April 1, 1939–June 22, 1941." M.A. thesis, Vanderbilt University, Nashville, Tenn., 1967.

THOMAS, HUGH. *The Spanish Civil War*. New York: Harper & Row, 1961.

WELLES, BENJAMIN. *The Gentle Anarchy*. New York: Praeger, 1965.

WHITAKER, ARTHUR P. *Spain and the Defense of the West: Ally and Liability*. New York: Harper, 1961.

Portugal

DERRICK, MICHAEL. *The Portugal of Salazar*. London, 1938.

FERRAZ DE SOUSA, ABEL. *Ressurgimento em Portugal*. São Paulo: Editora Lep S.A., 1962.

LIVERMORE, H. V. *A New History of Portugal*. New York: Cambridge University, 1966.

MARTINS, H. "Portugal," in S. J. Woolf (ed.), *European Fascism*. London: Weidenfeld & Nicolson, 1968.

MASSIS, HENRI. *Salazar face à face: Trois dialogues politiques*. Paris-Geneva: La Palatine, 1960.

Political Constitution of the Portuguese Republic. Lisbon: S.N.I., 1957.

Portugal: The New State in Theory and in Practice. Lisbon: S.P.N., 1938.

Salazar, Prime Minister of Portugal, Says . . . Lisbon: S.P.N., [1940].

SÉRANT, PAUL. *Salazar et son temps*. Paris: Les Sept Couleurs, 1961.

Index

71 72 73 74   12 11 10 9 8 7 6 5 4 3 2 1